VISUAL QUICKSTART GUIDE

OUTLOOK 2000

FOR WINDOWS

Michael J. Young

Peachpit Press

Visual QuickStart Guide

Outlook 2000 for Windows

Michael J. Young

Peachpit Press
1249 Eighth Street
Berkeley, CA 94710
(510) 524-2178
(510) 524-2221 (fax)

Find us on the World Wide Web at: http://www.peachpit.com

Peachpit Press is a division of Addison Wesley Longman

Editor: Lisa Theobald
Production Coordinator: Amy Changar
Compositors: Melanie Haage & Owen Wolfson
Indexer: Valerie Perry

ISBN: 0-201-69952-4

0 9 8 7 6 5 4 3 2 1

Printed and bound in the United States of America

Printed on recycled paper

Thank You!

To Lisa Theobald, for recruiting me as the author, for skillfully editing the whole manuscript, for smoothly handling formatting issues so I could focus on the content, for pushing through those special icons and other features I wanted, and for her friendliness and encouragement throughout the entire project.

To Kathie Werner, for kindly recommending me for writing this book.

To Nancy Ruenzel, for making negotiating and signing the contract a pleasant experience.

To Amy Changar, for efficiently coordinating the production of the book.

And to the Microsoft Outlook programmers, for continuing to make Outlook better and better.

TABLE OF CONTENTS

Introduction .... **ix**
New Features in Outlook 2000 xi
How to Use the Book xiii
How to Contact the Author xiv

Chapter 1: Setting Up Outlook 2000 **1**
Running Outlook 3
Supplying Setup Information 6

Chapter 2: Getting Started Using Outlook **15**
The Outlook Window 16
How Outlook Is Organized 17
Learning Basic Windows and Office Techniques 19
Consulting the Assistant 29
Getting Around in Outlook 32

Chapter 3: Working with Outlook Items **41**
Creating Items 43
Opening Items 47
Editing Items 49
Selecting Text 52
Formatting Text 53
Copying and Moving Text 54
Checking Spelling 55
Inserting Files, Items, and Objects 57
Copying and Moving Items 61
Removing and Archiving Items 64
Using Different Views 70
Sorting, Filtering, and Grouping Items 74
Using the Organize Page 80
Finding Outlook Items and Disk Files 82

Chapter 4: Working with Outlook Folders 87
Creating New Folders ... 88
Moving and Copying Folders ... 91
Renaming Folders ... 93
Removing Folders ... 94
Sharing Outlook Folders over the Internet ... 95
E/S Sharing Folders Over a Network ... 99
Other Outlook Folder Operations ... 103

Chapter 5: Using Outlook Today 107
Working with Outlook Today ... 108
Customizing Outlook Today ... 111

Chapter 6: Using the Inbox to Manage Messages 115
I/O Receiving E-mail Messages ... 117
C/W Receiving E-mail Messages ... 120
Reading E-mail Messages ... 123
Receiving Fax Messages ... 127
Sending E-mail Messages ... 132
Sending Fax Messages ... 148
Systematizing Your E-mail and Fax Messages ... 151
Modifying the Current View ... 154

Chapter 7: Using the Calendar 155
Creating Appointments ... 156
Defining Events ... 161
Scheduling Meetings ... 162
Working with Items in the Calendar Folder ... 165

Chapter 8: Using the Contacts Folder 171
Creating Contact Items ... 172
Working with Items in the Contacts Folder ... 177

Chapter 9: Using the Tasks Folder 181
Creating Task Items ... 182
Working with Items in the Tasks Folder ... 188

Chapter 10: Using the Journal 193
Recording Journal Entries ... 194
Working with Items in the Journal Folder ... 198

Chapter 11: Using the Notes Folder 203
Creating New Notes ... 204
Working with Items in the Notes Folder ... 206

Chapter 12: **Managing Your Disk Files and Folders** **209**
Working with Files 210
Working with File Folders 213

Chapter 13: **Exploring the Web in Outlook** **217**
Displaying a Web Page 218

Chapter 14: **Customizing Outlook** **223**
Customizing the Toolbars and Menus 224
Changing the Office Assistant 229
Modifying the Outlook Bar 230
Adjusting Views 233
Attaching a Home Page to an Outlook Folder 235

Appendix A: **Configuring Outlook** **237**
Changing Your Basic E-mail Configuration 238
I/O Setting Up and Modifying the Internet Only E-mail Configuration 240
C/W Setting Up and Modifying the Corporate Or Workgroup E-mail Configuration 248
C/W Using Several Profiles 254
Importing Settings or Data from Another E-Mail Program 255
Adding or Removing Outlook Components 256

Index **257**

TABLE OF CONTENTS

INTRODUCTION

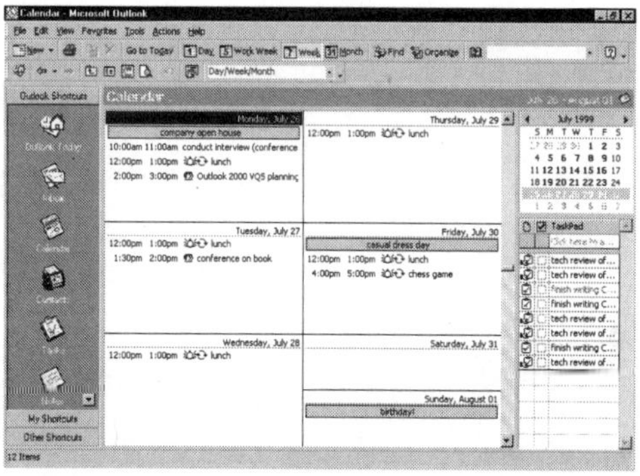

Figure i.1 Appointments and events stored in the Outlook Calendar folder.

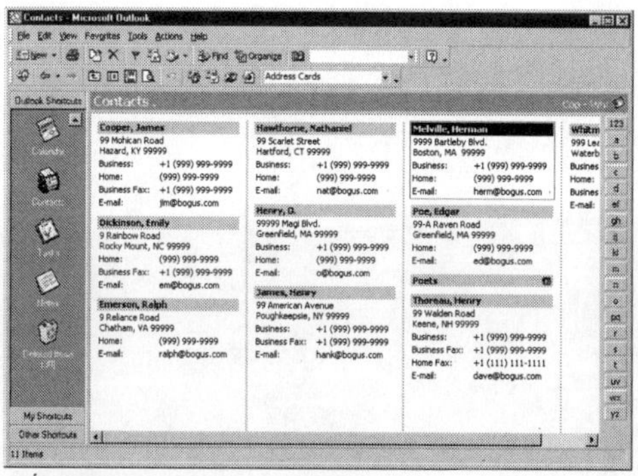

Figure i.2 Contact information stored in the Outlook Contacts folder.

You can use Microsoft Outlook 2000 to organize and plan your business or personal life, to communicate and share information with people in your company or anywhere on the Internet, and to collaborate with your co-workers on group projects.

Here's a more detailed sampling of what you can do with Outlook:

- Send, receive, store, and organize e-mail and fax messages.
- Keep a calendar of your personal appointments and events, and schedule meetings with other people (**Figure i.1**).
- Store names, addresses, and other information on your business and personal contacts (**Figure i.2**).
- Quickly send a message to a contact, dial a contact's phone number, or reach a contact in other ways.
- Keep track of the personal tasks you need to complete, and manage group projects.
- Maintain a record of activities or occurrences that take place in your business or personal life, such as receiving an e-mail message, creating a document, or making a phone call.

(continued on next page)

- Quickly type and store miscellaneous bits of information in electronic "sticky notes" (**Figure i.3**).
- Share any of your Outlook information with other people on a network or on the Internet.
- Manage your disk files and file folders right in the Outlook window, without having to switch to a separate file management program such as Windows Explorer.
- Explore Web pages in the Outlook window, without having to run a separate browser program.

Figure i.3 A note stored in the Outlook Notes folder.

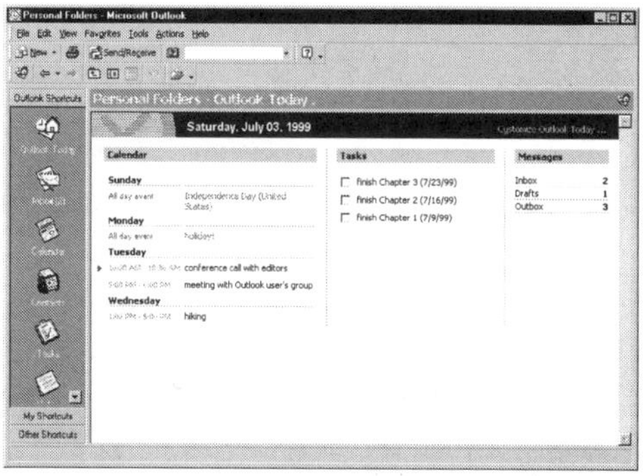

Figure i.4 Outlook displaying the Outlook Today folder.

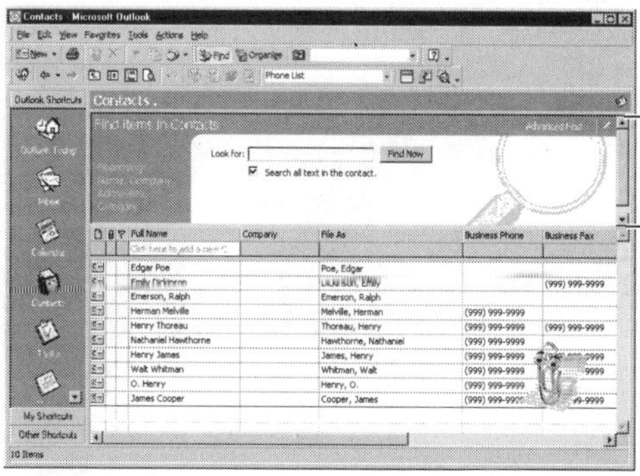

Figure i.5 The Find page displayed above the information in the opened Outlook folder.

New Features in Outlook 2000

The original version of Outlook was part of the Microsoft Office 97 suite of applications. Outlook has acquired many new features since then. Some of them were added with Outlook 98, the second version, and some are brand new in Outlook 2000, the third version. The following sections describe many of these new features.

New features in Outlook 98

- The **Outlook Today** folder, which displays a Web-style page that gives you an overview of the current information in several commonly used Outlook folders, and lets you quickly manage this information (**Figure i.4**).
- The **Find page**, a Web-style page that you can display in a separate pane and use to find Outlook items containing specific text (**Figure i.5**).
- The **Organize page**, a Web-style page that you can display in a separate pane and use to quickly work with Outlook items. For example, you can use this page to create rules for automatically moving or color-coding selected messages (messages from or to a particular person, junk messages, or adult-content messages).
- Support for the **HTML e-mail** format, which lets you include backgrounds, graphics, and other Web-page content in your e-mail messages. You can use predesigned **stationery** to get a head start in creating an attractive HTML e-mail message for a specific purpose (such as a party invitation or an announcement).

(continued on next page)

- Support for standard **Internet e-mail** protocols so that you can use Outlook with a wider variety of e-mail services (SMTP, POP3, and IMAP4).
- An enhanced **Preview pane** that lets you view the entire contents of an e-mail message.
- Automatic saving of messages while you compose them, in the **Drafts** folder.
- The use of **Internet directory (LDAP) services** for verifying or finding people's e-mail addresses.

New features in Outlook 2000

- **Folder home pages**, which let you display Web-style information in any Outlook folder.
- **Custom menus and toolbars**, which show only the commands you use most frequently.
- **Personal distribution lists**, which you can store in your Contacts folder and use to quickly send messages to entire groups of people.
- The **Find A Contact** list box on the Standard toolbar, which lets you rapidly find a contact wherever you are in Outlook (**Figure i.6**).
- Viewing **Web pages** right in the Outlook window, using the new **Favorites menu** or **Web-page shortcuts** in the Outlook Bar (**Figure i.7**).

Figure i.6 The Find A Contact list box.

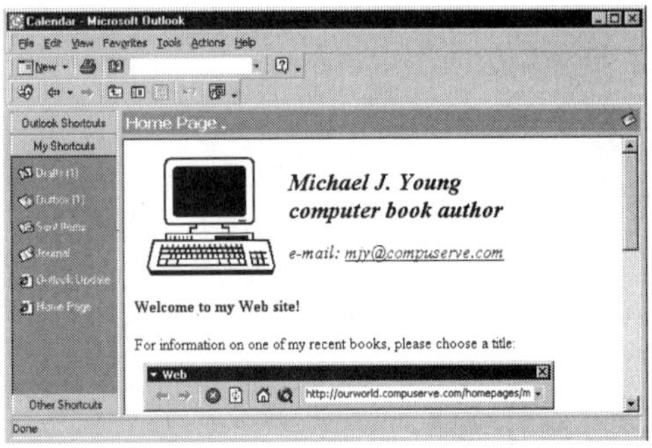

Figure i.7 A Web page displayed within the Outlook window.

How to Use the Book

I recommend that you read the book in the following way:

- If you haven't installed Outlook yet, read Chapter 1 for installation instructions and for help in making installation choices. This chapter refers you to Appendix A for instructions on some of the more involved configuration tasks you might need to complete during setup.
- Read Chapter 2, especially if you're new to Outlook or Office, to get an overview of Outlook's features and the types of information it manages, and to learn basic Windows and Office skills.
- Read through Chapters 3 and 4 to learn the basic Outlook techniques you'll need when you work with almost *any* of the types of information Outlook manages. Refer back to these chapters as you start to work with the different Outlook folders.
- Chapters 5 through 11 cover each of the main types of information that Outlook manages. You can read just those chapters that cover the information types you want to work with, and you can read them in any order.
- Read Chapter 12 if you want to use Outlook to manage your disk files and folders, rather than using Windows Explorer or another file-management program.
- Read Chapter 13 if you want to use Outlook to explore Web pages.
- Read Chapter 14 if you want to customize Outlook. I recommend, however, that you don't customize Outlook until you've finished working through the other chapters, so your program commands will match those described in the book.

Special Icons Used in This Book

As you'll learn in Chapter 1, you set up e-mail in Outlook using either the Internet Only configuration or the Corporate Or Workgroup configuration. Sections in this book that apply only to the Internet Only configuration are marked with the I/O icon, and sections that apply only to the Corporate Or Workgroup configuration are marked with the C/W icon. Sections without an icon apply to both configurations.

Also, some Outlook features are available only if your computer is attached to a Microsoft Exchange Server network and you have set up Outlook as an Exchange Server client, as explained in Chapter 1 and Appendix A. Sections covering features that require Exchange Server are marked with the E/S icon.

How to Contact the Author

You can e-mail me at **mjy@compuserve.com**. I welcome your comments and feedback. Although my schedule seldom permits me to answer questions that require research, if you have a question that I can answer readily, I'll be happy to share what I know.

You're also invited to visit my Web site at **http://ourworld.compuserve.com/homepages/mjy/**. There, you'll find book corrections, reader questions and answers, sources for getting additional help on Outlook and Office, descriptions of some of my other books, and additional information.

1 Setting Up Outlook 2000

This chapter shows you how to complete the three main steps for getting Outlook up and running:

- **Installing the Outlook software.** Whether you purchased Outlook 2000 as a part of Microsoft Office 2000 or obtained it as a separate product, your first step is to install the Outlook program.
- **Running Outlook for the first time.** You can run the Outlook program in several different ways, or you can have it run automatically whenever you start Windows.
- **Supplying setup information.** The first time you run Outlook it will prompt you for any setup information that it needs.

To install Outlook 2000:

1. Run the Setup program on the product CD, following the instructions provided (**Figure 1.1**).

   The Setup program will prompt you for the necessary setup information. At one point, it will allow you to select the Outlook components that will be installed (**Figure 1.2**).

2. Accept the default set of components.

   or

   Select the specific components you want to install.

3. Enter the other information that the Setup program requests.

The Setup program will now copy the Outlook software to your hard disk and install Outlook in Windows.

✔ Tips

- Like the other major Office applications, Outlook includes a set of separate installable components, such as Help, Stationery, and Integrated File Management.
- I recommend accepting the default set of Outlook components. You will then have everything you need to work with this book. If you later want to add or remove a component, follow the instructions in the section "Adding or Removing Outlook Components" in Appendix A.
- In the list of installable Outlook components, those marked with a disk symbol are installed by default. Note that the "1" next to a disk symbol means the component will be installed the first time you use it. The components marked with an "X" are not installed by default.

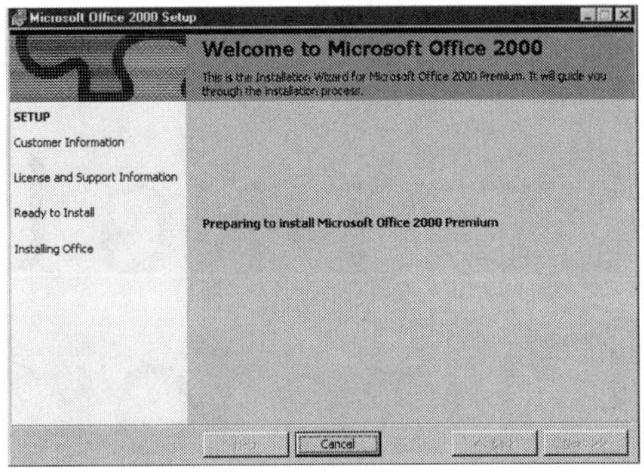

Figure 1.1 The opening Setup program dialog box, if you're installing Microsoft Office 2000 Premium.

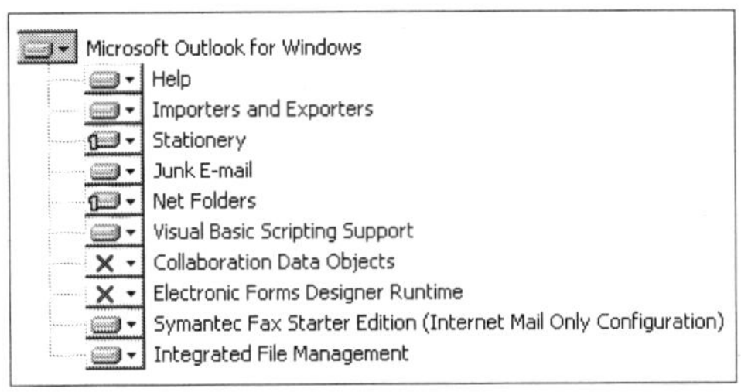

Figure 1.2 A list of the installable Outlook components. The ones marked with a disk symbol are installed by default.

Running Outlook

After you've finished the Setup program, you can start Outlook at any time. Keep in mind that the first time you run it, you'll probably have to enter some setup information.

To run Outlook:

- Open the Windows Start menu by clicking the Start button on your Windows Taskbar (**Figure 1.3**). Choose Microsoft Outlook from the menu.

  or

  Double-click the Microsoft Outlook icon on your Windows desktop.

  or

  If you have Windows 98 or later, click the Launch Microsoft Outlook button on the Windows Taskbar (**Figure 1.4**).

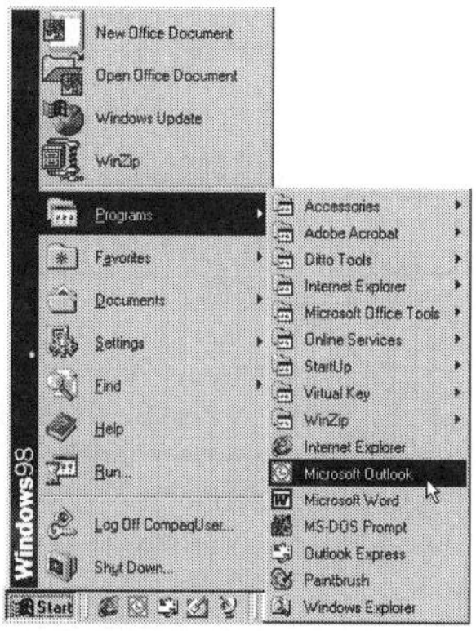

Figure 1.3: Starting Outlook from the Windows Start menu.

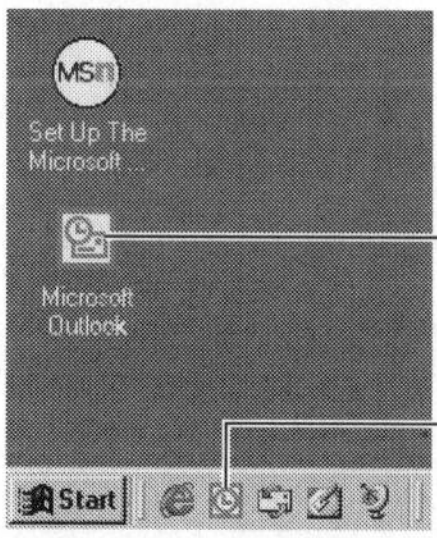

Double-click this icon....

...Or, click the Launch Microsoft Outlook button (Windows 98 or later).

Figure 1.4 Two additional ways to start Outlook.

✔ Tip

- For instructions on using the mouse and choosing menu commands, see the section "Learning Basic Windows and Office Techniques" in Chapter 2.

To have Outlook run automatically every time you start Widows:

1. Open the Windows Start menu, choose Settings, and then choose Taskbar (on Windows 95) or Taskbar & Start Menu (on Windows 98 or later) (**Figure 1.5**).
2. In the Taskbar Properties dialog box, select the Start Menu Programs tab and click the **Add** button (**Figure 1.6**).
3. In the Create Shortcut dialog box, click the **Browse** button (**Figure 1.7**).
4. In the Browse dialog box, locate and double-click the Outlook program file (listed either as Outlook or as Outlook.exe) (**Figure 1.8**).

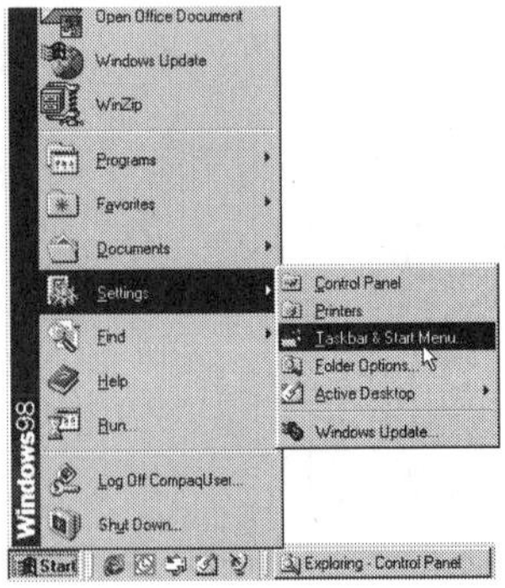

Figure 1.5 Choose the Taskbar & Start Menu command on the Settings submenu of the Windows 98 Start menu.

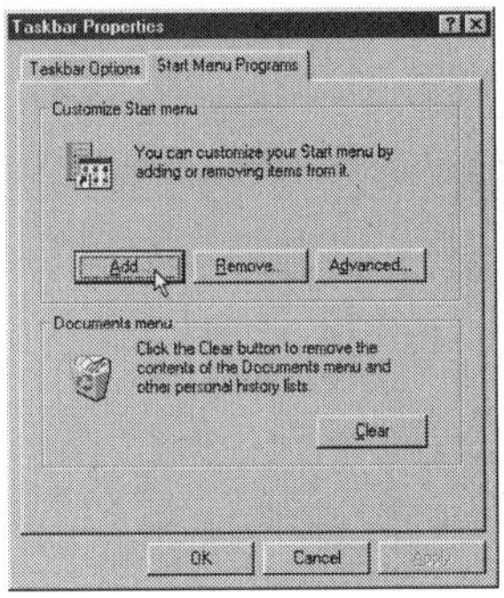

Figure 1.6 Cick the **Add** button in the Start Menu Programs tab of the Taskbar Properties dialog box.

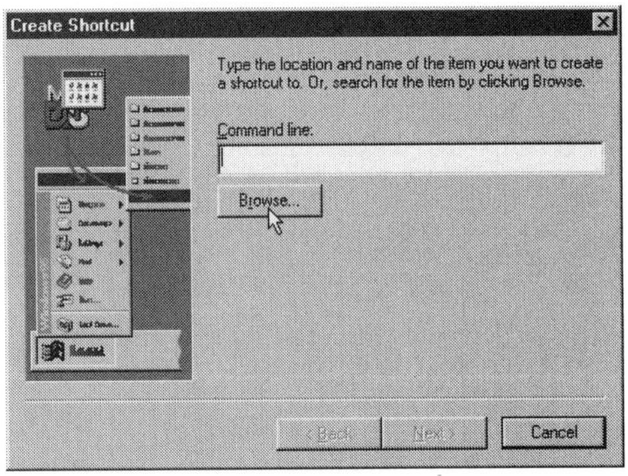

Figure 1.7 Click the **Browse** button in the Create Shortcut dialog box.

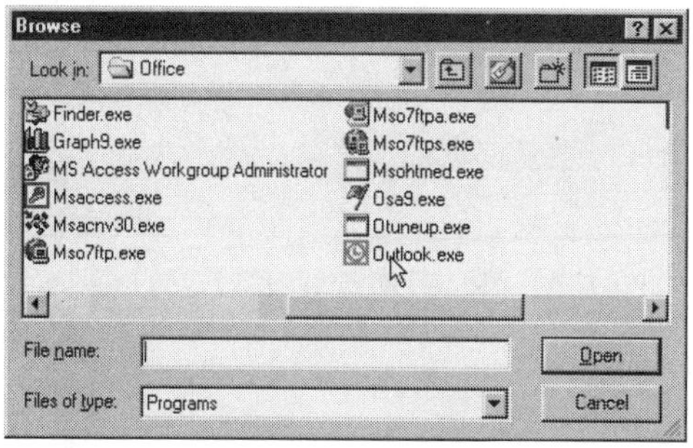

Figure 1.8 Double-click the Outlook program file in the Browse dialog box.

Figure 1-9 The usual location of the Outlook program file on your hard drive.

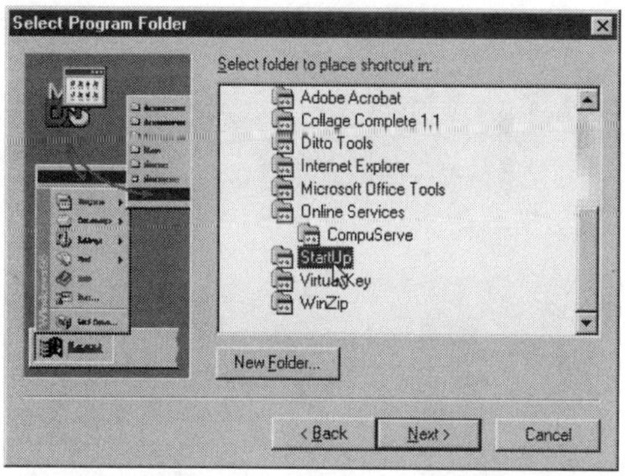

Figure 1.10 Select the StartUp folder.

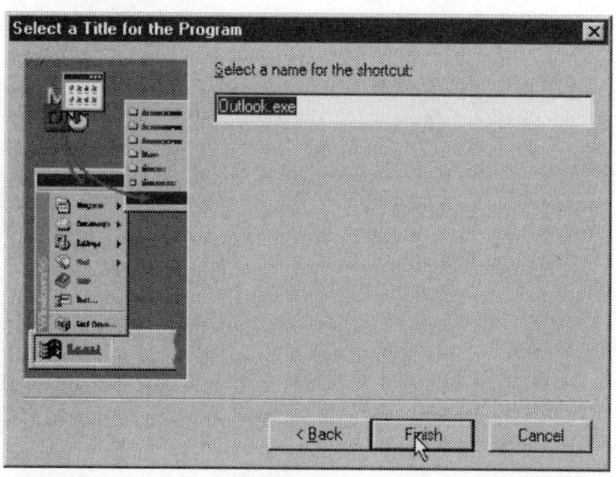

Figure 1.11 Click the **Finish** button to complete the operation.

This file is generally located in the following folder on your hard drive: Program Files\Microsoft Office\Office folder (**Figure 1.9**).

5. Click the **Next** button in the Create Shortcut dialog box.
6. In the Select Program Folder dialog box, select the StartUp folder (**Figure 1.10**) and then click the **Next** button.
7. In the Select a Title for the Program dialog box click the **Finish** button (**Figure 1.11**).

✔ Tip

- For instructions on working with the mouse, menus, and dialog boxes, see the section "Learning Basic Windows and Office Techniques" in Chapter 2.

Supplying Setup Information

The first time you run Outlook, it will generally display a series of wizard dialog boxes to prompt you for any required setup information. The particular setup dialog boxes you see—if you see any—depend upon any e-mail software you have previously installed on your computer, the way you've configured this software, and the choices you make as you begin supplying information.

✔ Tips

- The following instructions in this chapter describe the basic wizard dialog boxes that you might need to fill in during Outlook setup. Keep in mind that you might see all or none of these, depending on your particular situation.
- Appendix A provides instructions for some of the more involved configuration tasks you might need to complete during Outlook setup. The following instructions provide specific references to Appendix A where necessary.
- Outlook gathers only the minimal setup information required to get you started using the program and often makes choices for you. Keep in mind, however, that you can later change any configuration option by following the instructions given in Appendix A.
- If, after you set up and run Outlook, you encounter a problem that seems to be a program defect, choose the Detect and Repair command on the Help menu . This command will fix any errors that it finds in the Outlook program files (**Figure 1.12**).

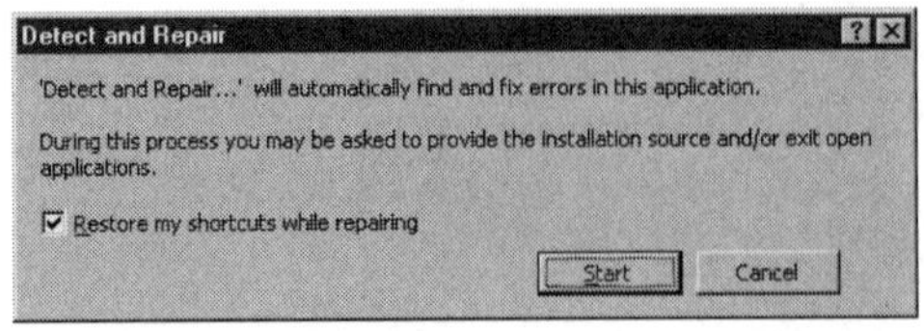

Figure 1.12 The Detect and Repair command will fix any errors that it finds in the Outlook program files.

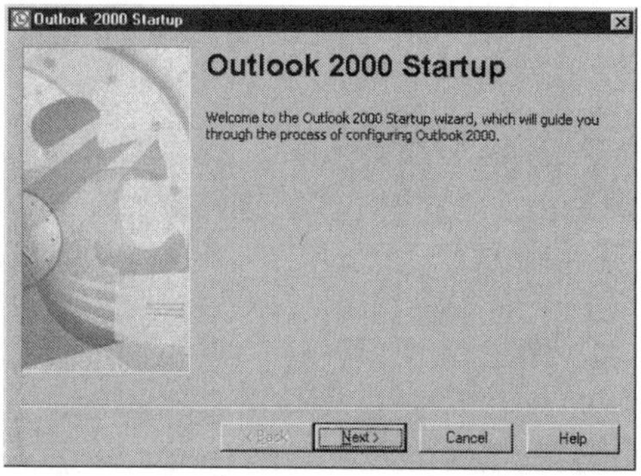

Figure 1.13 The Outlook 2000 Startup Wizard opening dialog box.

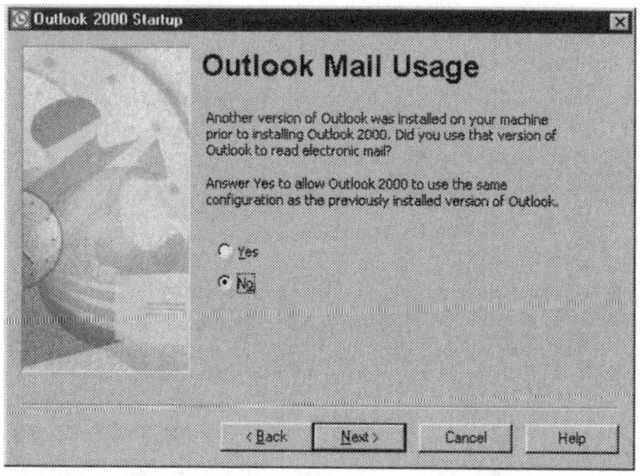

Figure 1.14 The Outlook Mail Usage dialog box.

The Outlook Startup Wizard

If you haven't previously installed Outlook 2000 on your computer, Outlook will begin by running the Outlook Startup Wizard the first time you start the program. The first dialog box is shown in **Figure 1.13**.

The Outlook Mail Usage dialog box

If you had a previous version of Outlook (Outlook 97 or Outlook 98) on your computer when you installed Outlook 2000, the Outlook 2000 Startup Wizard will display the Outlook Mail Usage dialog box (**Figure 1.14**).

To complete the Mail Usage dialog box:

1. Select **Yes** if you want to continue using your same e-mail service and e-mail settings, and to access any messages you saved in your previous Outlook version. If you make this choice and click the **Next** button, Outlook will set itself up and start running, and you're done with this chapter! Go right to Chapter 2. If you later want to change your e-mail setup, follow the instructions in Appendix A.

   or

   Select **No** if you want to specify a new Outlook e-mail setup. In this case, the wizard will display additional dialog boxes for you to fill in.
2. Click the **Next** button.

The E-mail Upgrade Options dialog box

If you currently have another e-mail program installed on your computer, Outlook might be able to "upgrade" it. In other words, it might be able to import the e-mail messages, address book, and settings from this program, so that you can continue to use your same e-mail service and setup in Outlook without interruption.

If the Outlook 2000 Startup Wizard detects the presence of a program that it can upgrade (these programs include Qualcomm Eudora, Netscape Mail, Microsoft Outlook Express, and other popular e-mail programs), it will display the E-mail Upgrade Options dialog box (**Figure 1.15**).

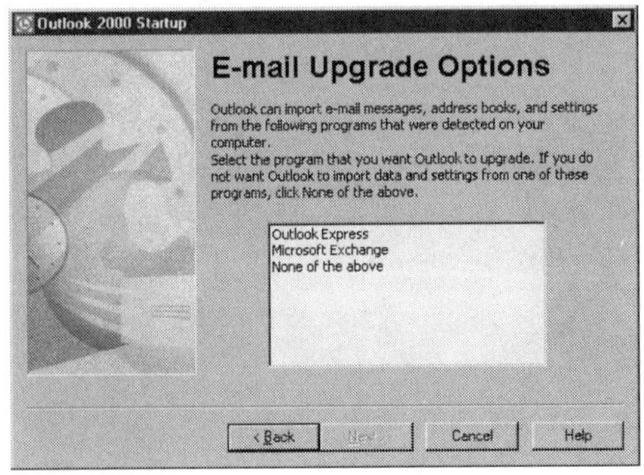

Figure 1.15 The E-mail Upgrade Options dialog box.

To complete the E-mail Upgrade Options dialog box:

1. Click the name of an e-mail program to upgrade it (**Figure 1.16**).

   When you click Next, Outlook will configure itself using the settings from the selected program and it will begin running. In this case, you're done with this chapter and you can go directly to Chapter 2! (If you later want to change your e-mail setup, follow the instructions in Appendix A.)

   or

   Click **None of the above** (**Figure 1.17**) if you don't want to upgrade an existing e-mail program.

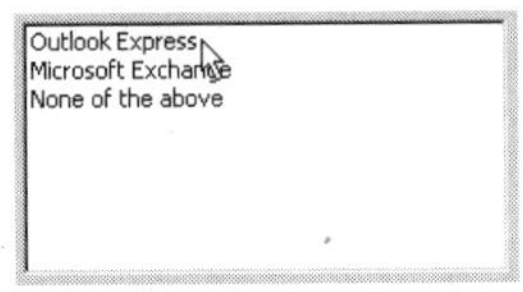

Figure 1.16 Click **Outlook Express** to upgrade this e-mail program.

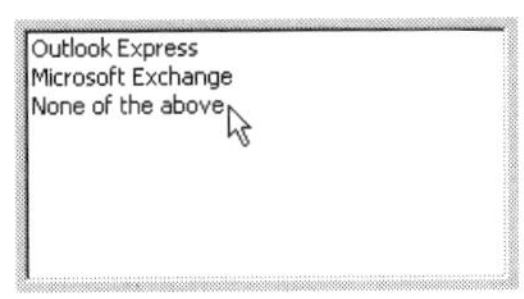

Figure 1.17 Click **None of the above** to forego upgrading an e-mail program.

Figure 1.18 Getting help on converting from Lotus cc:Mail.

If you make this choice, the wizard will display an additional series of dialog boxes so that you can specify new settings. Later, if you wish, you can import messages, addresses, and settings from your old e-mail program by following the instructions in "Importing Settings or Data from Another E-Mail Program" in Appendix A.

2. Click the **Next** button.

✔ Tips

- If you're switching from another e-mail or scheduling program to Outlook, you might find useful conversion information by typing the name of your previous program (for example, *Lotus cc:Mail* or *Schedule+*) into the Office Assistant and clicking the **Search** button (**Figure 1.18**).
- For instructions on using the Office Assistant, see the section "Consulting the Assistant" in Chapter 2.

E-mail Service Options dialog box

If you haven't chosen to use the settings from a previous version of Outlook or to upgrade an old e-mail program, the Outlook 2000 Startup Wizard will now display the E-mail Service Options dialog box, which lets you select your basic e-mail configuration (**Figure 1.19**).

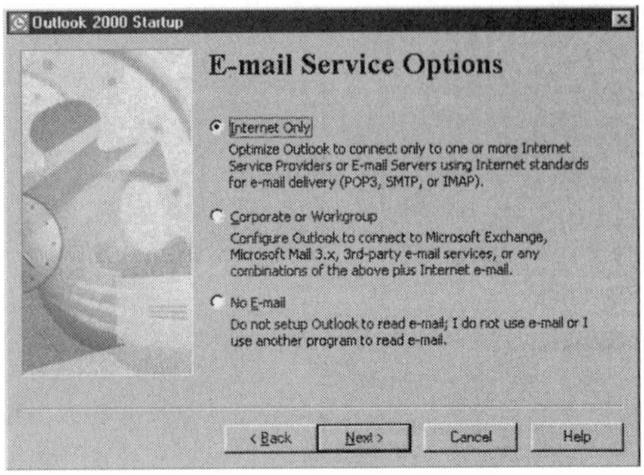

Figure 1.19 The E-mail Service Options dialog box.

To complete the E-mail Service Options dialog box:

1. Choose one of the three e-mail options.

   For help in making your choice, see the following tips and if necessary consult with your e-mail service provider or your corporate network administrator.

2. Click the **Next** button.

✔ Tips

- Select the **Internet Only** configuration (**Figure 1.20**) to get the fastest performance if your e-mail service uses standard Internet protocols (SMTP for outgoing e-mail and either POP3 or IMAP for incoming e-mail).

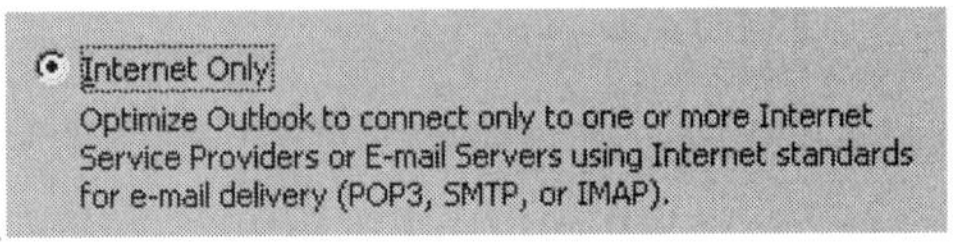

Figure 1.20 Selecting the Internet Only configuration.

- Select the **Corporate or Workgroup** configuration (**Figure 1.21**) if you want to use Outlook on a network with Microsoft Exchange Server, Microsoft Mail 3.x, or Lotus cc:Mail server. You should also choose this configuration if you use an e-mail service that doesn't employ standard e-mail protocols—for example, CompuServe or Classic MSN (MSN Version 1.x supplied with Windows 95). You can use this configuration for an e-mail service that employs the SMTP/POP3 protocols, but with slower performance than the Internet Only configuration.

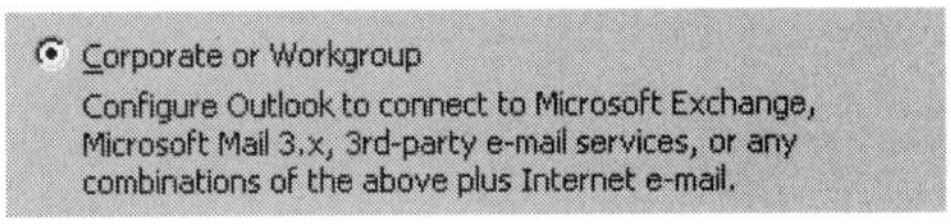

Figure 1.21 Selecting the Corporate or Workgroup configuration.

Figure 1.22 Selecting the No E-Mail configuration.

- Select the **No E-mail** configuration (**Figure 1.22**) if you don't want to use Outlook to manage e-mail or fax messages.
- You can later switch between the Internet Only and the Corporate or Workgroup configurations by following the instructions given in the section "Changing Your Basic E-mail Configuration" in Appendix A.
- The set of features available in Outlook depends upon your basic e-mail configuration. In the following chapters, I will point out the specific differences. Sections that apply to only one of the two configurations will be marked with the Internet Only icon I/O or the Corporate or Workgroup icon C/W.

Setting up e-mail in Outlook

If you're using either the Internet Only or the Corporate or Workgroup configuration, one of two things will now occur during setup:

- If e-mail has already been set up on your computer, Outlook will configure itself to use your previous e-mail settings and it will begin running. In this case, you're done with this chapter, and you can go to Chapter 2. (If you later want to modify your e-mail setup, follow the instructions in Appendix A.)
- If e-mail hasn't previously been set up on your computer, one of the following wizards will now run to set up e-mail:
  - The **Internet Connection Wizard** (**Figure 1.23**), if you're using the Internet Only configuration. For instructions on completing this wizard, see the section "I/O To add a mail account with the Internet Connection Wizard" in Appendix A.
  - The **Inbox Setup Wizard** (**Figure 1.24**), if you're using the Corporate or Workgroup configuration. For instructions on completing this wizard, see the section "C/W To Create a user profile with the Inbox Setup Wizard" in Appendix A.

✔ Tip

- If you're connected to a Microsoft Exchange Server network, you can use the Inbox Setup Wizard to set up Exchange Server as your e-mail service. In addition to e-mail, Exchange Server adds many workgroup features to Outlook—for example, sharing information, scheduling meetings, and managing group projects. Throughout this book, sections discussing features that require Exchange Server will be marked with the Exchange Server icon E/S.

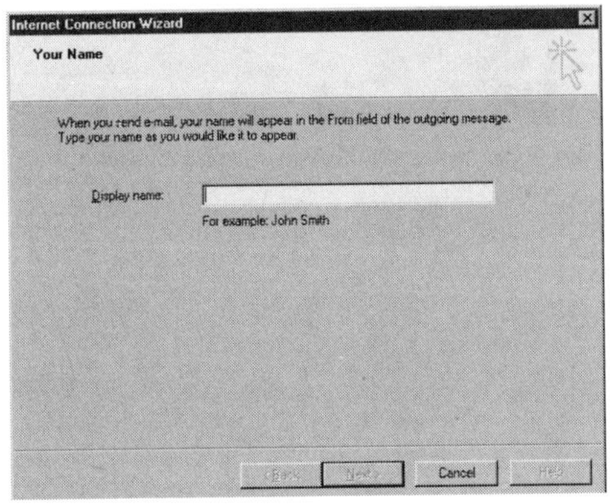

Figure 1.23 The first dialog box displayed by the Internet Connection Wizard.

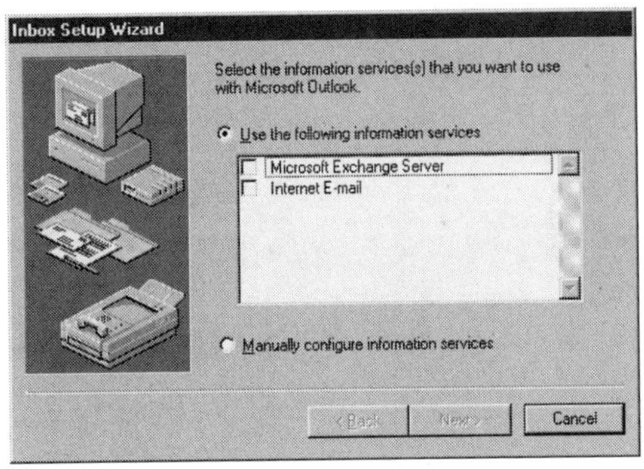

Figure 1.24 The first dialog box displayed by the Inbox Setup Wizard.

Setting up Outlook to send and receive faxes

If you have a fax modem installed on your computer (almost all newer modems are fax modems), you can use Outlook to send, receive, and store faxes within the same Inbox used for e-mail.

✔ Tip

- A fax modem is set up in a manner similar to an e-mail service. However, you normally use a special procedure (described next), rather than the Internet Connection Wizard or the Inbox Setup Wizard.

To set up a fax modem:

◆ If you're using the Internet Only configuration, follow the instructions in the section "I/O To add a fax account" in Appendix A.

or

If you're using the Corporate or Workgroup configuration, follow the instructions in the section "Setting Up and Modifying the Corporate or Workgroup E-mail Configuration" in Appendix A.

Getting Started Using Outlook

2

In this chapter, you'll get started using Outlook by learning the following:

- The various parts of the Outlook window and the way Outlook organizes information.
- How to perform basic Windows and Office techniques:
  - Using the mouse
  - Using menus, toolbars, and keyboard commands
  - Working with dialog boxes
  - Getting help
- How to navigate through Outlook and open folders containing different kinds of information.

✔ **Tip**

- The section "Running Outlook" in Chapter 1 described the different ways to start Outlook.

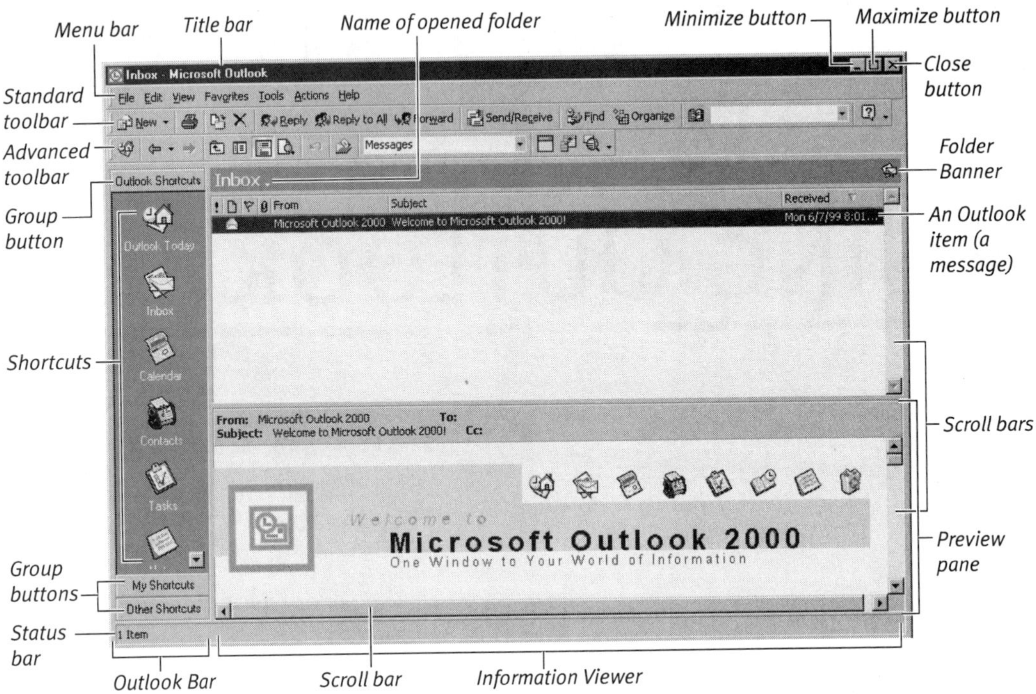

Figure 2.1 The Outlook program window.

The Outlook Window

Figure 2.1 shows the Outlook window as it might appear when you first start the program.

✔ Tips

- Your initial Outlook window might look different from the one shown in **Figure 2.1**, depending on the way you set up Outlook or the way you configured a previous version of Outlook. For example, your Outlook Bar might contain different shortcuts, the set of Outlook folders might vary, and your window might display different toolbars. Later in the book, you'll learn how to modify all of these features.
- You can show or hide the status bar at the bottom of the Outlook window by choosing the Status Bar command on the View menu. (See "To choose a menu command," later in the chapter.)

How Outlook Is Organized

The information Outlook manages is stored within a set of *Outlook folders*. Each Outlook folder stores, displays, and manages a particular type of information—for example, messages, appointments, names and addresses, tasks, or notes. The following are the default folders that Outlook initially creates for you and the types of information that each folder contains:

- **Outlook Today** displays a Web-style page that provides an overview of the current information in commonly used Outlook folders and lets you quickly manage this information.
- **Inbox** receives your incoming e-mail and fax messages.
- **Drafts** stores the messages you are composing, before you send them.
- **Outbox** temporarily holds the messages you have sent until they can be transmitted to the recipients.
- **Sent Items** keeps a copy of all messages you have sent.
- **Calendar** handles appointments, events, and meetings.
- **Contacts** manages information on your friends and business associates.
- **Tasks** keeps a list of the jobs you or others need to complete.
- **Notes** stores miscellaneous bits of information that you jot down.
- **Journal** maintains a record of various types of events, such as sending an e-mail message, accessing an Office file, or making a phone call.
- **Deleted Items** temporarily holds the Outlook items you've removed until they are permanently deleted.

A particular piece of information contained in an Outlook folder is called an *Outlook item*—for example, a message in the Inbox folder, an appointment in the Calendar folder, a pending task in the Tasks folder, or a note in the Notes folder.

Outlook also lets you access the files on your local or network disks. The integrated file management feature of Outlook provides an interface for working with disk files that's similar to the Windows Explorer.

As you can see in **Figure 2.1**, the Outlook program window is divided into two main parts:

- The *Outlook Bar* on the left, which displays groups of shortcuts. A shortcut consists of an icon plus a text label. You can click a shortcut to quickly open a particular Outlook folder or file folder.
- The *Information Viewer* on the right, which displays the contents of the open folder. Sometimes the Information Viewer is divided into smaller panes. For example, as shown in **Figure 2.1**, when the Inbox folder is open you can display a Preview pane at the bottom of the Information Viewer, which lets you immediately read your messages without opening them.

✔ Tips

- The Inbox, Drafts, Outbox, and Sent Items folders all store *mail items*—a category of Outlook items that includes e-mail messages and faxes.
- Don't confuse an *Outlook folder* with a *file folder*. An Outlook folder stores Outlook items strictly within Outlook, while a file folder stores disk files on a local or network disk and can be accessed by any program. In this book, the term *folder* refers to an Outlook folder unless it's otherwise qualified.
- Later in the chapter, you'll learn how to open Outlook folders, and in the next two chapters, you'll learn how to work with Outlook items and the folders that contain them.
- Later in the chapter, you'll also learn how to open file folders in Outlook, and in Chapter 12 you'll learn how to manage file folders and the disk files they contain.

Learning Basic Windows and Office Techniques

Before you can learn the techniques specific to Outlook, you must be familiar with basic Windows and Office techniques. These are described in the following instructions.

✔ Tips

- Often, you can perform an Outlook operation using the mouse, a menu command, a toolbar button, or a keyboard command. I generally describe all the different methods so that you can choose your favorite.
- Methods using menu commands or toolbar buttons are the easiest to remember because the menus and buttons provide visual cues. You need to memorize keyboard commands, but they are generally faster. So, as you work with Outlook, you might want to gradually learn the keyboard commands to speed up your work.

Using the mouse

These are the terms for basic mouse operations that are used in this book:

- To **point to** an object on the screen means to move the tip of the mouse pointer over the object (**Figure 2.2**).
- To **click** means to press and release the left mouse button.
- To **double-click** means to press and release the left mouse button twice in rapid succession.
- To **click on** an object (or just **click** an object) means to point to the object and then click (**Figure 2.3**).
- To **double-click on** an object (or just **double-click** an object) means to point to the object and then double-click (**Figure 2.4**).
- To **right-click** means to click using the right mouse button (**Figure 2.5**).
- To **drag** means to point to an object or location, press the left mouse button, and then move the pointer while holding down the button (**Figure 2.6**). To **drop** means to release the mouse button after dragging to a destination location.

✔ Tip

- The mouse pointer changes shape according to the part of the screen you point to, to indicate the particular action the mouse will perform. For instance, while over a toolbar button or menu the pointer is usually a left-pointing arrow, while over text it's usually an I-beam, and while over a hyperlink it's usually a hand with an extended index finger. (A *hyperlink* is an object you click to open a specific document, page, or Web page.)

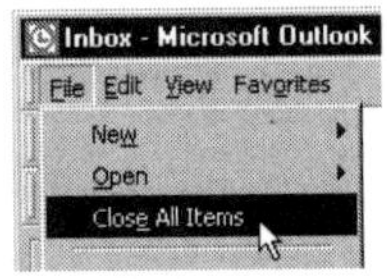

Figure 2.2 *Pointing to* a menu command.

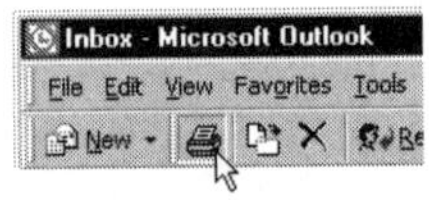

Figure 2.3 *Clicking* a toolbar button.

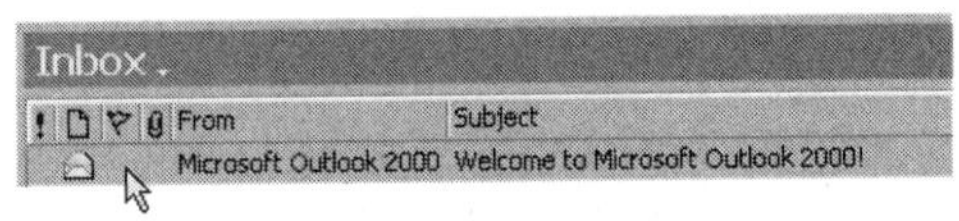

Figure 2.4 *Double-clicking* a message in the Inbox.

Figure 2.5 *Right-clicking* a blank area to open a pop-up menu.

Figure 2.6 The mouse pointer as it appears when you *drag* an Outlook item from one folder to another.

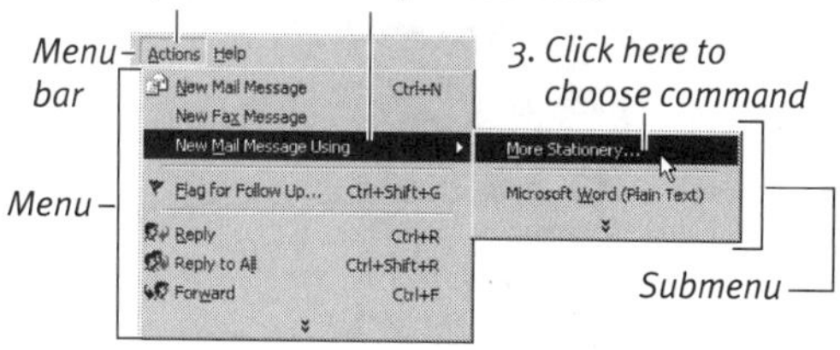

Figure 2.7 Choosing a menu command on a submenu.

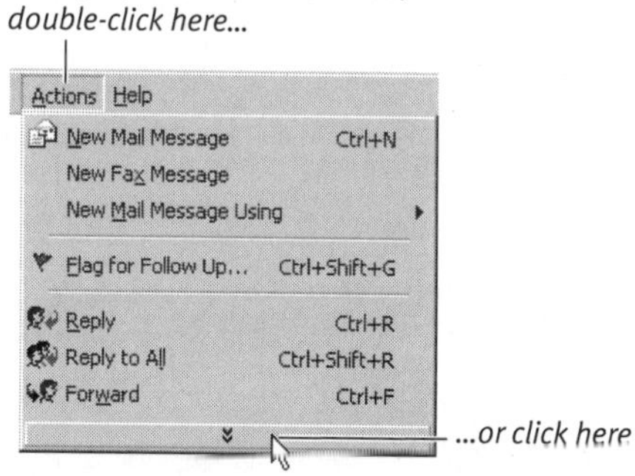

Figure 2.8 Displaying *all* commands on a menu.

To choose a menu command:

- Click the menu's label on the menu bar to open the menu, and then click the command. If the command is on a submenu, first point to the submenu label (marked with a triangle) to open the submenu, and then click the command (**Figure 2.7**).

✔ Tips

- In this book, the phrase "Choose Tools > Send" tells you to choose the Send command on the Tools menu. And "Choose Actions > New Mail Message Using > More Stationery" tells you to choose the command shown in **Figure 2.7**.
- A menu command followed by an ellipsis opens a dialog box to obtain additional information, rather than immediately carrying out an action.
- If a menu command is unavailable, the label is displayed in light gray letters and you can't choose it.

To show all commands on a menu:

- To see *all* commands on a particular menu, open the menu by *double*-clicking the menu's label. By default, Outlook shows only the menu commands you use most frequently.

  or

  Click the bottom of the menu (marked with double down-arrows) (**Figure 2.8**).

  or

  Pause about 5 seconds after opening the menu. All the commands will then appear.

(continued on next page)

✔ Tips

- When you show all menu commands, the commands that would normally be hidden are displayed on a lighter gray background.
- If you want Outlook to always show all commands on a menu, choose Tools > Customize, and in the Options tab of the Customize dialog box uncheck the **Menus show recently used commands first** option. (Dialog boxes are discussed later in this chapter.)
- In Chapter 14 (the section "Customizing the Toolbars and Menus") you'll learn how to customize the Outlook menus to suit your work habits. However, I recommend waiting to do this until you finish working through this book, so that your menus will match the instructions you see in the book.

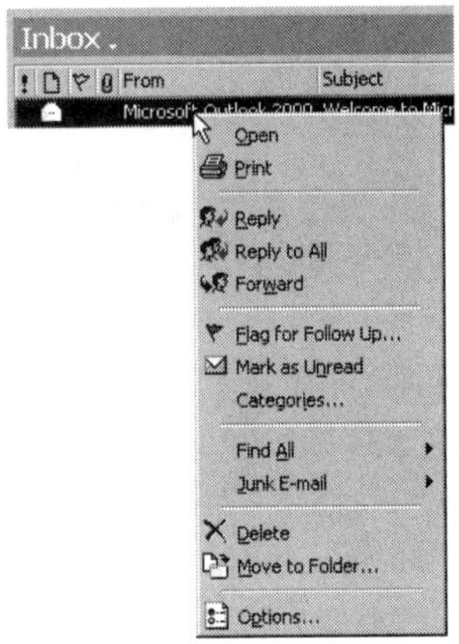

Figure 2.9 The pop-up menu displayed when you right-click a message in the Inbox.

To use a pop-up menu:

1. Right-click an object in the Outlook window.
   Outlook will display a pop-up menu of commands that are useful for working on whatever object underlies the mouse pointer. For example, if you right click a message in your Inbox, Outlook will show a pop-up menu of commands for working with a message (**Figure 2.9**).
2. Choose (that is, click) the command you want to carry out.

✔ Tip

- A pop-up menu is also known as a *shortcut menu* or a *context menu* (because the commands it shows depend upon the context of the object that you right-click).

Figure 2.10 The Standard toolbar.

Figure 2.11 The Advanced toolbar.

Figure 2.12 The Web toolbar.

Figure 2.13 Using the Toolbars submenu to display a toolbar.

Figure 2.14 Using the pop-up menu to display a toolbar.

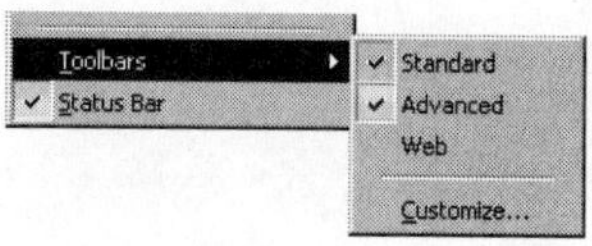

Figure 2.15 Check marks indicating that the Standard and Advanced toolbars are displayed.

Using toolbars

Outlook has three toolbars you can display:

- The **Standard** toolbar, which contains buttons for the most commonly used commands (**Figure 2.10**).
- The **Advanced** toolbar, which has buttons for less frequently used commands (**Figure 2.11**).
- The **Web** toolbar, which provides buttons for navigating through documents or Web pages (**Figure 2.12**). It's described in Chapter 13.

✔ Tip

- The buttons displayed on the Standard and Advanced toolbars change according to the folder that's currently open. The toolbars provide the commands that are most useful for working with each type of information.

To display a toolbar:

- If a toolbar you want to use isn't visible, choose View > Toolbars to open the Toolbars submenu, and then choose the name of the toolbar (**Figure 2.13**).

  or

  Right-click the toolbar area of the Outlook window and choose the name of the toolbar on the pop-up menu (**Figure 2.14**).

  A check mark will appear next to the toolbar name on the menu to indicate that the toolbar is displayed (**Figure 2.15**).

✔ Tip

- To hide a toolbar, choose the toolbar name from either the Toolbars submenu or the pop-up menu. The toolbar will be hidden and the check mark will be removed.

To execute a toolbar command:

- Click the toolbar button (**Figure 2.16**).

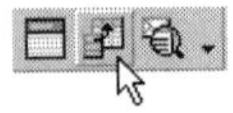

Figure 2.16 Clicking a toolbar button.

✔ Tips

- If the buttons belonging to a toolbar don't all fit within the area allotted to the toolbar in the program window, Outlook will display only the ones you've used most frequently. You can display the hidden buttons by clicking the right end of the toolbar (**Figure 2.17**).
- To see the purpose of a toolbar button, point to it for a few seconds and Outlook will display a *ScreenTip* describing the button (**Figure 2.18**), provided that the **Show ScreenTips on toolbars** option is checked. (Access this option by choosing Tools > Customize and opening the Options tab in the Customize dialog box.)
- Some toolbar buttons display a menu of commands or a list of items, rather than immediately carrying out an action. To display the menu or list, click the down-arrow to the right of the button (**Figure 2.19**). Then click the desired command or item.
- Buttons that turn an option on or off might appear normal when the option is off and appear pressed when the option is on. For example, when the Preview pane isn't displayed, the Preview Pane button appears normal . After you click this button to display the Preview pane, the button appears pressed .

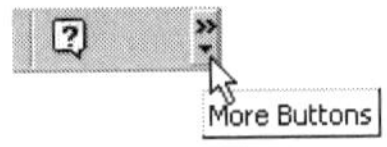

Figure 2.17 Displaying hidden toolbar buttons.

Figure 2.18 Displaying a ScreenTip.

Figure 2.19 A toolbar button that displays a menu of commands.

- If a button command isn't available, the button will be displayed in light gray, and clicking it will have no effect. For example, the Undo button on the Advanced toolbar will be displayed in light gray when there is no action to undo.
- In Chapter 14 (the section "Customizing the Toolbars and Menus") you'll learn how to move and customize the Outlook toolbars to suit your work habits. However, I recommend waiting to do this until you finish working through this book, so that the instructions you see in the book will match your toolbars.

Using keyboard commands

Many keyboard commands consist of a single key. For example, you can view help by pressing the F1 key or close a dialog box by pressing the Esc key.

Other keyboard commands consist of two or three keys that you must press simultaneously. For example, you can copy text by pressing Ctrl-C (that is, by pressing Ctrl and C simultaneously). And you can open the Address Book by pressing Ctrl- Shift-B (that is, by pressing Ctrl and Shift and B simultaneously).

✔ Tips

- You can execute any menu command by pressing Alt plus the underlined letters on the menu. For example, you can invoke the Edit > Copy menu command by first pressing Alt-E to open the Edit menu (*E* is underlined in the label for the Edit menu), and then pressing C (*C* is underlined in the Copy command label) (**Figure 2.20**).
- Many (but not all) of the Outlook menu commands display equivalent keyboard commands. For example, next to the Copy command on the Edit menu, Outlook displays an equivalent keyboard command, Ctrl-C (**Figure 2.20**).
- To obtain a concise list of Outlook keyboard commands, type "keyboard shortcuts" into the Office Assistant and then choose the topic "Keyboard shortcuts." To create a printed copy, you can print out each of the subtopics. For instructions on using the Assistant, see the section "Consulting the Assistant," later in this chapter.

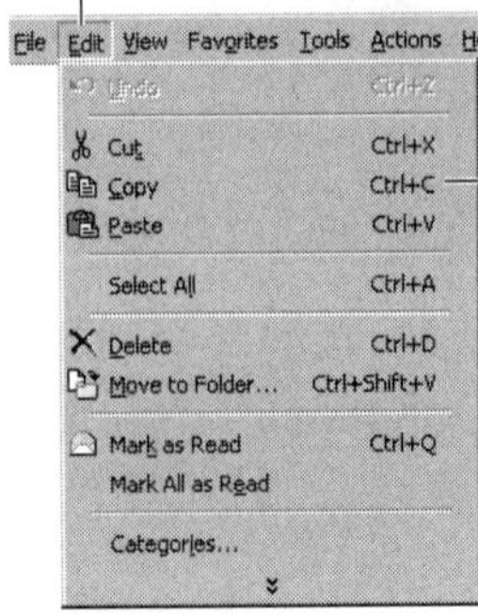

Figure 2.20 Executing a menu command using the keyboard.

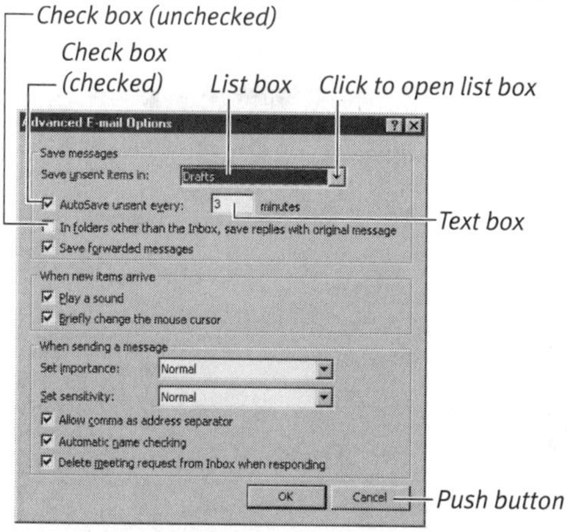

Figure 2.21 Dialog box controls.

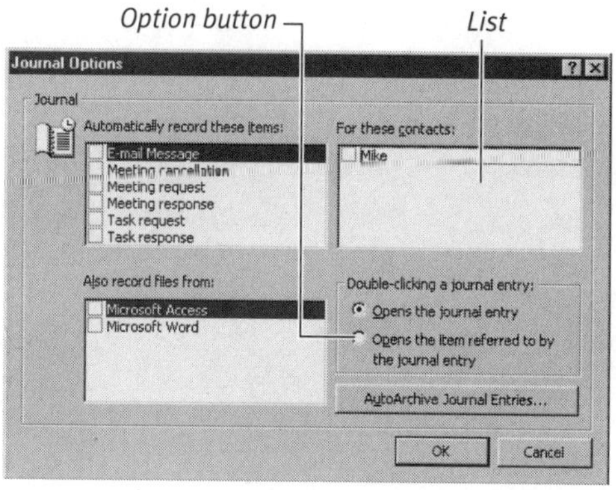

Figure 2.22 More dialog box controls.

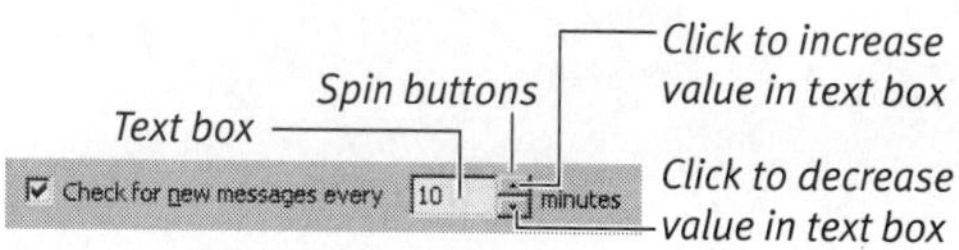

Figure 2.23 Even more dialog box controls.

Working with dialog boxes

A *dialog box* is a window that Outlook temporarily opens on top of its main window to display information or to obtain information from you (**Figure 2.21** and **Figure 2.22**). You enter information into a dialog box by using the different types of *controls* it displays:

- You click a **push button** to carry out an action, such as closing the dialog box and applying its settings (the **OK** button), closing the dialog box and discarding its settings (the **Cancel** button), or opening another dialog box (**Figure 2.21**).
- You check or uncheck a **check box** to turn an independent option on or off (**Figure 2.21**). To check or uncheck a check box, simply click on any part of the the label or the box itself.
- You select an **option button** (also quaintly known as a **radio button**) to choose one of a group of mutually exclusive options (**Figure 2.22**). To select an option button, click on any part of the label or the button itself. A dot will appear in the button, and the dot from the previously selected option button will be removed.
- You click and type into a **text box** to supply textual information (**Figure 2.21**).
- Sometimes, a pair of **spin buttons** are displayed to the right of a text box to help you enter a numeric value (**Figure 2.23**).
- You click an item displayed in a **list** to select it (**Figure 2.22**). Selecting a list item highlights it. Sometimes double-clicking a list item will select the item, close the dialog box, and apply the settings.

(continued on next page)

◆ You open a **list box** and then click an item in the list to select it (**Figure 2.21**). To open a list box (that is, to drop it down and display the list items), click the down-arrow at the right end.

◆ Some dialog boxes contain several **tabs**, each of which displays a separate set of controls. For example, the dialog box shown in **Figure 2.24** has three tabs. To open a tab and display the controls it contains, click the label at the top of the tab.

✔ Tips

■ With most dialog boxes, you must click the **OK**, **Close**, or **Cancel** button to remove the dialog box before you can continue working in Outlook.

■ Generally, pressing **Enter** while a dialog box is displayed is equivalent to clicking the **OK** button (the dialog box is closed and its settings are applied). And pressing Esc or clicking the **Close** button ☒ is equivalent to clicking the **Cancel** button (the dialog box is closed and its settings are discarded).

■ To get help while you're working with a dialog box, click the Help button ? near the upper-right corner of the dialog box and then click the control or area of the dialog box you want to learn about.

Click here to open the Commands tab.

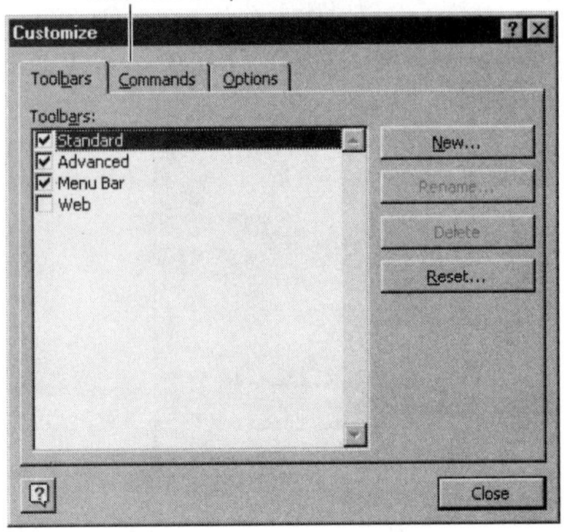

Figure 2.24 Opening a tab in a tabbed dialog box.

Figure 2.25 The Office Assistant, at your service.

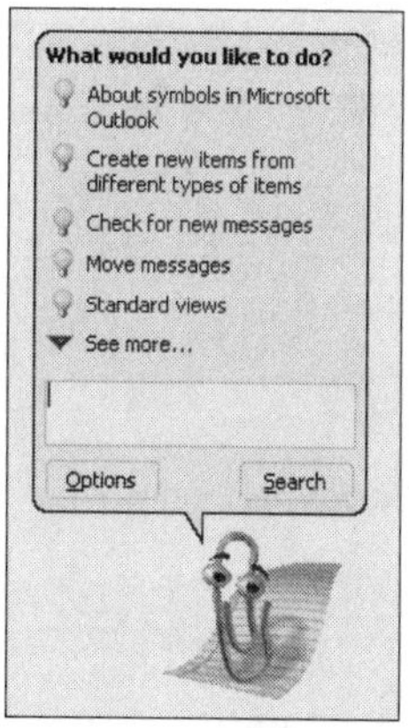

Figure 2.26 The Office Assistant displaying a balloon for you to ask your question.

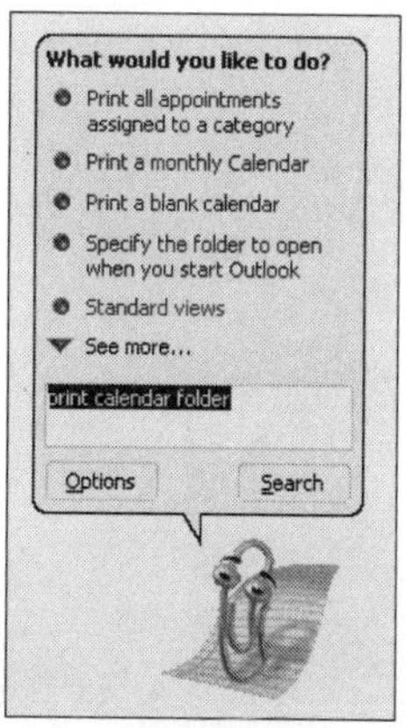

Figure 2.27 A list of topics matching the question that was typed.

Consulting the Assistant

You can get help on almost any feature of Outlook by using the Office Assistant (**Figure 2.25**).

✔ Tip

- If you want to start exploring Outlook on your own, before working though this book, I recommend that you read the instructions on using the Assistant and on opening folders—both given later in this chapter. You'll find most commands you need on the menus and on the Standard toolbar. Use the Assistant whenever you need help!

To use the Assistant:

1. If the Assistant is visible, click on it.

   or

   If the Assistant is hidden, click the Microsoft Outlook Help button on the Standard toolbar, choose Help > Microsoft Outlook Help, or press F1.

   If these methods fail, the Assistant is turned off. To turn on the Assistant and display it, choose Help > Show The Office Assistant.

   The Assistant will display a help balloon (**Figure 2.26**).

2. Type a question into the text box in the Assistant's balloon and click the **Search** button.

   You don't have to type a full sentence, but try to be specific so that the Assistant can find a shorter, more appropriate list of topics. (For example, if you want to print your Calendar folder, type "print calendar folder" rather than just "print.")

   The balloon will display a list of topics matching your question. **Figure 2.27** shows the topics displayed for "print calendar folder."

(continued on next page)

3. Click the most appropriate of the listed topics to view the help information. (If the topics don't all fit in the balloon, you can click **See more** to view additional topics.)

   The help text will generally be displayed in the Microsoft Outlook Help window (**Figure 2.28**).

4. When you're done reading the help text, remove the Microsoft Outlook Help window by clicking the Close button ☒ in the upper-right corner of the window.

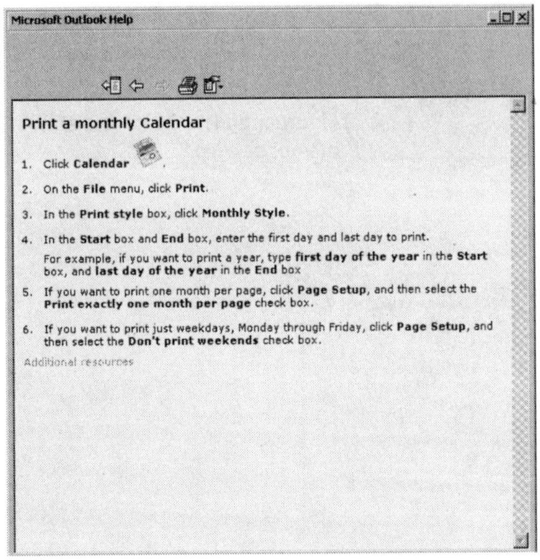

Figure 2.28 The Microsoft Outlook Help window.

✔ Tips

- Like a cat, the Assistant tends to perch right where you're working. To move it, drag the main Assistant body (not the balloon) to another part of the screen.
- You can temporarily hide the Assistant by choosing Help > Hide The Office Assistant.
- An Outlook form (described in Chapter 3) also has a Help menu, which you can use instead of the Help menu in the main Outlook window.
- The Assistant observes you working and occasionally offers a tip. When it has a tip to provide, a light bulb appears next to the Assistant (or next to the Microsoft Outlook Help button if the Assistant is hidden). Click the light bulb to see the tip.
- To print a help topic, click the Print button 🖶 at the top of the Microsoft Outlook Help window.

Figure 2.29 The pointer that's displayed when you choose the Help > What's This? menu command.

- For information on choosing a different Assistant character, or on modifying the Assistant's behavior, see the section "Changing the Office Assistant" in Appendix A. (Be sure to check this section if the Assistant isn't working as described here.)
- To get information on a particular object in the Outlook window (for example, a toolbar button, menu command, or piece of information), choose Help > What's This? A question mark will appear next to the mouse pointer (**Figure 2.29**). Then, click the object you want to learn about. If you click a toolbar button or choose a menu command, Outlook will display information on the command rather than carrying out the command.

Getting Around in Outlook

The first step in working with any kind of information in Outlook is to open the appropriate folder. For example, if you want to read or send e-mail messages, open the Inbox folder. If you want to see your appointments for the day, open the Calendar folder. If you want to find out what you need to get done this week, open the Tasks folder. And if you want to open a Word document contained in the My Documents file folder, open the My Documents file folder.

The following instructions show you the different ways to open an Outlook folder. They also show you how to open a file folder in Outlook so you can access the disk files it contains. These techniques will let you move around in Outlook and explore the different types of information it manages.

✔ Tips

- In Chapter 3 you'll learn how to work with Outlook items, and in Chapter 4 you'll learn how to modify the Outlook folders that contain items.
- In Chapter 12 you'll learn how to work with file folders and the files they contain.

Opening an Outlook folder

The Outlook shortcuts are divided into several groups. In the groups that Outlook creates, shortcuts to the Outlook folders are located within the following groups:

- **Outlook Shortcuts** contains shortcuts to the general-purpose Outlook folders: Outlook Today, Inbox, Calendar, Contacts, Tasks, Notes, and Deleted Items.
- **My Shortcuts** contains shortcuts to additional mail-item folders—Drafts, Outbox, and Sent Items—and a shortcut to the Journal folder and a shortcut to the Outlook Update page on Microsoft's Web site.

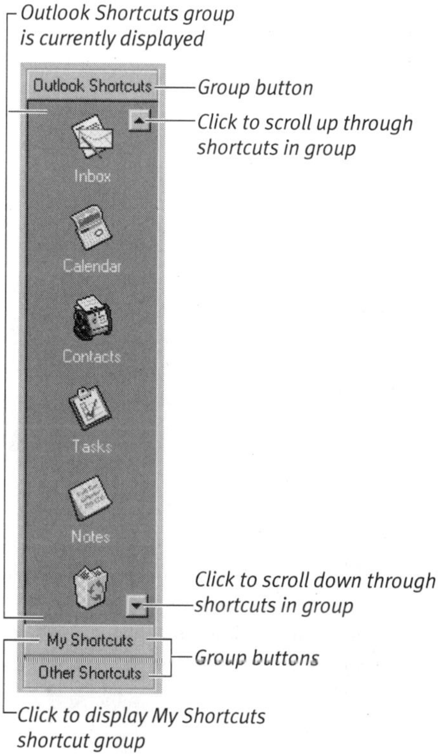

Figure 2.30 Opening a shortcut group in the Outlook Bar.

To open an Outlook folder:

1. In the Outlook Bar, if the group containing the shortcut to the folder you want to open isn't visible, click the button for that group (normally, Outlook Shortcuts or My Shortcuts).

   Outlook will then display the group. You can use the scroll arrows to scroll up and down through the shortcuts (**Figure 2.30**).

2. Click the shortcut for the folder you want to open.

   Outlook will then display the contents of that folder in the Information Viewer on the right. (For example, in **Figure 2.1**, the Inbox folder is opened and the message it contains is displayed in the Information Viewer.)

✔ Tips

- You can hide or display the Outlook Bar by choosing View > Outlook Bar.
- Your groups and shortcuts might be different from those described here. For example, if you had a previous version of Outlook on your computer when you installed Outlook 2000, Outlook might use your previous groups and shortcuts.
- Outlook Bar shortcuts can directly open disk files or Web pages, as well as folders. An example is the Outlook Update shortcut in the default My Shortcuts group, which opens the Outlook Update Web site when you click it.
- You can open an Outlook folder in a separate Outlook window by right-clicking the folder's shortcut in the Outlook Bar and then choosing Open In New Window from the pop-up menu. This technique allows you to work with a second folder without disturbing your view of the currently opened folder.

- In Chapter 14 (the section "Modifying the Outlook Bar") you'll learn how to add, remove, and modify groups and shortcuts in the Outlook Bar. However, I recommend waiting to do this until you finish working through this book so that your Outlook Bar will match the default one described in this book (unless, of course, your Outlook Bar is already different).

To open a file folder:

1. If the Other Shortcuts group isn't currently displayed in the Outlook Bar, click the Other Shortcuts group button to display this group (**Figure 2.31**).

   In the initial Outlook Bar setup, all shortcuts to file folders are located within the Other Shortcuts group.

2. Click the shortcut for the file folder you want to open (**Figure 2.32**).

   Outlook will then display the contents of that file folder—its files and subfolders—in the Information Viewer of the Outlook window (**Figure 2.33**).

Figure 2.31 Opening the Other Shortcuts group.

Figure 2.32 Opening the Favorites folder in the Other Shortcuts group.

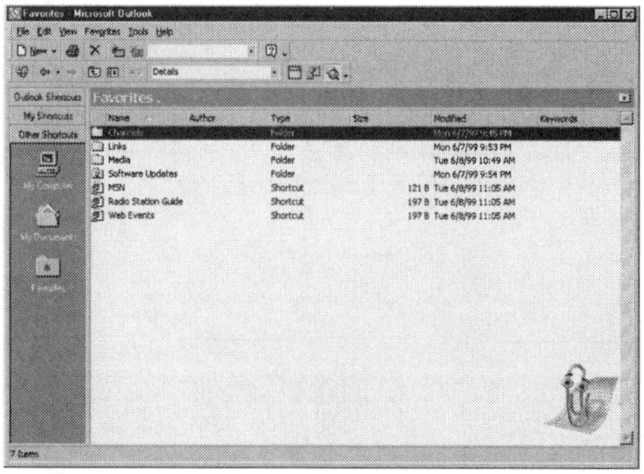

Figure 2.33 The Favorites folder displayed in the Information Viewer.

The following are the initial shortcuts in the Other Shortcuts group:

- **My Computer** opens the root folder containing all of your local disks.
- **My Documents** opens the My Documents folder on your hard disk, which is the default folder where the Office documents you create are stored.
- **Favorites** opens the Favorites folder on your hard disk, which stores the Internet addresses that you have saved using Microsoft Internet Explorer, Outlook, or other Office applications.

✔ Tip

- You can open a file folder in a separate Outlook window by right-clicking the folder's shortcut in the Outlook Bar and then choosing Open In New Window from the pop-up menu. This technique allows you to work with a second file folder without disturbing your view of the currently opened file folder.

Other ways to open folders

Outlook provides several additional ways to open either an Outlook folder or a file folder.

- You can select a folder in the **Folder List**, which displays a hierarchical list of folders. You can display the Folder List either temporarily or permanently in the left part of the Information Viewer. The Folder List lets you access *any* folder, not just those for which shortcuts have been created.

  Both Outlook folders and file folders are organized in a hierarchy. That is, folders can contain other folders, as well as items or files. And there is a single *root folder* at the top of the hierarchy (Outlook Today for your Outlook folders and Desktop for your file folders), which contains everything.

- You can use the **Go To Folder** dialog box to locate and open a specific folder. This method is useful for opening a folder that doesn't have a shortcut.

- You can **navigate** through folders that you've previously opened, using buttons on the Advanced toolbar or commands on the Go To submenu of the View menu.

- You can open the next folder up in the hierarchy of your Outlook or file folders by clicking the **Up One Level button**.

✔ Tips

- From anywhere in Outlook, you can open the Outlook Today folder by clicking the Outlook Today button on the Advanced toolbar, and you can open the Inbox folder by pressing Ctrl-Shift-I.

- You can open the Outlook Today, Inbox, Drafts, Calendar, Contacts, or Tasks folder by opening the View menu, pointing to Go To, and choosing the folder name from the submenu.

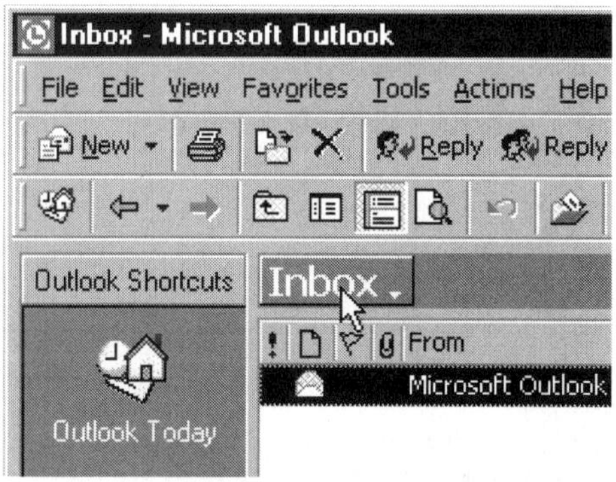

Figure 2.34 Open the Folder List temporarily by clicking the folder name at the left end of the Folder Banner.

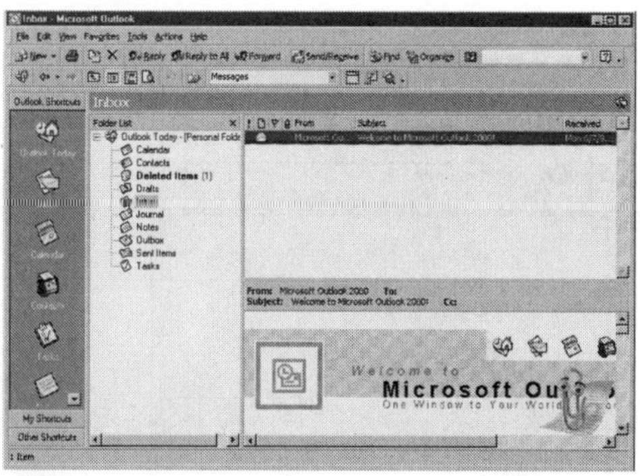

Figure 2.35 Permanently displayed Folder List displaying Outlook folders.

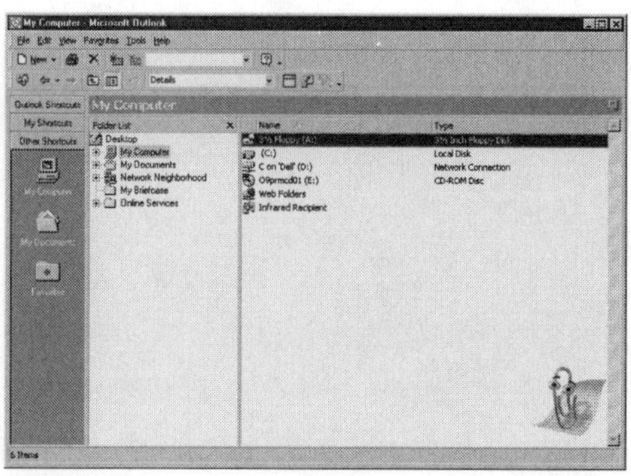

Figure 2.36 Permanently displayed Folder List displaying file folders.

To open a folder using the Folder List:

1. Display the Folder List temporarily by clicking the left end of the Folder Banner, where the name of the currently open folder is displayed (**Figure 2.34**).

   or

   Display the Folder List permanently by clicking the Folder List button on the Advanced toolbar or by choosing View > Folder List.

   If an Outlook folder is open, the folder list will display your Outlook folders (**Figure 2.35**). If a file folder is open, it will display your file folders (**Figure 2.36**).

2. To expand or collapse a branch of the folder hierarchy in the Folder List, click the + or – symbol next to the folder's name (**Figure 2.37**).

3. To open a folder, click on it in the Folder List.

   Outlook will then display the contents of that folder in the Information Viewer. If you displayed the Folder List temporarily, the list will be hidden and you'll have to open it again the next time you want to use it.

✔ Tips

- A temporarily displayed Folder List overlaps the information in the Information Viewer, while a permanently displayed Folder List occupies a separate pane.
- A temporary Folder List is hidden when you select a folder in it or click anywhere in Outlook outside of it.
- To hide a permanently displayed Folder List, click the Folder List button or choose the View > Folder List menu command again. Or, click the Close button in the upper-right corner of the Folder List.

(continued on next page)

- You can convert a temporary Folder List to a permanent one by clicking the push pin button in the upper-right corner of the Folder List.
- If an Outlook folder contains one or more unread messages, the Folder List displays the folder's name in bold and indicates the number of unread messages it contains. An example is the Deleted Items folder shown in **Figure 2.35**. (Exception: The Outbox or Drafts folder is displayed in bold if it contains *any* messages, and the number shown is the *total* number of messages it contains.)

Figure 2.37 Expanding and collapsing branches of the folder hierarchy in the Folder List.

To locate and open a specific folder using the Go To Folder dialog box:

1. Choose View > Go To > Folder or press Ctrl-Y to open the Go To Folder dialog box (**Figure 2.38**).
2. In the **Look in** list box, select Outlook if you want to open an Outlook folder or select File System if you want to open a file folder.
3. Type the name of the folder you want to open into the box of the **Folder name** list box.

   or

   Select the name of the folder from the drop-down list of the **Folder name** list box. This list contains the names of folders you've recently opened.

   or

   Select the name of the folder in the hierarchical list displayed below the **Folder name** list box.
4. Click the **OK** button.

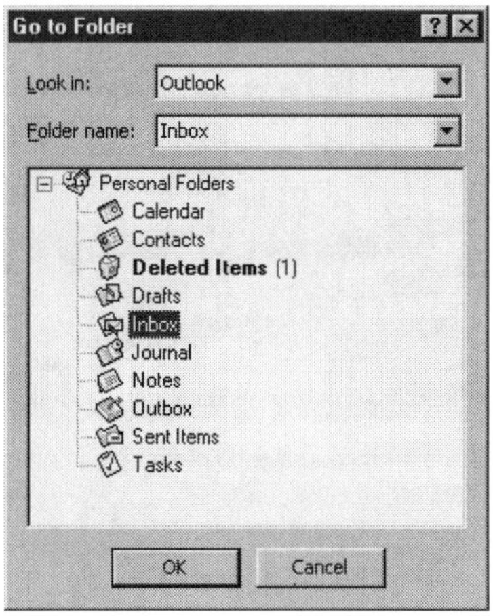

Figure 2.38 The Go To Folder dialog box.

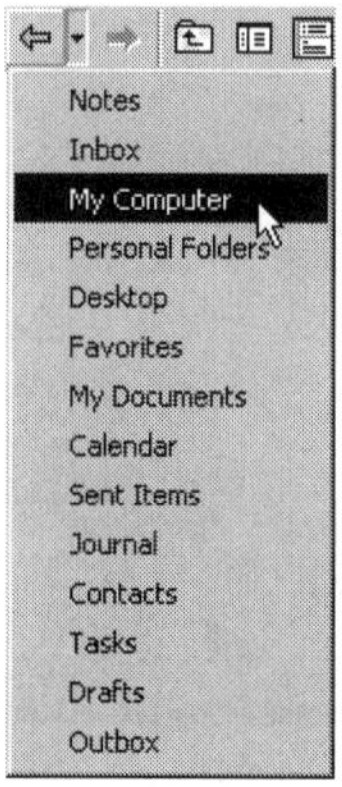

Figure 2.39 Open a previously opened folder by selecting it from the Previous Folder button's drop-down list.

To navigate through previously opened folders:

1. To reopen the folder you last had open, click the Previous Folder button on the Advanced toolbar.
2. To open a specific folder that you previously opened, click the down arrow on the Previous Folder button and select the name of the folder from the drop-down list (**Figure 2.39**).
3. After you've clicked the Previous Folder button one or more times to go back through previously opened folders, you can go forward again by clicking the Next Folder button on the Advanced toolbar.

To open the next folder up in the folder hierarchy:

- Click the Up One Level button on the Advanced toolbar.

  For example, if the Inbox is open, clicking this button will open Outlook Today, because Inbox is contained within Outlook Today in the hierarchy of Outlook folders (see the Folder List in **Figure 2.35**). Similarly, if the Favorites file folder is open, clicking this button will normally open the Windows file folder, because Favorites is usually contained within Windows in the file system hierarchy.

✔ Tip

- For a file folder only, you can open a subfolder of the currently opened folder by double-clicking the subfolder name in the Information Viewer.

WORKING WITH OUTLOOK ITEMS

3

Outlook *items* are the individual pieces of information stored in your Outlook folders—for example, e-mail messages in your Inbox folder, appointments in your Calendar folder, and task descriptions in your Tasks folder.

The first step in working with a particular type of Outlook item is to open the appropriate folder. Chapter 2 (the section "How to Get Around in Outlook") described the different ways to locate and open folders. Specifically, you should open the

- **Inbox**, **Drafts**, **Outbox**, or **Sent Items** folder to work with e-mail or fax messages.
- **Calendar** folder to work with appointments, events, or meetings.
- **Contacts** folder to work with contact descriptions (each of which stores information on a person or company) or distribution lists (each of which stores an entire set of addresses).
- **Tasks** folder to work with task descriptions.
- **Journal** folder to work with journal entries.
- **Notes** folder to work with text notes.
- **Deleted Items** folder to work with items you've removed from other folders.

In this chapter you'll learn how to

- Create new Outlook items
- Open items in an Outlook form
- Edit items
- Copy or move items
- Remove items, temporarily or permanently
- Archive items, automatically or manually
- Alter the overall organization of items by switching views
- Modify the way items are displayed in a particular view by sorting, filtering, or grouping them
- Work with items using the Organize Page
- Find Outlook items as well as disk files

✔ Tips

- This is the first of two chapters that cover the general Outlook techniques that you use when working with almost any type of information. In this chapter, you learn how to work with the items in Outlook folders, while in Chapter 4 you learn how to work with the folders themselves.
- I recommend quickly reading through Chapters 3 and 4 now and referring back to them frequently once you start working with the specific types of Outlook information in Chapters 5 through 11.
- The list of folders given above refers only to the default folders created by Outlook. In Chapter 4, you'll learn how to create new folders to store specific types of Outlook information.
- The **Outlook Today** folder is a special case. Rather than storing a particular type of Outlook item, it displays a page that gives you access to the current information in several commonly used folders.

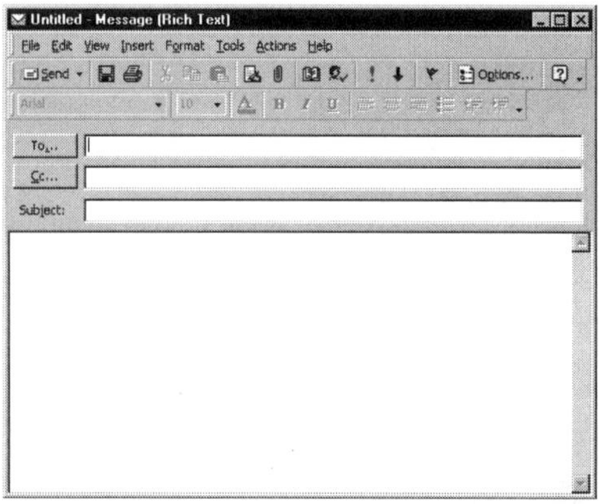

Figure 3.1 The form for defining a new e-mail message.

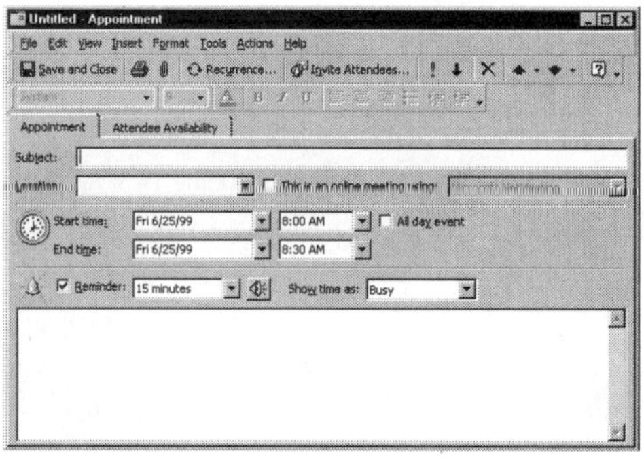

Figure 3.2 The form for defining a new appointment.

Figure 3.3 The form for defining a new note.

Creating Items

You enter information into Outlook by creating new Outlook items. You typically define the information for a new item in a separate window known as a *form*. A form displays a set of controls (text boxes, list boxes, option buttons, and so on) in which you enter the item information. Each piece of information that you enter through a control—such as the subject of an e-mail message, the start time of an appointment, or the priority of a task—is known as a *field*. A form also provides menu commands and toolbar buttons to assist you in adding, editing, and formatting the information and in working with the item in various ways.

Each type of item—for example, an e-mail message, an appointment, or a note—has a different form, one that's designed specifically for entering, editing, and viewing the item's information (**Figures 3.1 through 3.3**).

✔ Tips

- For a description of the different controls you use for entering information, see the section "Working with dialog boxes" in Chapter 2.
- In a form, if a toolbar you want to use isn't visible, choose View > Toolbars on the form's menu, and then choose the name of the toolbar from the submenu. Or, right-click the toolbar area of the form and choose the name of the toolbar from the pop-up menu.
- In addition to menu commands for working directly with the opened item, most forms also provide general-purpose commands that are the same as menu commands found on the main Outlook window.

(continued on next page)

These commands include

- The commands on the File > New submenu for creating new Outlook items
- Tools > Address Book for opening the Address Book dialog box
- Tools > Customize for customizing the Outlook toolbars and menus
- The commands on the Help menu for obtaining online help

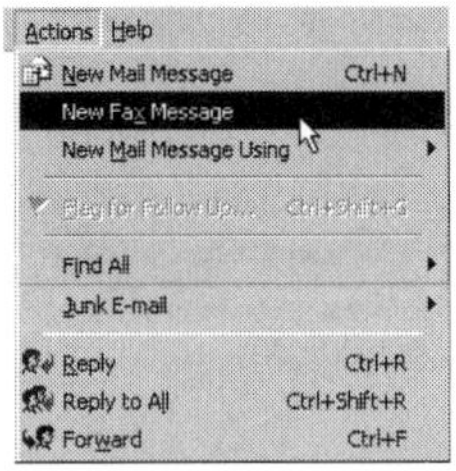

Figure 3.4 The Actions menu when the Inbox folder is opened.

Figure 3.5 The Actions menu when the Calendar folder is opened.

To create an item:

1. Open the folder in which you want to create the new item.

   (To create a new e-mail or fax message, you can open any mail-item folder—Inbox, Drafts, Outbox, or Sent Items.)

2. To create the default type of item for the opened folder, click the New button on the Standard toolbar or press Ctrl-N.

   The following are the default item types for the Outlook folders:

   - Inbox, Drafts, Outbox, or Sent Items: e-mail message
   - Calendar: appointment
   - Contacts: contact
   - Tasks: task
   - Journal: journal entry
   - Notes: note

   or

   If the folder manages several types of items, to create a specific type of item choose the appropriate command from the Actions menu. For example, if you've opened a mail-item folder such as Inbox, you can choose Actions > New Fax Message to create an outgoing fax message (**Figure 3.4**). Or, if you've opened the Calendar folder, you can choose Actions > New All Day Event to create an event (**Figure 3.5**).

Figure 3.6 The Actions menu when the Contacts folder is opened.

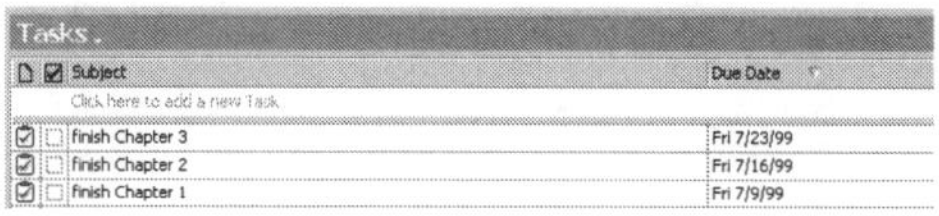

Figure 3.7 You can create a new task by clicking the top row of the information viewer and entering information.

Or, if you've opened the Contacts folder, you can choose Actions > New Distribution List to create a distribution list (**Figure 3.6**). (An Outlook form also has an Actions menu you can use.)

Outlook will then open an empty form of the appropriate type for you to fill in (**Figures 3.1 through 3.3**).

3. Enter the item's information and close the form.

   For instructions on entering the item's information, see "Editing Items," later in the chapter. You typically close the form by clicking the **Save and Close** button, but see "Editing Items" for exceptions.

   Once you've created a new item and closed the form, the item is displayed—along with the other items in the opened folder—in the Information Viewer of the Outlook window. In "Opening Items," later in the chapter, you'll learn how to reopen an item in a form so you can view or edit any of its information.

✔ Tips

- In a table view (a view with rows and columns such as the Phone List view shown in **Figure 3.46**, later in the chapter) you can create a new item and enter the basic item information right in the Information Viewer, without opening a form. To do this, you click the top table row (usually labeled **Click here to add a new item**), enter information into the fields shown, and press Enter (**Figure 3.7**). The **Show "new item"** row option, however, must be enabled for the current view. You access this option by choosing View > Current View > Customize Current View and clicking the **Other Settings** button.

(continued on next page)

- You can create almost any type of item, regardless of which folder is currently open, by clicking the down-arrow next to the New button on the Standard toolbar, and then choosing the item type from the drop-down menu (**Figure 3.8**). Alternatively, you can use the identical New submenu on the File menu in the Outlook window or in an Outlook form.

- You can create many different types of Outlook items, also regardless of which folder is open, by using the keyboard commands listed on the menu shown in **Figure 3.8**. Note, however, that if a mail-item folder isn't currently open, you'll need to press Ctrl-Shift-M to create a new e-mail message (rather than Ctrl-N).

- You can quickly create a new item based on an existing item of a different type by dragging the existing item from the opened folder and dropping it on the Outlook Bar shortcut for a folder of a different type. For example, if you open the Inbox, drag an e-mail message from the Inbox, and drop it on the Contacts shortcut, Outlook creates a new contact that already contains the name and e-mail address of the person who sent you the message. Similarly, if you drag an appointment from the Calendar folder and drop it on the Tasks shortcut, Outlook creates a new task that contains the description and date from the appointment (the appointment date becomes the due date of the task).

- You can get a head start in creating a new item by making a copy of an existing item in the same type of folder. For instance, to create a new contact that has the same address, telephone, and Web site as an existing contact, you could make a copy of the existing contact and then quickly edit the copy. See "Copying and Moving Items," later in the chapter.

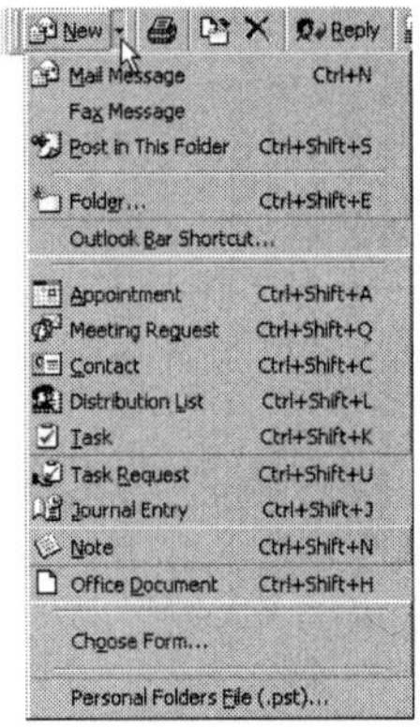

Figure 3.8 The menu that drops down from the New button. This is how the menu appears when a mail-item folder such as Inbox is open.

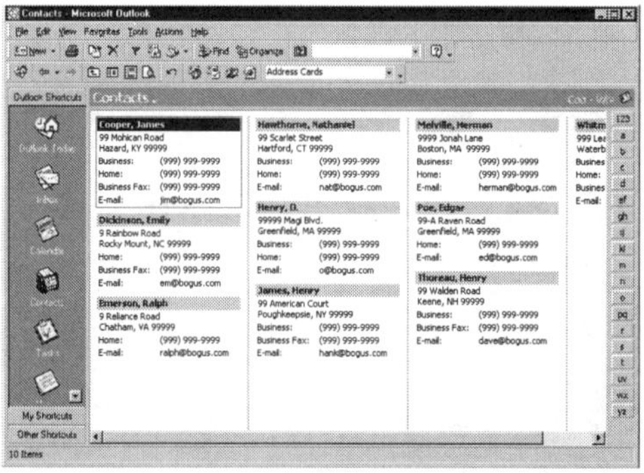

Figure 3.9 In the Address Cards view, the Contacts folder shows and lets you edit only a *portion* of the information for each contact.

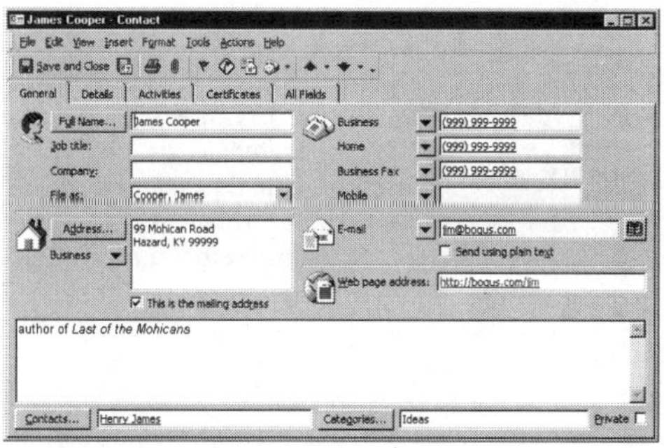

Figure 3.10 The Contact form, however, shows and lets you edit *all* contact information.

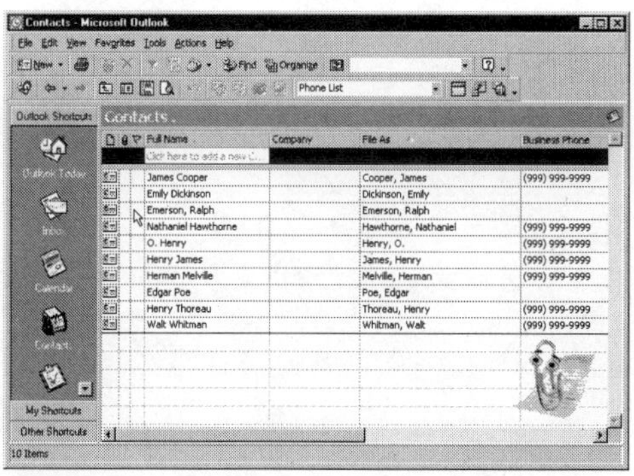

Figure 3.11 Double-click a Contact item displayed in the Information Viewer to open it.

Opening Items

When you open a folder, the Outlook Information Viewer displays the items it contains in a table, timeline, or other arrangement. Typically it shows only a portion of each item's information and allows only minor editing, if any (**Figure 3.9**). To view all of an item's information or to fully edit the item, you need to *open* it. When you open an item, Outlook displays it in the appropriate form for the particular type of item (**Figure 3.10**).

To open an item:

- Double-click on the item in the Information Viewer (**Figure 3.11**).

  or

  Click the item to select it (that is, highlight it), and press Enter or Ctrl-O.

(continued on next page)

or

Right-click the item and choose Open from the pop-up menu (**Figure 3.12**).

Once the item is opened in the form, you can view it or edit it as described in "Editing Items," later in the chapter.

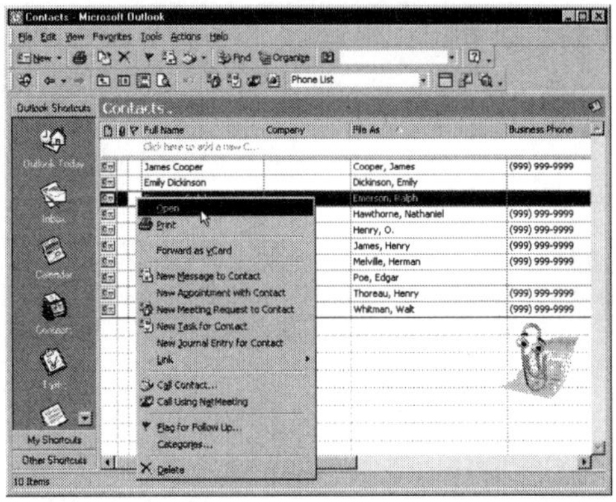

Figure 3.12 Open a Contact item by choosing Open from the pop-up menu.

✔ Tips

- You can open several items at once by selecting all of them before pressing Enter or Ctrl-O, or before right-clicking them and choosing Open from the pop-up menu. You can close all open items by choosing File > Close All Items.
- To select several adjoining items displayed in the Information Viewer, click the first one to select it and then expand the selection by pressing the appropriate arrow key while holding down Shift. Or, click the first item in the group and, while holding down the Shift key, click the last item.
- To select several non-adjoining items, click the first one to select it and then, while holding down the Ctrl key, click each additional item.
- To select *all* items in the open folder, choose Edit > Select All or press Ctrl-A.
- If you've opened an existing item in a form, you can view other items in the same folder within that form. To view the previous or next item in the folder, click the Previous Item button or the Next Item button on the form's Standard toolbar. To view a specific type of item, click the down arrow next to the **Previous Item** or **Next Item** button and choose a command from the drop-down menu (**Figure 3.13**). The commands on the drop-down menus are also found on the Previous and Next submenus of the form's View menu.

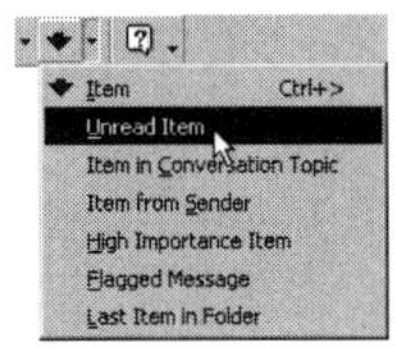

Figure 3.13 Opening the next unread item in the Inbox folder. (In this example, the form is displaying a message in the Inbox folder.)

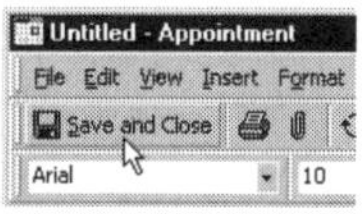

Figure 3.14 Saving your changes and closing an Appointment form.

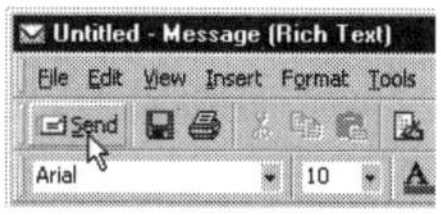

Figure 3.15 Saving and sending a message, and closing the Message form.

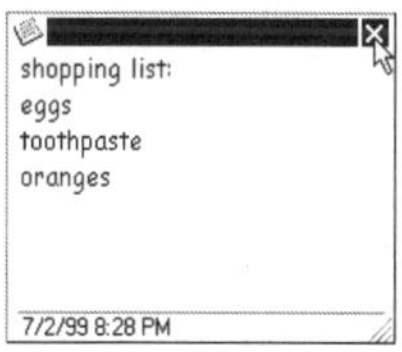

Figure 3.16 Saving your changes and closing a Notes form.

Editing Items

The following instructions show you how to edit a new item that you've just created in a empty form or an existing item that you've opened in a form.

✔ Tip

- You can edit fields displayed in the Information Viewer, without opening the item in a form, by clicking on the field and typing or selecting a new value. In the Calendar folder, for example, you can click on the subject field of an appointment and edit the text. To do this in most views, however, the **Allow in-cell editing** option must be checked. You access this option by choosing View > Current View > Customize Current View and clicking the **Other Settings** button.

To edit a new or existing item:

1. Open the item in a form. To open a new item in an empty form, follow the instructions given in "Creating Items." To open an existing item, follow the instructions given in "Opening Items."
2. Add, modify, or remove information within the controls displayed in the form.

   The following sections in this chapter explain the general techniques that you can use in almost any form. Chapters 3 through 11 describe in detail the forms for each type of Outlook item and explain the techniques unique to particular types of items.
3. Save your changes and close the form. You typically do this by clicking the Save And Close button on the form's Standard toolbar (**Figure 3.14**).

(continued on next page)

Some forms, however, have different procedures. For example, in the Message form you generally click the Send button on the Standard toolbar to save and send the message and to close the form (**Figure 3.15**). And in a Notes form, you click the Close button in the upper-right corner of the form to save the note and close the form (**Figure 3.16**).

✔ Tips

- You can save your work without closing the form by choosing File > Save. Or, you can close the form and discard any unsaved changes by clicking the Close button in the upper-right corner of the form, or by choosing File > Close, or by pressing Esc or Alt-F4. (Outlook will ask whether you want to save your changes. These instructions don't apply to a Notes form.)
- You can undo your most recent editing action in a form by choosing Edit > Undo or pressing Ctrl-Z. And you can reverse the effect of the Undo command by immediately choosing Edit > Redo or pressing Ctrl-Y. (In a Notes form, only the keyboard commands are available.)
- To enter a date or time into a date or time field (for example, the due date of an appointment or the starting time of an appointment), you can type a normal English expression such as "two weeks from now" or "noon" and Outlook will convert it to the actual date or time.

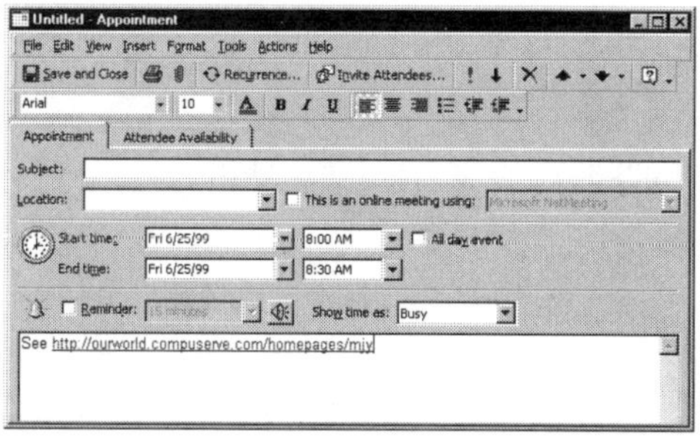

Figure 3.17 Typing a hyperlink into the large text box of an appointment.

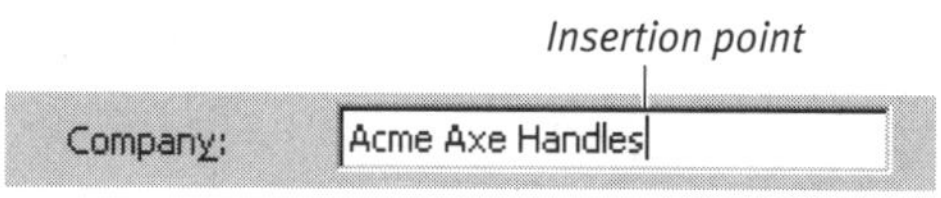

Figure 3.18 The insertion point that appears when you click a text box.

- In the large text box in a form (for example, the text box where you enter the body of your message in a Message form) or in a note, you can enter a link to a Web page or an e-mail address. To do this, just type the full Internet address (for example, *http://ourworld.compuserve.com/homepages/mjy/* or *mailto:mjy@compuserve.com*) and Outlook will convert it to a blue, underlined hyperlink that you can click to open the Web page in your browser or to send an e-mail message to the address (**Figure 3.17**).
- In the large text box in a form, you can search for specific text by choosing Edit > Find on the form's menu or by pressing F4. To find additional occurrences of the same text, choose Edit > Find Next or press Shift-F4.

To enter or edit text in a text box:

1. Click on the text box to activate it.

   The *insertion point*—a blinking vertical line—will appear in the box (**Figure 3.18**).
2. If you want to insert or delete text at a particular position within existing text, move the insertion point to that position by clicking on the position or by pressing the appropriate arrow key.
3. Type the text you want to enter.

   Each character will be inserted at the position of the insertion point.
4. To erase text, press Backspace to delete the character preceding the insertion point, or press Del to delete the character following the insertion point.

✔ Tip

- These instructions also apply to entering text into a Notes form, which consists of a single text box.

Selecting Text

To perform an operation on a block of text in a text box—for example, formatting it, copying it, deleting it, or checking its spelling—you must first *select* (that is, highlight) the text (**Figure 3.19**).

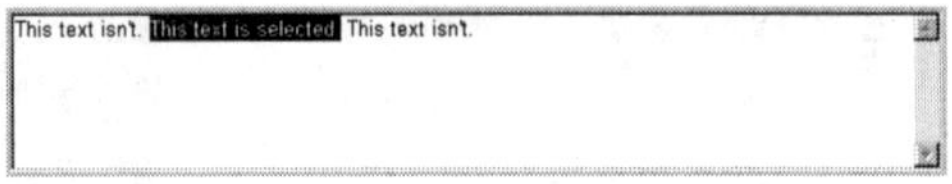

Figure 3.19 Selected text in a text box.

To select text:

- Place the insertion point at the beginning or end of the text, and extend the highlight over the text by pressing the appropriate arrow key while holding down Shift.

  or

  Use the mouse to drag the highlight over the text.

✔ Tips

- You can quickly select a single word by double-clicking it.
- You can select *all* text in the active text box by choosing Edit > Select All or pressing Ctrl-A. (In a Notes form, only the keyboard command is available.)

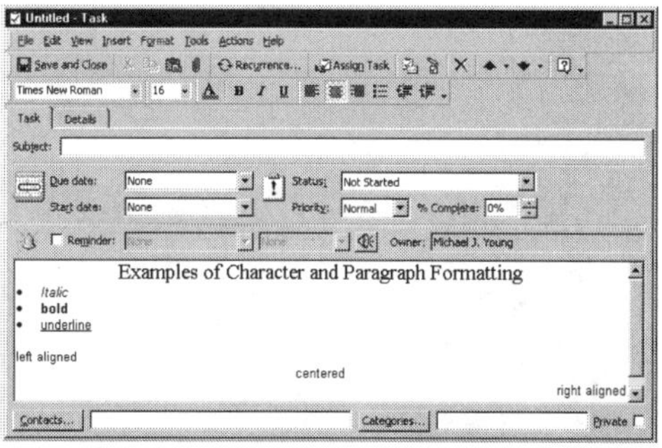

Figure 3.20 Formatted text in the large text box of a task.

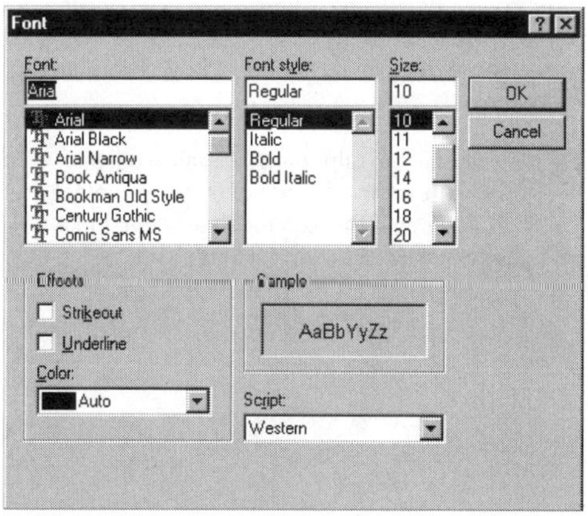

Figure 3.21 The Font dialog box.

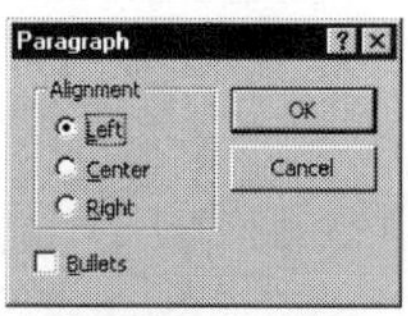

Figure 3.22 The Paragraph dialog box.

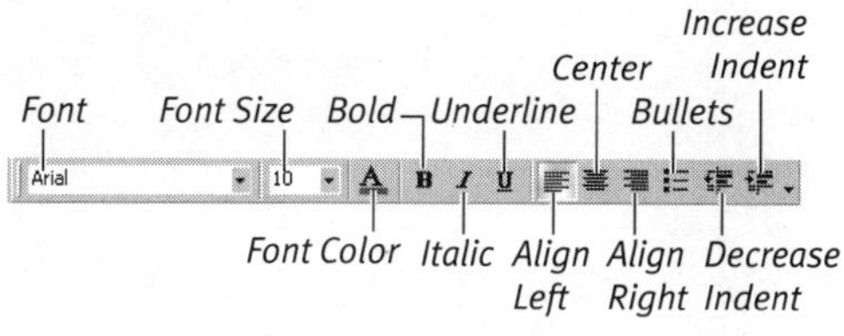

Figure 3.23 The Formatting toolbar displayed in a form.

Formatting Text

You can format—modify the appearance of—the text you type into the large text box in an Outlook form. You can format individual characters or paragraphs (**Figure 3.20**).

✔ Tips

- You can't format the text for a Notes item. You can only change the background color of the note.
- The available formatting commands for a message depend on the editor and e-mail format you're using, as explained in the section "Modifying the Format and Editor for E-mail Messages" in Chapter 6.

To format text in a form's large text box:

1. Select existing text to format.

   or

   Place the insertion point at the position where you want to type new text.
2. To format the individual characters, choose Format > Font to open the Font dialog box (**Figure 3.21**). Select character formatting options using the list boxes and check boxes until the text in the **Sample** area of the dialog box has the look you want, and then click the **OK** button.
3. To change the paragraph alignment or to create a bulleted list, choose Font > Paragraph, select the desired options in the Paragraph dialog box (**Figure 3.22**), and then click the **OK** button.

   Outlook will then apply the new formatting to the selection (if you selected text) or to the characters you subsequently type at the current position of the insertion point.

✔ Tip

- Rather than using a dialog box in steps 2 and 3, you can format by clicking buttons on the Formatting toolbar (**Figure 3.23**).

Copying and Moving Text

After you've typed information into a text box in an Outlook form, you can copy or move the text to another location within the same text box, within another text box, or even within a different Windows program.

To copy or move text:

1. In a text box, select the text that you want to copy or move.
2. To copy the text, choose Edit > Copy or press Ctrl-C.

   or

   To move the text, choose Edit > Cut or press Ctrl-X.
3. Place the insertion point where you want to insert the copied or moved text.

   This can be within *any* text box, not just the one in which you copied or cut the text. The easiest way is to just click on the target position.
4. Choose Edit > Paste, or press Ctrl-V.

✔ Tips

- Outlook stores your 12 most recently copied or cut blocks of text. If you have copied or cut several blocks of text, you can use the Clipboard toolbar to paste any of these blocks or all of them (**Figure 3.24**). (Pasting using Edit > Paste or Ctrl-V pastes only the most recently copied or cut block.)
- You can copy or move text *or graphics* between separate Windows programs. For example, you could copy a block of graphics from a paint program and then paste it into the large text box in an Outlook form.
- To *remove* the selected block of text, choose Edit > Clear or press Del.

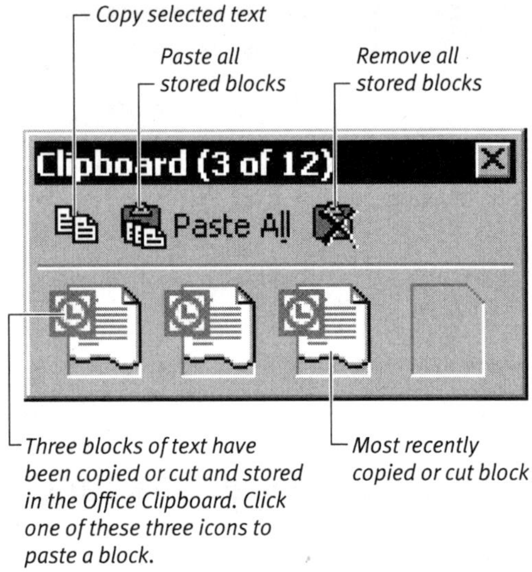

Figure 3.24 Use the Clipboard toolbar to paste a previously copied or cut block of text. If you place the mouse pointer over the icon for a particular block of text, the text will be shown in a ScreenTip.

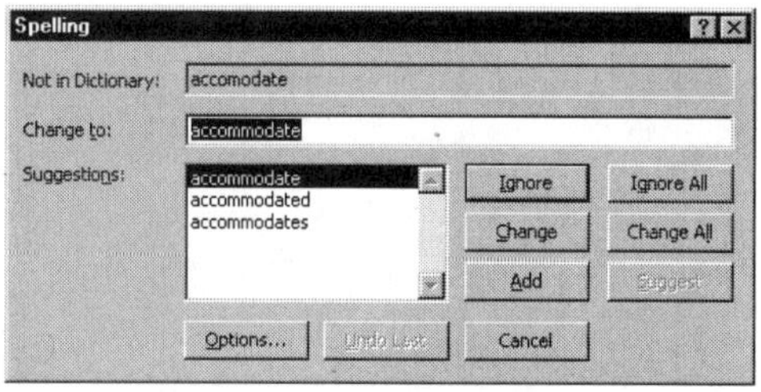

Figure 3.25 The Spelling dialog box.

Checking Spelling

Before you send an e-mail message or save an Outlook item such as an appointment or contact, you'd be wise to check your spelling.

To check your spelling:

1. To check the spelling of the text in *all* text boxes within a form, place the insertion point within any text box.

   or

   To check the spelling of a specific block of text within a text box, select that text.

2. Choose Tools > Spelling, or press F7.

   The spelling checker will then check the spelling of each word. For each word that the spelling checker can't find in its dictionary, it displays the Spelling dialog box (**Figure 3.25**).

3. Use the Spelling dialog box as follows.
   - To correct the spelling, click a spelling in the **Suggestions** list, or type a correct spelling into the **Change to** text box, and then click either **Change** to change the current occurrence of the word or **Change All** to change all occurrences.
   - To leave the word unchanged, click **Ignore** if you want to skip the current occurrence of the word or click **Ignore All** if you want to skip all occurrences.
   - To ignore the word and add it to the spelling checker's custom dictionary, so that it will no longer be flagged as a misspelling, click **Add**.
   - To undo the previous spelling correction or return to the last word you reviewed, click **Undo Last**.

(continued on next page)

- To open the Spelling tab of the Options dialog box (**Figure 3.26**), where you can set spelling options, click **Options**.
- To cancel the spelling check, click **Cancel**.

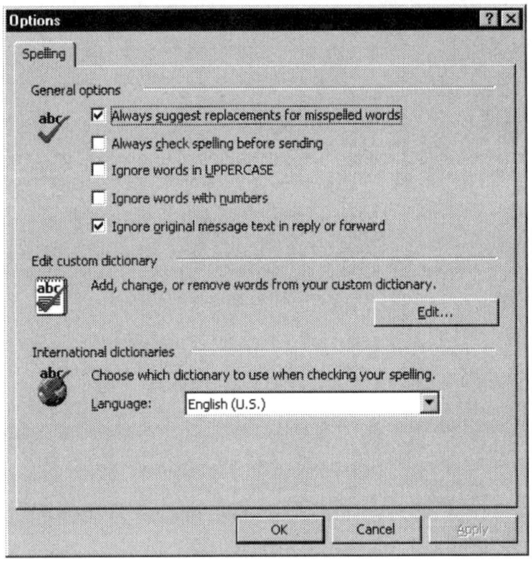

Figure 3.26 The Spelling tab of the Options dialog box.

✔ Tips

- You can also set spelling options by choosing Tools > Options and opening the Spelling tab.
- You can't check spelling in a Notes item.

Figure 3.27 An icon for an attached file.

Figure 3.28 An icon for a shortcut to a file.

Figure 3.29 An embedded object from the Clip Gallery inserted into a text box in a form.

Inserting Files, Items, and Objects

You can insert any of the following into the large text box in an Outlook form:

- A disk file, in any of the following ways:
  - **As text**: The full text from the file is inserted and displayed in the text box.
  - **As an attachment**: The text box stores a copy of the file, which it displays as an icon that you can double-click to open the copy (**Figure 3.27**).
  - **As a shortcut**: The text box stores only the location of the original file, which it displays as a shortcut icon that you can double-click to open the original file (**Figure 3.28**).
- Another Outlook item as text, as an attachment, or as a shortcut. For example, you might insert an appointment into an e-mail message sent to another Outlook user, so that the appointment can be added to his or her Calendar folder.
- A linked or embedded object.
  - A *linked object* displays data that is stored in a separate source document. If you modify the data in the source document, the linked object in the item is updated to match the source document. For example, you can insert a linked object that displays as an Excel workbook.
  - An *embedded object* is data that is stored and displayed within the Outlook item but is created and edited in a separate source program. For example, if you've installed the Microsoft Clip Gallery program, you could embed clip art that is created and modified by the Clip Gallery program (**Figure 3.29**).

(continued on next page)

INSERTING FILES, ITEMS, AND OBJECTS

✔ Tip

- If you're creating an e-mail message in the Message form, avoid inserting a shortcut or a linked or embedded object, because the message recipient might not have access to the data or program required to view or edit the information.

To insert a file:

1. Place the insertion point at the position where you want to insert the file in the large text box.
2. Choose Insert > File or click the Insert File button on the Standard toolbar.
3. In the Insert File dialog box (**Figure 3.30**), select the file you want to insert.
4. Click the **Insert** button to insert the file as an attachment.

   or

   Click the down arrow on the **Insert** button and select the way you want to insert the file (**Figure 3.31**). Note that when inserting a file into a form, clicking the button or selecting Insert has the same effect as selecting Insert As Attachment.

✔ Tips

- You can also insert a file as an attachment by dragging the file name from a file folder displayed in Outlook, or from the Windows Explorer or a file folder, and dropping it in the large text box in the form.
- When you drag an object from one window to another, if the target window is hidden on the screen, drag the object to the window's button on the Windows Taskbar and hold it there, keeping the mouse button pressed. After a few seconds, the target window will be activated and you can complete the drag operation.

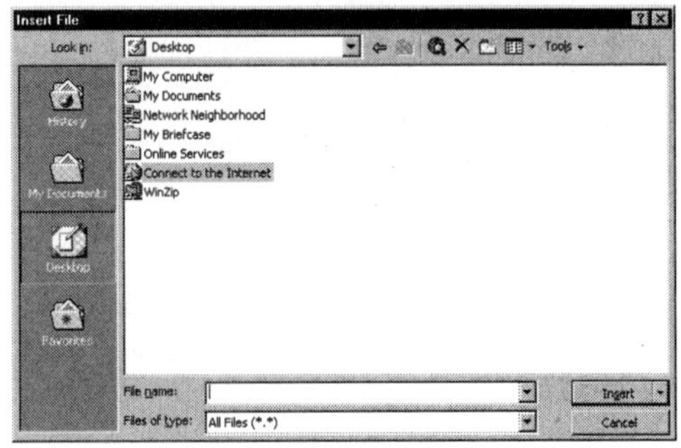

Figure 3.30 The Insert File dialog box

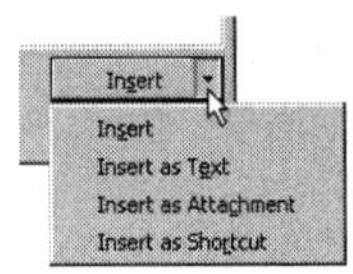

Figure 3.31 Opening the drop-down menu to choose the method for inserting the file

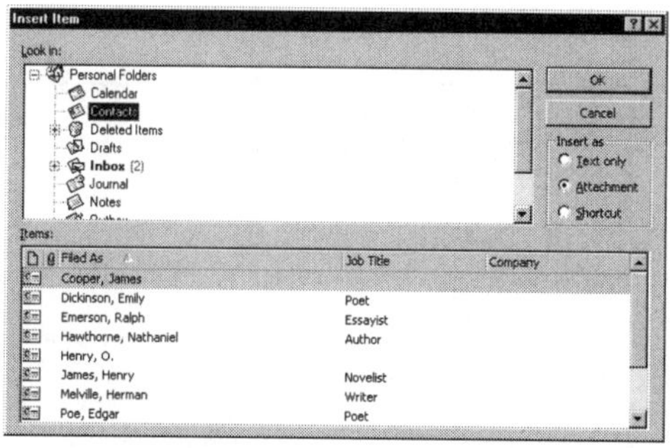

Figure 3.32 The Insert Item dialog box

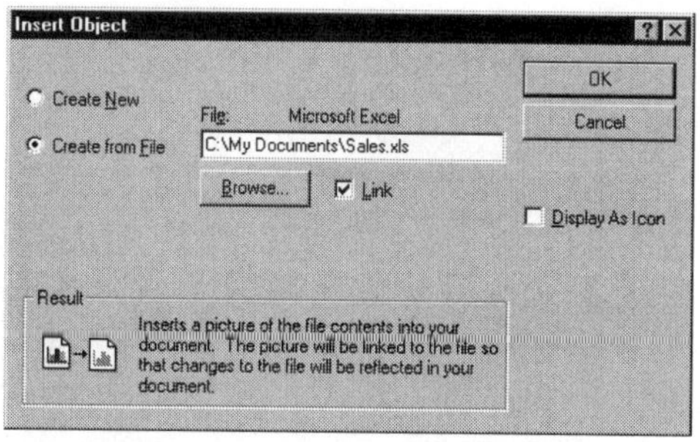

Figure 3.33 Inserting a linked object. In this example, the object will be linked to an Excel workbook.

To insert an Outlook item:

1. Place the insertion point where you want to insert the item in the large text box.
2. Choose Insert > Item.
3. In the Insert Item dialog box (**Figure 3.32**), select the item you want to insert:
   - In the **Look in** list select the Outlook folder.
   - In the **Items** list select the specific item in that folder.
   - In the **Insert as** area select an option button to specify the way you want the item to be inserted.
4. Click the **OK** button.

✔ Tips

- You can also insert an item by opening its folder in Outlook and then dragging the item from the Outlook window and dropping it in the text box in the form.
- A quick way to create an e-mail message and insert an Outlook item as an attachment is to select the item and choose Actions > Forward or press Ctrl-F. (For a contact, choose Actions > Forward As vCard.)

To insert a linked or embedded object:

1. Place the insertion point where you want to insert the linked or embedded object in the large text box.
2. Choose Insert > Object.

   Outlook will display the Insert Object dialog box.
3. To insert a *linked* object, select the **Create from File** option button, check the **Link** check box, and click the **Browse** button to select the file containing the data you want to link (**Figure 3.33**).

(continued on next page)

4. To insert an *embedded* object, select the **Create New** option button and select the type of object you want to embed in the **Object Type** list (**Figure 3.34**).

   After you click **OK** (in step 5), the source program will run and will let you create a new object. For example, if you selected the Microsoft Clip Gallery object type, the Clip Gallery program would run and would let you select a piece of clip art to embed in the Outlook item.

   or

   Select the **Create from File** option button, leave the **Link** check box unchecked, and click the **Browse** button to select the file that contains the existing data you want to embed (**Figure 3.35**).

5. Click the **OK** button in the Insert Object dialog box.

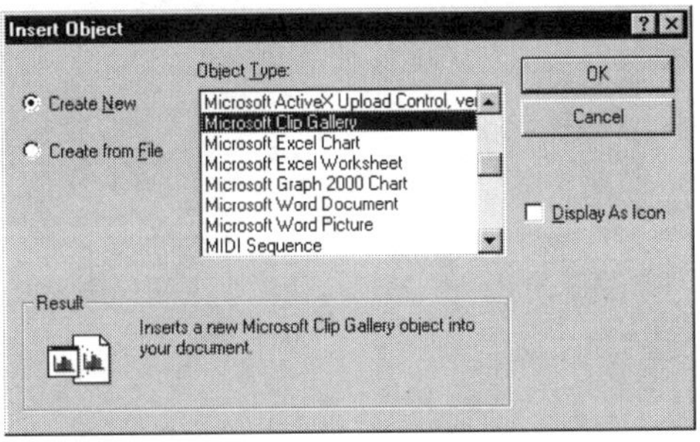

Figure 3.34 Inserting an embedded object. In this example, a new object will be created in the Microsoft Clip Gallery program.

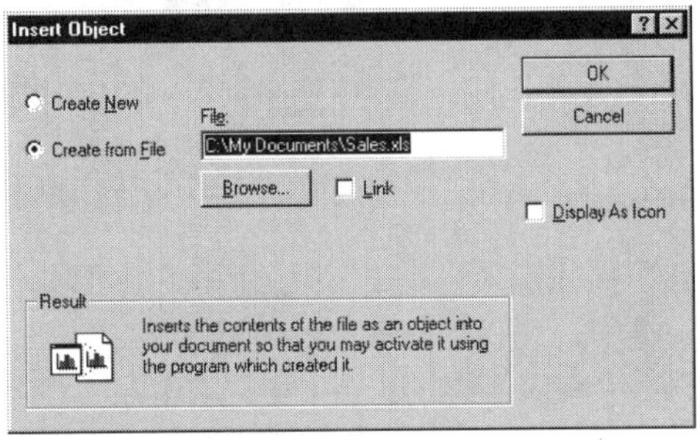

Figure 3.35 Inserting an embedded object. In this example, the object will come from the existing data in an Excel workbook.

✔ Tips

- If you want to display an icon representing the linked or embedded object, rather than displaying the data itself, check the **Display As Icon** check box in the Insert Object dialog box.
- To edit a block of linked or embedded data, double-click it. (If this doesn't work for an embedded object, click on the object and choose Edit > *Object Name* Object > Edit, where *Object Name* is the name of the particular object, such as Worksheet.)
- To modify the properties of an embedded or linked object, right-click it and choose Properties from the pop-up menu.

Copying and Moving Items

The following are some of the ways in which you might want to copy or move an Outlook item:

- You can make a copy of an item in the same folder as the original to get a head start in creating a similar new item. For example, if you want to create a new item in your Contacts folder for a person who has the same address and phone number as an existing contact, you could make a copy of the existing contact and quickly edit it.
- You can copy an item to a different folder of the same type to create a backup. For example, you might make copies of your important incoming e-mail messages in a separate mail-item folder for safe keeping.
- You can move items to different folders of the same type to organize your Outlook information. For example, to organize the messages you receive, you might move them from the Inbox to various mail-item folders, perhaps named Business E-mail, Personal E-mail, and Faxes.
- You can copy an item to a folder of a different type to get a head start in creating a new item based on the existing item. As explained in a tip earlier in the chapter (under "To create an item"), when you copy an item to a folder of a different type, Outlook creates a new item in the target folder that contains information from the existing item. For example, you could copy an incoming e-mail message to your Contacts folder to create a new contact that already contains the name and e-mail address of the person who sent you the message.

✔ **Tip**

- See Chapter 4 for instructions on creating new folders.

To copy or move an item:

1. Open the folder containing the item you want to copy or move, and select the item in the Outlook window. If you wish, you can select several items to copy or move them all at once.
2. To copy the item, choose Edit > Copy To Folder.

   or

   To move the item, choose Edit > Move To Folder or press Ctrl-Shift-V.
3. In the Copy Items dialog box (if you're copying) or in the Move Items dialog box (if you're moving), select the destination folder (**Figure 3.36**).

   If you want to create a new folder in which to store the copied or moved item, click the **New** button and specify the folder name, type, and location (as explained in Chapter 4).
4. Click the **OK** button.

Or

- To copy an item, hold down the Ctrl key and drag the item from the Information Viewer in the Outlook window and drop it on the Outlook Bar shortcut for the destination folder. If the shortcut isn't currently visible, while you drag, hold the item over the top or bottom of the current group to scroll through the shortcuts in that group, or hold it over the button for another group to open that group (keep the mouse button pressed the whole time!).
- To move an item, drag it the same way but *without* pressing the Ctrl key.

Or

1. Open the folder containing the item you want to copy or move and select the item in the Outlook window.

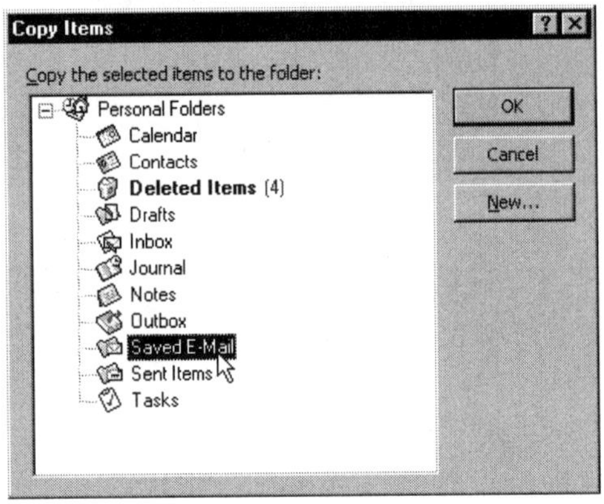

Figure 3.36 Copying an item to the Saved E-Mail folder.

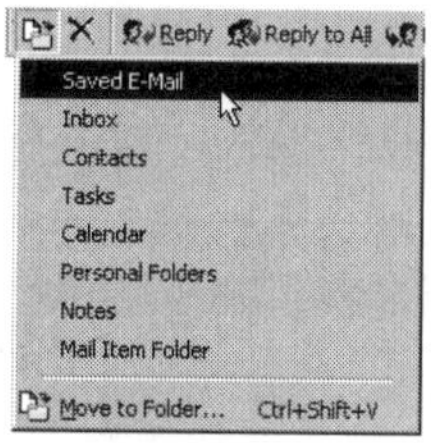

Folders to which you've recently moved or copied an item

Figure 3.37 Moving an item to a folder using the Move To Folder toolbar button.

If you wish, you can select several items to copy or move them all at once.

2. To copy the item, choose Edit > Copy or press Ctrl-C.

   or

   To move the item, choose Edit > Cut or press Ctrl-X.

3. Open the destination folder and choose Edit > Paste or press Ctrl-V.

✔ Tips

- You can also move an item by selecting it in the Outlook window, clicking the Move To Folder button on the Standard toolbar, and choosing one of the folders you've recently copied or moved an item to (**Figure 3.37**), or by choosing **Move To Folder** to open the Move Items dialog box (the same dialog box opened by choosing Edit > Move To Folder).
- If you've opened an item in a form, you can copy or move it to a different folder by choosing File > Copy To Folder or File > Move To Folder in the form (or by pressing Ctrl-Shift-V to move). These commands work just like the identically named commands on the Edit menu in the Outlook window.
- You can reverse an item copy or move operation by immediately clicking the Undo button on the Advanced toolbar, or by choosing Edit > Undo Copy or Edit > Undo Move, or by pressing Ctrl-Z. If you immediately reissue the Undo command, the copy or move will be restored.

Removing and Archiving Items

When you remove an item from an Outlook folder, Outlook initially moves it to the Deleted Items folder rather than permanently deleting it. As long as the item remains in Deleted Items you can easily recover it. You can permanently delete a removed item by removing it from Deleted Items; you will then no longer be able to recover it (unless you've made a backup copy somewhere else).

You can use the Outlook archiving feature to permanently delete items older than a specified period of time. You can also use the archiving feature to move your older items to an archive file, so that they'll be out of the way but yet you'll be able to recover them. You can set up the archive feature to run automatically at specified intervals, or you can run it manually at any time.

To remove an Outlook item:

1. Select the item in the Outlook window. You can select several items to remove all of them (**Figure 3.38**).
2. Press Del or Ctrl-D, or click the Delete button on the Standard toolbar, or choose File > Delete.

   Outlook will then move the item to your Deleted Items folder.

Or

- If the item is opened in a form, click the Delete button on the form's Standard toolbar, choose File > Delete, or press Ctrl-D. (Some forms don't have all of these commands.)

  Outlook will then move the item to your Deleted Items folder.

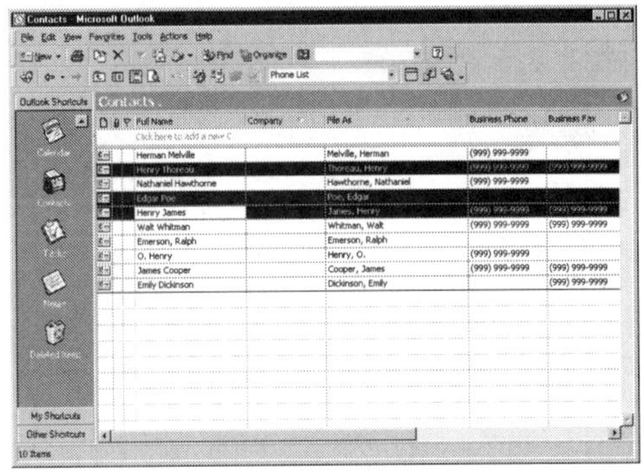

Figure 3.38 Selecting several Contacts items prior to deleting them.

Figure 3.39 Outlook's warning before it removes an item from Deleted Items.

Figure 3.40 Outlook's warning before it removes all items from Deleted Items.

✔ Tips

- You can restore an item you've removed by *immediately* clicking the Undo button on the Advanced toolbar, choosing Edit > Undo Delete, or pressing Ctrl-Z. (Immediately reissuing this command removes the item again.)
- As long as an item remains in the Deleted Items folder, you can recover it by simply moving the item from Deleted Items back to its original folder, using any of the methods described in "Copying and Moving Items," earlier in the chapter.
- You can permanently delete an item by removing it from the Deleted Items folder, using any of the methods explained in "To remove an Outlook item," earlier in the chapter.
- Outlook will warn you when you attempt to remove an item from Deleted Items and will give you the chance to cancel the deletion (**Figure 3.39**), provided that the **Warn before permanently deleting items** option is checked. To access this option, choose Tools > Options, open the Other tab, and click the **Advanced Options** button.
- You can remove *all* items from the Deleted Items folder—thereby permanently deleting them—by choosing Tools > Empty "Deleted Items" Folder. Outlook will display a warning and let you cancel the deletion (**Figure 3.40**). I recommend avoiding this command and using archiving instead to remove only your older items.

(continued on next page)

- Outlook will remove all items from Deleted Items whenever you exit the program if the **Empty the deleted items folder upon exiting** option is checked. To access this option, choose Tools > Options and open the Other tab. I recommend that you leave this option off, so that you'll have more time in which you can recover any removed items.
- You can also have the Outlook archive feature (described next) permanently delete items that are older than a certain time period. You can have it delete items from Deleted Items or directly from other folders.
- If you're using Outlook with Microsoft Exchange Server and are storing your files in a mailbox on the server, the server might delete older items from your Deleted Items folder.

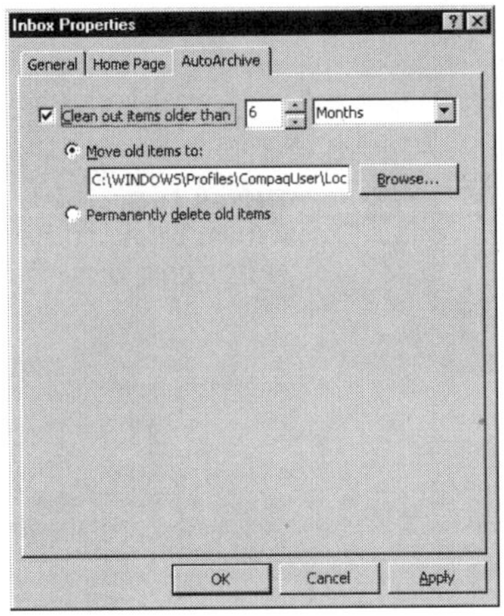

Figure 3.41 The AutoArchive tab in the Inbox Properties dialog box.

To archive automatically:

1. For each folder that you want to archive, right-click the folder's icon in the Outlook Bar, choose Properties on the pop-up menu, open the AutoArchive tab in the *Folder* Properties dialog box (where *Folder* represents the folder that you want to archive) (**Figure 3.41**), select the desired options. Here are the options you can select:
   - To enable automatic archiving for this folder, check **Clean out items older than** and specify a time period in the following text box and list box.
   - To have old items removed from the folder but saved in an archive (.PST) file on your disk, select **Move old items to** and specify an archive (.PST) file in the following text box or just accept the default file name and location. I recommend selecting this option for all folders except Deleted

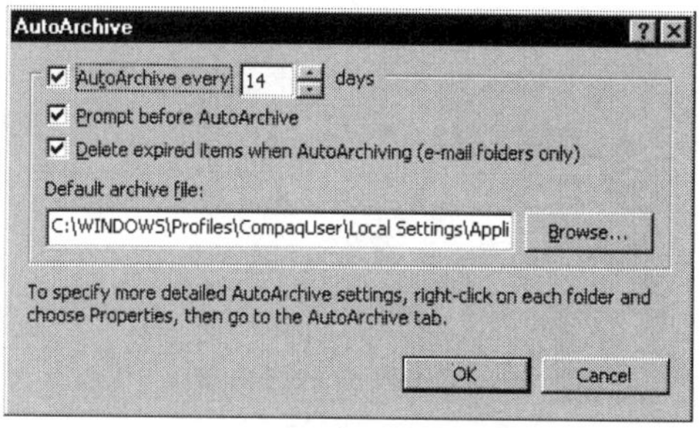

Figure 3.42 The AutoArchive dialog box.

Items, because you'll later be able to recover any archived item.

- To have old items removed from the folder and discarded, select **Permanently delete old items.** I recommend selecting this option only for your Deleted Items folder, because it's unlikely that you'll need to recover any of these items.

2. Click the **OK** button.
3. Choose Tools > Options, open the Other tab, and click the **AutoArchive** button to open the AutoArchive dialog box (**Figure 3.42**).
4. In the AutoArchive dialog box, select options as desired. Here are the options you can select:
   - To enable automatic archiving, check **AutoArchive every** and enter a number of days in the following text box to indicate the archiving frequency.
   - Check **Prompt before AutoArchive** if you want to be able to choose whether or not to perform each scheduled archiving.
   - Check **Delete expired items...** to have Outlook delete—rather than archive—expired messages in mail-item folders when it performs automatic archiving (as you'll learn in Chapter 6, a message can be assigned an expiration date).
   - Specify a default archive (.PST) file in the **Default archive file** text box, or just accept the current file name and location. Outlook will move all archived items to that file, except items in folders for which you have specified a different archive file (in step 1).

(continued on next page)

5. Click the **OK** button.

   Outlook will automatically archive all folders for which you have enabled archiving (in step 1).

✔ Tips

- You can't enable automatic archiving for your Contacts folder. Outlook doesn't automatically archive Contacts items because they don't usually become obsolete with time, as messages, appointments, and other types of items do.
- You can prevent an individual item from being archived when its folder is automatically archived. To do this, open the item in a form, choose File > Properties in the form, and in the *Item* Properties dialog box (*Item* represents the name of the item) check **Do not AutoArchive this item** (**Figure 3.43**).
- To recover an archived item, choose File > Open > Personal Folders File (.pst) and select the archive file in the Open Personal Folders dialog box. Outlook will then open the archive file and display its folders in the Folder List. You can use the Folder List to open the folder containing the archived item, and copy the item back to its original folder.

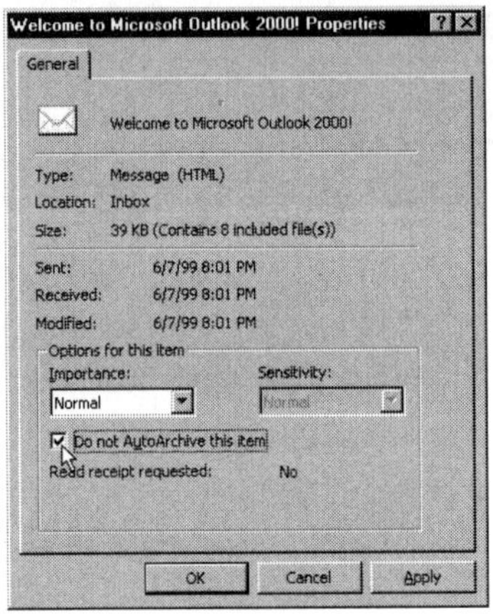

Figure 3.43 Checking the **Do not AutoArchive this item** item property.

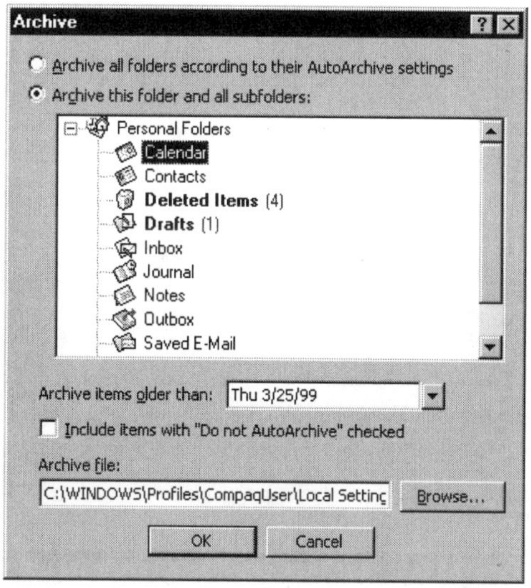

Figure 3.44 The Archive dialog box.

To archive manually:

1. Choose File > Archive to open the Archive dialog box (**Figure 3.44**).
2. Select options as desired in the Archive dialog box:
   - Select **Archive all folders according to their AutoArchive settings** to have Outlook archive just as if an automatic archiving session were running, using the settings described in the previous section, "To archive automatically." If you select this option, the other options in the Archive dialog box will have no effect.
   - To manually archive a specific folder and its subfolders, select **Archive this folder and all subfolders** and select the folder in the following list.
   - Enter the archive date into the **Archive items older than** box (click the down-arrow to display a calendar). Only items older than the date you specify will be archived.
   - Normally, you can prevent an individual item from being archived by opening the item in a form, choosing File > Properties in the form, and checking **Do not AutoArchive this item**. However, you can have Outlook archive items regardless of this setting by checking **Include items with "Do not AutoArchive" checked**.
   - Specify the archive (.PST) file in the Archive File text box, or accept the default file name and location.
3. Click the **OK** button.

Using Different Views

When you've opened an Outlook folder, you can change the overall way you view and work with the information it displays by switching to a different *view*. Each type of Outlook folder provides a unique set of views, designed specifically for working with the items it contains.

For example, in the Contacts folder you can select the Address Cards view to display each item in a format that resembles a business card (**Figure 3.45**). You can select the Phone List view to display all items in a table, where each row displays a different contact and each column displays a particular field of information (such as the name or company) for all contacts (**Figure 3.46**). Or, you can select the By Category view to display all items in a table where the items are grouped according to their categories (**Figure 3.47**).

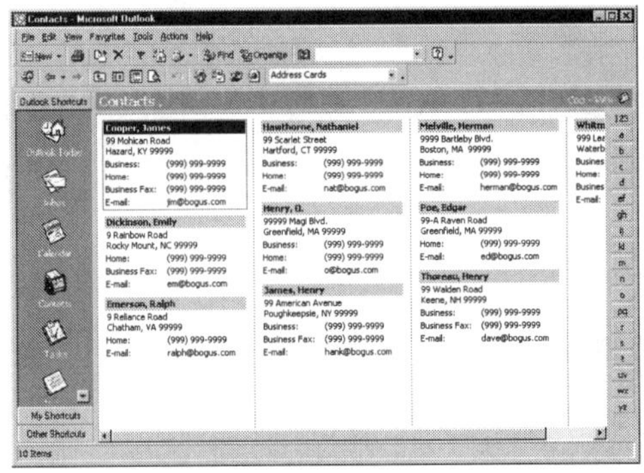

Figure 3.45 The Contacts folder in the Address Cards view.

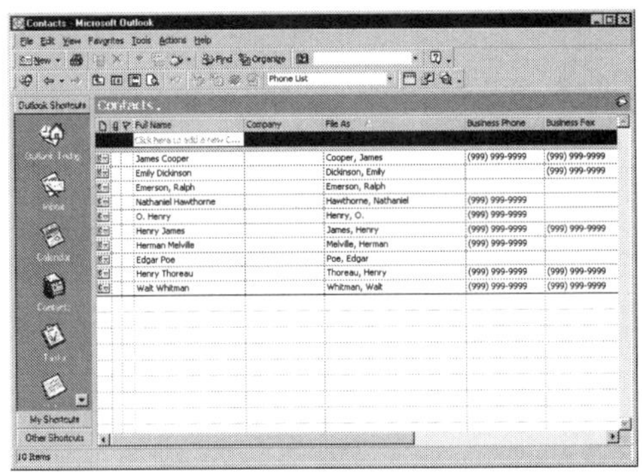

Figure 3.46 The Contacts folder in the Phone List view.

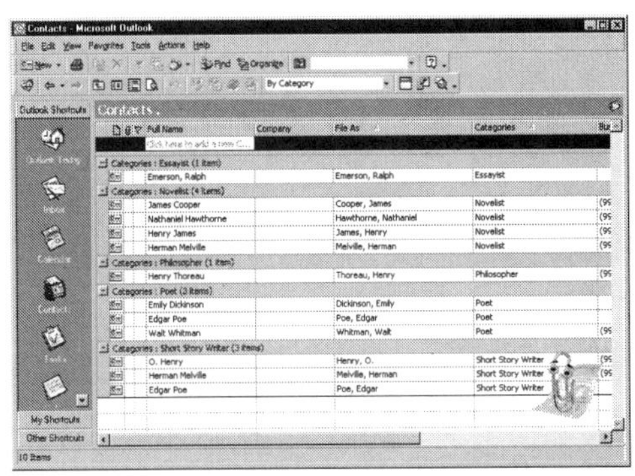

Figure 3.47 The Contacts folder in the By Category view.

✔ Tips

- As you'll learn later in the book, you can assign one or more categories to any type of Outlook item. Categories can be used for sorting, filtering, grouping, or finding items.
- In "Adjusting Views" in Chapter 14 you'll learn how to modify a standard view (such as those shown in **Figures 3-45 through 3-47**) as well as how to create a new custom view.

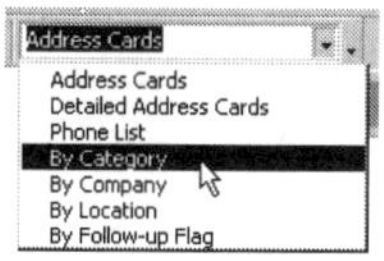

Figure 3.48 Select a view in the Current View list box on the Advanced toolbar.

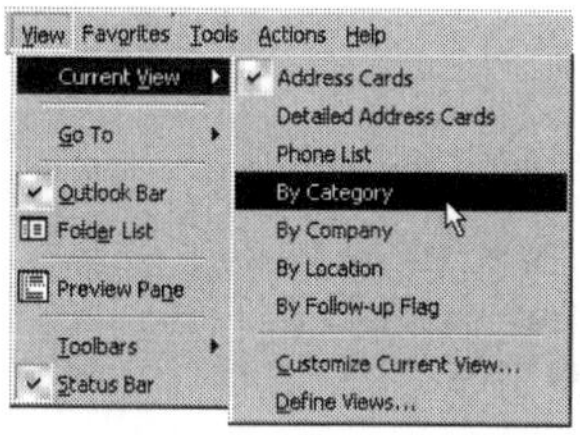

Figure 3.49 Choose a view from the Current View submenu.

Column header *Drag right edge to adjust column width*

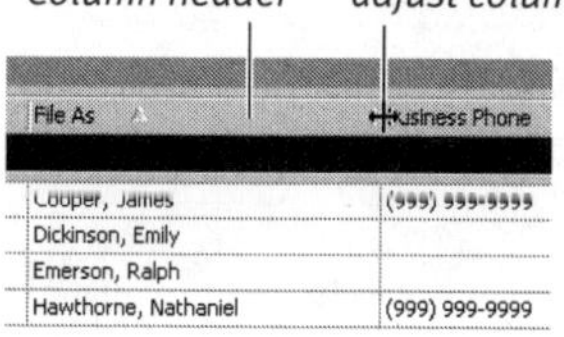

Figure 3.50 Adjust the width of the "File As" column in a table view.

To change the view:

◆ Click the down-arrow on the Current View list box on the Advanced toolbar, and select a new view in the list by clicking on it (**Figure 3.48**).

or

Choose View > Current View, and then choose a view from the submenu (**Figure 3.49**).

✔ Tip

- In a table view (a view with rows and columns such as the Phone List view shown in **Figure 3.46**), you can adjust the width of a column by dragging the right edge of the header above that column to the right or left (**Figure 3.50**). You can also quickly adjust the width to exactly fit the column's contents by double-clicking the right edge of the header, or by right-clicking anywhere on the header and choosing **Best Fit** from the pop-up menu.

Displaying the Preview pane

With any view, you can display a *Preview pane* at the bottom of the Information Viewer in the Outlook window. The main area of the Preview pane displays the contents of the large text box of the selected item (or the entire contents of a Notes item), and the header displays selected item fields (**Figure 3.51**).

To display the Preview pane:

1. Activate the view in which you want to display the Preview pane.
2. Click the Preview Pane button on the Advanced toolbar or choose View > Preview Pane.

   If you click the button or choose the menu command again, the Preview pane will be hidden.

✔ Tips

- Once you display the Preview pane in a particular view, it will always be displayed whenever that view is active, until you explicitly turn off the Preview pane in the view.
- You can adjust the height of the Preview pane by dragging its top border up or down (**Figure 3.52**).
- You can hide the Preview pane header by double-clicking it. You can redisplay the header by double-clicking the dark bar at the top of the pane (**Figure 3.53**).

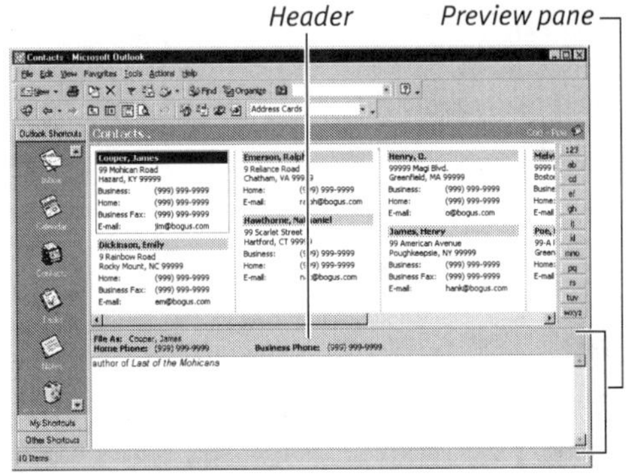

Figure 3.51 The Preview pane displayed in the Address Cards view of the Contacts folder.

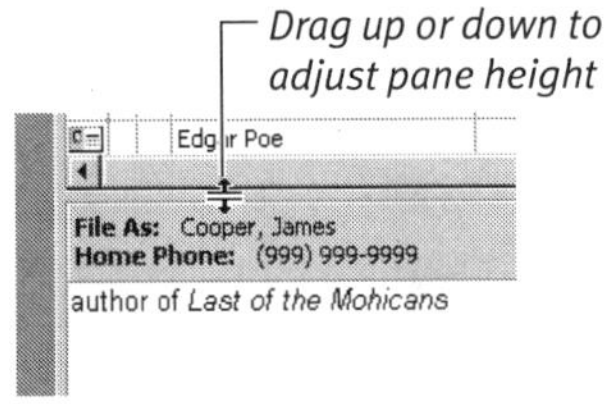

Figure 3.52 Adjusting the height of the Preview pane by dragging the top edge.

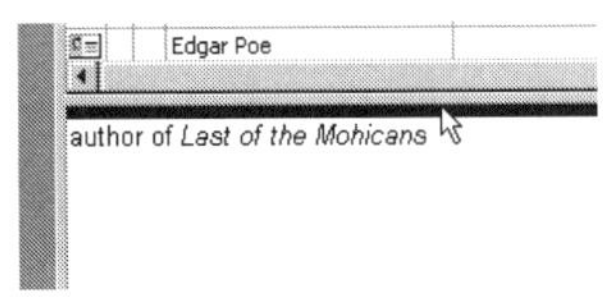

Figure 3.53 Redisplaying the Preview pane header by double-clicking the dark bar at the top of the pane.

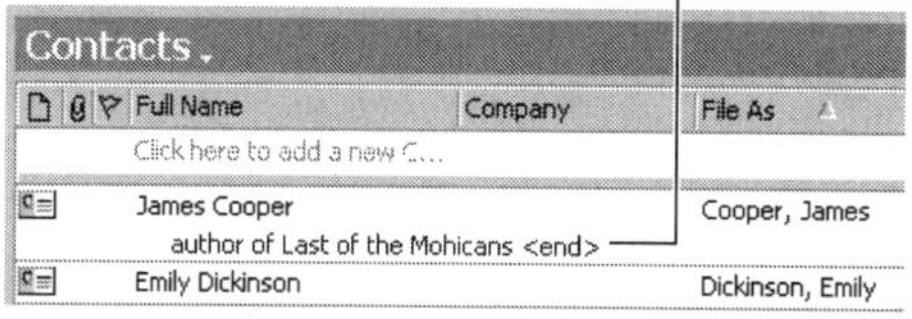

Figure 3.54 A Contacts item with AutoPreview on, showing the contents of the large text box.

- In a table view (a view with rows and columns such as the Phone List view shown in **Figure 3.46**), you can display the first part of the text contained in the item's large text box, right below each item (**Figure 3.54**). To do this, click the AutoPreview button on the Advanced toolbar or choose View > AutoPreview. Reissuing this command turns off the preview display.
- You can modify features of the Preview pane—such as the font used in the header—by choosing Tools > Options, opening the Other tab, and clicking the **Preview Pane** button.

Sorting, Filtering, and Grouping Items

You can control the way Outlook displays the items in a particular view in the following three ways:

- **Sorting**, which means to change the order in which items are displayed. You can sort using up to four different item fields. For example, using three fields, you could sort your e-mail messages by the senders' names, with all messages from the same sender sorted by date, and all messages sent on the same date sorted by subject.
- **Filtering**, which means to limit the items that are displayed. For example, you could filter your Contacts items so that only contacts from your home town are shown.
- **Grouping**, which means to divide the items into separate sets, where all the items in a set have the same value in a particular field. For example, if you grouped tasks using the priority field, all tasks in each group would have the same priority value (low, normal, or high). You can have groups within groups, using as many as four fields. For example, using two fields, you could group your tasks by priority, with the items within each priority group grouped by status (not started, in progress, and so on). Grouping is like sorting, but the different sets are labeled with headers and you can individually expand or collapse them.

Figure 3.55 shows the Phone List view of the Contacts folder, with the default settings—that is, before sorting, filtering, or grouping have been applied. Notice that the items are sorted by the File As field (usually the last name followed by the first name), all

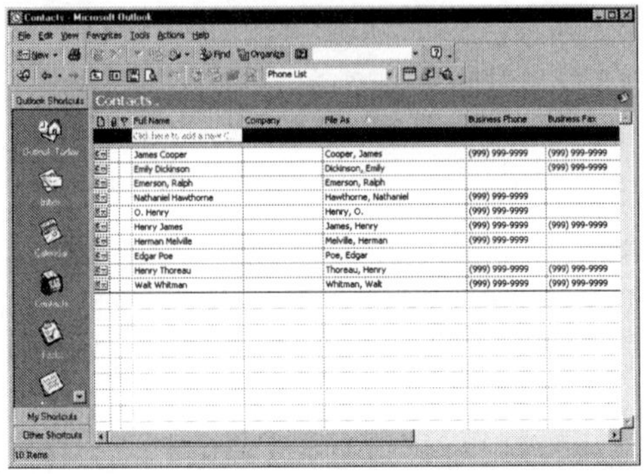

Figure 3.55 The Phone List view of the Contacts folder, before sorting, filtering, or grouping has been applied.

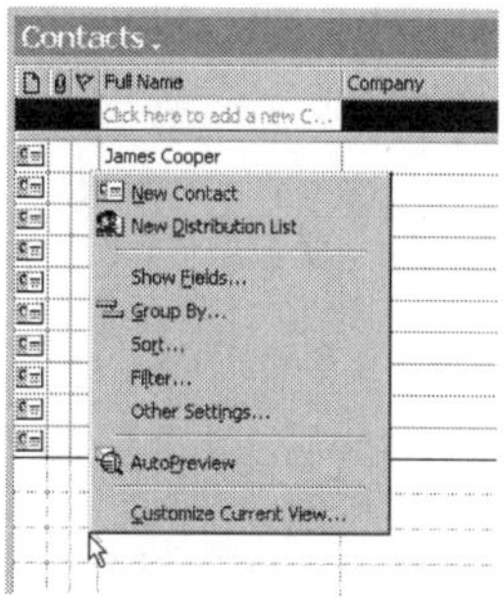

Figure 3.56 Right-clicking a blank area to display the pop-up menu.

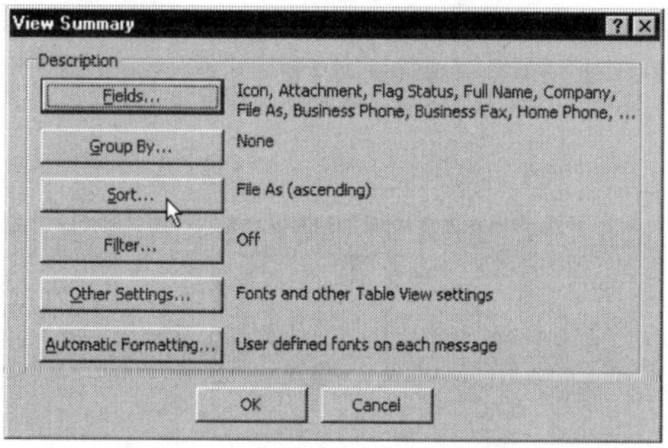

Figure 3.57 Clicking the **Sort** button in the View Summary dialog box.

items in the folder are shown, and the items aren't grouped. In the following instructions, you'll see the effects of applying sorting, filtering, and grouping to this view.

✔ Tips

- You apply sorting, filtering, and grouping to a particular view. Each view of a folder can have different sorting, filtering, or grouping settings.
- The availability of sorting, filtering, and grouping depends upon the particular view. For example, you can apply grouping only to a table view (such as the Phone List view shown in **Figure 3.55**) or a timeline view (such as Task Timeline view of the Tasks folder). Also, you can't apply any of these settings to the Day/Week/Month view of the Calendar folder.

To sort items:

1. Activate the view in which you want to set the sorting order of the items.
2. Right-click a blank area in the Information Viewer (not on an item!) (**Figure 3.56**) and choose Sort from the pop-up menu.

   or

   If you can't find a blank spot, choose View > Current View > Customize Current View, and click the **Sort** button in the View Summary dialog box (**Figure 3.57**).

(continued on next page)

3. In the Sort dialog box (**Figure 3.58**), specify the primary sorting criterion by selecting the field you want to use for sorting in the **Sort items by** list box and selecting either an **Ascending** or **Descending** sort.

4. If you want to sort using additional fields, specify each one in a **Then by** area of the Sort dialog box.

5. Click the **OK** button.

   Figure 3.59 shows the Phone List view of the Contacts folder after an ascending sort using the Full Name field has been applied (as shown in **Figure 3.58**), which sorts the items by first name.

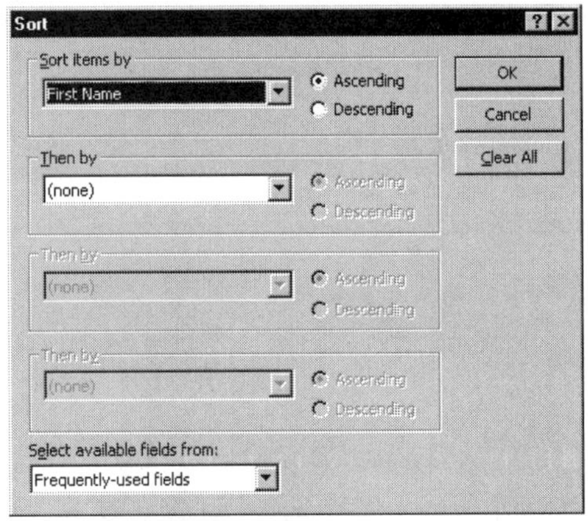

Figure 3.58 The Sort dialog box.

✔ Tips

- In the Sort dialog box, you can change the fields that are available for sorting by selecting an item in the **Select available fields from** list box.
- You can't sort items in a time-based view, such as the Task Timeline view of the Task folder or the Day/Week/Month view of the Calendar folder.
- In a table view, you can quickly sort the items using a particular field by clicking the corresponding column header (**Figure 3.60**). Subsequent clicks toggle between an ascending sort (indicated with an up-pointing triangle in the header) and a descending sort (indicated with a down-pointing triangle). To use one or more additional fields for sorting, click each header while pressing Shift; Outlook will use the fields in the order you click them.
- If a column header is too narrow, you won't see the triangle indicating that the field is being used for sorting.

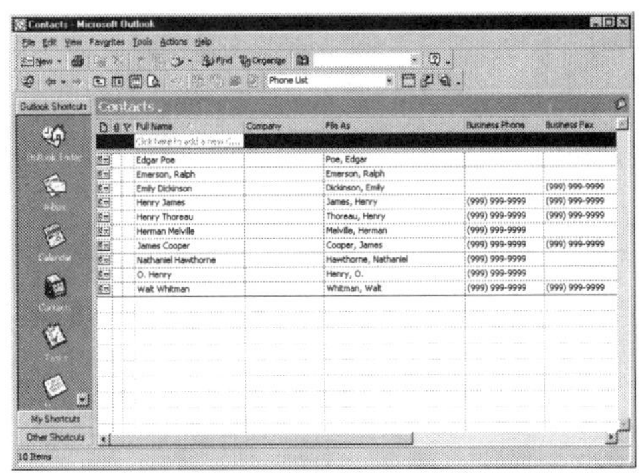

Figure 3.59 The Phone List view of the Contacts folder, sorted by Full Name.

Indicates an ascending sort using this field

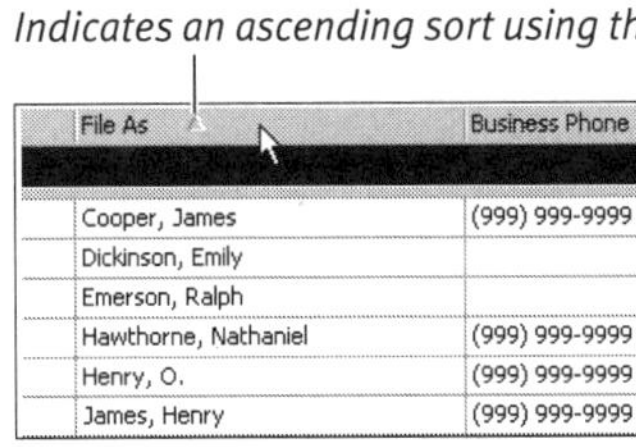

Figure 3.60 Sorting by the File As field by clicking the column header.

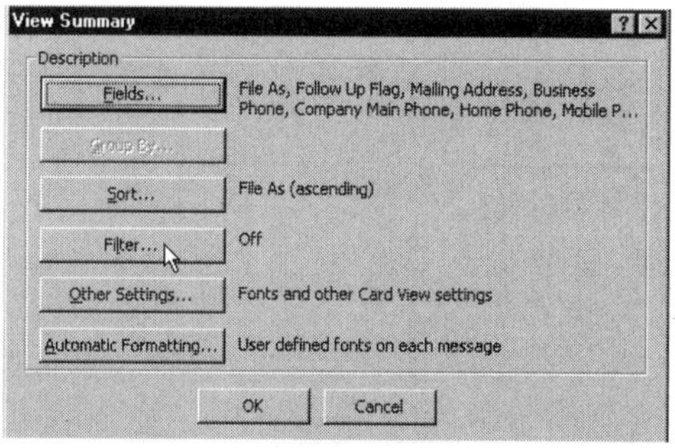

Figure 3.61 Clicking the **Filter** button in the View Summary dialog box.

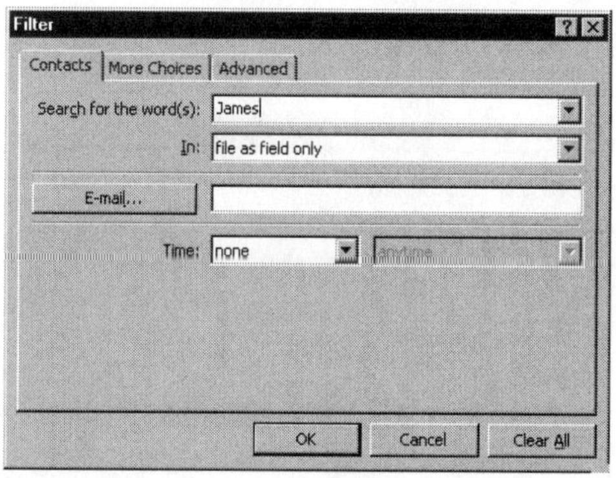

Figure 3.62 Entering filter criteria into the Filter dialog box.

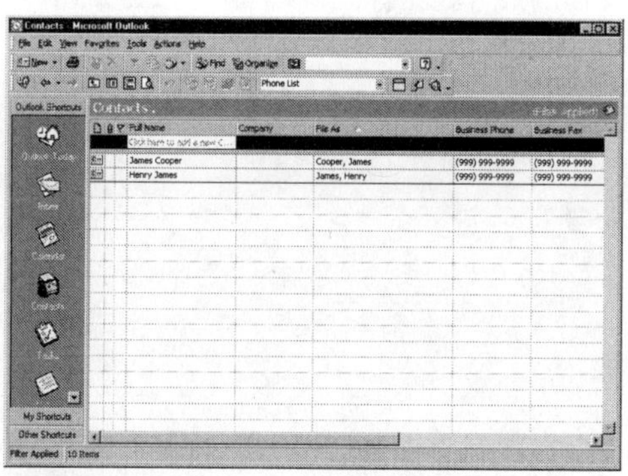

Figure 3.63 The effect of applying the filter criteria shown in Figure 3.62 to the Phone List view.

To filter items:

1. Activate the view in which you want to filter the items.
2. Right-click a blank area in the Information Viewer (not on an item!) (see **Figure 3.56**) and choose Filter from the pop-up menu.

   or

   If you can't find a blank spot, choose View > Current View > Customize Current View and click the **Filter** button in the View Summary dialog box (**Figure 3.61**).
3. Select the filter criteria in the tabs of the Filter dialog box.

   For example, if you typed the name *James* in the **Search for the word(s)** text box and selected *file as field only* in the **In** list box (**Figure 3.62**), Outlook would display only the items that have the word *James* in the File As field (**Figure 3.63**).
4. Click the **OK** button.

✔ Tips

- The Filter dialog box displays the same tabs and controls as the Advanced Find dialog box, described later in the chapter.
- When the items in the current view are filtered, the message "Filter Applied" appears both on the right end of the Folder Banner and on the left end of the Status bar (see **Figure 3.63**), letting you know that not all items are displayed.
- To remove a filter and display all items, reopen the Filter dialog box, as explained in step 2 above, click the **Clear All** button, and then click the **OK** button.

To group items:

1. Activate the view in which you want to group the items. You must activate a table view.
2. Right-click a blank area in the Information Viewer (not on an item!) (**Figure 3.56**) and choose Group from the pop-up menu.

   or

   If you can't find a blank spot, choose View > Current View > Customize Current View and click the **Group By** button in the View Summary dialog box (**Figure 3.64**).
3. In the Group By dialog box (**Figure 3.65**), specify the primary grouping criterion by selecting the field you want to use for grouping in the **Group items by** list box, and selecting either **Ascending** or **Descending** to set the order in which the groups are listed.
4. If you want groups within groups, specify each nested group in a **Then by** area of the Group By dialog box.
5. Select an option in the **Expand/collapse defaults** list box to specify how the groups will be shown when you first display the view.
6. Click the **OK** button.

As an example, the Group By dialog box settings shown in **Figure 3.66** would divide the items in the Phone List view of the Contacts folder as shown in **Figure 3.67**.

✔ Tips

- In the Group By dialog box, you can change the fields that are available for grouping by selecting an item in the **Select available fields from** list box.

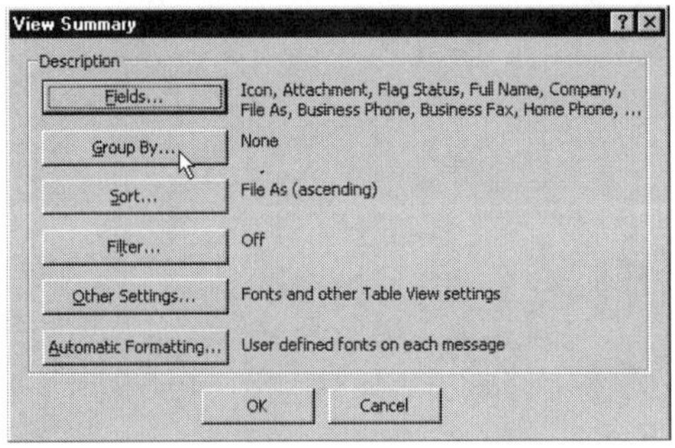

Figure 3.64 Clicking the **Filter** button in the View Summary dialog box.

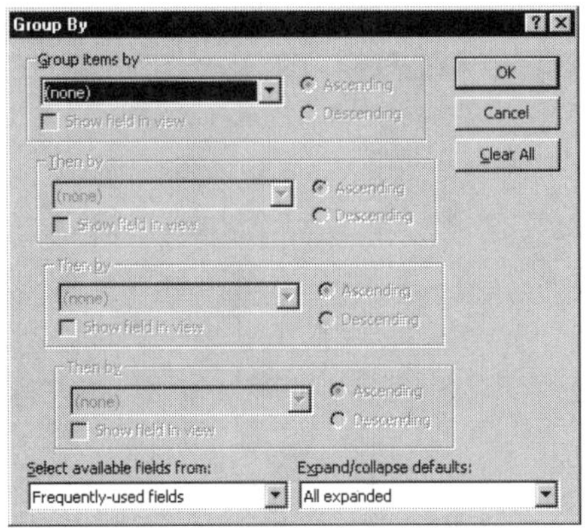

Figure 3.65 The Group By dialog box.

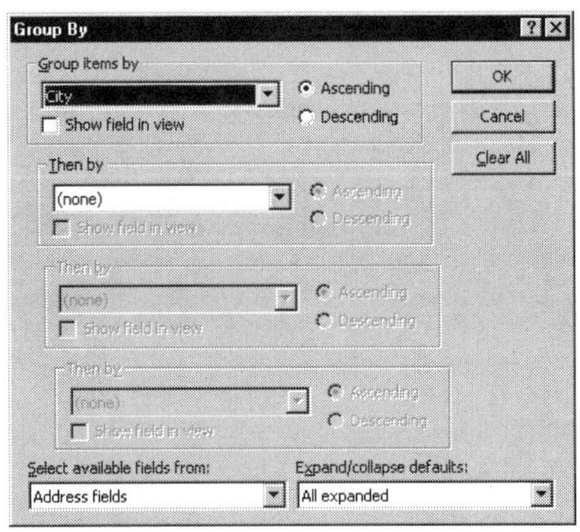

Figure 3.66 Settings for grouping contacts by city.

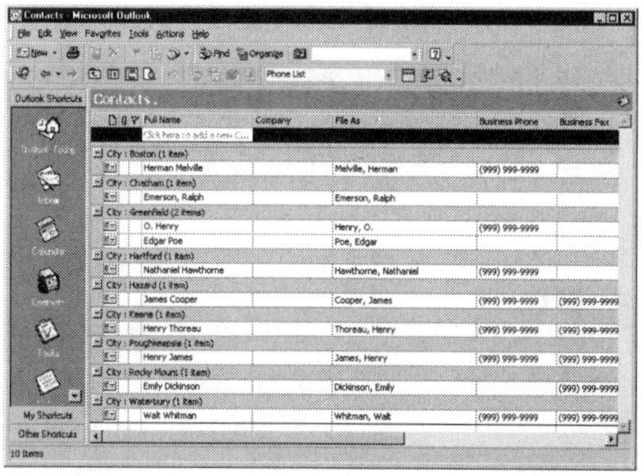

Figure 3.67 The result of the settings shown in Figure 3.66.

Right-clicked here to open pop-up menu

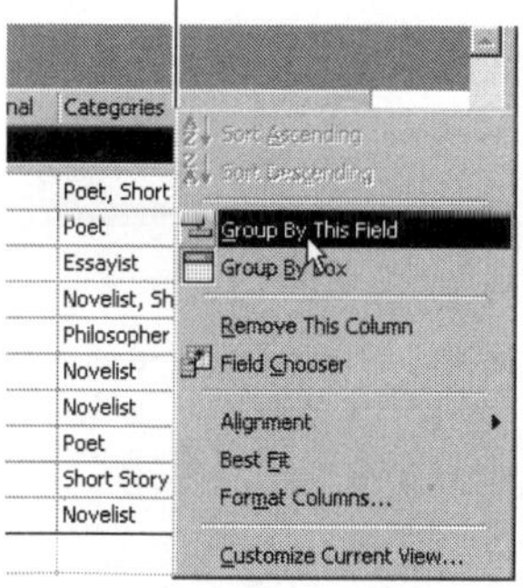

Figure 3.68 Using the Categories field for grouping items.

- A quick way to group items using a field that's displayed in a column of the Information Viewer is to right-click the column header and choose Group By This Field from the pop-up menu (**Figure 3.68**). Repeat this operation for any nested groups you wish to add; Outlook will group using the fields in the order in which you designate them.
- You can collapse or expand a group of items displayed in the Information Viewer by clicking the − or + button at the top of the group. You can collapse or expand *all* groups by choosing View > Expand/Collapse Groups > Collapse All or View > Expand/Collapse Groups > Expand All.
- Some standard views already have grouping applied. For example, the By Category view of the Contacts folder groups records using the Category field.
- To remove all grouping, open the Group By dialog box, as explained in step 2 above, click the **Clear All** button, and then click the **OK** button.

Using the Organize Page

The Organize Page is a Web-style page that you can display in a pane at the top of the Information Viewer (**Figure 3.69**). It contains a set of controls that you can use to work with items in various ways. The particular controls that are available—and the things you can do in the Organize Page—depend upon the Outlook folder in which it's displayed. Here's an overall list of what you can do using the Organize Page:

- Switch views.
- Move an item to a different folder.
- Assign a category to an item or create a new category.
- Create a rule for automatically moving selected messages.
- Automatically color-code messages.
- Automatically move or color-code junk or adult-content messages.

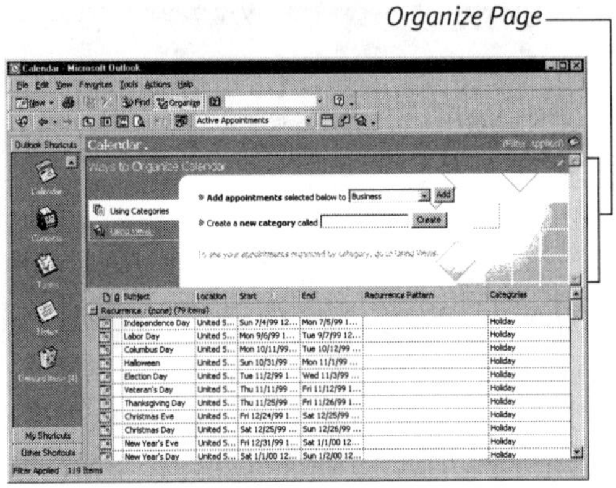

Figure 3.69 The Organize Page displayed in the Active Appointments view of the Calendar folder.

✔ Tips

- The last three functions in the list (automatically moving messages, color-coding messages, and handling junk e-mail) are described in "Systematizing Your E-mail and Fax Messages" in Chapter 6.
- The Organize Page doesn't let you do anything you can't do through conventional program commands. However, it's sometimes easier to use than conventional commands.

First, click a command category here... *...then, use the controls here to carry out a command*

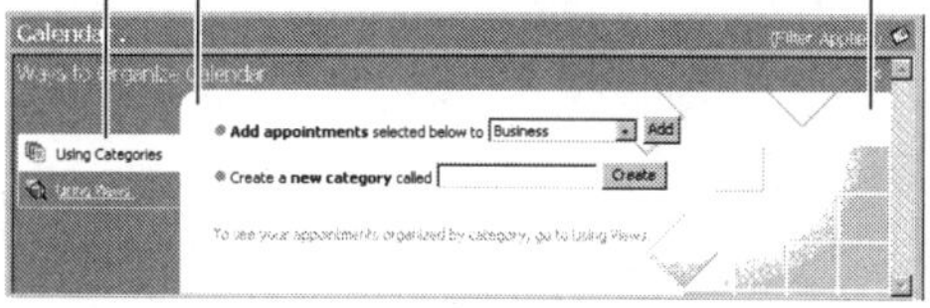

Figure 3.70 Using the Organize Page.

To use the Organize Page:

1. Open the folder containing the items you want to work with, and activate the desired view.
2. Click the Organize button on the Standard toolbar or choose Tools > Organize.

   Outlook will display the Organize Page (**Figure 3.69**).
3. Click the desired category of commands on the left side of the page.
4. Use the controls to issue the commands you want (**Figure 3.70**).

✔ Tip

- To remove the Organize Page, click the Organize button on the Standard toolbar again, or click the **Close Organize** button in the upper-right corner of the page.

Finding Outlook Items and Disk Files

Outlook provides the following search tools:

- The easiest way to locate Outlook items containing specific text is to use the Find Page, which is a Web-style page that you can display in a pane at the top of the Information Viewer (**Figure 3.71**).
- To locate Outlook items using more exacting search criteria, to search through more than one Outlook folder, or to find files on local or network disks, you need to use the Advanced Find dialog box (**Figure 3.72**).

To use the Find Page:

1. Open the Outlook folder where you want to search for items. (The Find Page searches only in the opened Outlook folder.)
2. Click the Find button on the Standard toolbar or choose Tools > Find. Outlook will display the Find Page (**Figure 3.73**).
3. Type the text you want to search for in the **Look for** text box.
4. Click the **Find Now** button.

   Outlook will now display only those items—if there are any—that contain the text you typed (**Figure 3.74**).
5. If you didn't find the item you were looking for, in the Find Page you can click **Go to Advanced Find** to display the Advanced Find dialog box (described next). Or, you can click **Clear Search** to restore the items that were displayed before you performed the search, and to empty the **Look for** list box so you can perform another search.

Find Page

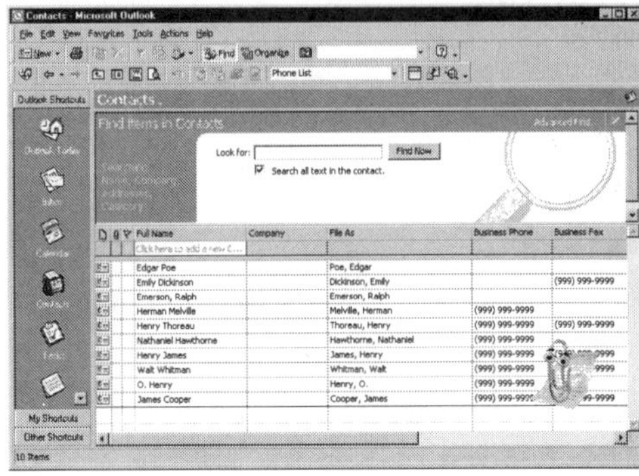

Figure 3.71 The Find Page displayed in the Contacts folder.

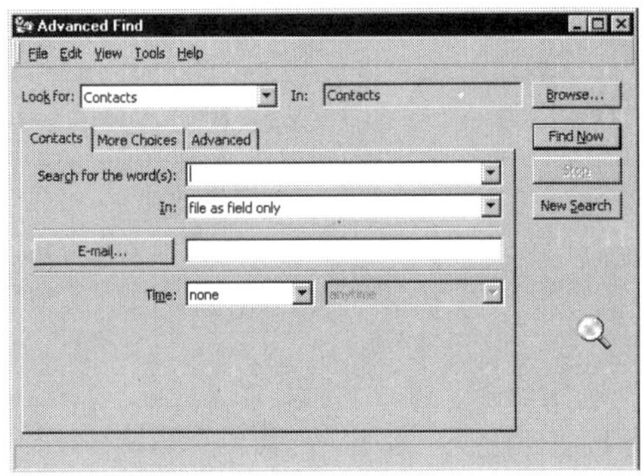

Figure 3.72 The Advanced Find dialog box (searching for contacts).

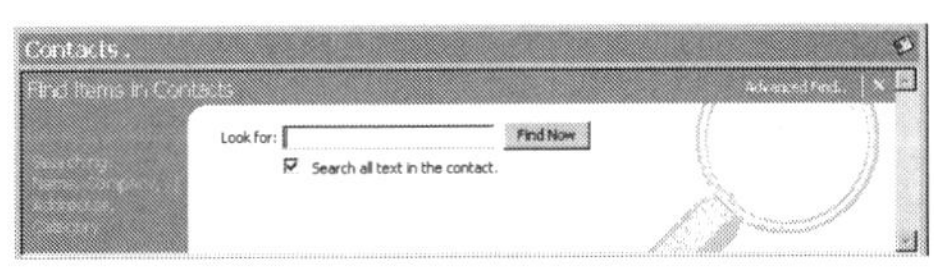

Figure 3.73 The Find Page.

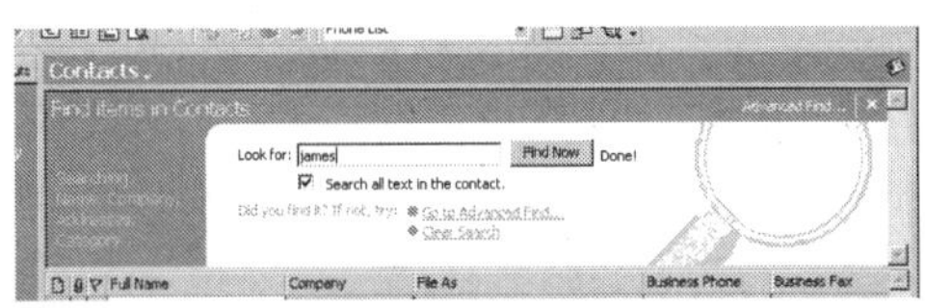

Figure 3.74 The Contacts folder after searching for all items that contain the text *james*.

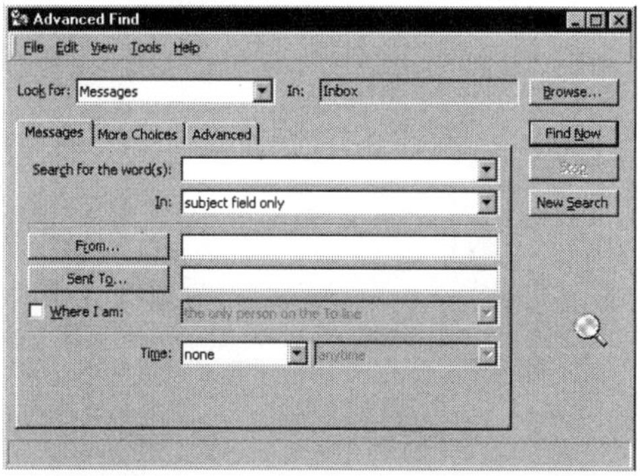

Figure 3.75 The Advanced Find dialog box (searching for messages).

✔ Tips

- For faster searches, you can uncheck the **Search all text in the *item*** check box in the Find Page (where *item* is the type of item in the folder, such as *contact* or *appointment*), which causes Outlook to search only the most common item fields. (Notice that the names of the specific fields that Outlook searches when this option is unchecked are displayed to the left of the Find Page.) If you don't find what you're looking for, you can then check **Search all text in the *item*** to do a more thorough search.
- To remove the Find Page (and restore the display of all items, if you performed a search), click the Find button on the Standard toolbar again, or click the **Close Find** button in the upper-right corner of the page.

To use the Advanced Find dialog box:

1. Choose Tools > Advanced Find or press Ctrl-Shift-F.

   or

   If you've displayed the Find Page, you can click the **Advanced Find** button near the upper-right corner of the page.

   Outlook will open the Advanced Find dialog box (**Figure 3.75**). It doesn't matter which folder is open when you display this dialog box—you can always search for any kind of item or disk file in any Outlook folder or disk folder.

2. In the **Look for** list box in the Advanced Find dialog box, select the type of item or file you want to search for:
   - Select **Any type of Outlook item** to search for all types of items.

(continued on next page)

- Select a specific type of Outlook item (such as **Messages**, **Contacts**, or **Journal entries**) to narrow your search to just that type of item.
- Select **Files** to search for disk files in local or network file folders.
- Select **Files (Outlook/Exchange)** to search for disk files that are stored in Outlook mail-item folders. (Storing files in Outlook is useful mainly for public folders provided by Exchange Server and is briefly discussed in the section "E/S To access a public folder" in Chapter 4.)

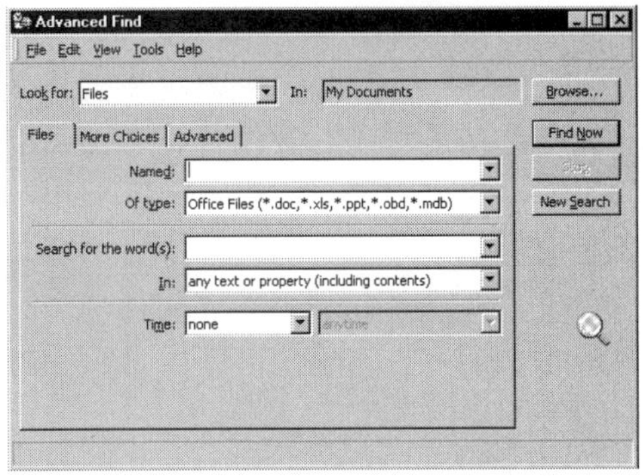

Figure 3.76 The Advanced Find dialog box (searching for disk files).

3. Click the **Browse** button to select one or more folders that you want to search (Outlook folders or disk folders), or just accept the default folder displayed in the **In** box. (Outlook selects a default folder to be searched, based upon the type of item or file that you select in the **Look for** list box.)
4. Enter your search criteria into the tabs of the Advanced Find dialog box.

   The tabs you see and the controls they contain depend upon the type of item you are searching for. **Figures 3.72**, **3.75**, and **3.76** show the Advanced Find dialog box as it appears when you search for contacts, messages, and disk files.

   For help entering information into a particular control, choose Help > What's This? on the dialog box's menu and then click the control.
5. Click the **Find Now** button.

   Outlook will then perform the search and will display the items or files it finds—if any—at the bottom of the Advanced Find dialog box. The items are displayed in the same way they would be displayed in the Outlook window. **Figure 3.77** shows search criteria entered into the Advanced Find dialog box with the results of the search displayed at the bottom.

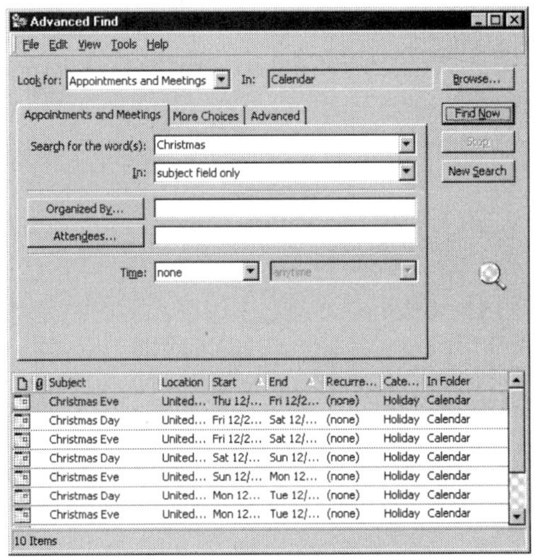

Figure 3.77 The Advanced Find dialog box, after a search has been performed.

✔ Tips

- The Advanced Find dialog box provides many of the same commands as the Outlook window for sorting, grouping, changing the view, or customizing the view.
- You can open or work with the items displayed in the Advanced Find dialog box using many of the techniques described in this chapter, working within the dialog box.
- After you've entered a set of search criteria into the Advanced Find dialog box (which might be fairly involved), you can save your criteria by choosing File > Save Search in the dialog box. If you later want to perform the same search again, you can retrieve your saved search criteria by choosing File > Open Search.
- You can use the Advanced Find dialog box even if you aren't running Outlook! To display it, choose Find > Using Microsoft Outlook on your Windows Start menu (opened by clicking the **Start** button on the Windows taskbar).

Working with Outlook Folders

4

As explained in Chapter 2, Outlook *folders* are the places where information is stored, displayed, and managed. When you set up Outlook, it creates a default set of folders, one for each basic type of information that it manages. As you begin working with Outlook and organizing your personal information, however, you'll soon want to start adding, rearranging, or renaming folders, just as you would if you were storing information in a file cabinet.

In Chapter 2, you learned different ways to locate and open an Outlook folder. In this chapter, you'll learn how to

- Create new folders
- Move or copy folders
- Rename folders
- Remove folders
- Share folders over the Internet
- Share folders over a network (Exchange Server)
- Print folders
- Change folder properties

Creating New Folders

You might want to create one or more new Outlook folders for a variety of reasons. For example, you might want to do the following:

- Create one or more additional mail-item folders for storing and organizing the messages you've received—perhaps one folder for personal e-mail messages, one for business e-mail messages, and one for faxes.
- Create an additional calendar-item folder so that you can keep your personal appointments in one folder and your business appointments and meetings in another.
- Create a task-item folder for each major project that you're managing. (Later in the chapter, you'll learn how you can share such a folder over the Internet.)
- Create a new folder in the Public Folders area on the server to use for sharing information with other people on your network (Exchange Server).

✔ Tip

- Outlook folders are organized in a hierarchy. That is, folders can contain other folders, as well as items. A single *root folder* at the top of the hierarchy is named Outlook Today (sometimes labeled "Personal Folders" or "Mailbox"), which contains all other folders (**Figure 4.1**).
- When you create a new Outlook folder, you can place it within any other Outlook folder, making it a *subfolder* of the original folder.

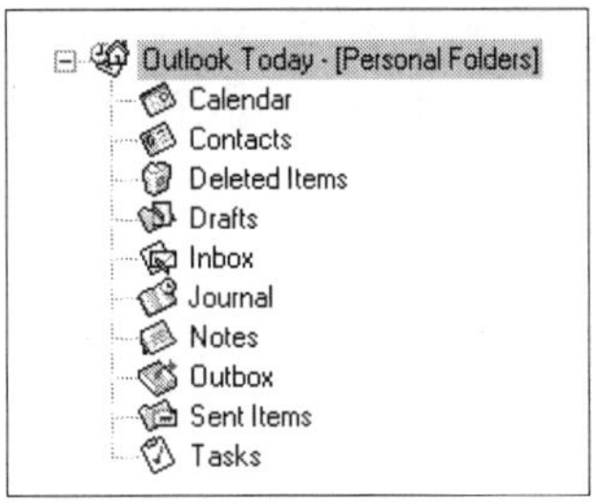

Figure 4.1 The hierarchy of the default Outlook folders.

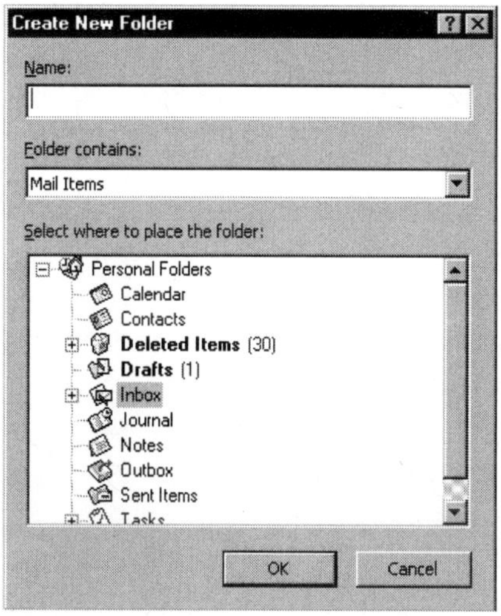

Figure 4.2 The Create New Folder dialog box.

To create a new folder:

1. Choose File > Folder > New Folder, or press Ctrl-Shift-E.

   Outlook opens the Create New Folder dialog box (**Figure 4.2**).

2. In the **Name** text box, enter a name for your new folder.

3. In the **Folder contains** list box, select the type of items you want to store in your new folder:

   - **Appointment Items** are appointments, events, or meetings. The is the item type that is stored in the default Calendar folder.
   - **Contact Items** are contacts (descriptions of your personal or business contacts) or distribution lists (sets of contacts). This is the item type that is stored in the default Contacts folder.
   - **Journal Items** are journal entries (records of events that have occurred). This is the item type that is stored in the default Journal folder.
   - **Mail Items** are e-mail messages, fax messages, and other items. This is the item type that is stored in the default Inbox, Drafts, Outbox, and Saved Items folders.
   - **Note Items** are text notes that you jot down. This is the item type that is stored in the default Notes folder.
   - **Task Items** are tasks (descriptions of jobs or projects you need to complete). This is the item type that is stored in the default Tasks folder.

(continued on next page)

4. In the **Select where to place the folder** list, select (click on) the folder in which you want to store your new folder.

   Your new folder will become a subfolder of the selected folder. If necessary, click the + symbol to expand the branch of the hierarchy that contains the folder you want to select. **Figure 4.3** shows an example of a completed Create New Folder dialog box.

5. Click the **OK** button.

6. In the message box that Outlook displays (**Figure 4.4**), click **Yes** if you want to add a shortcut for your new folder to the My Shortcuts group of the Outlook Bar. Or click **No** if you don't.

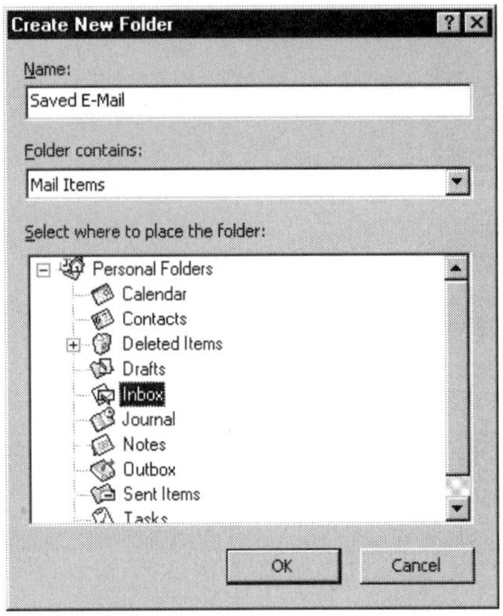

Figure 4.3 Settings for creating a new folder for saving e-mail messages. The folder will be named Saved E-Mail and will be located within the default Inbox folder.

✔ Tips

- If you opt not to create a shortcut for your new folder, you can open it using the Folder List, as described in "To open a folder using the Folder List" in Chapter 2. You can also create a shortcut later, using the method outlined in "Modifying the Outlook Bar" in Chapter 14.
- You can get a head start in creating a new folder that's similar to an existing one by making a copy of the existing folder. Instructions are given in the next section.

Figure 4.4 Prompt for creating an Outlook Bar shortcut for your new folder.

Creating New Folders

Moving and Copying Folders

You can move an Outlook folder from its current position in the Outlook folder hierarchy to another position. Doing so can help you organize your Outlook folders, just as you might move a paper file folder to a different file drawer.

For example, if you created several folders for storing e-mail messages and you initially made them subfolders of Outlook Today (like all of the default Outlook folders), you might later decide to move them to your Inbox (making them subfolders of Inbox), so that all your new e-mail folders would be grouped in a single location (see **Figures 4.5** and **4.6**).

Figure 4.5 The folder hierarchy *before* moving Saved Business E-Mail and Saved Personal E-Mail.

Figure 4.6 The folder hierarchy *after* moving Saved Business E-Mail and Saved Personal E-Mail to the Inbox folder.

You can also make a copy of an Outlook folder, placing the copy in the same folder as the original or in a different folder.

For example, you might make a backup copy of your Sent Items folder for safekeeping. Or, if you wanted to create a separate calendar-item folder for your personal appointments, you could make a *copy* of your Calendar folder—rather than creating a new folder—so you wouldn't have to reenter information already contained in Calendar.

✔ Tips

- You can't move a default Outlook folder (Inbox, Calendar, and so on), although you can make a copy of it.
- When you move or copy a folder, you also move or copy all items contained in the folder.

To move or copy a folder:

1. Open the folder you want to move or copy.
2. To move the folder, chose File > Folder > Move "*Folder*," where *Folder* is the name of the currently opened folder (such as Saved E-Mail).

   or

   To copy the folder, choose File > Folder > Copy "*Folder*."

   Outlook will open the Move Folder dialog box (**Figure 4.7**) or the Copy Folder dialog box (**Figure 4.8**).
3. In the dialog box, select the folder in which you want to store the moved or copied folder. If necessary, click the + symbol to open the branch of the folder hierarchy containing the target folder.
4. Click the **OK** button.

✔ Tips

- In the permanently displayed Folder List (see "To open a folder using the Folder List" in Chapter 2), you can right-click any folder in the list and choose Move "*Folder*" or Copy "*Folder*" from the pop-up menu to move or copy that folder, without having to first open the folder (**Figure 4.9**).
- In the permanently displayed Folder List, you can also quickly move a folder by dragging it to the destination folder. To copy the folder, press Ctrl while you drag.
- In the next section, you'll learn how to assign a different name to your moved or copied folder.

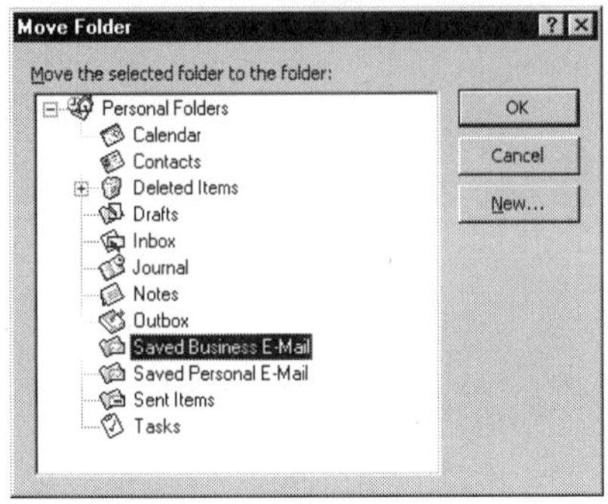

Figure 4.7 The Move Folder dialog box.

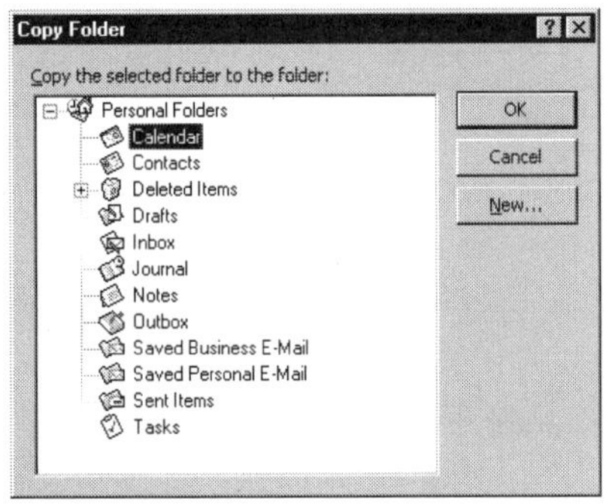

Figure 4.8 The Copy Folder dialog box.

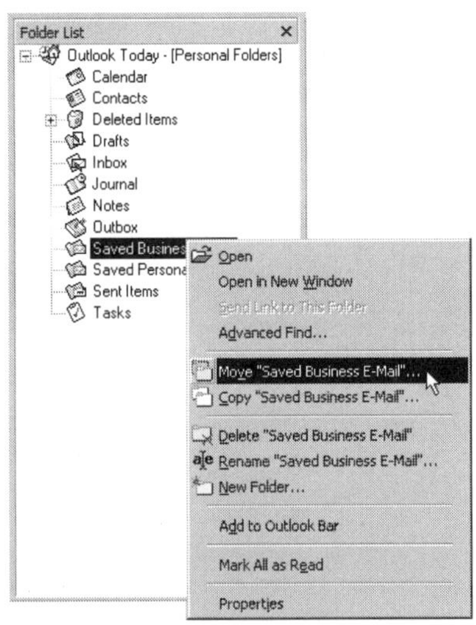

Figure 4.9 Using the pop-up menu in the Folder List to move a folder.

Figure 4.10 The Rename dialog box.

Type a new name in this box

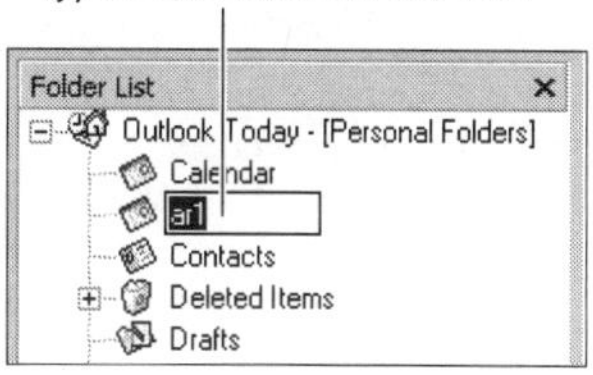

Figure 4.11 Editing a folder name in the Folder List.

Renaming Folders

You can rename any Outlook folder that you have created. (You *can't* rename a default Outlook folder, such as Inbox or Calendar, however.)

For example, if you have made a copy of the Calendar folder in the same folder as the original, Outlook will name the copy Calendar1. You'll probably want to give it a more descriptive name, such as Business Schedule or Personal Appointments.

To rename a folder:

1. Open the folder you want to rename.
2. Choose File > Folder > Rename "*Folder*," where *Folder* is the name of the currently opened folder.

   Outlook will display the Rename dialog box (**Figure 4.10**).
3. Type the name you want into the **New name** text box.
4. Click the **OK** button.

✔ Tips

- If the Folder List is displayed permanently (see "To open a folder using the Folder List" in Chapter 2), when you choose File > Folder > Rename "*Folder*," Outlook will highlight the folder name in the Folder List and let you edit the name right there (**Figure 4.11**).
- In the permanently displayed Folder List, you can rename *any* folder that you've created (without first opening the folder), by right-clicking the folder in the list and choosing Rename "*Folder*" from the pop-up menu. Or, you can simply click the folder and press F2. In either case, Outlook will then let you edit the name in place, as shown in **Figure 4.11**.

Renaming Folders

Removing Folders

You can remove any Outlook folder that you have created. (You *can't* remove a default Outlook folder, such as Inbox or Calendar, however.) When you remove a folder, Outlook initially moves the folder and all its contents to the Deleted Items folder. As long as the folder remains in Deleted Items, you can easily recover it. If it gets permanently deleted from Deleted Items, you'll no longer be able to recover it.

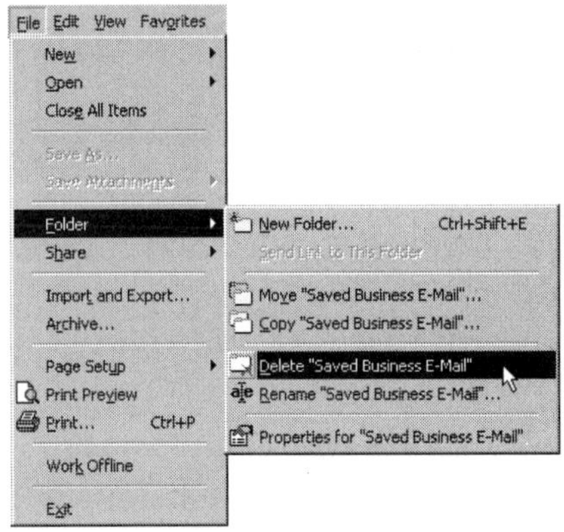

Figure 4.12 Choosing the menu command for deleting the opened folder.

To remove a folder:

1. Open the folder you want to remove.
2. Choose File > Folder > Delete "*Folder*," where *Folder* is the name of the currently opened folder (**Figure 4.12**).

   Outlook will warn you before deleting the folder (**Figure 4.13**).
3. Click **Yes** in the warning dialog box to proceed with the deletion.

Figure 4.13 The warning message Outlook displays before deleting a folder.

✔ Tips

- If you've permanently displayed the Folder List (see "To open a folder using the Folder List" in Chapter 2), you can delete *any* folder that you've created (without first opening the folder) by right-clicking the folder in the list and choosing Delete "*Folder*" from the pop-up menu. Or, you can simply click the folder and press Del.
- To recover a removed folder that's still in Deleted Items, simply move it from Deleted Items back to its original location.
- To permanently delete a removed folder, remove it from Deleted Items. To do this, you can use any of the methods provided in this section or any of the methods for permanently removing an item that are presented in "To permanently delete a removed item" in Chapter 3.

Sharing Outlook Folders over the Internet

You can share one or more of your Outlook folders over the Internet using Outlook's Net Folders feature. You can share a folder with anyone who meets the following requirements:

- The person must be able to exchange e-mail with you (but see first tip below).
- The person must be using Outlook (but see first tip below).
- You must add that person to your member list for the folder, and the person must accept membership.

Say, for example, that you're working on a project with a group of people scattered across the country. You could share your Calendar folder (or another calendar-item folder) with these people so that they would all have access to the appointments, deadlines, and meetings that it contains.

Outlook sends by e-mail a copy of a shared folder to each new *member* (a person with whom you share the folder). Then, whenever you make changes to the folder, Outlook automatically sends those changes to each member and updates the member's copy of the folder. If a member has the required permission level, he or she can add or modify items in the folder, and Outlook will send those changes back to you and automatically update your copy.

✔ Tips

- If an intended member doesn't have Outlook, or if the member uses an e-mail service that doesn't transmit the required information (such as CompuServe), only limited sharing of messages is possible.

(continued on next page)

- Both you and the people with whom you share a folder must have the Net Folders component of Outlook installed. For information on adding a component, see "Adding or Removing Outlook Components" in Appendix A.
- You can't share the default Inbox folder.
- If you're using Outlook with Exchange Server, you can't share folders stored in an Exchange Server mailbox or Public Folders area on the server. You can, however, share any folders you've stored in a Personal Folders (.PST) file.
- Outlook items that have the Private option checked won't be shared with others. (In later chapters, you'll learn about checking this option.)

To share a folder:

1. Open the folder you want to share.
2. Choose File > Share > This Folder.

   Outlook will then run the Net Folder Wizard, which will prompt you for the information required to share the folder.
3. In the first wizard dialog box (**Figure 4.14**), click the **Next** button.
4. In the second wizard dialog box (**Figure 4.15**), click the **Add** button. In the Add Entries To Subscriber Database dialog box (**Figure 4.16**), select the names of the people you want to share the folder with and click **OK**.

   For more information on using the Add Entries To Subscriber Database dialog box, see the instructions for using the similar Select Names dialog box in the section "I/O To address a message" or "C/W To address a message" in Chapter 6.

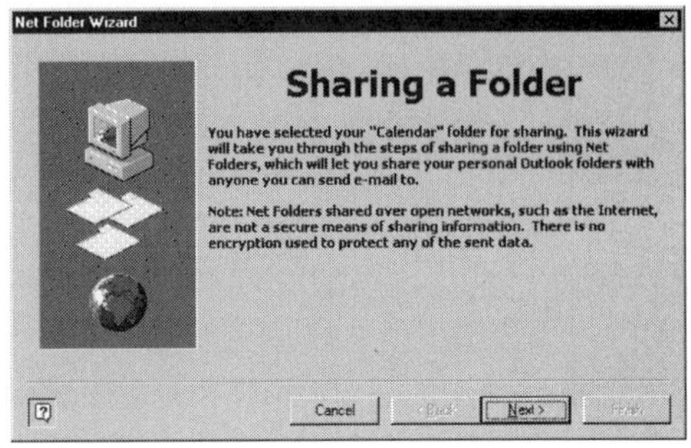

Figure 4.14 The first Net Folder Wizard dialog box.

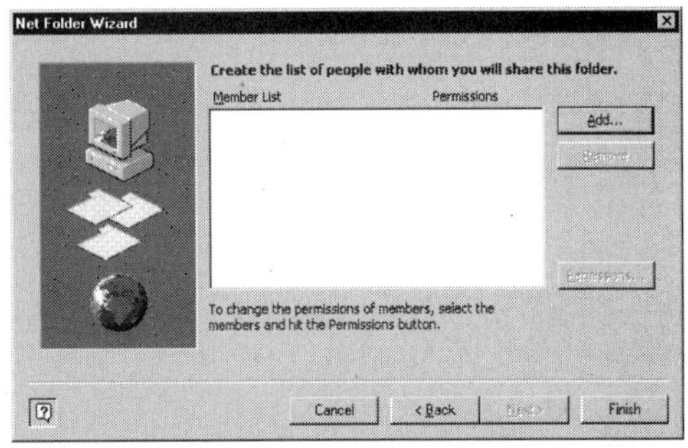

Figure 4.15 The second Net Folder Wizard dialog box.

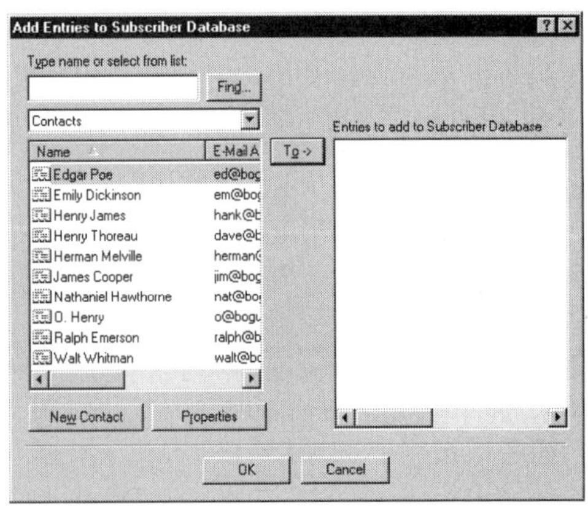

Figure 4.16 The Add Entries to Subscriber Database dialog box, as it appears with the Internet Only configuration (the dialog box is laid out differently with the Corporate or Workgroup configuration).

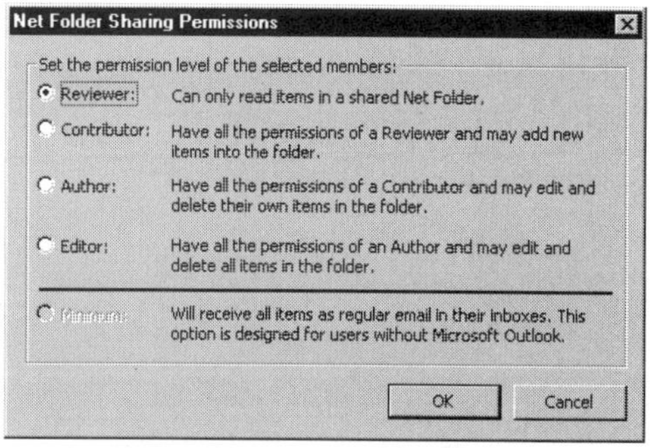

Figure 4.17 The Net Folder Sharing Permissions dialog box.

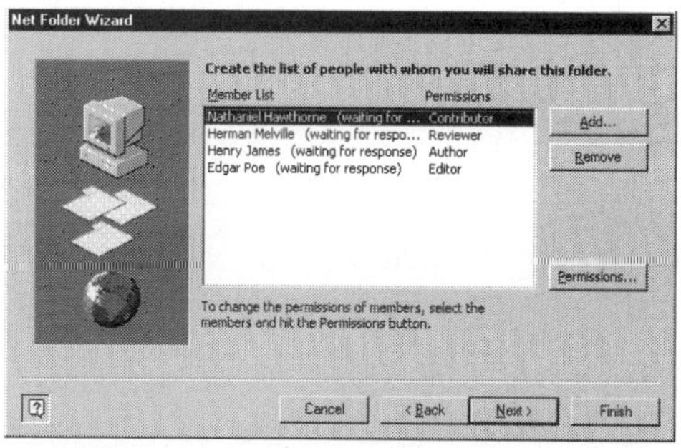

Figure 4.18 The completed second Net Folder Wizard dialog box.

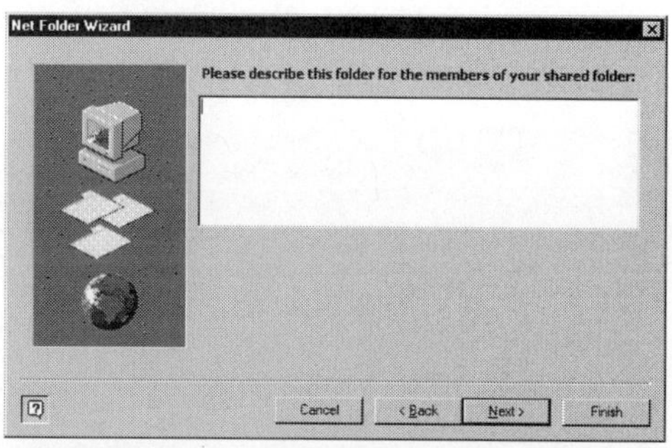

Figure 4.19 The third Net Folder Wizard dialog box.

5. Back in the second wizard dialog box, if you want to adjust a member's permission level, select the name, click the **Permissions** button, select the new level of permission in the Net Folder Sharing Permissions dialog box (**Figure 4.17**), and click **OK**.

   Initially, all members have the **Reviewer** permission level, meaning that they can only read the items in the shared folder. You should change a member's permission if you want the member to be able to add new items, to edit and delete items the member has created, or to edit and delete any items in the folder.

   Figure 4.18 shows the second wizard dialog box after four members have been added and permissions have been set.

6. Click the **Next** button in the second wizard dialog box.

7. In the third wizard dialog box (**Figure 4.19**) type information on the shared folder and click **Next**.

   Here, you might type a description of the folder, a greeting to folder members, or brief instructions. The information you type will appear in the e-mail messages sent to members as well as in the **Description** text box of the folder's Properties dialog box (as shown in **Figure 4.31**, later in the chapter).

(continued on next page)

8. In the fourth wizard dialog box (**Figure 4.20**), just click the **Finish** button, and you're done!

Outlook will now send e-mail messages to all the potential members you specified. After one or more members accept the invitation by clicking the Accept button in the message, Outlook will automatically share the folder with them.

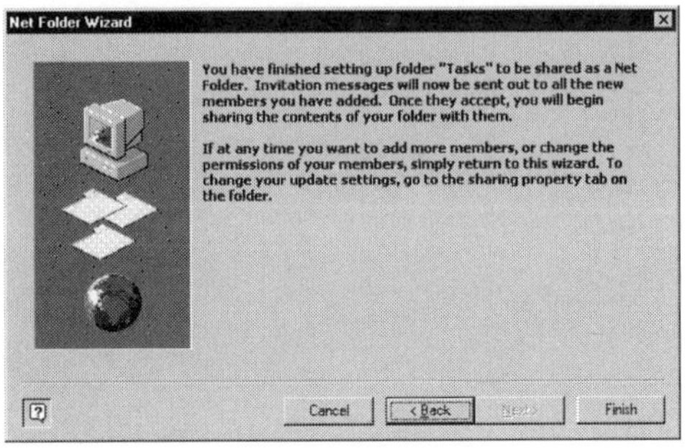

Figure 4.20 The fourth Net Folder Wizard dialog box.

✔ Tips

- If a member doesn't have Outlook, or uses an e-mail service that doesn't support full folder sharing (such as CompuServe), you should assign that member the Minimum permission level, which causes Outlook to exchange information using e-mail, without automatic folder updating. This option works only for a mail-item folder.
- To add or remove members for a shared folder, open that folder and run the Net Folder Wizard again.
- To change other settings for a shared folder, open the Sharing tab of the folder's Properties dialog box as explained in "To change a folder's properties," later in the chapter.

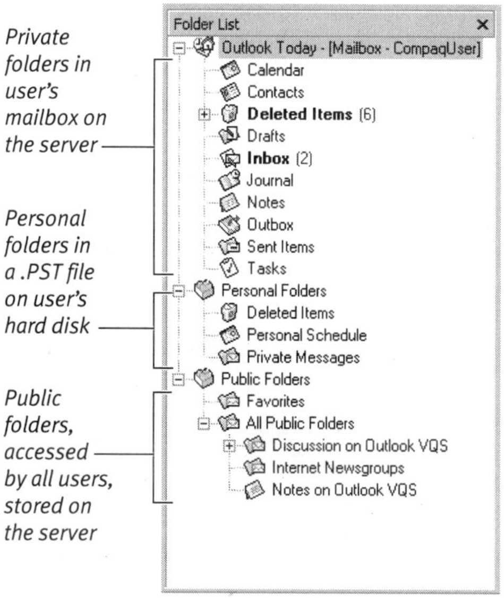

Figure 4.21 The Folder List for an Exchange Server user.

E/S Sharing Folders Over a Network

If you're using Outlook with Microsoft Exchange Server, you can share Outlook folders with other Outlook users on the network in either of the following ways:

- You can share a *private folder* with one or more specific users, or with all users. A private folder is one that is stored in your mailbox on the server. Exchange Server creates a personal mailbox for each user on the network. It's the usual location for your default Outlook folders (Inbox, Calendar, Contacts, and so on), as well as the folders you create to store your personal information.
- You can create a *public folder*, which is stored in the Public Folders area of the server. Exchange Server provides a single Public Folders area on the server. All users can easily access folders in the Public Folders area using the Folder List or shortcuts (although, if desired, the folder creator can limit access).

Figure 4.21 shows the Folder List for a setup in which Outlook is being used with Exchange Server. Notice that the default Outlook folders (including Inbox, where e-mail messages are delivered) are all private folders located in the user's mailbox on the server. Three additional folders are stored in a Personal Folders (.PST) file on the user's hard disk. The Public Folders are stored on the server and are shared by all Outlook users on the network.

E/S To share a private folder:

1. Open the folder you want to share. It must be a private folder in your mailbox.
2. Choose File > Folder > Properties For "*Folder*" (where *Folder* is the name of the currently opened folder) and open the Permissions tab (**Figure 4.22**).
3. To share the folder with *everyone* on the network, assign the desired permission level to the **Default** user by selecting that user in the list and selecting the desired permission level in the **Roles** list box.

   Initially, the Default user is assigned the **None** level of permission, which denies sharing. When you select a permission level, the options for that level are automatically selected in the **Permissions** area. If you want to create a custom level of permission, you can select individual options in this area.
4. To share the folder with one or more specific users, click the **Add** button, select the users in the Add Users dialog box (**Figure 4.23**) and click **OK**. Then, in the Permissions tab assign the desired permission level to each user.
5. Click the **OK** button in the Properties dialog box.

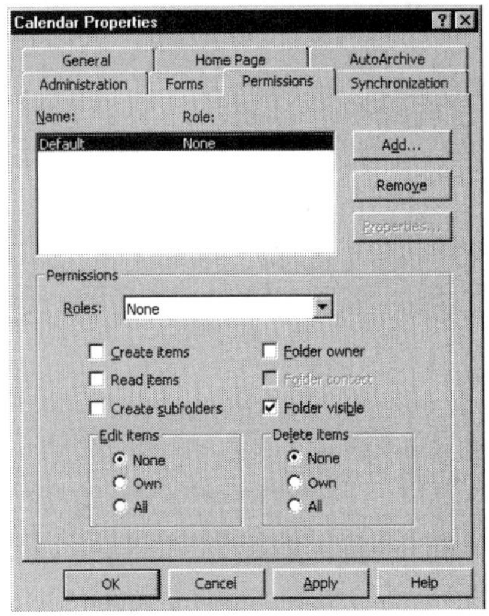

Figure 4.22 The Permissions tab of the Calendar Properties dialog box.

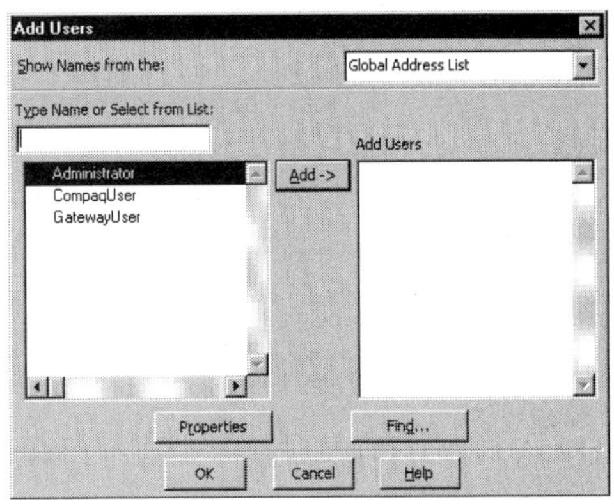

Figure 4.23 The Add Users dialog box.

✔ Tips

- You can open the Properties dialog box for any folder, without first opening that folder, by right-clicking the folder in the permanently displayed Folder List or by right-clicking the folder's shortcut in the Outlook Bar, and then choosing Properties from the pop-up menu.
- Outlook items that have the Private option checked won't be shared with others. (In later chapters, you'll learn about checking this option.)

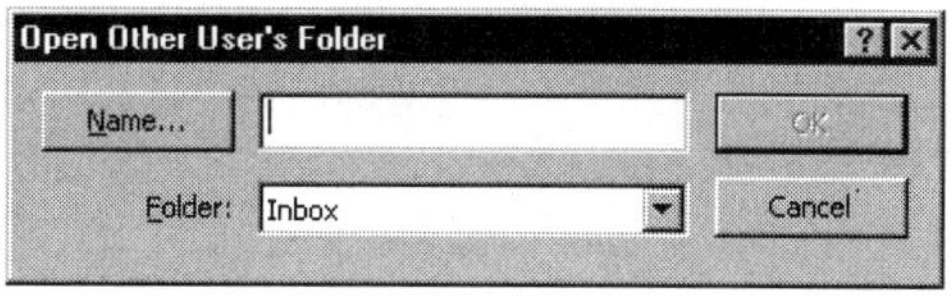

Figure 4.24 The Open Other User's Folder dialog box.

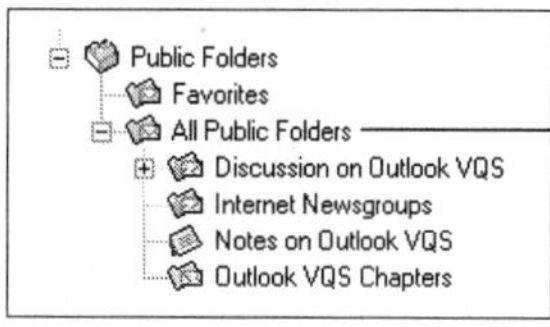

Figure 4.25 Creating a public folder.

E/S To access another user's shared private folder:

1. Choose File > Open > Another User's Folder.

   Outlook will open the Open Other User's Folder dialog box (**Figure 4.24**).
2. Type the user's name into the text box, or click the **Name** button to select the name from a list of Outlook users on the network.
3. Select the folder you want to access in the **Folder** list box.
4. Click the **OK** button.

Outlook will open the shared folder in a separate window. You can then view, open, or work with the items it contains, according to your level of permission.

E/S To create a public folder:

- Follow the instructions for creating a new folder given in the section "To create a new folder," earlier in the chapter. In step 4, simply place your new folder within All Public Folders in the Public Folders area, or within one of its subfolders (**Figure 4.25**).

✓ Tip

- When you create a public folder, all other users are initially granted the **Author** level of permission, which lets them create items, read items, and edit or delete the items they create. You can change permissions in the Permissions tab of the folder's Properties dialog box. (For instructions on opening this tab, see "To change a folder's properties," later in the chapter.)

To access a public folder:

- To open a public folder, use the Folder List, or click a shortcut if you've created one. (Creating shortcuts is discussed in "Modifying the Outlook Bar" in Chapter 14.)
- To work with the items in the folder, use the techniques discussed in Chapter 3.
- To work with the folder itself, use the techniques described in this chapter.

✔ Tips

- If someone else has created the folder, your permission level will determine which operations you can perform.
- You can use a public folder that stores mail items to carry on a group discussion (much like a discussion on an online bulletin board). To post a new discussion item, choose File > New > Post In This Folder or press Ctrl-Shift-S. To reply to a discussion item, open it and click the Post Reply button on the form's Standard toolbar.
- You can also share Office documents and other types of disk files by storing them in a public mail-item folder. To store a file, simply drag it from Windows Explorer or a file folder and drop it on the public folder name in the Folder List or on the folder's shortcut in the Outlook Bar. The file can be opened the same way you open a regular Outlook item.
- To locate a public folder, choose Tools > Find Public Folder and enter search criteria into the Find Public Folders dialog box (**Figure 4.26**).

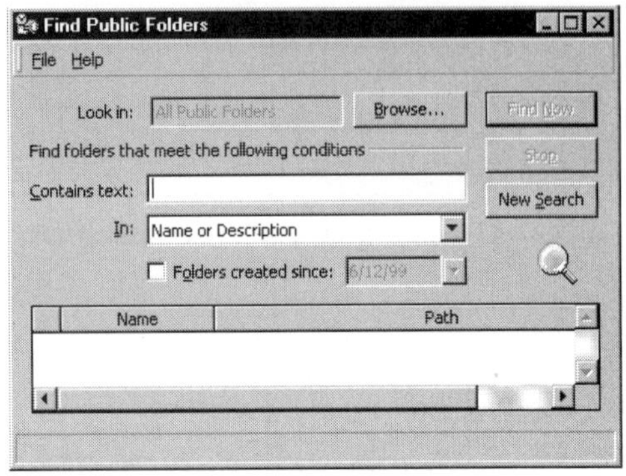

Figure 4.26 The Find Public Folders dialog box.

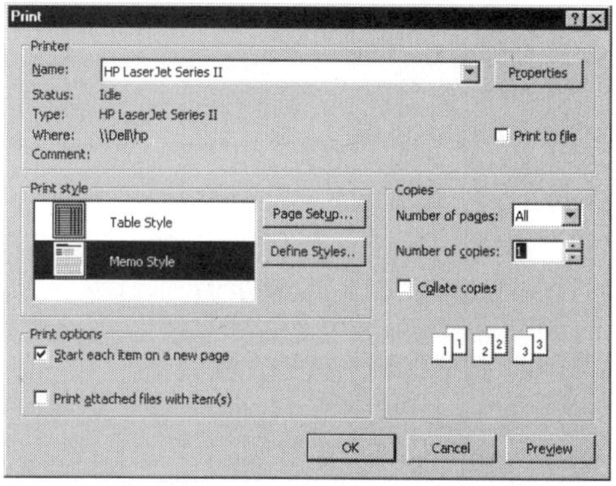

Figure 4.27 The Print dialog box as it appears when the Messages view (a table view) of the Inbox folder is active.

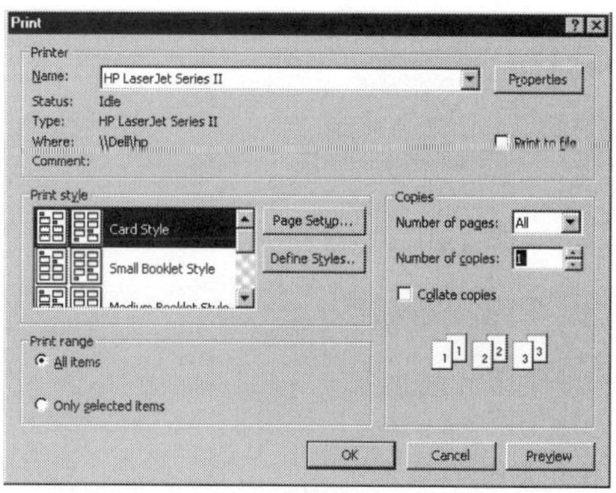

Figure 4.28 The Print dialog box as it appears when the Address Cards view of the Contacts folder is active.

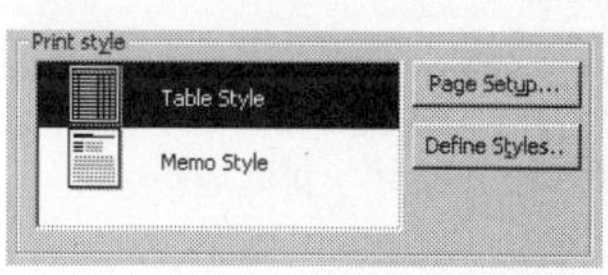

Figure 4.29 The **Print style** area of the Print dialog box.

Other Outlook Folder Operations

In the following sections, you'll learn how to print an entire Outlook folder—or one or more individual items within a folder. You'll also learn how to change an Outlook folder's properties.

To print an Outlook folder or folder items:

1. Open the Outlook folder you want to print or the folder containing the items you want to print.
2. Switch to the view that displays the items the way you want to print them.

   Even if you're printing just a single item (rather than a whole folder), the current view affects the print styles that will be available.
3. If you want to print one or more individual items (rather than the entire folder), select them now.
4. Choose File > Print or press Ctrl-P to open the Print dialog box (**Figures 4.27** and **4.28**).
5. Choose the style you want for the printed output by selecting it in the **Print style** list of the Print dialog box (**Figure 4.29**). The available styles depend upon the opened folder and the current view:
   - If a table view is active, you can select the **Table Style**, which prints the list of items in the folder, just as they appear in the Outlook window. Or, you can select the **Memo Style**, which prints the full contents of the individual item or items that you selected in step 2. (The Memo Style won't be available if you didn't select one or more items.)

(continued on next page)

- If another type of view is active, you'll probably have a wider choice of print styles. For example, with the Address Cards view of the Calendar folder, you can select the Card Style, Small Booklet Style, Medium Booklet Style, Memo Style, or Phone Directory Style.

6. In the **Copies** area of the Print dialog box (**Figure 4.30**), specify the pages to be printed, the number of copies, and whether the pages are to be collated. Or, just accept the defaults.

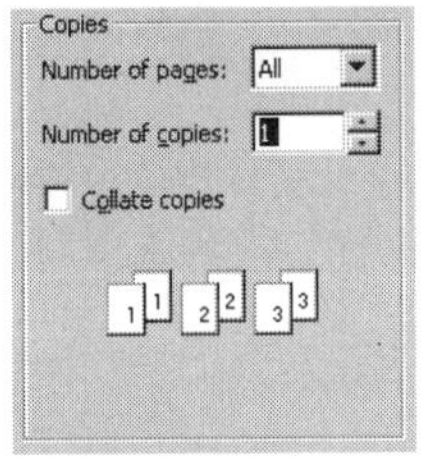

Figure 4.30 The **Copies** area of the Print dialog box.

7. If necessary, in the **Printer** area of the Print dialog box (**Figure 4.31**), select a different printer in the **Name** list box or change the printer settings by clicking the **Properties** button.

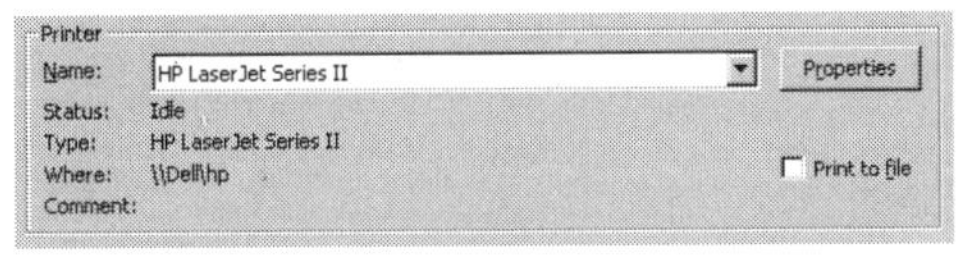

Figure 4.31 The **Printer** area of the Print dialog box.

8. In the area below the **Print style** list, labeled **Print range** or **Print options**, select the options you want. The available options depend on the print style that's currently selected.

9. If you want to see what the printed output will look like before you start using paper, click the **Preview** button. Outlook will display the printed appearance of each page in the Print Preview window (**Figure 4.32**), reflecting the current settings in the Print dialog box. When you're ready to print—or to adjust print settings—click the Print button on the toolbar at the top of the window to return to the Print dialog box.

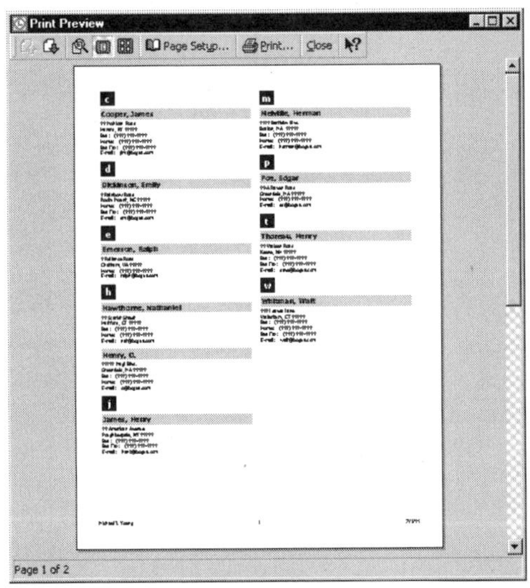

Figure 4.32 The Print Preview window, showing the printed appearance of the Address Cards view of the Calendar folder (with the Card Style print style).

10. Click the **OK** button in the Print dialog box to start printing.

✔ Tips

- I recommend that you don't print in the Outlook window by clicking the Print button on the Standard toolbar, because the results are unpredictable.

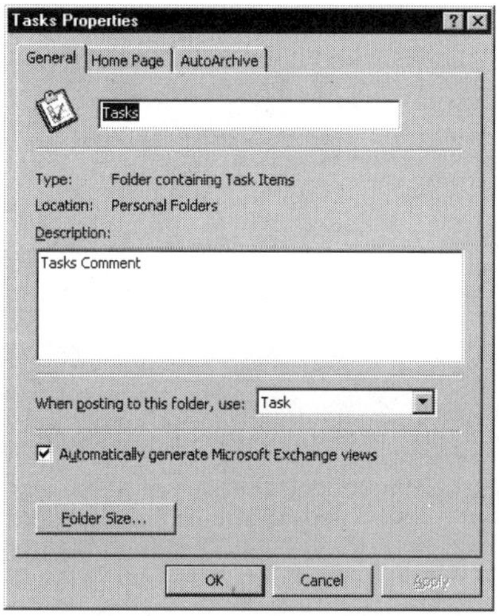

Figure 4.33 The Properties dialog box for the Tasks folder.

Sometimes Outlook opens the Print dialog box so you can adjust settings and preview the output, but other times it immediately prints.

- In the Print dialog box, you can click the **Page Setup** button to customize the currently selected print style. You can adjust the format, paper size, headers and footers, and other features of the printed output.
- In the Print dialog box, you can click the **Define Styles** button to modify any of the available print styles or to create new custom print styles.
- If you've opened an item in a form, you can print just that item by choosing File > Print in the form, which opens the Print dialog box. Or, you can just click the Print button on the form's Standard toolbar to immediately print the item using the default settings, without opening the Print dialog box. When you print an item in a form, Outlook uses the Memo Style print style.

To change a folder's properties:

1. Open the folder whose properties you want to change.
2. Choose File > Folder > Properties For "*Folder*," where *Folder* is the name of the currently opened folder.

   Outlook will open the *Folder* Properties dialog box (**Figure 4.33**).
3. Change properties in the tabs of the Properties dialog box as desired:
   - In the **General** tab, you can modify the folder's name (but only for a folder you have created) or the folder's description. You can also click the **Folder Size** button to determine the size of the folder and any subfolders it contains

(continued on next page)

(**Figure 4.34**). Unless you're an expert, I recommend that you don't alter any of the other settings in this tab.

- The **Home Page** tab lets you assign a home page to the folder. See the section "Attaching a Home Page to an Outlook Folder" in Chapter 14.
- The **AutoArchive** tab lets you define settings for automatically archiving the folder. This tab is explained in the section "To archive automatically" in Chapter 3. (This tab isn't included in the Properties dialog box for a contact-item folder because you can't automatically archive this folder type.)
- The **Sharing** tab is present only if you're sharing folders over the Internet or over a network, as described previously in the chapter.
- The Properties dialog box for a contact-item folder also includes Outlook Address Book and Activities tabs (the purpose of the Outlook Address Book tab is described in "Setting Up and Modifying the Corporate Or Workgroup E-mail Configuration" in Appendix A).
- If you're using Outlook with Exchange Server, the Properties tab might include four additional tabs: Administration, Forms, Permissions, and Synchronization. The Permissions tab was explained in the section "Sharing Outlook Folders over a Network," earlier in the chapter. The others are advanced features that aren't covered in this book.

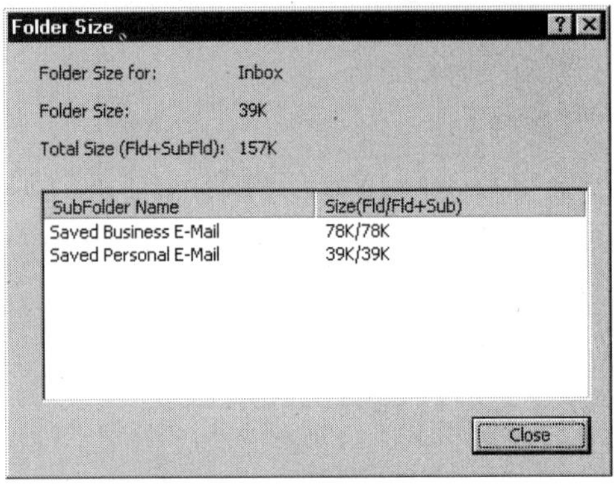

Figure 4.34 The information displayed when you click **Folder Size** in the General tab of the Properties dialog box.

✔ Tip

- You can open the Properties dialog box for any folder, without first opening that folder, by right-clicking the folder in the permanently displayed Folder List or by right-clicking the folder's shortcut in the Outlook Bar, and then choosing Properties on the pop-up menu.

5 Using Outlook Today

The Outlook Today folder displays a Web-style page that lets you quickly view current information in several commonly used Outlook folders:

- **Calendar**. Outlook Today displays your appointments, meetings, and all-day events for the next five days.
- **Tasks**. Outlook Today displays a list of all your tasks.
- **Messages**. Outlook Today shows the number of unread messages in your Inbox and the total numbers of messages in your Drafts and Outbox folders.

You can use Outlook Today to open any folder or item that it displays, as well as to mark tasks as completed.

In this chapter, you'll learn how to

- Work with the Outlook Today folder
- Customize Outlook Today

✔ **Tip**

- The Outlook Today techniques in the first main section of this chapter apply to the default Outlook Today setup. You should wait until you finish working through these instructions before you customize Outlook Today.

Working with Outlook Today

Figure 5.1 shows Outlook with the Outlook Today folder opened. The page consists of three main columns, one for each of the types of information it displays.

✔ Tips

- If you look at your Outlook folders in the Folder List, you'll see that Outlook Today is at the top of the hierarchy of folders in your Personal Folders file (**Figure 5.2**), or—if you're using Exchange Server—in your mailbox (**Figure 5.3**). That is, it's the folder that contains all of your other folders.

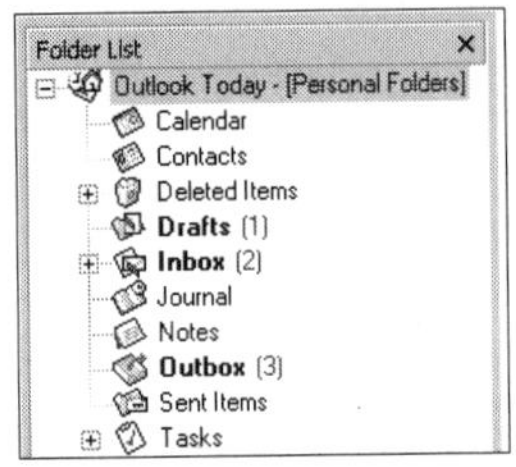

Figure 5.2 Hierarchy of folders in your Personal Folders (.PST) file.

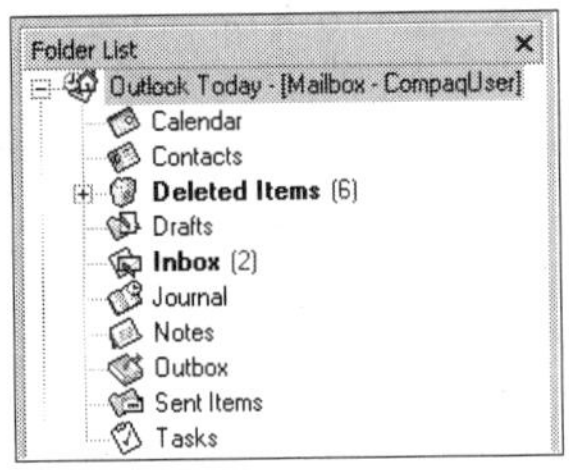

Figure 5.3 Hierarchy of folders in your mailbox (Exchange Server).

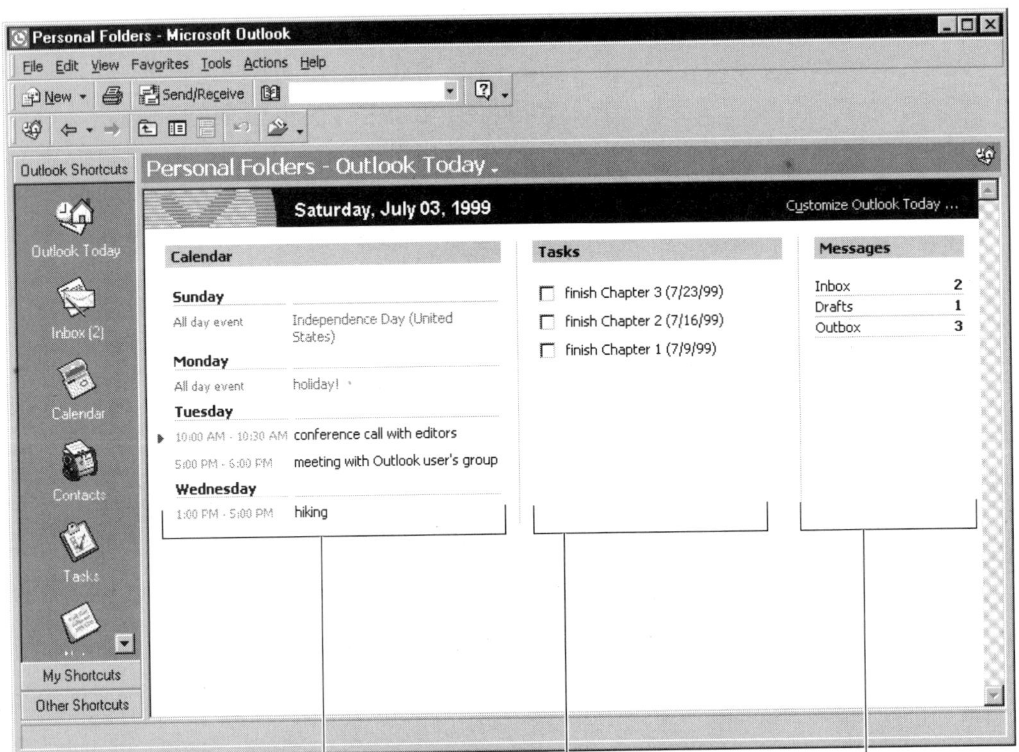

Your appointments, meetings, and all-day events for the next five days

Your tasks

The number of unread messages in your Inbox, and the total numbers of messages in your Drafts and Outbox folders

Figure 5.1 Outlook Today.

Figure 5.4 The Outlook Today shortcut.

- Outlook Today is a mail-item folder that has been assigned a home page. (As you'll learn in "Attaching a Home Page to an Outlook Folder" in Chapter 14, any folder can be assigned a home page.) Normally, you don't store items in Outlook Today. Rather, you work with its home page, which contains the elements that are described in this chapter.
- If the Outlook Today folder is open and the page described in this chapter isn't visible, or if it disappears, choose View > Show Folder Home Page to display the folder's home page.

To open Outlook Today:

- Click the Outlook Today shortcut in the Outlook Bar (**Figure 5.4**), or use any of the other techniques for opening a folder that were given in "How to Get Around in Outlook" in Chapter 2.

  or

  Click the Outlook Today button on the Standard toolbar. (This is a convenient method for opening Outlook Today when its shortcut isn't visible.)

✔ Tip

- You can have Outlook automatically open the Outlook Today folder whenever you start the program. See "To customize Outlook Today," later in the chapter.

To work with your Calendar items:

- Open any of the Calendar items that are displayed—an appointment, event, or meeting—by clicking on it. You can click on the date or the subject (**Figure 5.5**).

  or

  Open the Calendar folder by clicking on the gray Calendar header at the top of the column.

✔ Tip

- When you point to an item or folder name in Outlook Today, the text is underlined and the mouse pointer turns into a hand, indicating that you can click to open the item or folder (**Figure 5.6**).

To work with your tasks:

- To open a task, click on the task description. You can click on the subject or due date—*not* on the check box (**Figure 5.7**).

  or

  To mark a task as completed, click on the check box to its left. Outlook will check the box and draw a line through the task, marking it as completed (**Figure 5.8**).

  or

  To open the Tasks folder, click on the gray Tasks header at the top of the column.

To work with your messages:

- Click a folder name to open the folder (**Figure 5.9**). You can open the Inbox by clicking Inbox or by clicking the gray Messages header at the top of the column.

Figure 5.5 Working with your Calendar items.

Figure 5.6 Opening your Wednesday afternoon appointment by clicking the date.

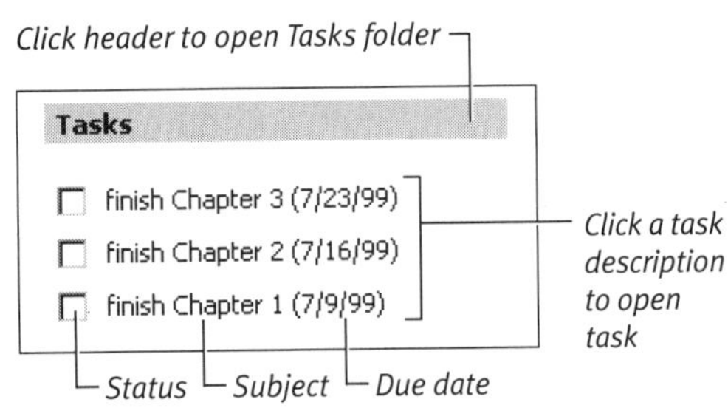

Figure 5.7 Working with your tasks.

Figure 5.8 A task that's been checked as completed.

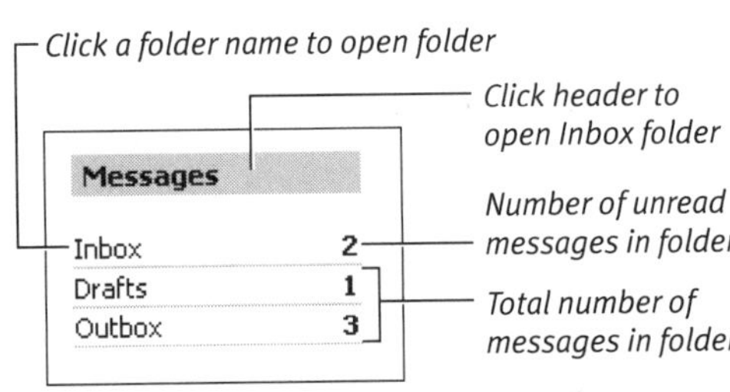

Figure 5.9 Working with your messages.

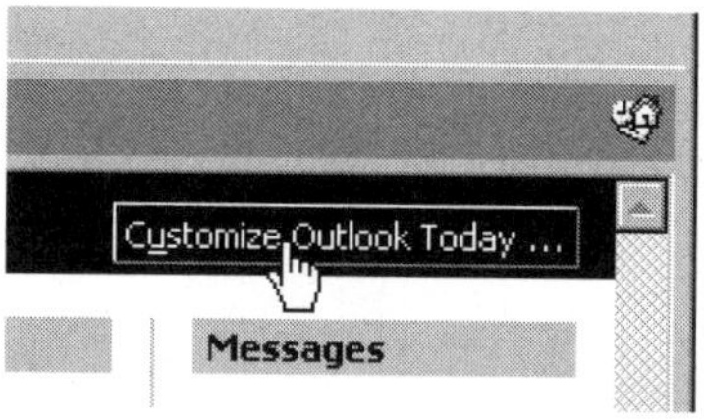

Figure 5.10 Clicking the button that opens the Customize Outlook Today page.

Customizing Outlook Today

You can customize Outlook Today according to your preferences and work habits. Specifically, you can do the following:

- Have Outlook automatically open the Outlook Today folder whenever you start the program.
- Specify the mail-item folders that are listed in the Messages column of Outlook Today.
- Change the number of days of Calendar items that are displayed in Outlook Today.
- Choose which tasks are displayed and the way they're sorted.
- Modify the overall style of the Outlook Today page.

To customize Outlook Today:

1. Open the Outlook Today folder and click the **Customize Outlook Today** button in the upper-right corner of the page (**Figure 5.10**).

(continued on next page)

Outlook will open the Customize Outlook Today page of the Outlook Today folder (**Figure 5.11**).

2. In the Customize Outlook Today page, select customization options as desired:
   - To have Outlook automatically open Outlook Today each time you start the program, check **When starting, go directly to Outlook Today**.
   - To change the folders displayed in the Messages column, click the **Choose Folders** button, and in the Select Folder dialog box (**Figure 5.12**), check each folder you want to be displayed and then click the **OK** button.
   - To change the number of days of Calendar items that are displayed in the Calendar column, select a number in the **Show this number of days in my calendar** list box.

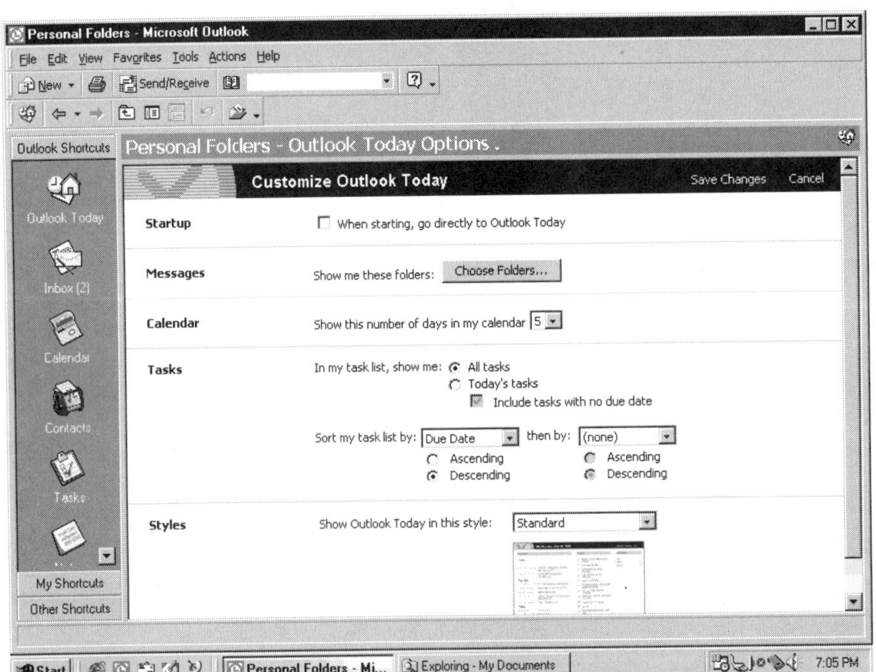

Figure 5.11 The Customize Outlook Today page of the Outlook Today folder.

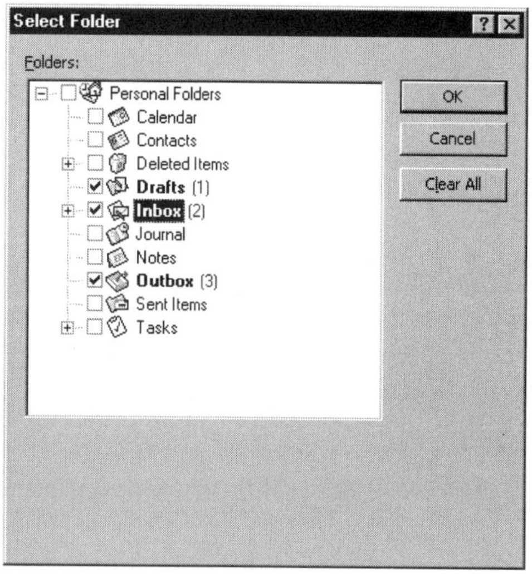

Figure 5.12 The Select Folder dialog box.

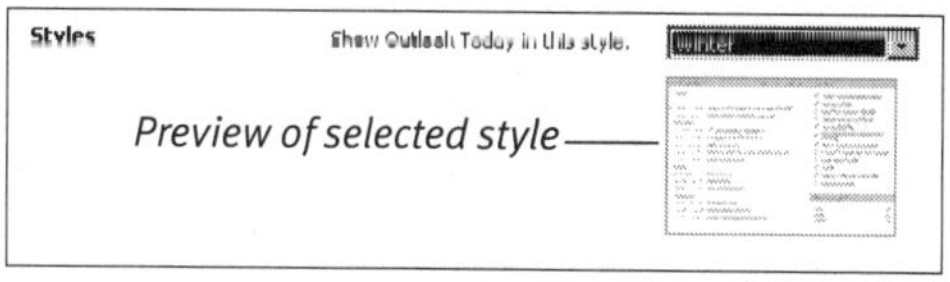

Figure 5.13 Selecting a style.

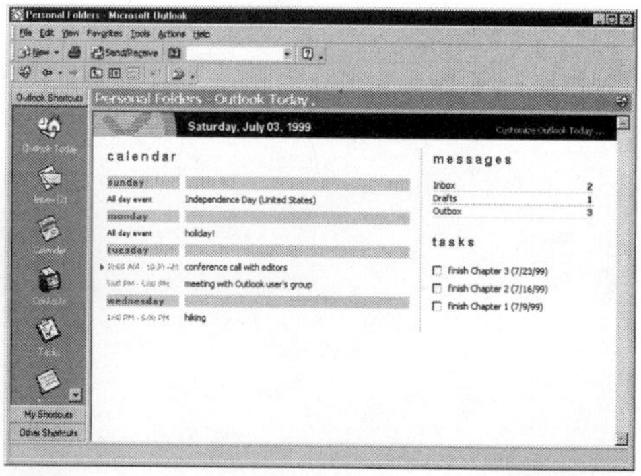

Figure 5.14 Outlook Today with the Summer style.

- To show only the current day's tasks, select the **Today's tasks** option. If you want to display *all* of the day's tasks check **Include tasks with no due date**.
- To change the sorting order of tasks, select a primary sorting field in the **Sort my task list by** list box, and select a secondary sorting field in the **then by** list box. Under each list box, select either **Ascending** or **Descending** to specify the sorting order used with the field.
- To change the overall look of the Outlook Today folder, select a new style in the **Show Outlook Today in this style** list box. The default style shown in Figure 5.1 is Standard. When you select a style, Outlook displays a preview image of that style below the list box (**Figure 5.13**). The Summer style is shown in **Figure 5.14**.

3. Click the **Save Changes** button  in the upper-right corner to save the new settings you made, return to the main page of Outlook Today, and apply the changes.

   or

   Click the **Cancel** button  to discard your settings and return to the main page of Outlook Today.

USING THE INBOX TO MANAGE MESSAGES

6

You can use the Outlook Inbox folder—as well as the other mail-item folders (Drafts, Outbox, and Sent Items)—to receive, send, and manage e-mail and fax messages. Here's how these folders are normally used:

- Incoming e-mail and fax messages are delivered to your Inbox by a mail account (Internet Only configuration) or by an e-mail information service (Corporate Or Workgroup configuration).
- While you are composing a message, before you send it, it's normally stored in the Drafts folder.
- When you send a message, it's temporarily stored in the Outbox folder until you actually transmit it to the recipient. (Sometimes messages are transmitted immediately and aren't stored in your Outbox.)
- A copy of each message you send is normally stored in your Sent Items folder.

In this chapter, you'll learn:

- How to receive e-mail messages in your Inbox.
- How to read e-mail messages and open or save file attachments.

- How to receive and read fax messages.
- How to send e-mail messages.
- How to send fax messages.
- How to systematize your e-mail and fax messages.

✓ Tips

- The instructions in this chapter assume that you've already set up your e-mail and fax accounts or information services, as explained in Chapter 1 (basic setup techniques) and Appendix A (advanced setup techniques).
- The instruction also assume that you've opened your Inbox or another mail-item folder. (Otherwise, you won't find some of the commands mentioned.)
- The different ways to open folders are explained in "Opening an Outlook folder" in Chapter 2. Keep in mind that with the initial Outlook setup, the shortcut for the Inbox folder is in the Outlook Shortcuts group, and those for the Drafts, Outbox, and Sent Items folders are in the My Shortcuts group.
- When you work with messages, there are many differences between the Internet Only configuration and the Corporate Or Workgroup configuration. Sections marked with the Internet Only icon I/O or the Corporate Or Workgroup icon C/W apply to the indicated configuration only. Sections without either of these icons apply to both configurations. You can find out which configuration you have by choosing Help > About Microsoft Outlook.

Receiving E-mail Messages

You can have Outlook automatically receive your e-mail messages from one or more accounts at specified intervals, or you can manually receive them at any time. If you don't set up automatic receiving, then you'll have to receive manually.

The procedure for setting up automatic receiving depends upon whether an e-mail account uses a full-time Internet connection or a dial-up connection. A *full-time* connection is one that provides access to the Internet at all times, usually through a company local area network (LAN) connected to your computer. A *dial-up* connection uses a modem in your computer and is typically made only when you are actually exchanging e-mail or accessing an Internet site.

✔ Tips

- The different types of connections are described in the section "To add a mail account with the Internet Connection Wizard" in Appendix A.
- When Outlook receives e-mail messages, it might also transmit outgoing e-mail messages from your Outbox, as described later in the chapter.

To receive e-mail messages automatically:

1. Choose Tools > Options and open the Mail Delivery tab in the Options dialog box.
2. Check the **Check for new messages every** option.

(continued on next page)

3. In the adjoining text box, enter the desired interval in minutes at which you want Outlook to automatically receive your e-mail messages.
4. If one or more of your e-mail accounts uses a dial-up connection, check the **Automatically dial when checking for new messages** option (**Figure 6.1**). (If you don't check this option, a dial-up account will be skipped when Outlook automatically receives e-mail.)
5. Click the **OK** button.

   Outlook will then begin receiving your e-mail messages at the interval you specified, automatically dialing your modem for any account that uses dial-up access (**Figure 6.2**). It will place any messages you receive in your Inbox folder.

✔ Tips

- Outlook will automatically receive e-mail *only* from accounts that have the **Include this account when receiving mail or synchronizing** option checked. To access this option, choose Tools > Accounts, select the account name on the All or Mail tab, click the **Properties** button, and open the General tab (**Figure 6.3**).
- If you are *working offline*, Outlook will *not* automatically receive e-mail from an account with full-time Internet access. It will, however, continue to automatically dial up and receive e-mail from an account with dial-up access. To switch between working online and working offline, choose File > Work Offline. When you're working offline, a broken-connection icon appears at the right end of the status bar (**Figure 6.4**).
- If you're working offline and manually receive e-mail messages (as described next), Outlook switches you back to working online.

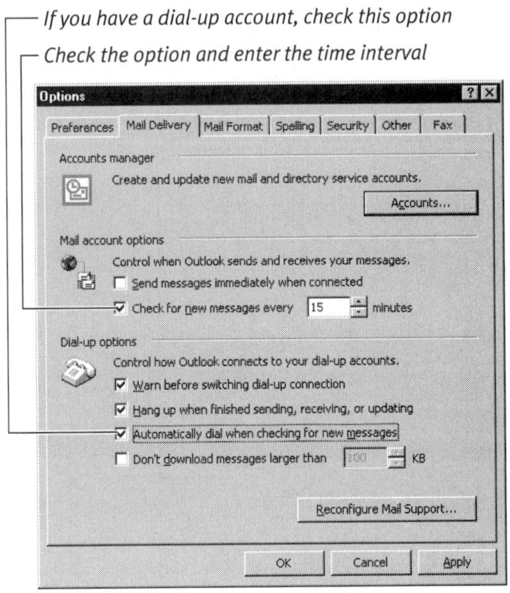

Figure 6.1 Selecting options on the Mail Delivery tab of the Options dialog box to have Outlook automatically receive your e-mail messages (via a full-time or dial-up account).

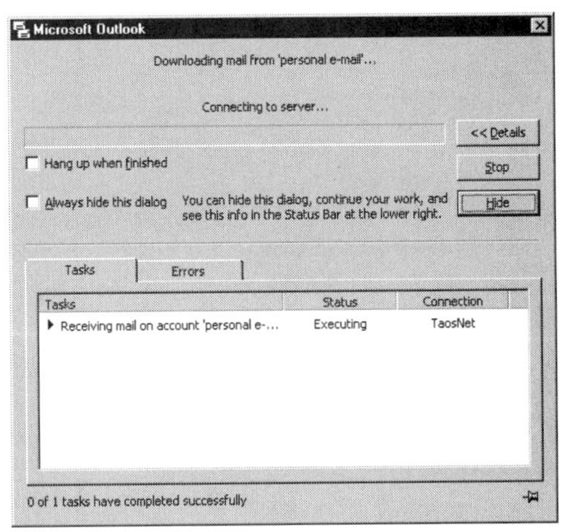

Figure 6.2 The dialog box that Outlook displays when it's receiving and sending e-mail.

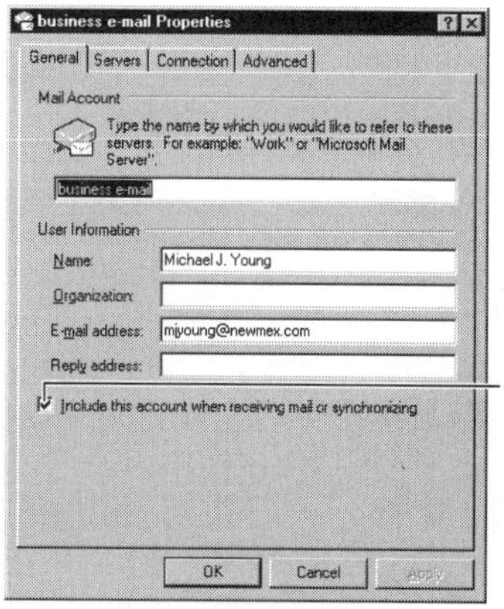

Figure 6.3 The General tab of the Account Properties dialog box.

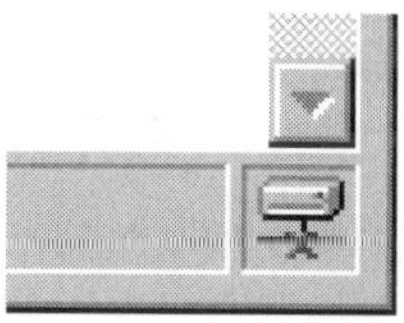

Figure 6.4 The broken-connection icon on the Status bar indicating that you're working offline.

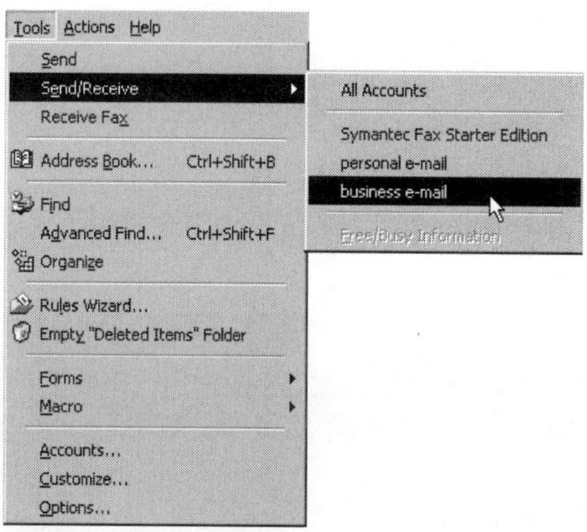

Figure 6.5 Receiving messages from just the **business e-mail** account.

To receive e-mail messages manually:

- To receive e-mail from all your *enabled* e-mail accounts (see the following tip), click the Send/Receive button on the Standard toolbar, or choose Tools > Send/Receive > All Accounts, or press F5.

  or

  To receive e-mail from a specific account (whether or not it's enabled), choose Tools > Send/Receive and then choose the name of the account from the submenu (**Figure 6.5**).

  Outlook will then connect with the e-mail account or accounts (**Figure 6.2**), and it will place any messages you receive in your Inbox folder.

✔ Tip

- In this instruction, an *enabled* e-mail account means one that has the **Include this account when receiving mail or synchronizing** option checked. To access this option, choose Tools > Accounts, select the account name on the All or Mail tab, click the **Properties** button, and open the General tab (**Figure 6.3**).

Receiving E-mail Messages

You can have Outlook automatically receive your e-mail from your e-mail information services, or you can manually receive e-mail at any time. If you don't set up automatic receiving, then you'll have to receive manually.

The procedure for setting up automatic receiving depends upon whether an e-mail information service uses a full-time Internet connection or a dial-up connection. A *full-time* connection is one that provides access to the Internet at all times, usually through a company local area network (LAN) connected to your computer. A *dial-up* connection uses a modem in your computer and is typically made only when you are actually exchanging e-mail or accessing an Internet site.

Receiving e-mail messages automatically

The method for setting up automatic receiving of e-mail messages varies with each e-mail information service you're using.

If you're using the Microsoft Exchange Server information service, e-mail messages are always received automatically so long as you're connected to the Exchange Server network. Each message arrives in your Inbox shortly after it's sent. You don't have to do anything to set up automatic receiving.

The following sections give the procedures for the Internet E-mail and the CompuServe Mail information services. Other e-mail information services typically provide similar procedures for scheduling automatic receiving of e-mail.

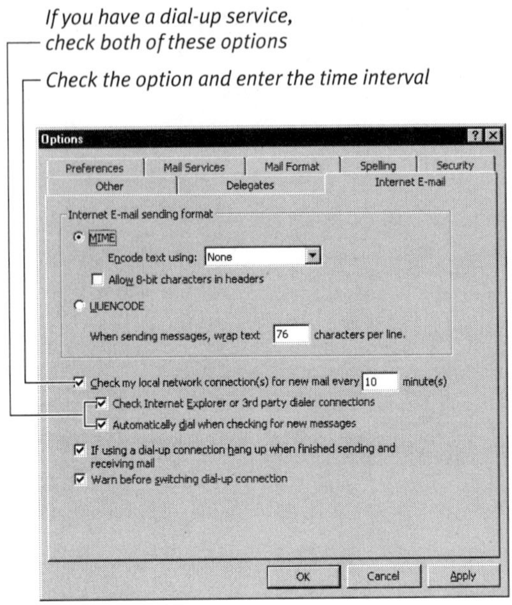

Figure 6.6 Turning on automatic receiving of e-mail messages with the Internet E-mail information service.

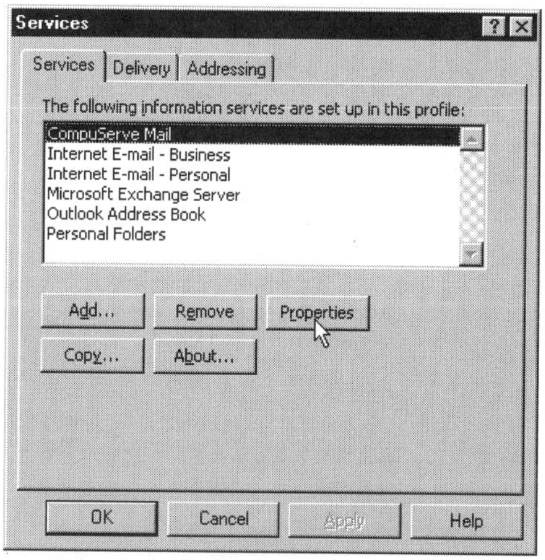

Figure 6.7 The Services tab of the Services dialog box.

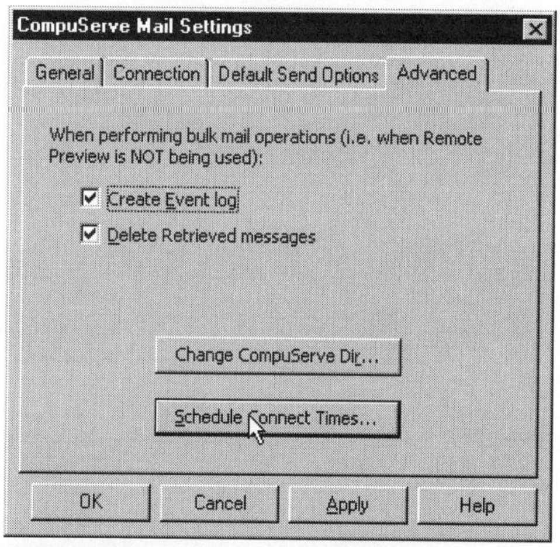

Figure 6.8 The Advanced tab of the CompuServe Mail Settings dialog box.

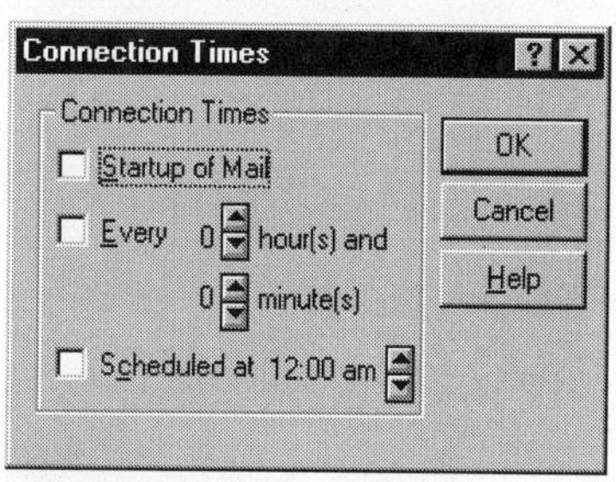

Figure 6.9 The Connection Times dialog box.

To receive e-mail automatically with the Internet E-mail information service:

1. Choose Tools > Options and open the Internet E-mail tab in the Options dialog box.
2. Check the **Check my local network connection(s) for new mail every** option.
3. In the adjoining text box, enter the desired interval in minutes at which you want Outlook to automatically receive your e-mail messages.
4. If your Internet E-mail information service uses a dial-up connection, check both the **Check Internet Explorer or 3rd party dialer connections** option and the **Automatically dial when checking for new messages** option (**Figure 6.6**). (Checking both options ensures that Outlook will make the needed connection regardless of the type of dial-up connection you have.)
5. Click the **OK** button.

To receive e-mail automatically with the CompuServe Mail information service:

1. Choose Tools > Services to open the Services dialog box.
2. On the Services tab, select **CompuServe Mail** in the list and click the **Properties** button (**Figure 6.7**) to open the CompuServe Mail Settings dialog box.
3. Open the Advanced tab and click the **Schedule Connect Times** button (**Figure 6.8**) to open the Connection Times dialog box (**Figure 6.9**).

(continued on next page)

4. In the Connection Times dialog box, specify the times you want the information service to dial CompuServe to receive your e-mail messages.

5. Close all three dialog boxes by clicking the **OK** button in each.

C/W To receive e-mail messages manually:

- To receive e-mail from all your *enabled* e-mail information services (see the following tip), click the Send/Receive button 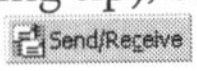 on the Standard toolbar, or choose Tools > Send/Receive > All Accounts, or press F5.

  or

  To receive e-mail from a specific e-mail information service (whether or not it's enabled), choose Tools > Send/Receive and then choose the name of the information service from the submenu (**Figure 6.10**).

  Outlook will then connect with the e-mail information service or services, and it will place any messages you receive in your Inbox folder.

✔ Tip

- In this instruction, an *enabled* e-mail information service means one that is checked in the **Check for new mail on** list. To access this list, choose Tools > Options and open the Mail Services tab (**Figure 6.11**).

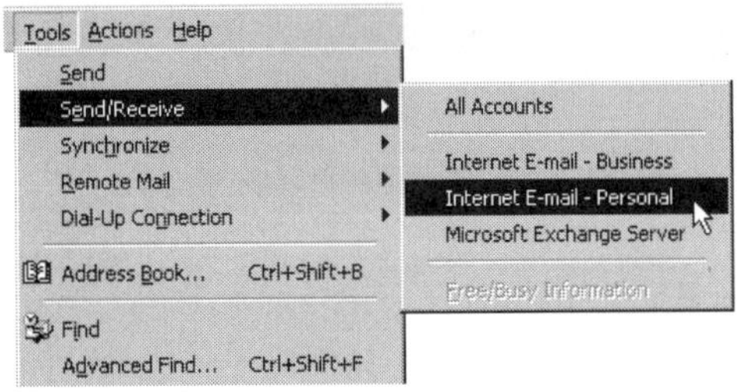

Figure 6.10 Receiving e-mail from just the Internet E-mail - Personal information service.

Information services checked in this list are enabled for receiving e-mail

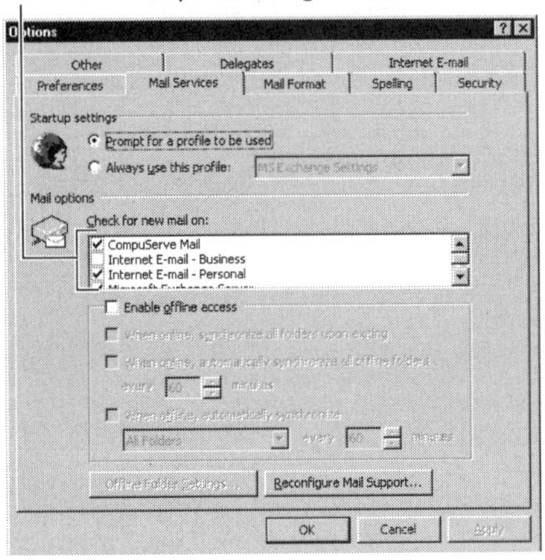

Figure 6.11 Enabling e-mail information services for receiving e-mail.

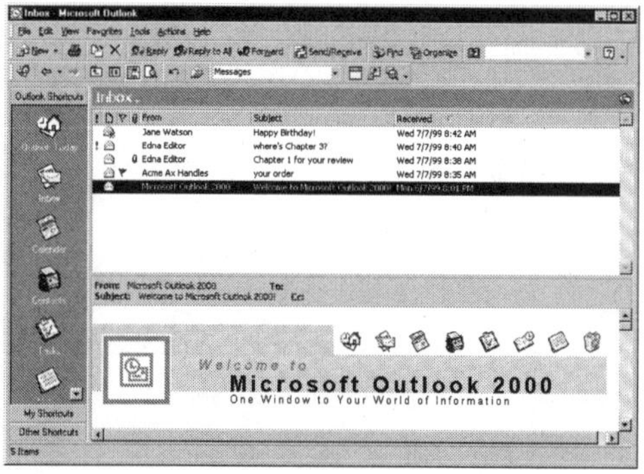

Figure 6.12 Reading a message in the Preview pane.

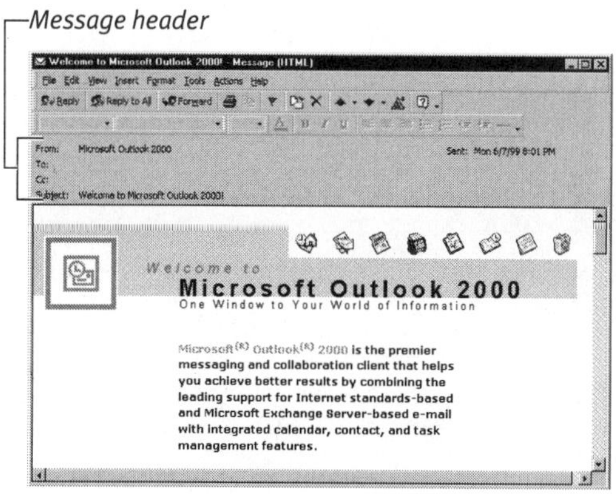

Figure 6.13 Reading a message in the Message form.

Reading E-mail Messages

With either e-mail configuration, Outlook will deliver your incoming e-mail messages to your Inbox (**Figure 6.14**), and you can read any e-mail message it contains either by using the Preview pane or by opening the message in a Message form.

To read an e-mail message:

1. Open the Inbox folder and click the e-mail message to select it.
2. If the Preview pane isn't currently displayed, click the Preview Pane button on the Advanced toolbar or choose View > Preview Pane. You can then view the selected message in this pane, without having to open it (**Figure 6.12**).

   or

   Double click the message, or use one of the other methods for opening an item described in "To open an item" in Chapter 3. The message will then be displayed in a Message form (**Figure 6.13**).

✔ Tips

- In the Outlook window, an unread message is marked with bold formatting. You can change the marking of a message by selecting it and choosing Edit > Mark As Read or Edit > Mark As Unread, or you can choose Edit < Mark All As Read to remove the bold marking from all messages in the folder.

(continued on next page)

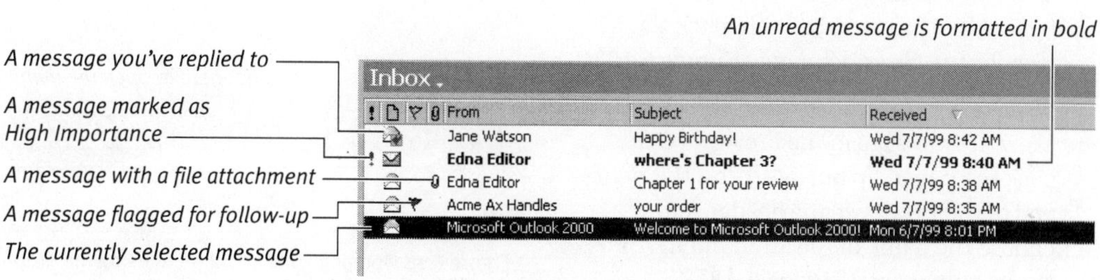

Figure 6.14 E-mail messages listed in the Inbox, using the Messages view.

- If you've chosen Word as your e-mail editor, a message will be opened in Word rather than in the Outlook Message form (unless the message is in HTML format). See "E-mail editors and formats," later in the chapter.
- You can edit a message that you've opened in the Outlook Message form by choosing Edit > Edit Message in the form. (If a message is in Rich Text Format or if it's opened in Word, you can edit it without choosing this command.)
- If you want to flag a message for special attention, open the message and click the Flag For Follow Up button on the form's toolbar. Then define the flag in the Flag For Follow Up dialog box (**Figure 6.15**).
- You can hide or show the message header in the Message form (**Figure 6.14**) by choosing View > Message Header. When you hide the header, only the From and Sent fields are shown.
- You can set other options for a message by opening the message in a form and choosing View > Options to open the Message Options dialog box (**Figure 6.16**). This dialog box also lets you view the message's Internet headers, which show technical information on the sending and routing of the message.

To open a file attachment included in an e-mail message:

1. View the message in the Preview pane or open it in a form, and double-click the icon for the file attachment (**Figure 6.17**).

   or

   View the message in the Preview pane, click the paperclip button on the right end of the Preview pane header, and choose the name of the attachment from the pop-up menu (**Figure 6.18**).

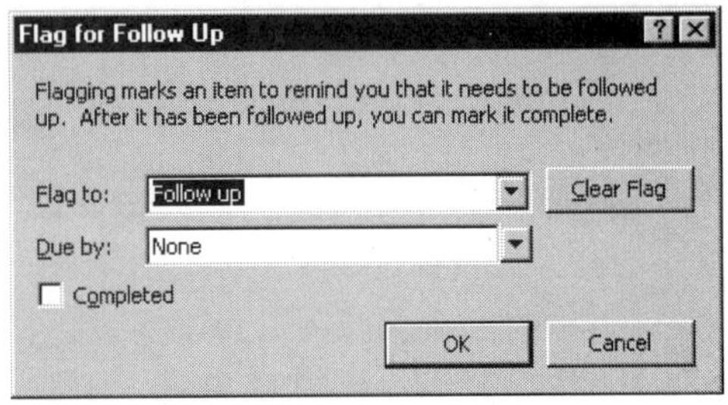

Figure 6.15 The Flag For Follow Up dialog box.

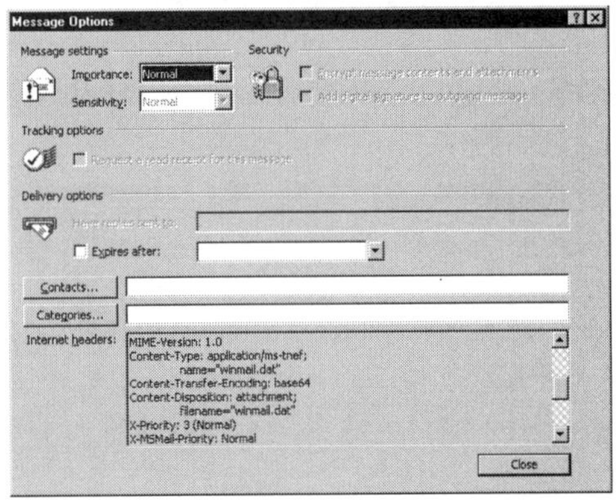

Figure 6.16 The Message Options dialog box for an incoming message in the Inbox.

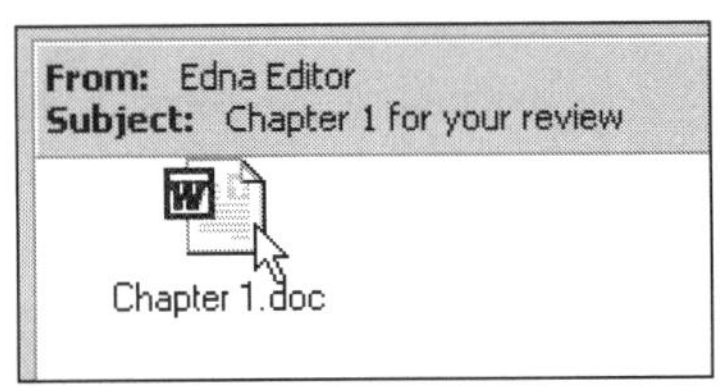

Figure 6.17 Double-clicking a file attachment icon to open the file.

Click here to open the menu

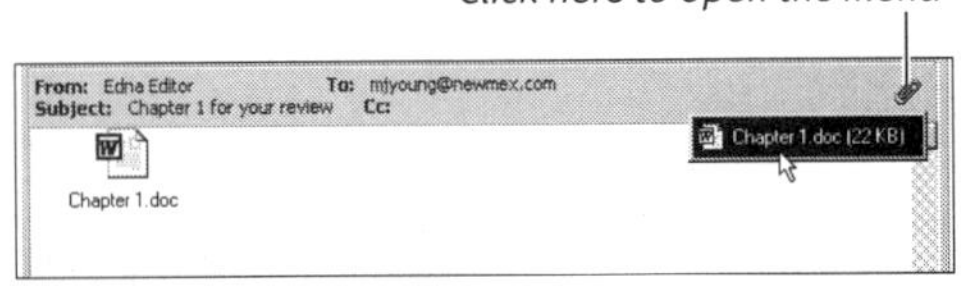

Figure 6.18 Opening a file attachment using the drop-down menu on the Preview pane header.

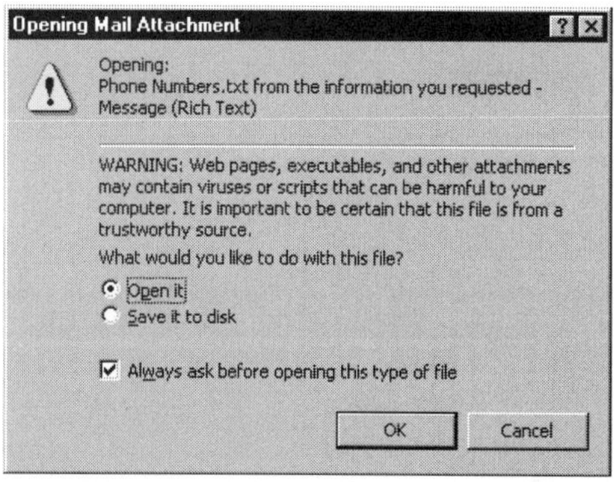

Figure 6.19 Choosing to open a file attachment in the Opening Mail Attachment dialog box.

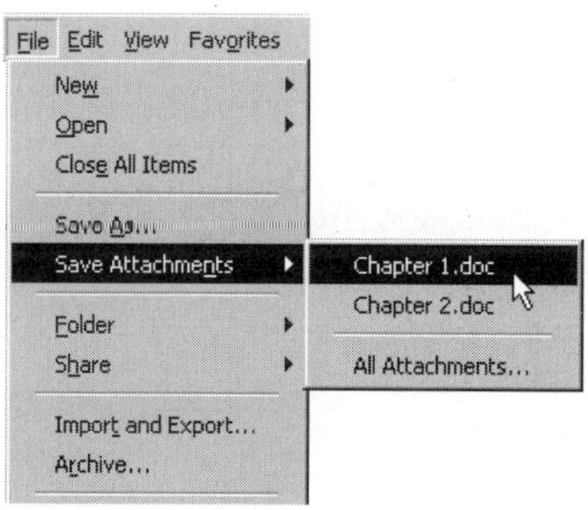

Figure 6.20 Saving the Chapter 1.doc file attachment.

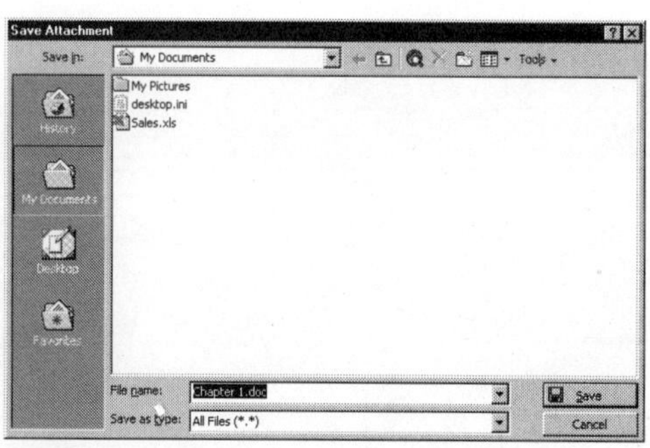

Figure 6.21 Selecting a disk location for a file attachment in the Save Attachment dialog box.

2. If Outlook displays the Opening Mail Attachment dialog box (**Figure 6.19**), select **Open it** and click the **OK** button.

The file attachment will then be opened in the appropriate program. For example, if you have Microsoft Word installed, a file attachment with the .doc extension will be opened in Word.

✔ Tip

- *Don't open a file attachment in a message from an unknown source!* Certain types of attachments can contain viruses, and opening an attachment might allow a virus to harm your computer.

To save a file attachment in a disk file:

1. In the Outlook window, select the message that has the attachment you want to save.
2. Choose File > Save Attachments and then from the submenu choose the name of the attachment you want to save (**Figure 6.20**).
3. In the Save Attachment dialog box (**Figure 6.21**), select the disk location where you want to save the file. If you wish, you can change the name of the file by typing a new name in the **File name** text box.
4. Click the **Save** button.

✔ Tips

- *Don't save a file attachment in a message from an unknown source!* Certain types of attachments can contain viruses. Saving the attachment in a disk file and then later opening that file might allow a virus to harm your computer.

(continued on next page)

- If a message has more than one file attachment, you can save several attachments at once by choosing File > Save Attachments > All Attachments in step 2 and then selecting the specific attachments you want to save in the Save All Attachments dialog box (**Figure 6.22**).
- If a message is open in a form, you can save one or more attachments by choosing File > Save Attachments.
- If a message is displayed in the Preview pane or opened in a form, you can save a single file attachment by right-clicking the attachment's icon and choosing Save As from the pop-up menu (**Figure 6.23**).

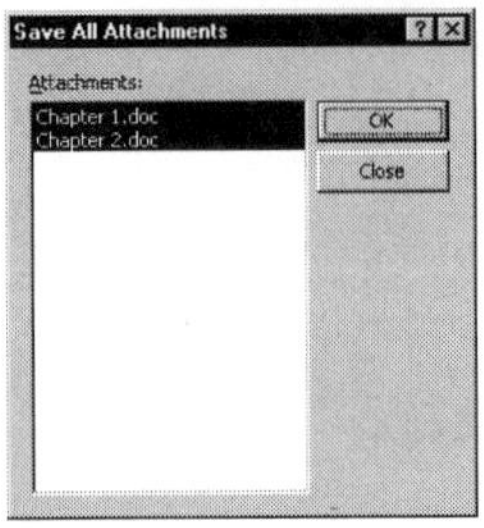

Figure 6.22 The Save All Attachments dialog box.

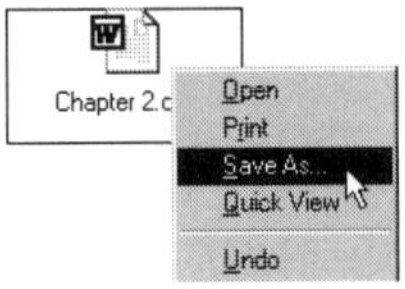

Figure 6.23 Saving the Chapter 2.doc file attachment.

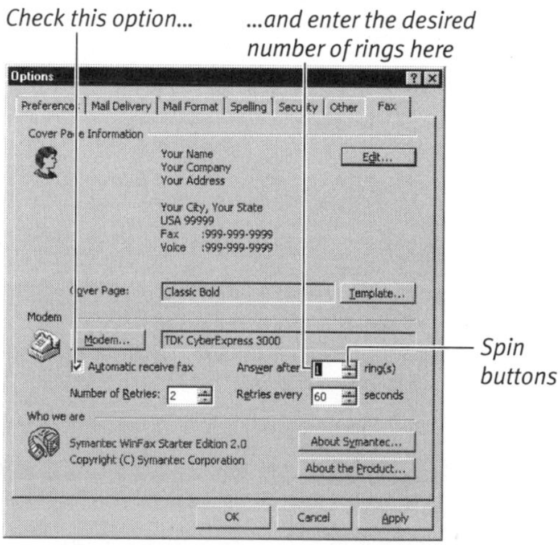

Figure 6.24 Selecting options to have Outlook automatically answer incoming fax calls.

Figure 6.25 The message box Outlook displays while it's receiving a fax.

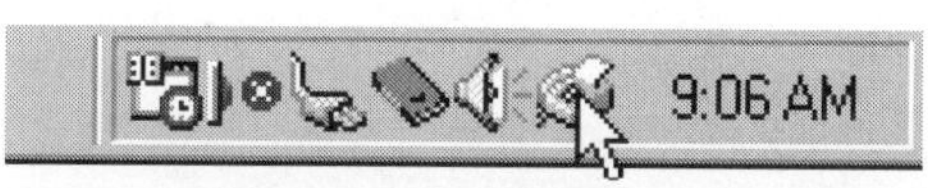

Figure 6.26 Clicking the Microsoft Fax icon.

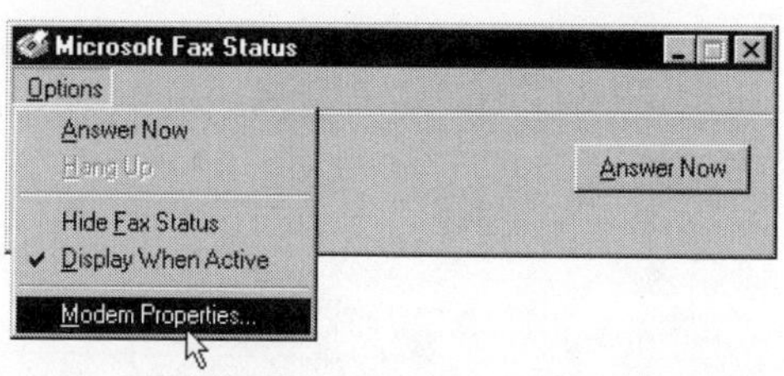

Figure 6.27 Choosing Options > Modem Properties in the Microsoft Fax Status dialog box.

Receiving Fax Messages

You can receive faxes in either of the following two ways:

- **Automatically**. With this method, whenever the phone rings, Outlook automatically answers and receives the fax. Normally, you use this method if your fax modem is attached to a separate phone line that you use only for faxes.
- **Manually**. With this method, when the phone rings, you have to manually issue a command to have Outlook answer the call and receive the fax. Generally, you use this method if you have a single phone line for receiving both voice and fax calls, and you have both a telephone and a fax card attached to the line.

I/O To receive faxes automatically:

1. Choose Tools > Options and open the Fax tab in the Options dialog box.
2. Check the **Automatic receive fax** option.
3. In the **Answer after** text box, enter the number of rings you want Outlook to wait before answering (type or use the spin buttons) (**Figure 6.24**).
4. Click the **OK** button.

   Outlook will begin automatically receiving your incoming faxes and delivering them to your Inbox (**Figure 6.25**).

C/W To receive faxes automatically:

1. Click the Microsoft Fax icon on the right end of your Windows taskbar (**Figure 6.26**).
2. In the Microsoft Fax Status dialog box that appears, choose Options > Modem Properties (**Figure 6.27**).

(continued on next page)

3. In the Fax Modem Properties dialog box, select the **Answer after** option, and in the adjoining list box, select the number of rings you want the fax modem to wait before answering (**Figure 6.28**).
4. Click the **OK** button in the Fax Modem Properties dialog box.
5. Click the **Close** button ☒ in the Microsoft Fax Status dialog box to remove this dialog box.

   Outlook will begin automatically receiving your incoming faxes and delivering them to your Inbox (**Figure 6.29**).

To start receiving faxes manually:

1. Choose Tools > Options and open the Fax tab in the Options dialog box.
2. Uncheck the **Automatic receive fax** option (**Figure 6.30**).
3. Click the **OK** button.

   You'll now have to receive each fax manually.

To receive a fax manually:

- If your phone rings and you know it's a fax (perhaps someone just arranged to send you one), immediately choose Tools > Receive Fax. Outlook will answer the call, receive the fax (**Figure 6.31**), and deliver it to your Inbox.

  or

  If your phone rings and you don't know whether it's a voice call or a fax call, pick up the receiver. If you hear a beep, beep, beep sound indicating that a fax machine is calling (known as a CNG tone), immediately choose Tools > Receive Fax, and after Outlook answers (wait at least 5 seconds or until you hear Outlook answer), hang up the receiver. Outlook will then receive the fax and deliver it to your Inbox.

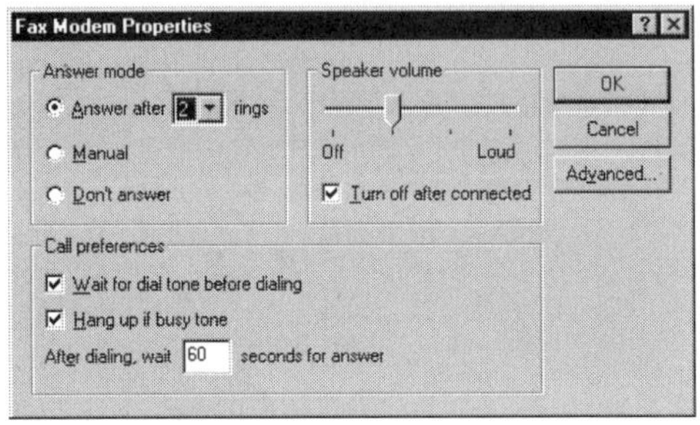

Figure 6.28 Setting up the modem to answer automatically after two rings.

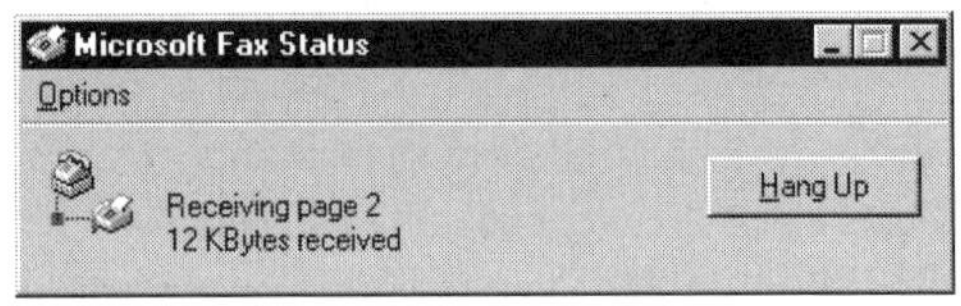

Figure 6.29 The message box Outlook displays while it's receiving a fax.

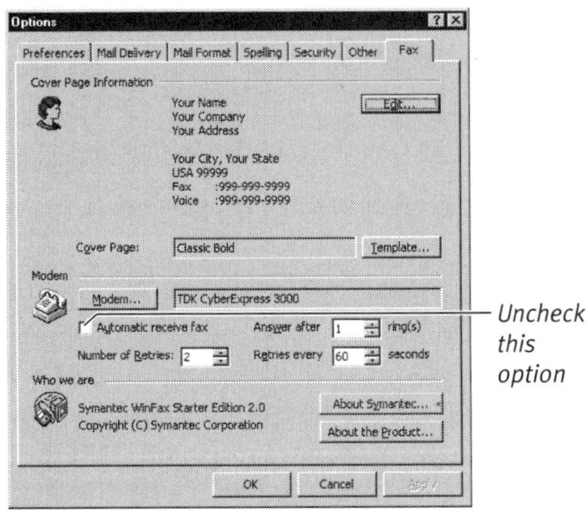

Figure 6.30 Preventing Outlook from automatically answering incoming fax calls, so that you can answer them manually.

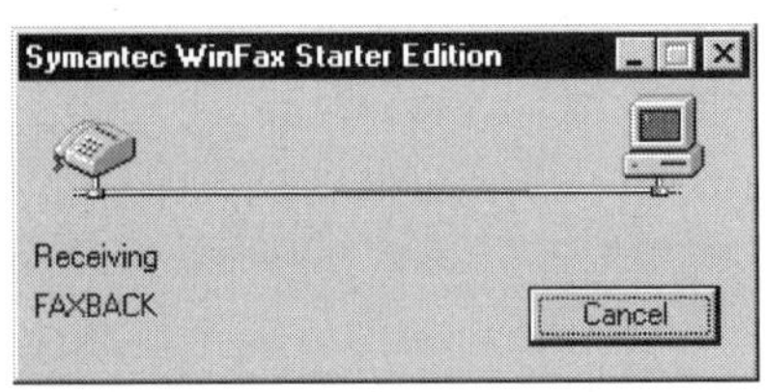

Figure 6.31 The message box Outlook displays while it's receiving a fax.

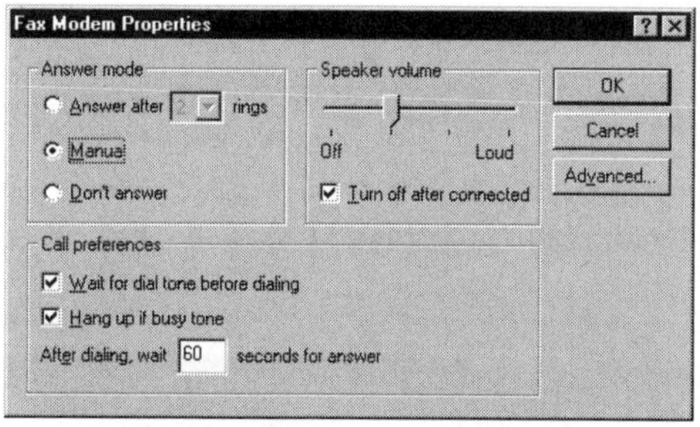

Figure 6.32 Preventing Outlook from automatically answering incoming fax calls, so that you can answer them manually.

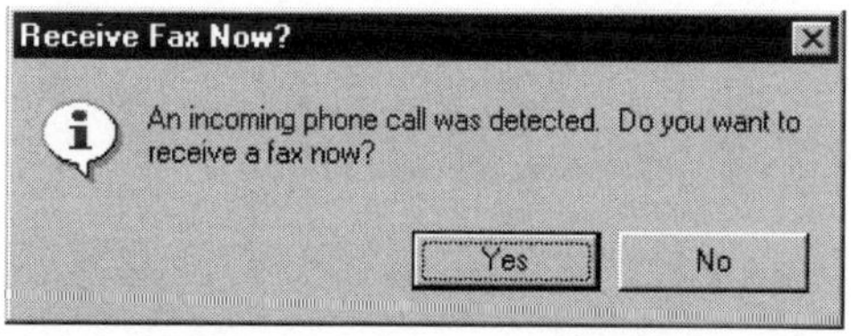

Figure 6.33 The message box Outlook displays when you're receiving fax calls manually and the phone rings.

To start receiving faxes manually:

- Follow the instructions given in the earlier section, "To receive faxes automatically," except in step 3 select the **Manual** option rather than **Answer after** (**Figure 6.32**).

  You'll now have to receive each fax manually.

To receive a fax manually:

- When your phone rings, Outlook will display a message box (**Figure 6.33**). If you know the call is a fax (perhaps someone just arranged to send you one), click the **Yes** button. Outlook will answer the call, receive the fax (**Figure 6.31**), and deliver it to your Inbox.

  or

  If you don't know whether the call is a voice call or a fax, first pick up the receiver. If you hear a beep, beep, beep sound indicating that a fax machine is calling (known as a CNG tone), click the **Yes** button, and after Outlook answers (wait at least 5 seconds or until you hear Outlook answer), hang up the receiver. Outlook will then receive the fax and deliver it to your Inbox. If the call is a voice call, click **No**.

To read a fax:

1. Open your Inbox.

   A fax message will have the subject "Fax Received" and will display a paperclip icon indicating that it has a file attachment (**Figure 6.34**).

2. Either view the fax message in the Preview pane (**Figure 6.35**) or open it in a form (**Figure 6.36**). For instructions, see "To read an e-mail message," earlier in the chapter.

   You'll notice that the message text contains only a fax status report. The fax itself is contained in the file attachment.

3. Open the file attachment by clicking the paperclip button on the right end of the Preview pane header and choosing the attachment name from the drop-down menu (**Figure 6.37**), or by using any of the other methods for opening a file attachment given in "To open a file attachment included in an e-mail message," earlier in the chapter. If Outlook displays the Opening Mail Attachment dialog box, select the **Open it** option and click the **OK** button.

   The fax will be opened in the Quick Fax Viewer window (**Figure 6.38**). You can use the menu and toolbar commands in this window to scroll through the pages of your fax, to zoom the fax image to various sizes, to rotate the image, or to print the fax.

Figure 6.34 A fax message in the Inbox.

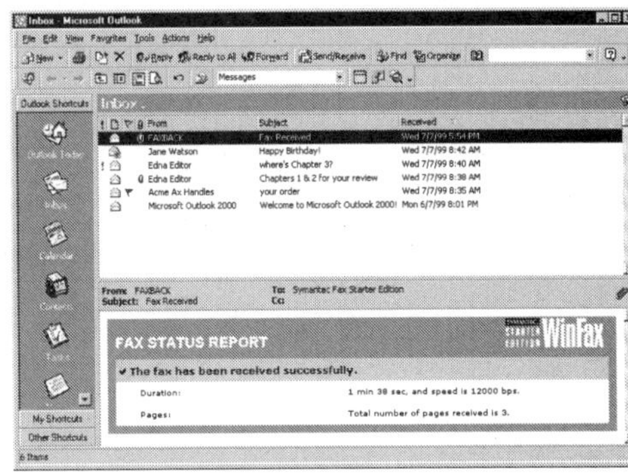

Figure 6.35 Viewing a fax message in the Preview pane.

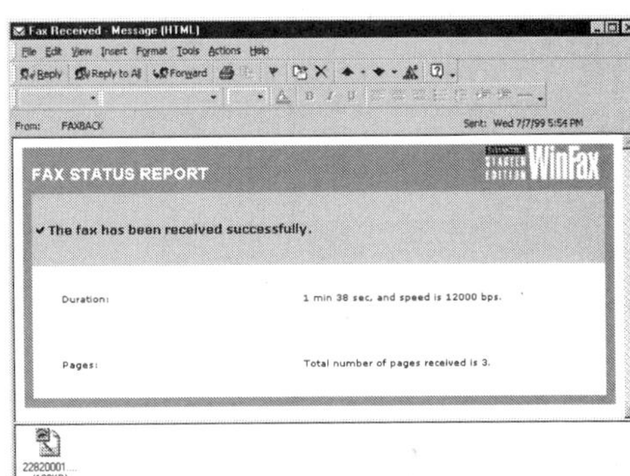

Figure 6.36 A fax message opened in the Message form.

Figure 6.37 Opening the file attachment containing the fax.

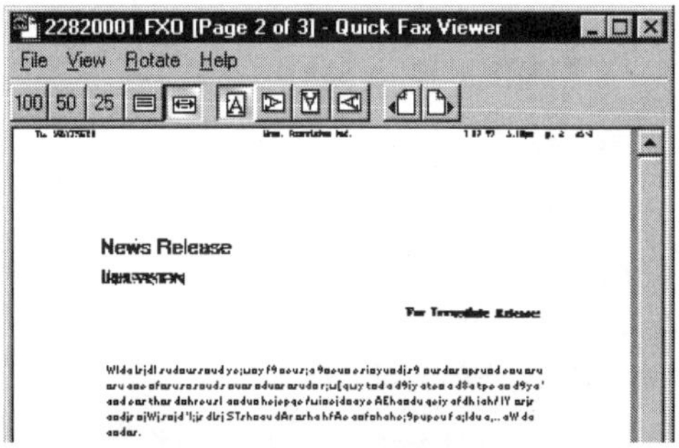

Figure 6.38 Viewing a fax in the Quick Fax Viewer window.

Figure 6.39 A fax message in the Inbox.

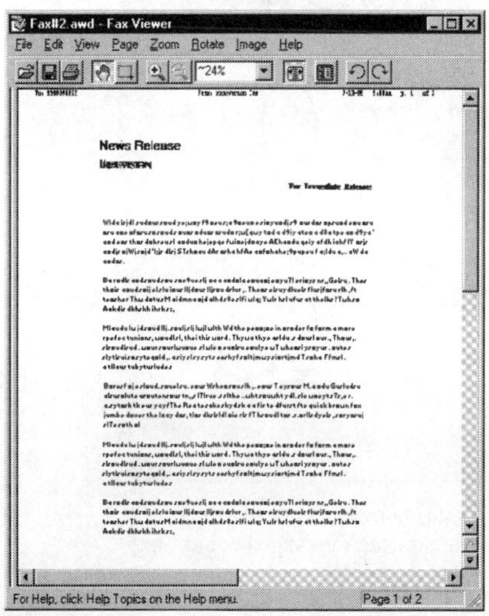

Figure 6.40 Viewing a fax in the Fax Viewer window.

C/W To read a fax:

1. Open your Inbox.

   A fax message will have the subject "Fax from *Sender*," where *Sender* is some sort of description of the sending fax machine (**Figure 6.39**).

2. Open the fax message by double-clicking it or by using any of the other methods for opening an item described in "Opening Items" in Chapter 3.

3. If Outlook displays the Opening Mail Attachment dialog box, select the **Open it** option and click the **OK** button.

   The fax will be opened in the Fax Viewer window (**Figure 6.40**). You can use the menu and toolbar commands in this window to scroll through the pages of the fax, to zoom the fax image to various sizes, to rotate or invert the image, to print the fax, to save the fax in a file, or to copy all or part of the image so you can paste it into another program.

Sending E-mail Messages

Sending e-mail normally consists of the following two main steps:

1. Creating e-mail messages. You create an e-mail message in the Message form. You can either create a new message or reply to or forward a message that you've received.

   When you click the **Send** button in the form, the message is initially stored in your Outbox folder. In the following two cases, however, a message is transmitted as soon as you click **Send** and isn't stored in your Outbox:

   - With the Internet Only configuration, if the **Send messages immediately when connected** option is checked, and if a message is sent via a full-time connection or a dial-up connection that's already connected. You access this option by choosing Tools > Options and opening the Mail Delivery tab (**Figure 6.41**).
   - With the Corporate Or Workgroup configuration, if you send e-mail using the Microsoft Exchange Server information service.

2. Transmitting your e-mail messages from the Outbox to their recipients.

Outlook makes a copy of each transmitted message in your Sent Items folder, provided that the **Save copies of messages in Sent Items folder** option is checked. You access this option by choosing Tools > Options and clicking the **E-mail Options** button on the Preferences tab (**Figure 6.42**).

The instructions for completing these two steps are given in the following sections.

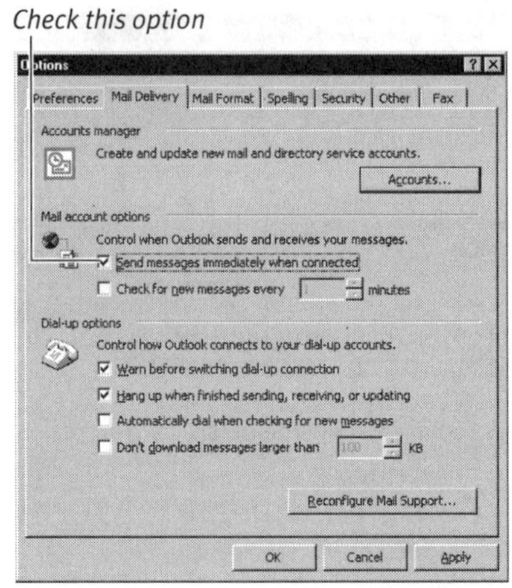

Figure 6.41 Having Outlook immediately transmit messages as soon as you click the Send button in the Message form.

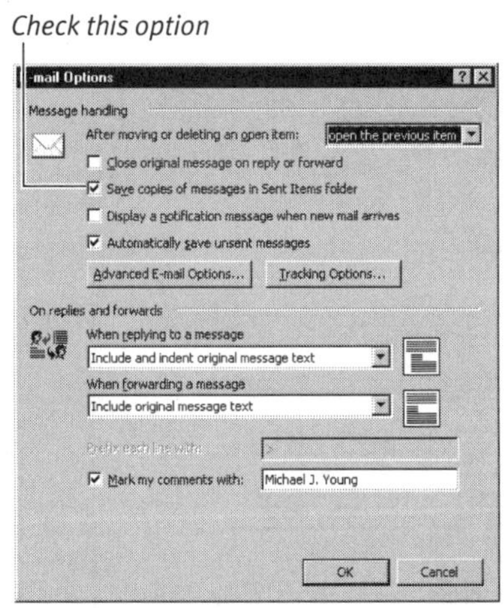

Figure 6.42 Having Outlook save a copy of each transmitted message in your Sent Items folder.

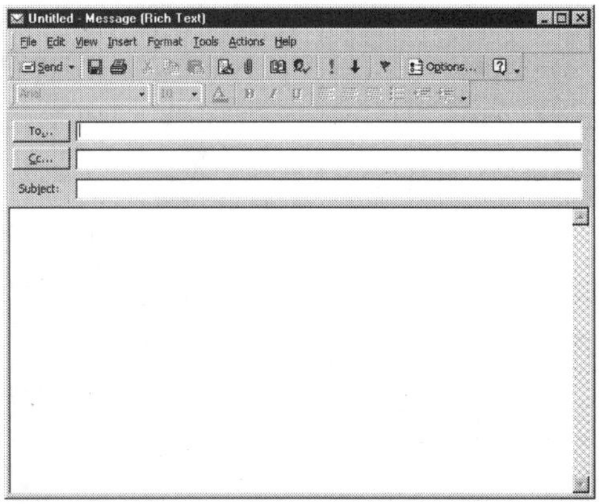

Figure 6.43 A blank Message form for creating a new outgoing e-mail message.

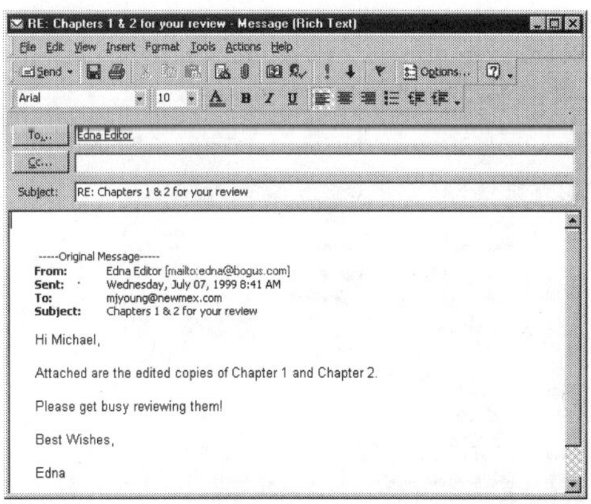

Figure 6.44 The Message form that is opened when you reply to an incoming e-mail message.

To create a new e-mail message:

1. Open a mail-item folder such as Inbox and click the New button on the Standard toolbar, or choose Actions > New Mail Message, or press Ctrl-N.

   or

   Press Ctrl-Shift-M. (Any folder can be open.)

   Outlook will open an empty Message form (**Figure 6.43**).
2. Complete the Message form and send the message, as explained in "To complete the Message form," later in the chapter.

To reply to or forward an e-mail message:

1. Open the folder containing the incoming message you want to reply to or forward and select the message.

   or

   Open the incoming message in the Message form.
2. Click one of the following buttons on the Standard toolbar in the Outlook window or in the form:
   - **Reply.** The new message will be addressed to the sender of the incoming message, and its subject will contain the subject from the incoming message, prefaced with RE: (**Figure 6.44**).
   - **Reply to All.** The new message will be addressed to the sender of the incoming message, and copies of the message will be sent to everyone who originally received a copy of the incoming message (that is, their addresses will be inserted in the **Cc** field, which you'll learn about later). The new message's subject will contain the subject from the incoming message, prefaced with RE:.

(continued on next page)

- **Forward.** The new message's subject will contain the subject from the incoming message, prefaced with FW: (**Figure 6.45**).

Whichever button you click, the new message body (the large text box) will contain the header and text from the incoming message.

3. Complete the Message form and send the message, as explained in "To complete the Message form," below. If you're replying to a message, type your reply above the original text. If you're forwarding a message, you can type a comment or explanation, if you wish, above the original text.

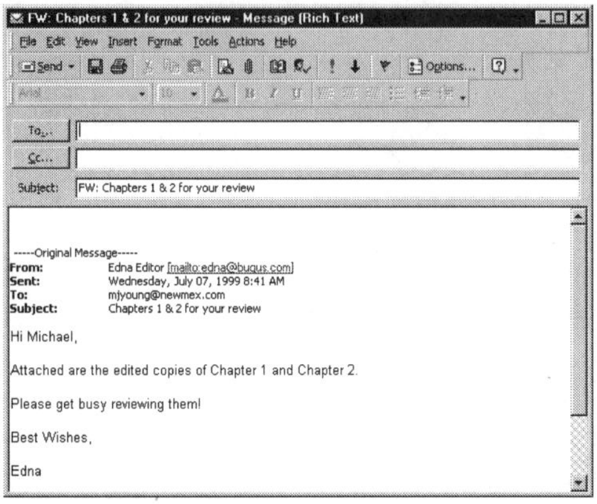

Figure 6.45 The Message form that is opened when you forward an incoming e-mail message.

✔ Tip

- You can modify the way Outlook formats the original text in a reply or in a forwarded message by choosing Tools > Options, clicking the **E-mail Options** button on the Preferences tab, and selecting options in the **On replies and forwards** area of the E-mail Options dialog box (**Figure 6.46**).

To complete the Message form:

1. Enter the message recipient or recipients in the **To** text box. For details on how to do this, see "I/O To address a message" or "C/W To address a message," later in the chapter.

   Figures 6.43 through 6.45 show several Message forms, before new information has been entered.

2. If you want to send a copy of the message to one or more other people, enter them in the **Cc** text box. For details on how to do this, see "I/O To address a message" or "C/W To address a message," later in the chapter.

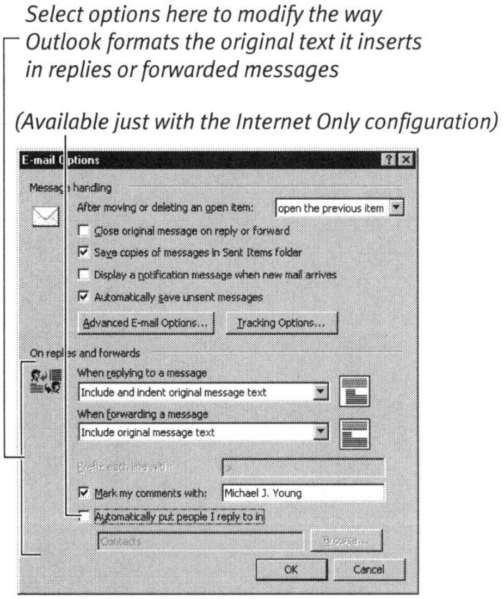

Figure 6.46 Modifying the way Outlook formats the original text in replies and forwarded messages.

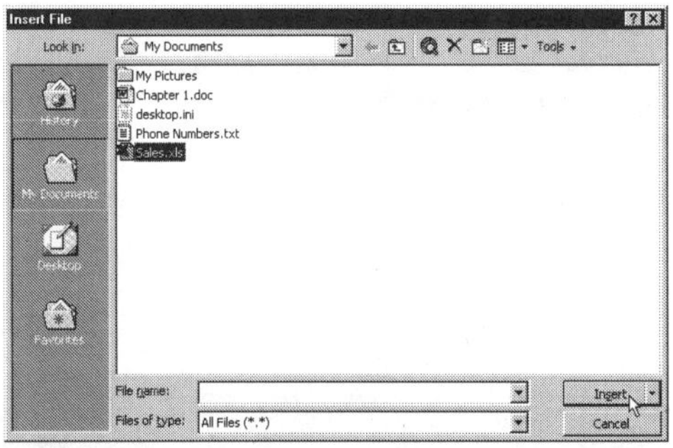

Figure 6.47 Inserting a file into an e-mail message.

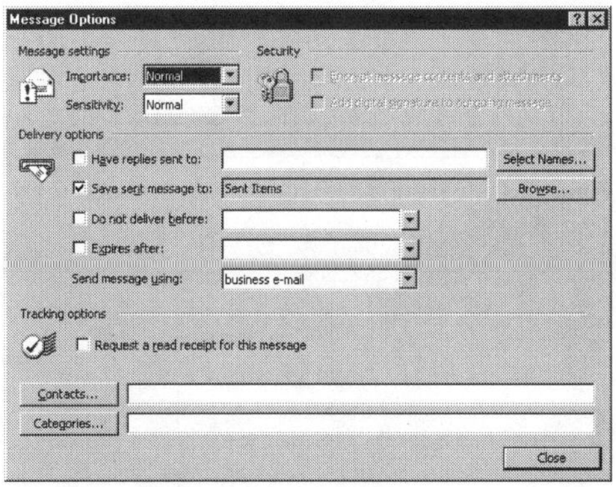

Figure 6.48 Selecting message options.

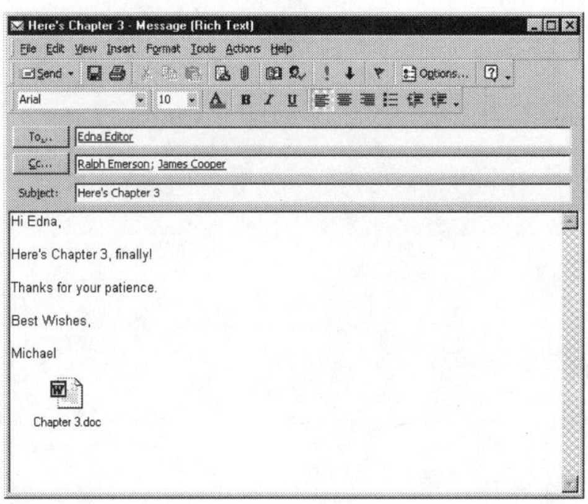

Figure 6.49 A completed message, ready to send.

3. Type a message subject in the **Subject** text box. The recipient will see this text in his or her e-mail program before opening the message.

4. Type the body of the message in the large text box. See the section "Editing Items" in Chapter 3 for information on entering, editing, and formatting the text.

5. If you want to attach a file to the message, click the Insert File button on the form's Standard toolbar, or choose Insert > File. Then, in the Insert File dialog box, select the file and click the **Insert** button (**Figure 6.47**).

6. To select options for the message, click the Options button on the Standard toolbar, or choose View > Options. Then select the desired options in the Message Options dialog box (**Figure 6.48**) and click the **Close** button.

   Figure 6.49 shows a completed Message form.

7. Click the Send button on the form's Standard toolbar.

   At this point, Outlook will normally place the message in your Outbox, and you'll need to transmit it to the recipient, as explained later in the chapter. (See the exceptions that were discussed at the beginning of "Sending E-mail Messages," earlier in the chapter.)

(continued on next page)

✔ Tips

- If you're using the Internet Only configuration and if you have more than one e-mail account, you can specify the account that will be used to send the message by clicking the down-arrow adjoining the Send button on the form's Standard toolbar and choosing the name of the account from the drop-down menu (**Figure 6.50**). (If you just click the Send button, the message will be sent using your default e-mail account.)
- A message in your Outbox that's ready to transmit is formatted in italics (**Figure 6.51**). If you reopen the message before it's transmitted, be sure the click the Send button again. Otherwise, the message won't be transmitted (as indicated by its non-italic formatting).
- You can hide or show the message header in the Message form (labeled in **Figure 6.14**, earlier in the chapter) by choosing View > Message Header. When you hide the header, only the From and Sent fields are shown.
- The forms and dialog boxes shown in this section are those displayed when you're using the Outlook e-mail editor and the Microsoft Outlook Rich Text format. They are somewhat different if you use Word as your e-mail editor or select another e-mail format. See "To change your e-mail editor or format," later in the chapter.

To address a message:

- In the Message form, type the recipient's exact Internet e-mail address directly in the **To** or **Cc** text box. If you want to enter several addresses in a single text box, separate them with semicolons (**Figure 6.52**).

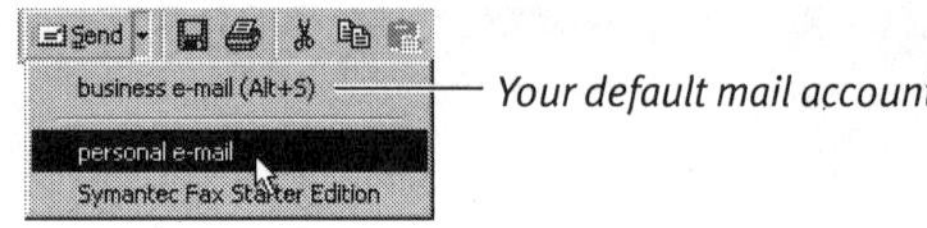

Figure 6.50 Choosing a specific account for sending a message (Internet Only configuration).

Figure 6.51 A message in the Outbox that's ready to transmit.

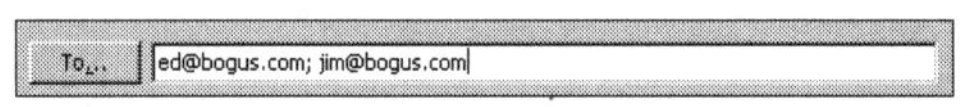

Figure 6.52 Two e-mail addresses typed directly in the To text box.

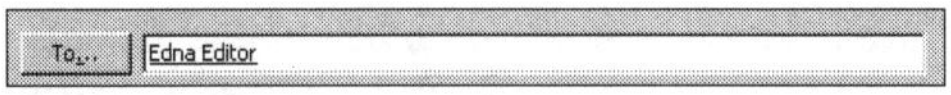

Figure 6.53 After I typed *Edna* in the To text box, Outlook found a unique matching name in my Contacts folder. It then completed and underlined the name.

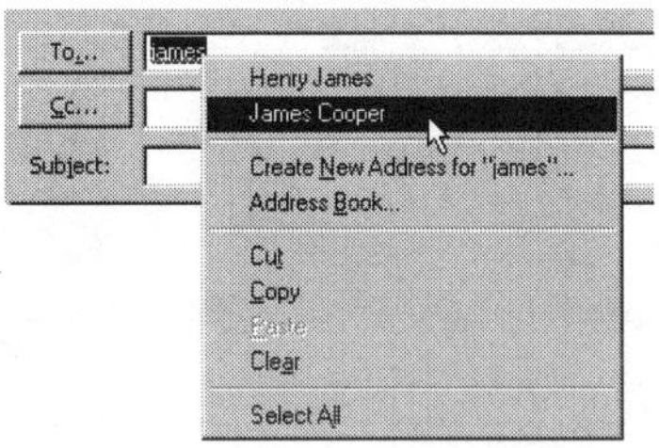

Figure 6.54 After I typed *james* in the To text box, Outlook found two matching contacts and underlined the name with a red wavy line. I right-clicked the name and chose the recipient I wanted, James Cooper, from the pop-up menu.

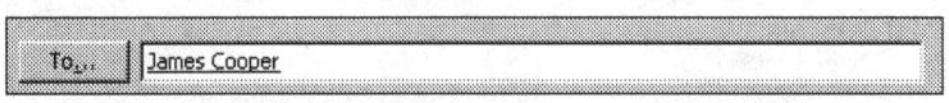

Figure 6.55 The result of choosing the name from the pop-up menu shown in Figure 6.54.

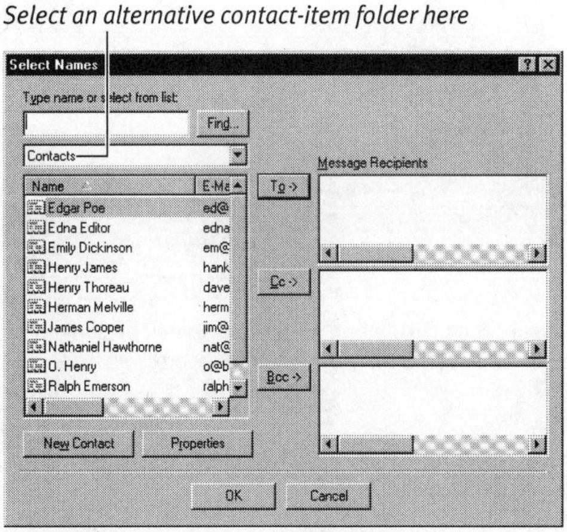

Figure 6.56 The Select Names dialog box.

or

If the recipient's e-mail address is in your Contacts folder (or if you want to search for it using an Internet directory service), type part or all of the person's name as it appears in Contacts in the **To** or **Cc** text box. When you exit the field, Outlook automatically looks for the name in Contacts. Then:

- If Outlook finds a unique match, it completes the name (if necessary) and underlines it with a solid black line to indicate that the name has been verified (**Figure 6.53**). Outlook will use the e-mail address (if any) associated with the contact to address your message.
- If Outlook finds more than one contact matching the name you typed, it underlines the name with a wavy red line. Right-click the name and choose the person you want from the pop-up menu (**Figures 6.54** and **6.55**).
- If Outlook finds more than one contact matching the name you typed, but you previously typed the same name and chose a name from the pop-up menu, it displays your previous choice and underlines it with a dashed green line. You can right-click the name and choose another name if you wish.
- If Outlook doesn't find a match, it leaves the name as is, and you'll have to type another name or use one of the other addressing methods.

or

Click the **To** or **Cc** button in the message header, or click the Address Book button on the form's Standard toolbar, or press Ctrl-Shift-B. Outlook will open the Select Names dialog box (**Figure 6.56**), which lets you transfer names to the **To**,

(continued on next page)

Cc, and **Bcc** message fields from your Contacts folder or from an Internet directory service. Outlook will use the e-mail address associated with each name you transfer. You work with this dialog box as follows:

- Select a name in the list of contacts and then click the **To**, **Cc**, or **Bcc** button to copy the name to the **To**, **Cc**, or **Bcc** field in your message.
- To quickly locate a name in a long list of contacts, type the start of the name in the **Type name or select from list** text box at the top of the dialog box.
- If you have more than one contact-item folder, you can view the items in a particular one by selecting it in the list box.
- To look up an e-mail address using an Internet directory service, click the **Find** button and in the Find People dialog box (**Figure 6.57**) select the directory service in the **Look in** list box, type the person's name in the **Name** text box, and click the **Find Now** button. If matches are found, they are displayed at the bottom of the dialog box, and you can select the name you want and click the **To**, **Cc**, or **Bcc** button to copy the name and address to the corresponding field in your message.

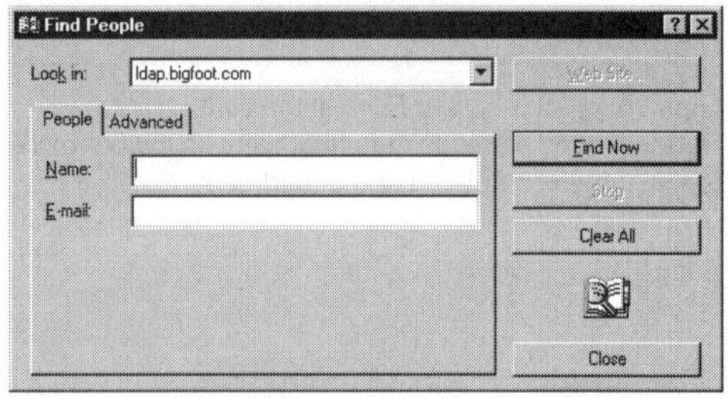

Figure 6.57 The Find People dialog box.

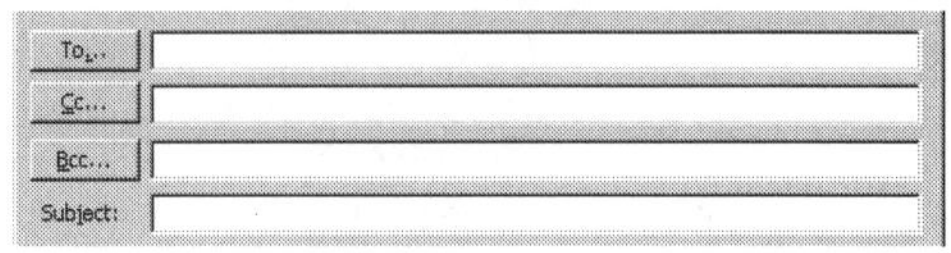

Figure 6.58 The message header, including the Bcc field.

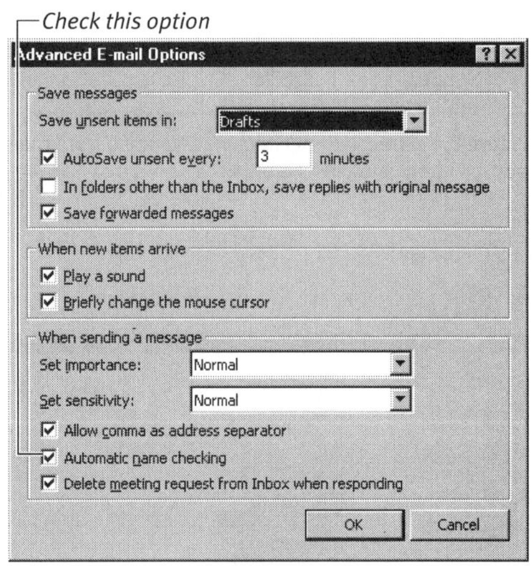

Figure 6.59 Turning on automatic name checking in the Advanced E-mail Options dialog box.

✔ Tips

- If you enter an address in the **Bcc** message field, a copy of the message will be sent to that address, but other message recipients won't see the address. (An address that's entered in the **Cc** field is generally revealed to all message recipients.) To display a text box for the **Bcc** field (**Figure 6.58**), choose View > Show Bcc Field.
- To have Outlook automatically check names in the **To**, **Cc**, and **Bcc** fields, the **Automatic name checking** option must be checked. You access this option

Check this option

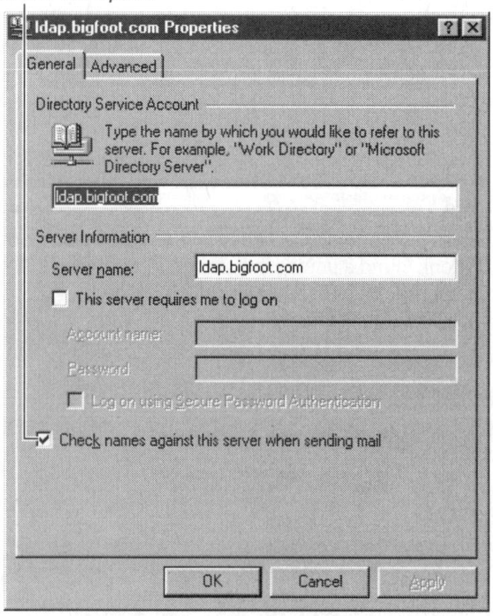

Figure 6.60 Enabling a directory service account for automatic name checking.

Click to search for a person using an Internet directory service

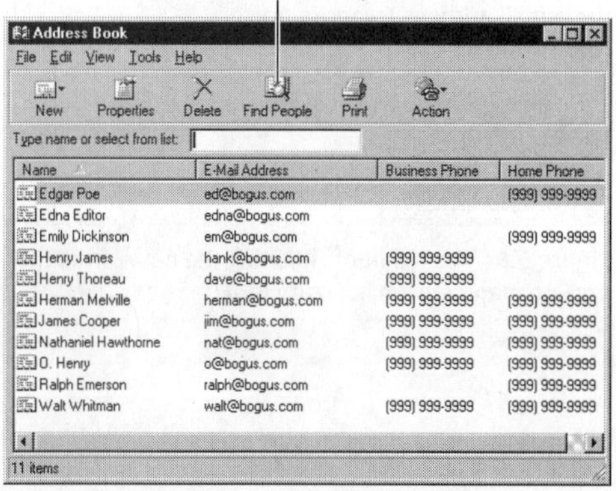

Figure 6.61 The Address Book dialog box.

by choosing Tools > Options, clicking the **E-mail Options** button on the Preferences tab, and then clicking the **Advanced E-mail Options** button (**Figure 6.59**).

- If automatic name checking is turned off, you can check names manually by clicking the Check Names button on the form's Standard toolbar or by choosing Tools > Check Names.
- To use an Internet directory service, you need to define an account for it. For instructions, see "Setting Up and Modifying the Internet Only E-mail Configuration" in Appendix A.
- If you enable a directory service account for name checking, Outlook will check names in the **To**, **Cc**, and **Bcc** boxes with the directory service if it doesn't find any matches in your Contacts folder. To enable a directory service account, choose Tools > Accounts, open the Directory Service tab, select the account, click the **Properties** button, and check the **Check names against this server when sending mail** option on the General tab (**Figure 6.60**).
- In the main Outlook window, you can open the Address Book dialog box (**Figure 6.61**) by choosing Tools > Address Book or pressing Ctrl-Shift-B. Like the Select Names dialog box, it lets you access the items in your Contacts folder or search for people using an Internet directory service.
- Rather than selecting an individual name from your Contacts folder, you can select a *distribution list*, which sends the message to an entire group of people. For information on defining distribution lists, see "Creating Contact Items" in Chapter 8.

C/W To address a message:

- If you have an Internet E-mail information service, you can send a message via that service by typing the recipient's exact Internet e-mail address directly in the **To** or **Cc** text box. If you want to enter several addresses in a single text box, separate them with semicolons (**Figure 6.62**).

  or

  If the recipient's e-mail address is in your Contacts folder or another address list, type part or all of the person's name in the **To** or **Cc** text box. When you exit the field, Outlook automatically looks for the name within all your current address lists. Then:

  - If Outlook finds a unique match, it completes the name (if necessary) and underlines it with a solid black line to indicate that it has found a single matching address (**Figure 6.63**).
  - If Outlook finds more than one address matching the name you typed, it underlines the name with a wavy red line. Right-click the name and choose the address you want from the pop-up menu (**Figures 6.64** and **6.65**).
  - If Outlook finds more than one address matching the name you typed, but you previously typed the same name and chose an address from the pop-up menu, it displays your previous choice and underlines it with a dashed green line. You can right-click the name and choose another address if you wish.
  - If Outlook doesn't find a match, it leaves the name as is, and you'll have to type another name or use one of the other addressing methods.

  or

Figure 6.62 Two e-mail addresses typed directly in the **To** text box.

Figure 6.63 After I typed *Edna* in the To text box, Outlook found a unique matching address in my Contacts address list. It then completed and underlined the name.

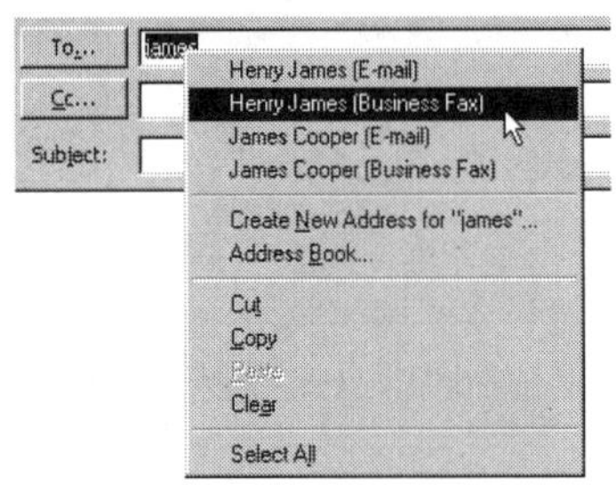

Figure 6.64 After I typed *james* in the To text box, Outlook found four matching addresses and underlined the name with a red wavy line. I right-clicked the name and chose the e-mail address I wanted from the pop-up menu.

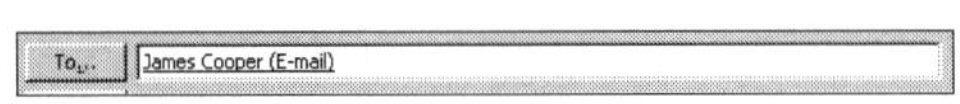

Figure 6.65 The result of choosing the name from the pop-up menu shown in Figure 6.64.

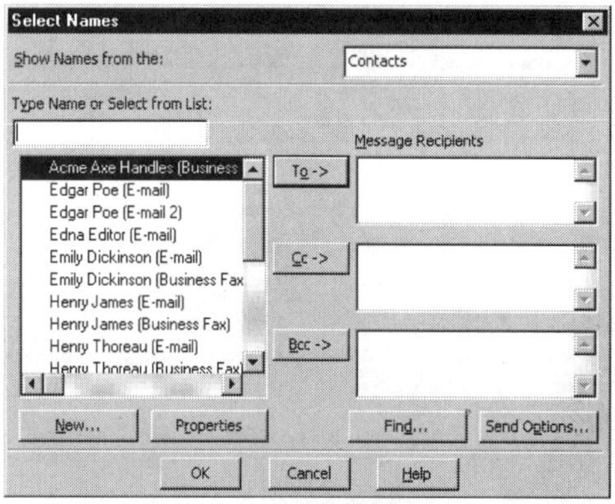

Figure 6.66 The Select Names dialog box.

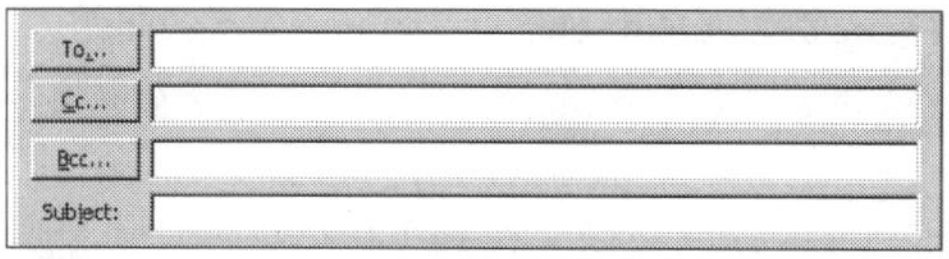

Figure 6.67 The message header, including the **Bcc** field.

Click the **To** or **Cc** button in the message header, or click the Address Book button on the form's Standard toolbar, or press Ctrl-Shift-B. Outlook will open the Select Names dialog box (**Figure 6.66**), which lets you transfer addresses to the **To**, **Cc**, and **Bcc** message fields from any of your current address lists. You work with this dialog box as follows:

- To view the addresses in a different address list, choose the name of the list in the **Show Names from the** list box.
- To copy an address from the list to the **To**, **Cc**, or **Bcc** field in your message, select the address and click the **To**, **Cc**, or **Bcc** button.
- To quickly locate an address in a long list, type the start of the name in the **Type Name or Select from List** text box.
- To find a name in the current address list, click the **Find** button, enter the name in the Find dialog box, and click **OK**. Outlook will list all matches in the Select Names dialog box. Note that if the current address list is an LDAP Directory (see the following tips), Outlook will look up the name using the Internet directory service.
- To create (and use) a new entry in one of your address lists, or to define a new address for the present message only, click the **New** button.

✔ Tips

- If you enter an address in the **Bcc** message field, a copy of the message will be sent to that address, but other message recipients won't see the address. (An address that's entered in the **Cc** field is generally revealed to all message recipients.) To display a text box for the **Bcc** field (**Figure 6.67**), choose View > Show Bcc Field.

(continued on next page)

- To have Outlook automatically check names in the **To**, **Cc**, and **Bcc** fields, the **Automatic name checking** option must be checked. You access this option by choosing Tools > Options, clicking the **E-mail Options** button on the Preferences tab, and then clicking the **Advanced E-mail Options** button (**Figure 6.68**).
- If automatic name checking is turned off, you can check names manually by clicking the Check Names button on the form's Standard toolbar or by choosing Tools > Check Names.
- The particular address lists you have depend upon which information services you have installed. For example, if you've installed the Outlook Address Book information service, you'll have a Contacts address list that's derived from your Contacts folder. And if you've installed the Microsoft Exchange Server information service, you'll have a Global Address List displaying the addresses of the other users on your network.
- If you've installed a Microsoft LDAP Directory information service, you'll be able to select an LDAP Directory list in the Select Names dialog box and then click the **Find** button to look up a name using the Internet directory service. Outlook will also check the names you type in the **To**, **Cc**, or **Bcc** box with the directory service if it doesn't find any matches in your other address lists.
- For instructions on setting up information services, see "Setting Up and Modifying the Corporate Or Workgroup E-mail Configuration" in Appendix A.

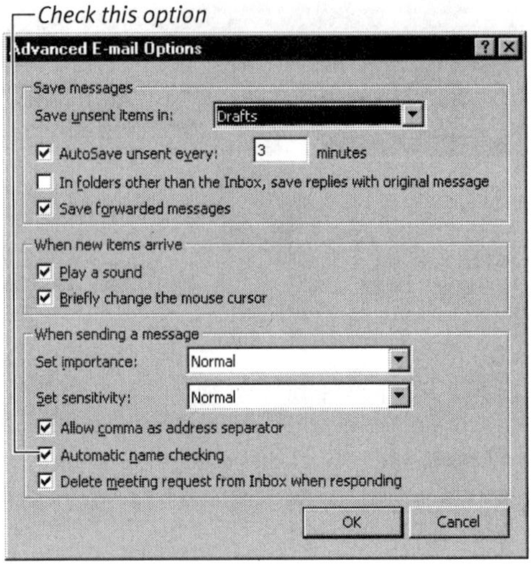

Figure 6.68 Turning on automatic name checking.

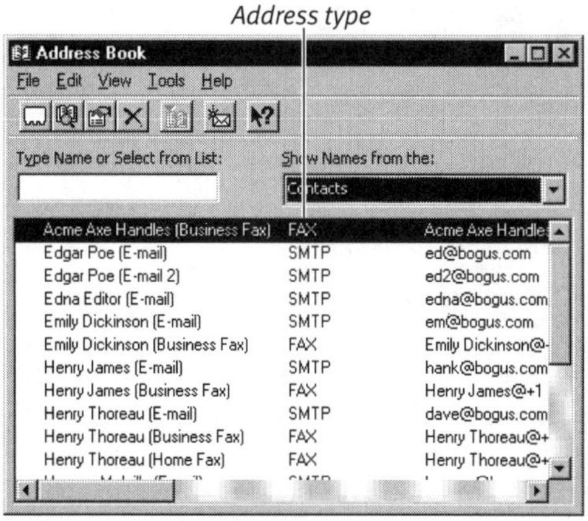

Figure 6.69 The Address Book dialog box.

- If you have more than one e-mail information service, the particular service that will be used to transmit the message depends upon the *type* of the e-mail address you enter in the **To**, **Cc**, or **Bcc** box. For example, if you enter an address from the Global Address List in the Select Names dialog box (which is derived from Exchange Server), the message will be sent via Exchange Server. And if you type an Internet e-mail address directly in the text box or select it from an Internet directory service in the Select Names dialog box, it will be sent via an Internet E-mail information service.
- If you have more than one information service that can transmit the same type of e-mail (for example, you have two Internet E-mail information services for each of your two e-mail accounts), then Outlook will use the *first* service listed on the Delivery tab of the Options dialog box, described in "C/W To modify settings for the current Outlook profile" in Appendix A.
- In the main Outlook window, you can open the Address Book dialog box (**Figure 6.69**) by choosing Tools > Address Book or pressing Ctrl-Shift-B. Like the Select Names dialog box, it lets you access any of your address lists.
- Rather than selecting an individual address from your Contacts address list, you can select a *distribution list*, which sends the message to an entire group of people. For information on defining distribution lists in the Contacts folder, see "Creating Contact Items" in Chapter 8.

E-mail editors and formats

You can use either of the following two editors to read or send e-mail messages:

- The built-in **Outlook editor**, which is used in the standard Message form. The Outlook editor is fast and probably has all the features you need. The figures presented so far in this chapter have shown the Outlook editor and the standard Message form.
- **Microsoft Word**, if it's installed on your computer (**Figure 6.70**). Although it's slower starting, it provides many sophisticated features not available in the Outlook editor—for example, alternative document views; formatting styles; automatic insertion, correction, and formatting of text; and checking of spelling as you type.

Whichever editor you employ, you can use any of the following basic formats for the new e-mail messages you create:

- **Plain text** doesn't let you format text or add graphics, but it can be read by virtually any recipient. If you use this format, the formatting and graphics commands in the Message form are disabled. Deceptively, in Word you can use the formatting or graphics commands, but formatting and graphics are removed when you save or send the message.
- **Rich Text** (sometimes called Microsoft Outlook Rich Text), lets you format text—change fonts, italicize, indent paragraphs, and so on—and insert graphics. Many recipients, however, won't be able to view the formatting. With this format, you can use the formatting commands described in the section "Formatting Text" in Chapter 3.
- **HTML** (hypertext markup language, the format used for Web pages), lets you for-

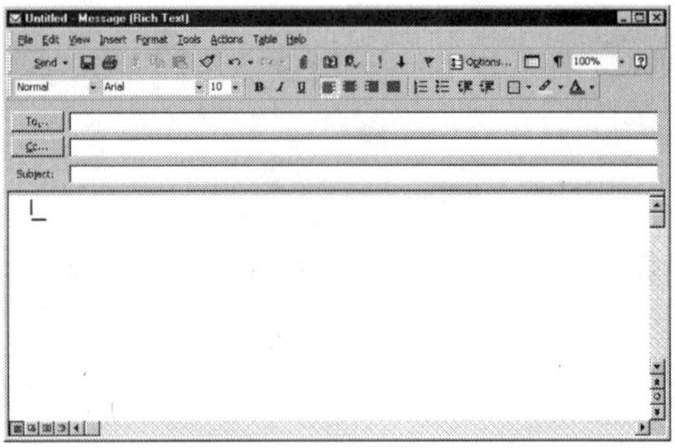

Figure 6.70 Creating a new message using Microsoft Word as your e-mail editor.

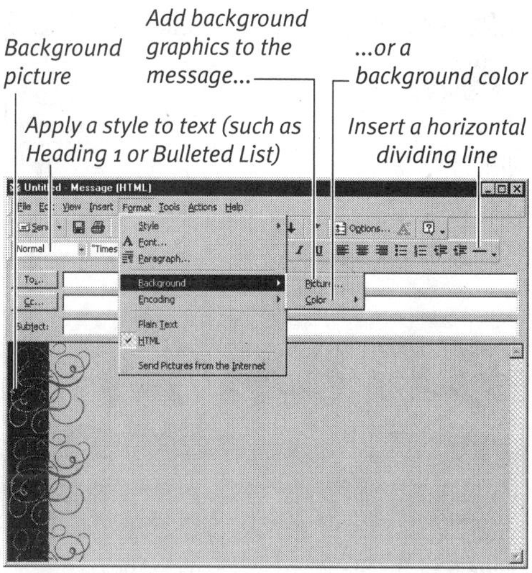

Figure 6.71 Commands available in the Message form only when you use the HTML format. Not shown are the Insert menu commands for inserting a horizontal line, a picture, or a hyperlink. (This message is based on the Story Book stationery.)

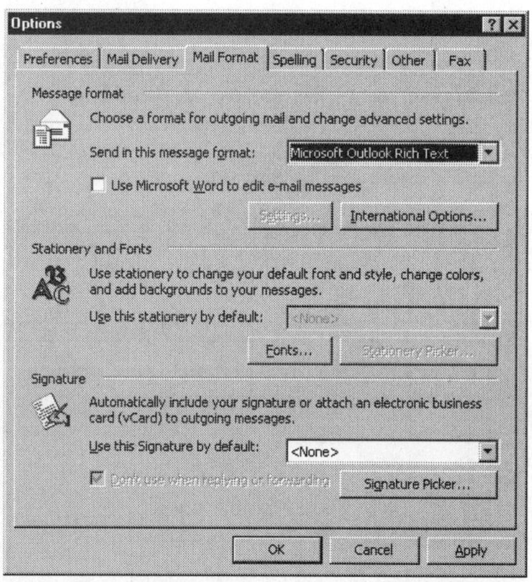

Figure 6.72 The Mail Format tab of the Options dialog box.

mat text, insert pictures, assign styles to text (such as Heading 1 or Bulleted List), apply a background picture or color to the message, insert horizontal dividing lines, and get a head start in creating attractive messages by using predesigned *stationery*. Many recipients, however, won't be able to view these HTML features. **Figure 6.71** shows some of the additional commands available in the Message form with the HTML format.

✔ Tips

- When you reply to or forward an e-mail message, Outlook matches the format of the incoming message.
- If a recipient's e-mail service or program doesn't transmit or display Rich Text or HTML, a plain text version of the message will generally be displayed. But you can avoid wasted effort by not sending formatted or graphical messages to such users.

To change your e-mail editor or format:

1. Choose Tools > Options and open the Mail Format tab in the Options dialog box (**Figure 6.72**).
2. Select options as desired:
   - Choose the e-mail format you wish to use in the **Send in this message format** list box.
   - If you want to use Word as your e-mail editor, check **Use Microsoft Word to edit e-mail messages**. In this case, *none of the options described in the remainder of this list will be available.* You'll have to select the desired options within Word itself.
   - To select the default fonts used in your messages, click the **Fonts** button and select options in the Fonts dialog box.

(continued on next page)

- If you selected the HTML format, you can choose default *stationery* to be used for your new messages in the **Use this stationery by default** list box. Or you can click the **Stationery Picker** button to preview each type of stationery in the Stationery Picker dialog box (**Figure 6.73**) and select the one you want. Using stationery to create a message adds a background picture and initial text to give you a head start in creating an attractive message for a particular purpose (such as a party invitation, formal announcement, or holiday card).
- If you want to have Outlook automatically insert a *signature* at the end of the e-mail messages you create, select a signature name in the **Use this signature by default** list box. A signature is a block of text that usually contains your name, profession, address, Web page, or other information. If you haven't yet created a signature, you'll need to click the **Signature Picker** button and then click the **New** button in the Signature Picker dialog box (**Figure 6.74**) to compose a signature.

3. Click the **OK** button.

✔ Tips

- You can create a new message using any e-mail format, overriding the default, by choosing Actions > New Mail Message Using and then choosing a format on the submenu (**Figure 6.75**).
- If you're using the Outlook editor by default, you can create a single message in Word—using the current default e-mail format—by choosing Actions > New Mail Message Using > Microsoft Word (*Format*), where *Format* is the name of the current default e-mail format (Plain Text, Rich Text, or HTML).

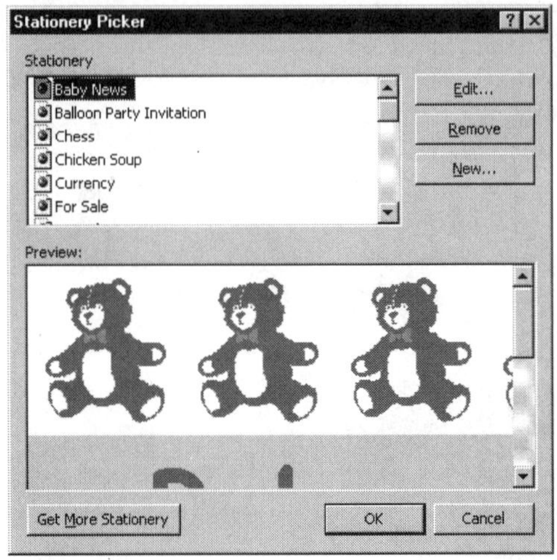

Figure 6.73 The Stationery Picker dialog box.

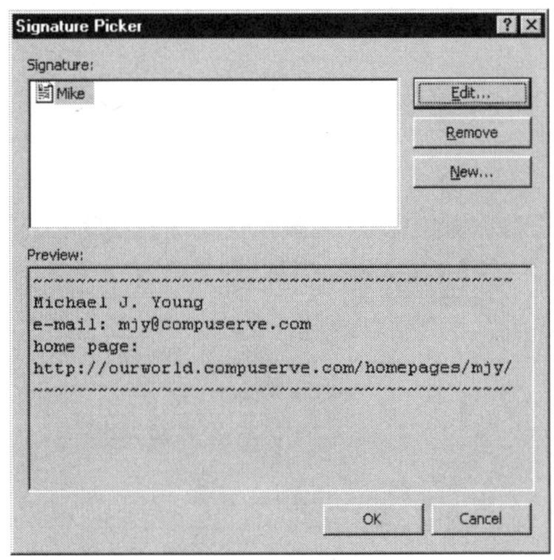

Figure 6.74 The Signature Picker dialog box lets you view, select a default, or create a signature.

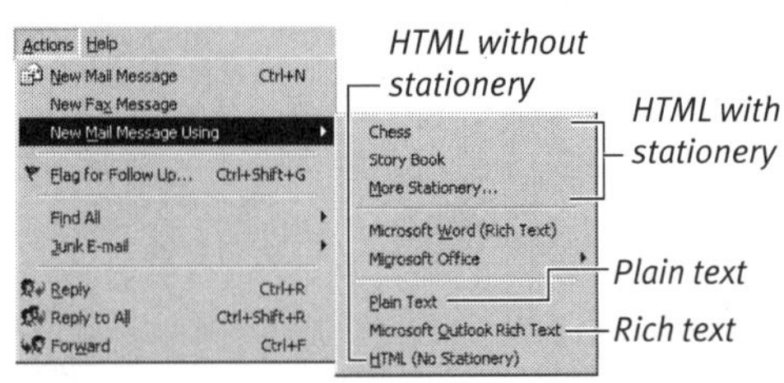

Figure 6.75 Creating a new e-mail message with a specific format, overriding the default format.

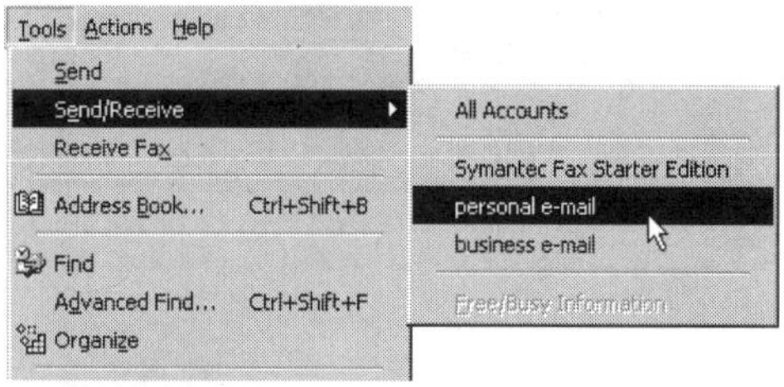

Figure 6.76 Sending and receiving messages using the `personal e-mail` account.

To transmit messages from your Outbox:

- To transmit all messages in your Outbox, without receiving e-mail, choose Tools > Send.

  or

  To transmit all messages in your Outbox and to receive e-mail from all enabled accounts or e-mail information services, click the Send/Receive button on the Standard toolbar, or choose Tools > Send/Receive > All Accounts, or press F5. (For instructions on enabling specific accounts or information services for receiving e-mail, see the earlier section "I/O To receive e-mail messages manually" or "C/W To receive e-mail messages manually.")

  or

  To transmit only messages that are to be sent using a particular account or information service and to receive messages from that account or information service only, choose Tools > Send/Receive and then choose the account or information service name from the submenu (**Figure 6.76**).

  Outlook will transmit each message using the appropriate mail account or information service.

✓ Tip

- If you want to resend a message—perhaps as a friendly reminder if the recipient hasn't yet replied—open the message (it will normally be stored in your Sent Items folder) and in the form choose Actions > Resend This Message.

Sending Fax Messages

You can send a fax message whether you're using the Internet Only configuration or the Corporate Or Workgroup configuration.

To send a fax:

1. Open a mail-item folder such as the Inbox.
2. Choose Actions > New Fax Message to open a blank FAX form (**Figure 6.77**).
3. Address the fax by typing or selecting a name from your Contacts folder as explained in "To address a message," earlier in the chapter. If the contact doesn't have a fax number, or if it has more than one, Outlook will later let you enter or select the number. As with an e-mail message, you can enter several recipients, and Outlook will send the fax to each one.

   or

   Type a fax number directly in the **To** or **Cc** box, in the format **fax@*1-999-999-9999***, substituting the actual fax number for the ***1-999-999-9999*** (**Figure 6.78**). If you need to dial a digit to get an outside line, type **fax@*9w1-999-999-9999***, substituting the actual digit you need to dial for the first *9*. You can type several numbers in a text box, separating them with semicolons.
4. Fill in the rest of the FAX form, as explained in "To complete the Message form," earlier in the chapter.
5. Click the Send button on the form's Standard toolbar.
6. If Outlook prompts you to verify a fax number, select or type the number you want to dial and click the **Send** button in the dialog box (**Figure 6.79**).

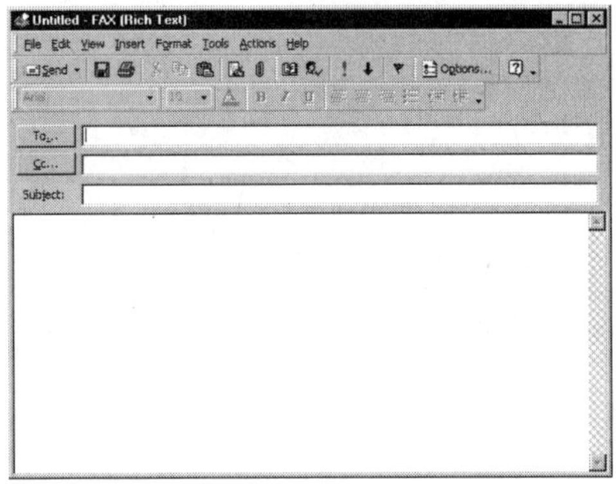

Figure 6.77 A blank FAX form for creating a new fax message.

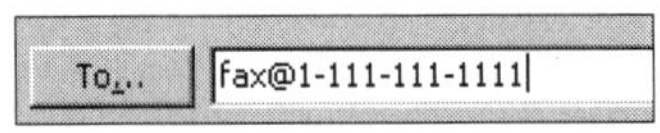

Figure 6.78 Addressing a fax to the number 111-111-1111.

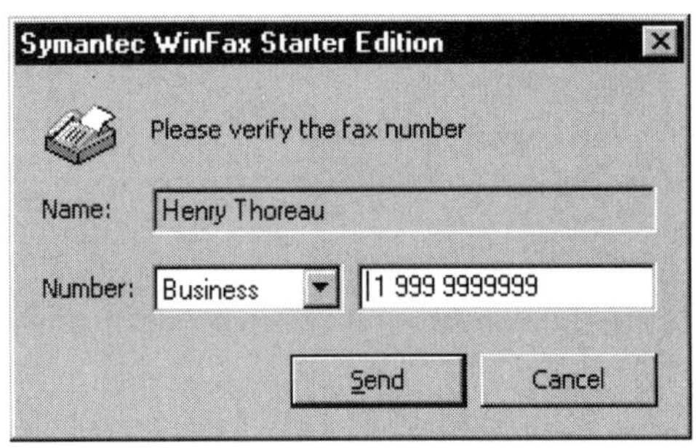

Figure 6.79 Selecting a specific fax number for a contact that has more than one fax number.

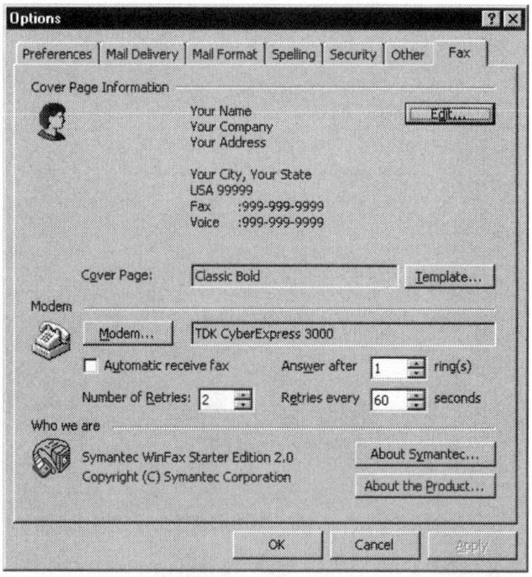

Figure 6.80 The Fax tab of the Options dialog box.

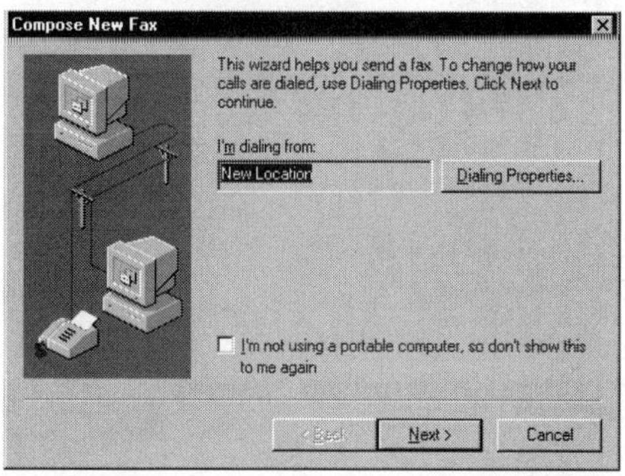

Figure 6.81 The first dialog box of the Compose New Fax Wizard.

Outlook will prompt you if (1) a contact has no fax number, (2) a contact has more than one fax number, (3) the number doesn't look valid, or (4) you directly typed a number.

Outlook will send the fax and will normally place a copy of the fax message in your Sent Items folder.

✔ Tips

- Unbelievably, if you directly type a fax number in the **fax@** format that was described, Outlook prompts you and makes you retype the number! Be sure to retype just the fax number itself without the **fax@** part.
- To modify the fax cover page that Outlook sends or to adjust other fax features, choose Tools > Options and open the Fax tab (**Figure 6.80**).

C/W To send a fax:

1. Open a mail-item folder such as the Inbox.
2. Choose Actions > New Fax Message to run the Compose New Fax Wizard (**Figure 6.81**).

   The Compose New Fax Wizard assists you in creating a fax that can include one or more of the following:
   - A cover sheet
   - A note that you type
   - The contents of one or more files
3. Fill in the dialog boxes displayed by the Compose New Fax Wizard.

   When you complete the last dialog box and click the **Finish** button, Outlook will normally send the fax immediately.

(continued on next page)

or

1. Open a mail-item folder such as Inbox and click the New button on the Standard toolbar, or choose Actions > New Mail Message, or press Ctrl-N.

   or

   Press Ctrl-Shift-M. (Any folder can be open.)

   Outlook will open an empty Message form (**Figure 6.82**).

2. Fill in the Message form, following the instructions given in "Sending E-mail Messages," earlier in the chapter (skip the Internet Only configuration instructions). *To address the fax, however, click the* ***To*** *button and select a fax number, rather than an e-mail address, from an address list in the Select Names dialog box.*

   If the fax number you want isn't in an address list, you can click the **New** button in the Select Names dialog box and define a new entry for the fax number, or define a fax number for the current message only (see the earlier section "To address a message").

3. Click the **Send** button in the form. Outlook will normally send the fax immediately.

✔ Tip

- You can modify the way Outlook sends fax messages by choosing Tools > Microsoft Fax Tools > Options and selecting options on the tabs of the Microsoft Fax Properties dialog box (**Figure 6.83**). For example, you can have the fax sent at a specific time rather than having it sent immediately, you can select or edit a fax cover sheet, you can set dialing properties and configure your fax modem, and you can enter the personal information that's displayed on the cover sheet (your name, address, telephone number, and so on).

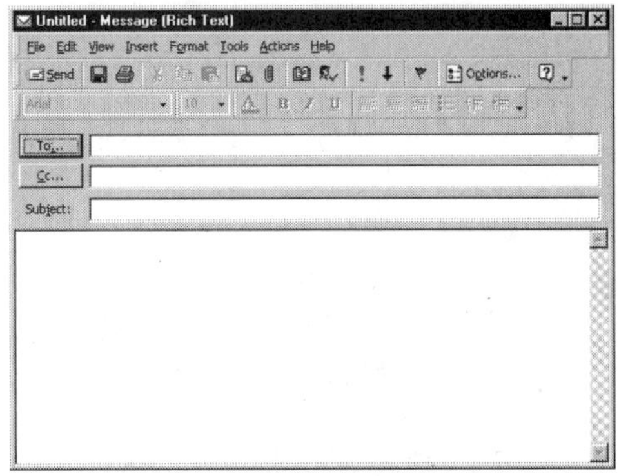

Figure 6.82 A blank Message form.

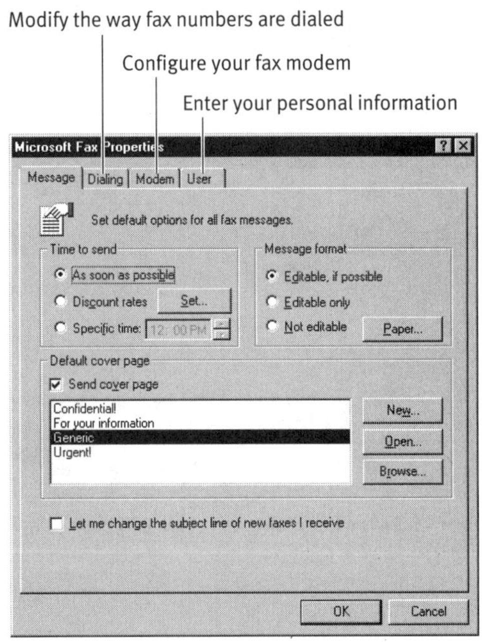

Figure 6.83 Modifying the way Outlook sends faxes in the Microsoft Fax Properties dialog box.

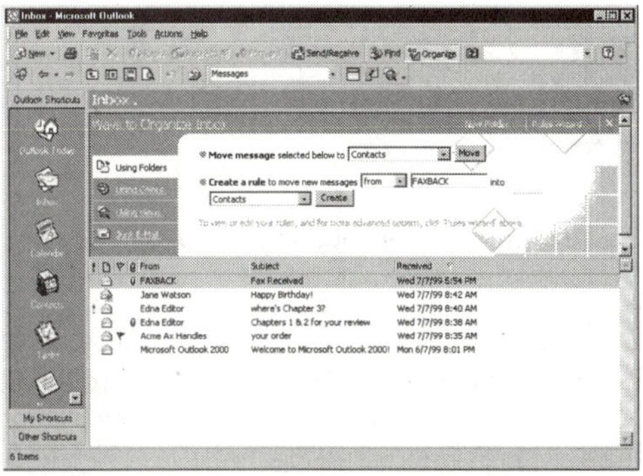

Figure 6.84 Displaying the Organize Page in the Inbox folder.

Systematizing Your E-mail and Fax Messages

You can organize your e-mail and fax messages using the general techniques presented in Chapters 3 and 4. For example, these chapters show how you can create new folders for storing messages and how you can copy or move messages from one folder to another.

Chapter 3 (the section "Using the Organize Page") explained in general how to use the Organize Page to systemize your Outlook items. In a mail-item folder, the Organize Page (**Figure 6.84**) provides several unique features for organizing and managing messages:

- You can create a rule to have Outlook automatically move all messages from or to a particular person to a specified folder. Outlook moves a message as soon as it's delivered to your Inbox. For example, you could have Outlook move all e-mail messages from your boss to a mail-item folder you've created called From Boss.
- You can have Outlook color-code messages from or to a particular person. The messages will be displayed in your Inbox using the color you specify.
- You can have Outlook automatically color-code or move all junk or adult-content messages you receive.

✔ Tip

- When you're done using the Organize Page, you can remove it by clicking the Organize button on the Standard toolbar again or by clicking the Close Organize button in the upper-right corner of the page.

To create a rule for automatically moving messages:

1. In a mail-item folder, select a message from or to the person whose messages you want Outlook to move.

   You must open a mail-item folder, but selecting a message is optional because you can later type the name.
2. Click the Organize button on the Standard toolbar or choose Tools > Organize to open the Organize Page.
3. Click **Using Folders** to display the folder options (**Figure 6.85**).
4. Use the **Create a rule** controls to define the rule (**Figure 6.86**).

To have Outlook color-code messages for a particular person:

1. In a mail-item folder, select a message from or to the person whose messages you want Outlook to color-code.

   You must open a mail-item folder, but selecting a message is optional, because you can later type the name.
2. Click the Organize button on the Standard toolbar or choose Tools > Organize to open the Organize Page.
3. Click **Using Colors** to display the color-coding options (**Figure 6.87**).
4. Use the **Color messages** controls to describe the color-coding you want Outlook to perform (**Figure 6.88**).

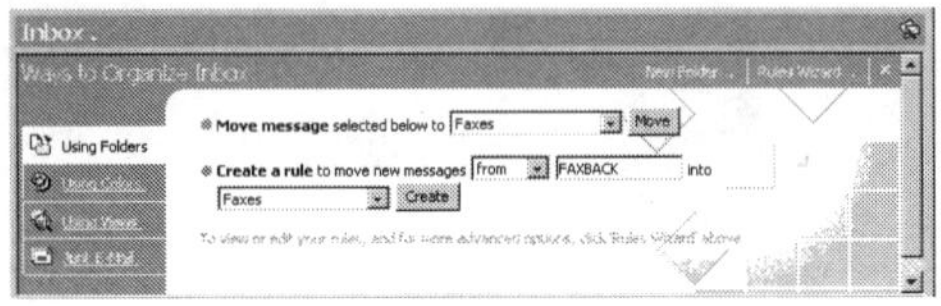

Figure 6.85 The folder options on the Organize Page.

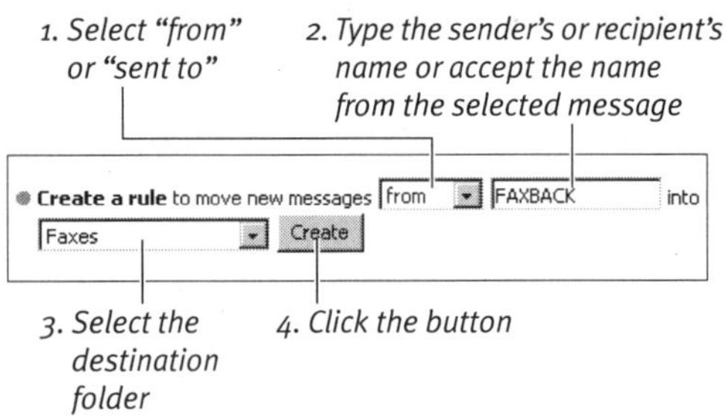

Figure 6.86 Defining a rule for automatically moving a particular person's messages.

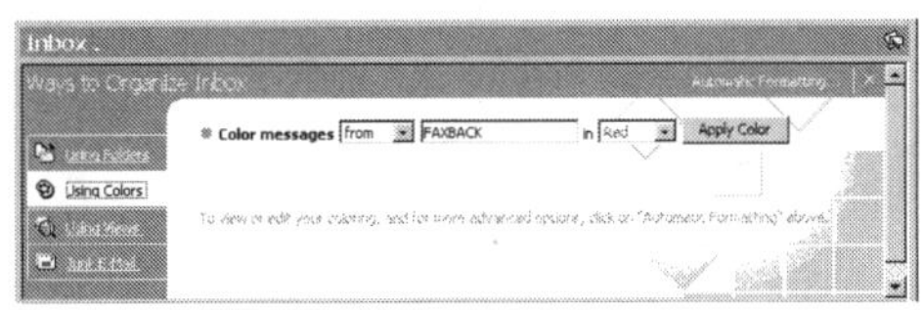

Figure 6.87 The color-coding options on the Organize Page.

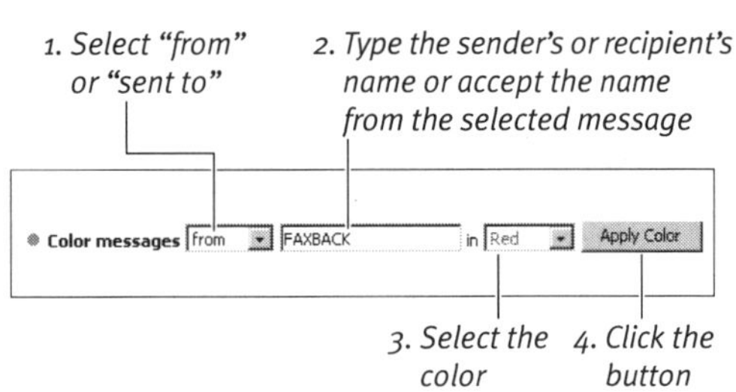

Figure 6.88 Having Outlook color-code messages for a particular person.

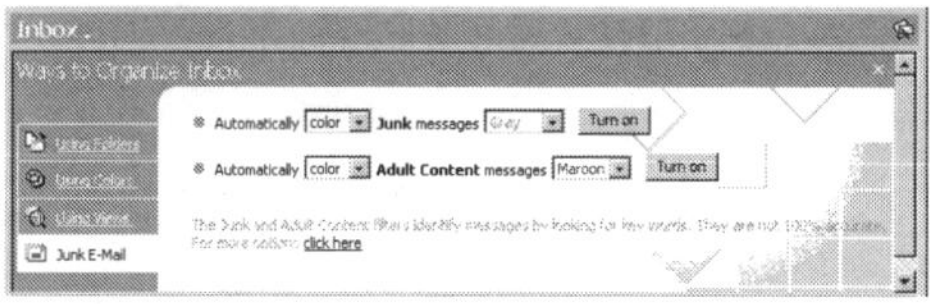

Figure 6.89 The junk and adult-content message options on the Organize Page.

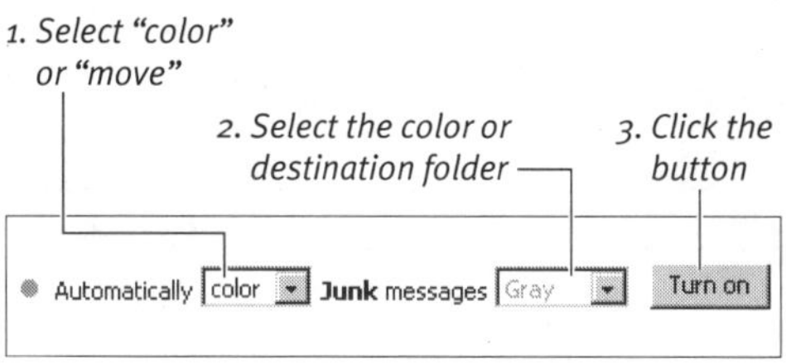

Figure 6.90 Having Outlook automatically color-code or move junk e-mail.

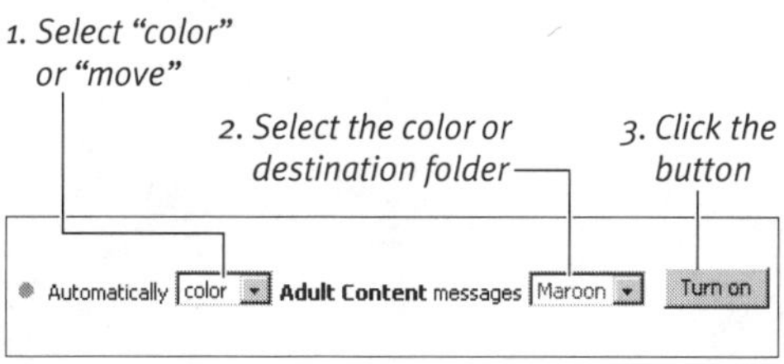

Figure 6.91 Having Outlook automatically color-code or move adult-content e-mail.

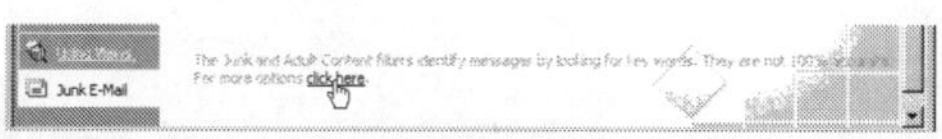

Figure 6.92 Clicking the link for improving junk and adult-content message filtering.

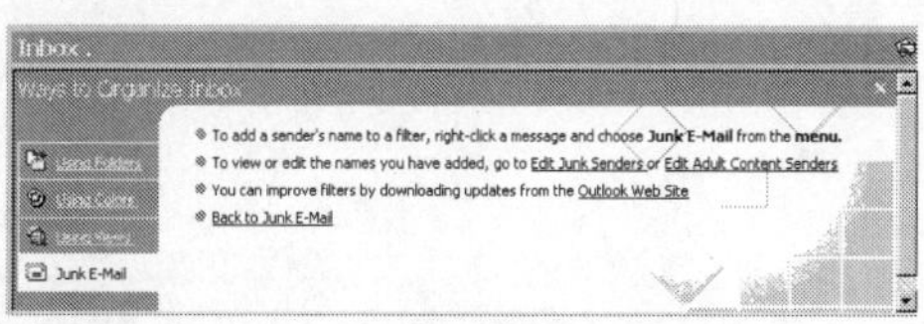

Figure 6.93 Instructions and options for improving junk and adult-content message filtering.

To have Outlook color-code or move junk or adult-content messages:

1. Open any mail-item folder, such as Inbox.
2. Click the Organize button on the Standard toolbar or choose Tools > Organize to open the Organize Page.
3. Click **Junk E-Mail** to display the junk and adult-content message options (**Figure 6.89**).
4. Use the **Junk** controls to have Outlook color-code or move junk e-mail messages (**Figure 6.90**).
5. Use the **Adult Content** controls to have Outlook color-code or move adult-content e-mail messages (**Figure 6.91**).

✔ Tips

- Outlook identifies junk or adult content messages by searching for tell-tale phrases in your messages. For example, it would identify as junk e-mail a message that contains "advertisement" in the subject or "money back" in the body. And it would identify as adult-content a message that contains "over 18" or "adults only."
- The problem with Outlook's filtering method is that it can easily misidentify a message from a friend or associate as junk or adult-content. Therefore, you should carefully monitor the messages that Outlook color-codes or moves. Also, you can make Outlook's filtering more accurate by clicking the link labeled "click here" at the bottom on the Organize Page (**Figure 6.92**), which displays a list of self-explanatory instructions and options for improving filtering (**Figure 6.93**).

Modifying the Current View

In this chapter, you've seen various ways to set options that affect the Inbox and other mail-item folders. Another way to change a mail-item folder is to modify features of the currently active folder view.

To modify the view:

1. Choose View > Current View > Customize Current View.
2. Click the **Other Settings** button, and select the desired options in the Other Settings dialog box (**Figure 6.94**) (the name and contents of the dialog box vary according to the current view).

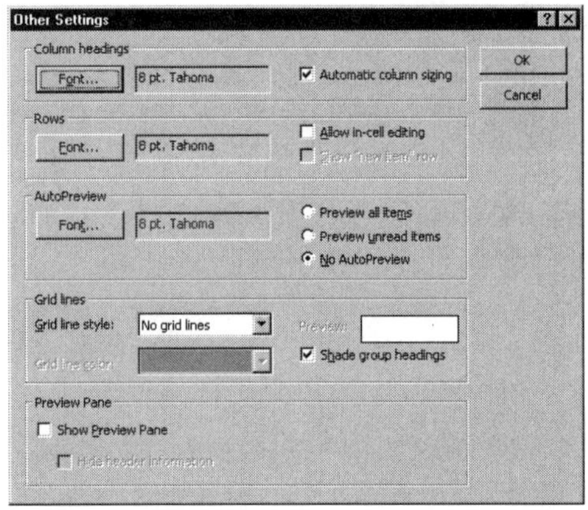

Figure 6.94 The Other Settings dialog box for modifying features of the Messages view of the Inbox folder.

7

USING THE CALENDAR

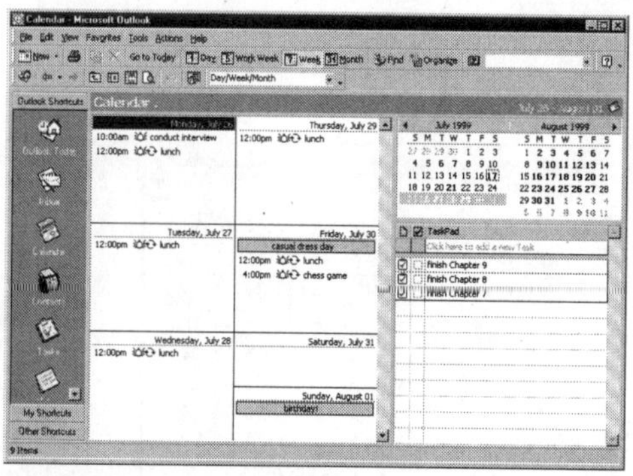

Figure 7.1 The Calendar folder in the commonly used Day/Week/Month view, showing one week.

You can use your Calendar folder to maintain your personal schedule or to schedule meetings with others (**Figure 7.1**). The Calendar folder stores three types of items:

- **Appointments**. An appointment is an activity that consumes a block of your time—for example, an interview that you will conduct on Monday, your daily lunch break, or your weekly chess game.
- **Events**. An event is an occurrence that lasts one or more complete days, but doesn't fully consume your time—for example, your birthday, a holiday, or casual dress day at your company.
- **Meetings**. A meeting is like an appointment, but it includes other people or resources that you schedule using Outlook.

In this book, *calendar item* is the general term used to refer to any of these items.

In this chapter, you'll learn:

- How to create appointments
- How to define events
- How to schedule meetings
- How to work with items in the Calendar folder when viewing a day, a week, or a month
- How to set Calendar folder options

✔ Tip

- The techniques given in this chapter apply to the default Calendar folder as well as to any new calendar-item folders that you've created.

Creating Appointments

You can create either a one-time appointment or a recurring appointment. A recurring appointment is one that occurs at regular intervals—daily, weekly, monthly, or yearly.

To create a one-time appointment:

1. Open the Calendar folder.
2. Click the New button  on the Standard toolbar, or choose Actions > New Appointment, or press Ctrl-N.

   Outlook will open an Appointment form (**Figure 7.2**).
3. Describe the appointment by entering information into the controls in the Appointment form:
   - Enter a brief description of the appointment in the **Subject** text box and, if you wish, a more detailed description in the large text box.
   - Type the appointment location in the **Location** list box or select a location that you've previously typed from the drop-down list.
   - Type the appointment starting date in the first **Start time** list box, or click the down-arrow and select a date from the drop-down calendar (**Figure 7.3**). Type the appointment starting time in the second **Start time** list box or select a time from the drop-down list (**Figure 7.4**).
   - In a similar manner, specify the appointment ending date and time in the two **End time** list boxes.

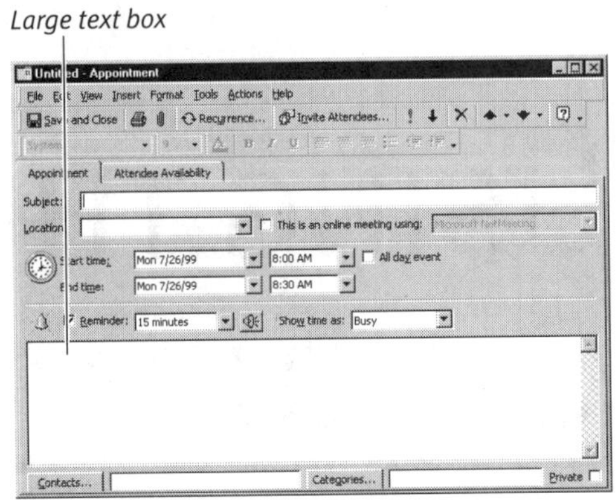

Figure 7.2 A blank Appointment form for defining a new appointment.

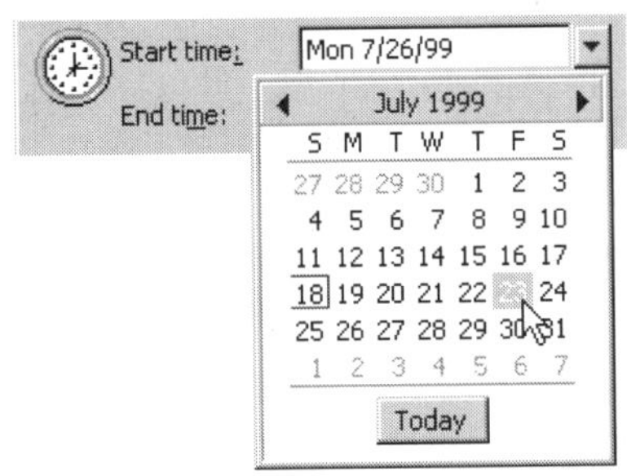

Figure 7.3 Selecting an appointment starting date from the drop-down calendar.

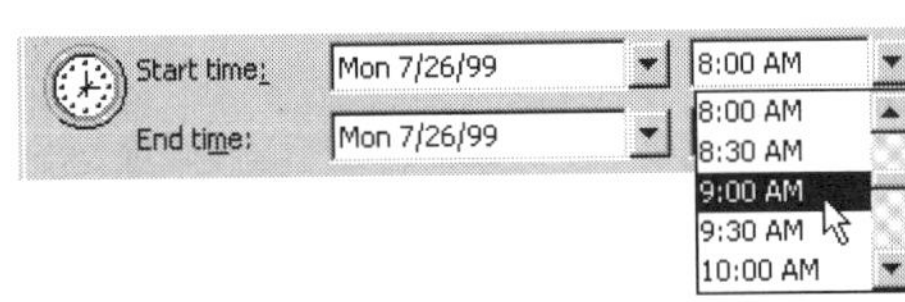

Figure 7.4 Selecting an appointment starting time from the drop-down list.

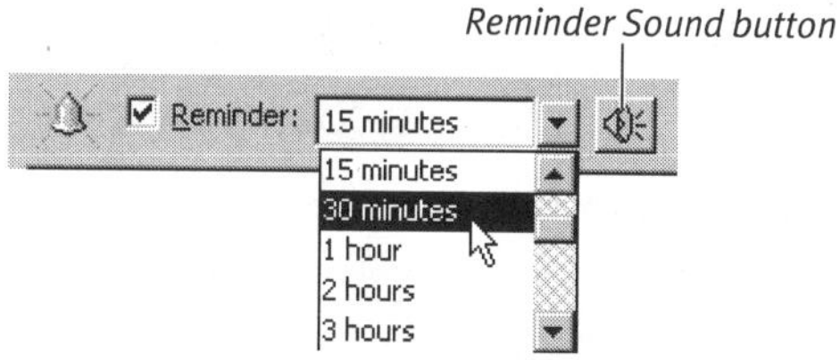

Figure 7.5 Selecting the reminder time from the drop-down list.

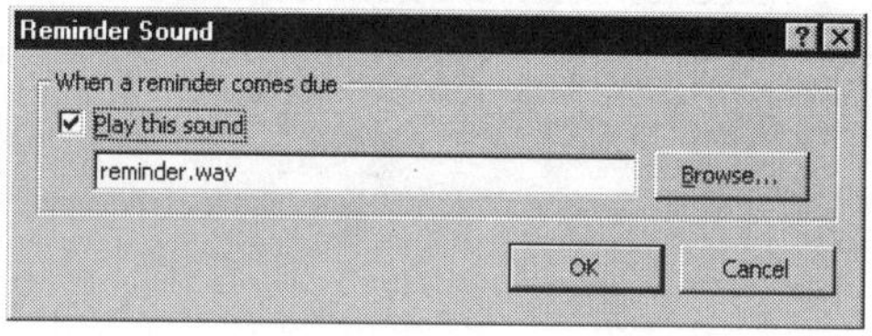

Figure 7.6 The Reminder Sound dialog box.

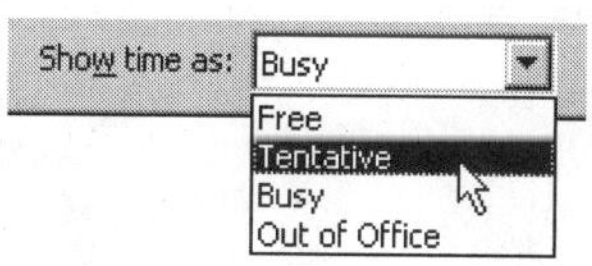

Figure 7.7 Selecting the way Outlook will mark the appointment in the Calendar folder.

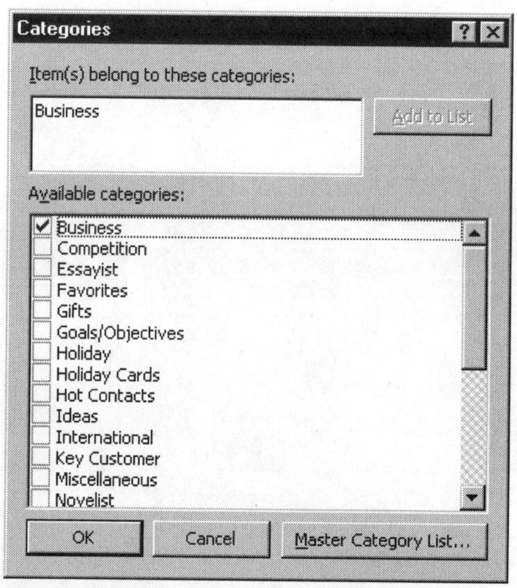

Figure 7.8 Selecting one or more categories for an appointment in the Categories dialog box.

- If you want Outlook to display a reminder message box just before the appointment starting time, check the **Reminder** option. Also, specify the amount of time before the start of the appointment that the reminder is to be displayed. You can do this by typing a time in the list box or selecting a time from the drop-down list (**Figure 7.5**). If you want to turn the reminder sound off or on or select a different sound, click the Reminder Sound button to open the Reminder Sound dialog box (**Figure 7.6**).
- To indicate how the time will be marked in your Calendar folder (see the second tip in the following set), select an item from the **Show time as** list box (**Figure 7.7**).
- If a contact in your Contacts folder is associated with the appointment (for example, the person you're going to be meeting), type the contact's name in the **Contacts** text box, or click the **Contacts** button to select that contact from your Contacts folder. This will link the appointment to the contact. You'll then be able to open the contact by double-clicking the name in the **Contacts** list box. Also, the Activities tab of the Contact form for that contact will list the appointment, along with any other linked Outlook items.
- If you want to assign a category to the appointment, type it in the **Categories** text box, or click the **Categories** button to select a category from the Categories dialog box (**Figure 7.8**). You can use a category to sort, filter, group, or find appointments (these operations are discussed in Chapter 3).

(continued on next page)

- If you're sharing your Calendar folder but you want the appointment to be hidden, check the **Private** option. (Sharing folders is discussed in "Sharing Outlook Folders over the Internet" and "E/S Sharing Outlook Folders over a Network" in Chapter 4.)
- If the meeting is going to be an online meeting using Microsoft NetMeeting or NetShow Services, check the **This is an online meeting using** option and select the online meeting software you're using from the adjoining list box (Microsoft NetMeeting or NetShow Services) (**Figure 7.9**). When you check **This is an online meeting using**, the Appointment form displays several additional controls for which you'll need to make selections (the particular options you see depend upon the online meeting software you select).

  A completed Appointment form is shown in **Figure 7.10**.

4. Click the Save And Close button Save and Close on the form's Standard toolbar to save your new appointment in the Calendar folder and to close the Appointment form.

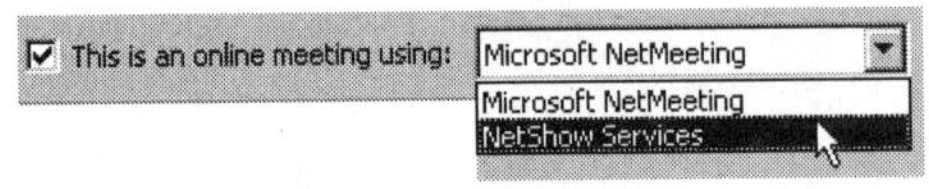

Figure 7.9 Setting up an online meeting.

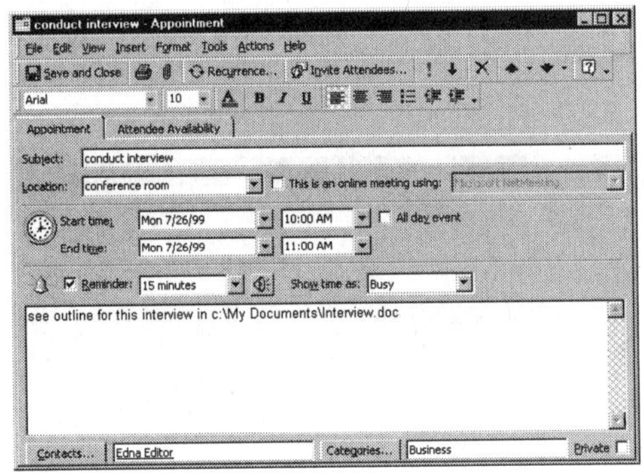

Figure 7.10 A completed Appointment form.

✔ Tips

- You can quickly specify the starting and ending dates and times for an appointment by selecting the time in the Day/Week/Month view of the Calendar folder prior to opening the Appointment form. You select times just like you select items.
- When you display a single day or work week in the Day/Week/Month view of the Calendar folder, Outlook color codes the border around each appointment according to your selection in the **Show time as** list box, as follows: Free is white, Tentative is light blue, Busy is dark blue, and Out Of Office is dark magenta.

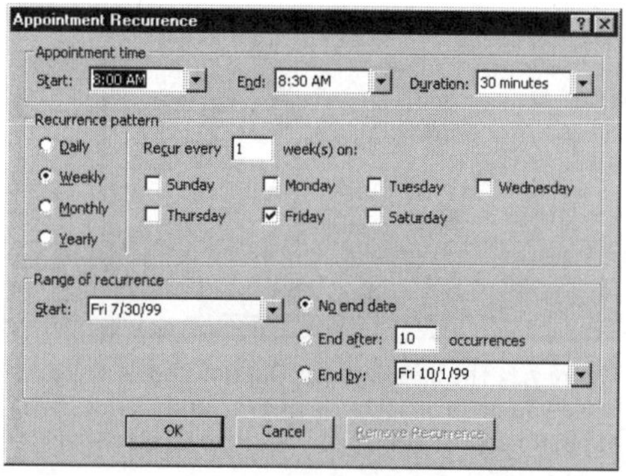

Figure 7.11 The Appointment Recurrence dialog box.

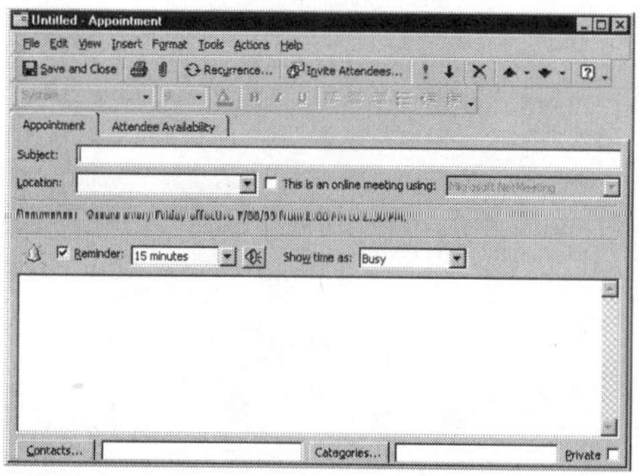

Figure 7.12 The Appointment form for a recurring appointment.

- You can enter several names in the Contacts or Categories text boxes. If you type the names, separate them using commas or semicolons.
- Clicking the Recurrence toolbar button Recurrence... or choosing Actions > Recurrence opens the Appointment Recurrence dialog box, which lets you convert a one-time appointment into a recurring appointment, as discussed in the next section.
- Checking the **All day event** option converts the appointment into an event, which is described in "Defining Events," later in the chapter.
- Clicking the Invite Attendees toolbar button Invite Attendees... or choosing Actions > Invite Attendees, or adding one or more attendees on the Attendee Availability tab converts the appointment into a meeting, which is described in "Scheduling Meetings," later in the chapter.

To create a recurring appointment:

1. Open the Calendar folder.
2. Choose Actions > New Recurring Appointment.

   Outlook will open the Appointment Recurrence dialog box (**Figure 7.11**).
3. Define the appointment time, recurrence pattern, and range of recurrence by selecting options in the Appointment Recurrence dialog box. Click the **OK** button when you're done.

   Outlook will now open an Appointment form. The form will be the same as the one used for defining a one-time appointment, but will lack the controls for setting the starting and ending dates and times (**Figure 7.12**), because with a recurring appointment, all dates and times are set in the Appointment Recurrence dialog box.

(continued on next page)

4. Describe the appointment by entering information into the controls on the Appointment form, following the instructions given in "To create a one-time appointment," earlier in the chapter.

5. Click the Save And Close toolbar button to save your new recurring appointment in the Calendar folder and to close the Appointment form.

✔ Tips

- To change an appointment's recurrence information or to remove the recurrence, reopen the Appointment Recurrence dialog box by clicking the Recurrence toolbar button or choosing Actions > Recurrence on the Appointment form. To remove the recurrence, thereby converting the appointment to a one-time appointment, click the **Remove Recurrence** button in the Appointment Recurrence dialog box.

- If you open an occurrence of a recurring appointment to view or edit it, Outlook will give you the opportunity to open the specific occurrence or to open (and thereby modify) the appointment information for the entire series (**Figure 7.13**).

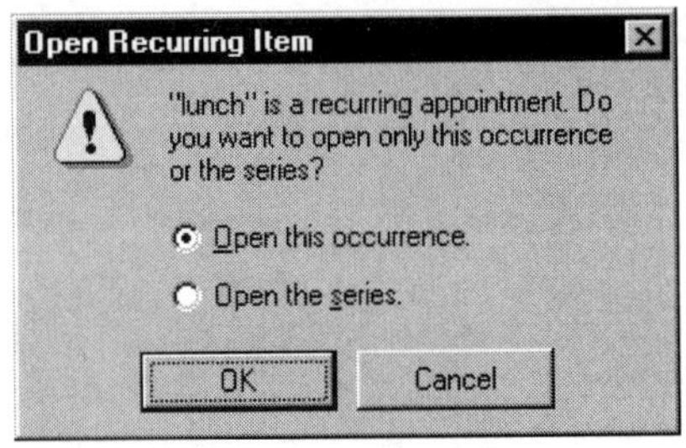

Figure 7.13 The message box Outlook shows when you open an instance of a recurring appointment.

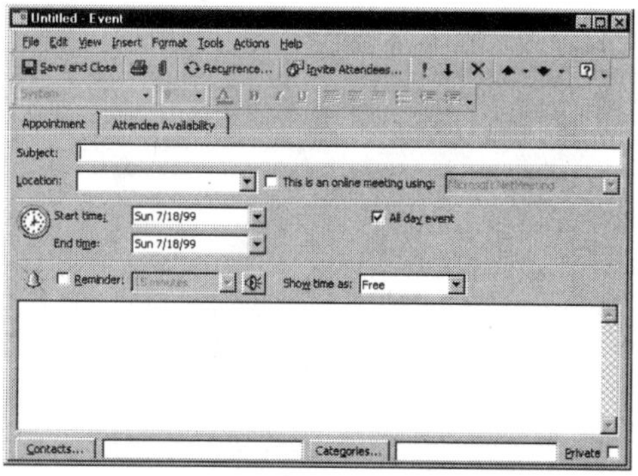

Figure 7.14 The Event form.

Defining Events

As with an appointment, you can define either a one-time event or a recurring event. The following procedure shows you how to define either type of event.

To define an event:

1. Open the Calendar folder.
2. Choose Actions > New All Day Event.

   Outlook will open the Event form (**Figure 7.14**), which is the same as the Appointment form except that **All day event** is checked. Also, the form lets you specify starting and ending dates, but not specific starting and ending times (that's because an event always lasts one or more complete days).
3. Describe the event by entering information into the controls in the Event form, following the instructions given in "To create a one-time appointment," earlier in the chapter. Be sure to leave the **All day event** button checked (otherwise the event will be converted to an appointment).
4. If you want to create a recurring event, which is analogous to a recurring appointment, click the Recurrence toolbar button or choose Actions > Recurrence, and in the Appointment Recurrence dialog box define the event time, recurrence pattern, and range of recurrence (see **Figure 7.11**, earlier in the chapter).
5. Click the Save And Close toolbar button to save your new event in the Calendar folder and to close the Event form.

Scheduling Meetings

You can use Outlook to schedule meetings with other people. When you do this, Outlook stores a meeting item in your Calendar folder, and it sends copies of the meeting item to the people you invite.

✔ Tip

- Scheduling a meeting allows you to share a specific calendar item (a meeting) with other people. Keep in mind that you can also share an entire Calendar folder with other people using the techniques discussed in "Sharing Outlook Folders over the Internet" and "E/S Sharing Outlook Folders over a Network" in Chapter 4.

To schedule a meeting:

1. Open the Calendar folder.
2. Choose Actions > New Meeting Request, or press Ctrl-Shift-Q.

   Outlook will open the Meeting form (**Figure 7.15**), which is the same as an Appointment form except that it includes a **To** button and a text box.
3. In the **To** text box, enter the address or addresses of all meeting *attendees* (the people you want to invite to the meeting). Follow the instructions given in "I/O To address a message" or "C/W To address a message" in Chapter 6.
4. Describe the meeting by entering information into the controls on the Meeting form, following the instructions given in "To create a one-time appointment," earlier in the chapter.

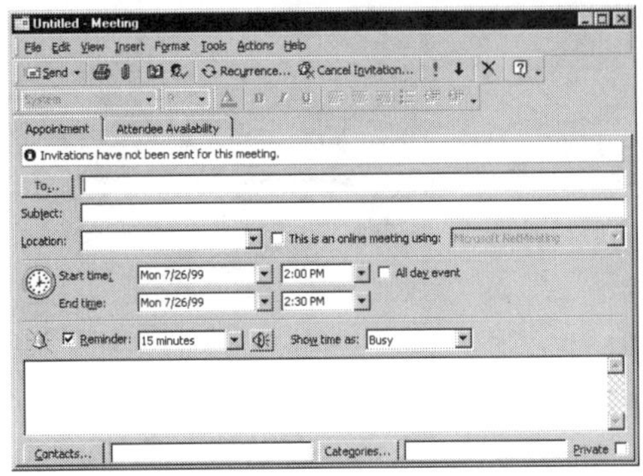

Figure 7.15 The Meeting form.

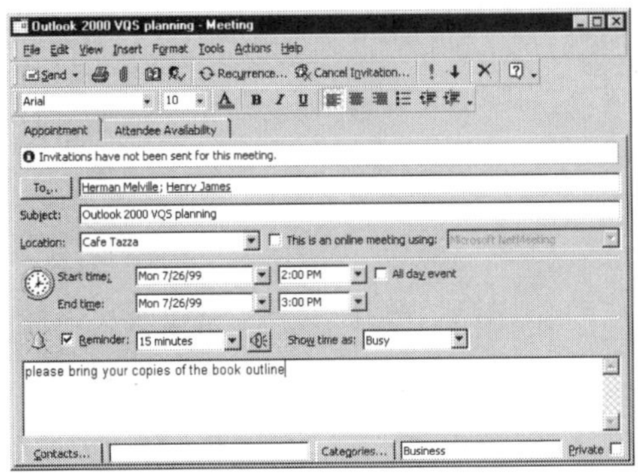

Figure 7.16 A completed Meeting form, ready to send to attendees.

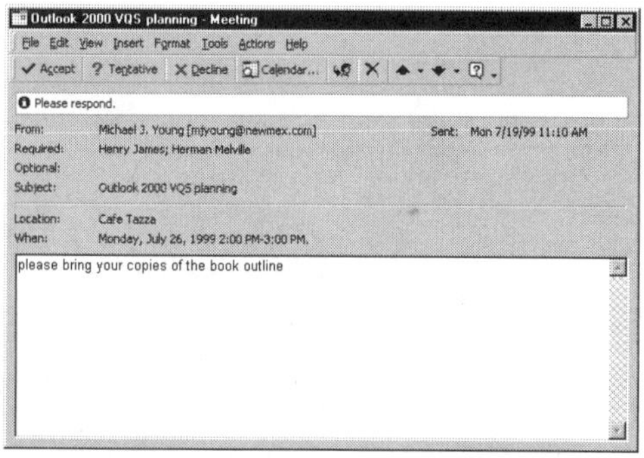

Figure 7.17 A meeting request in an attendee's Inbox.

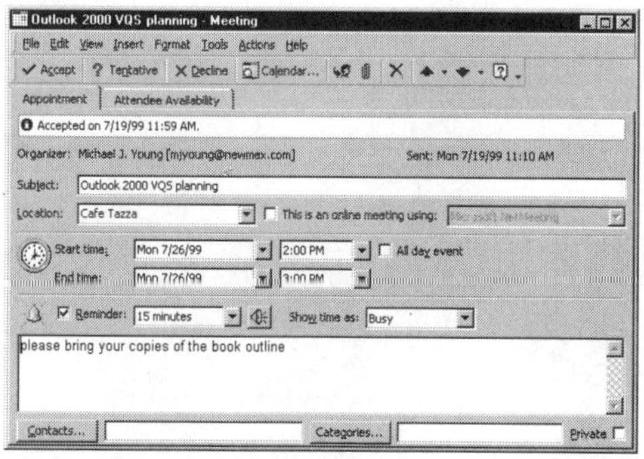

Figure 7.18 A meeting item that was automatically added to an attendee's Calendar folder.

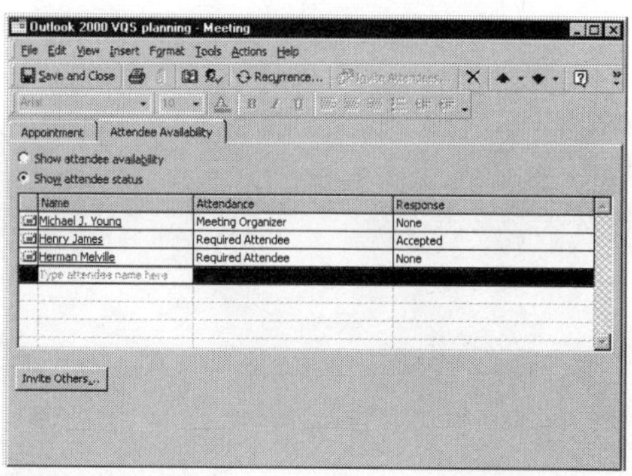

Figure 7.19 Viewing the responses from the meeting attendees.

5. If you want to create a recurring meeting, which is analogous to a recurring appointment, click the Recurrence toolbar button or choose Actions > Recurrence, and in the Appointment Recurrence dialog box define the meeting time, recurrence pattern, and range of recurrence (see **Figure 7.11**, earlier in the chapter). (You can also create a recurring meeting by choosing Actions > New Recurring Meeting to open the form in step 2.)

   Figure 7.16 shows a completed Meeting form.

6. Click the Send toolbar button.

   Outlook will save the meeting in your Calendar folder, close the Meeting form, and send a meeting request to each attendee.

   The meeting request will appear in the Inbox of each attendee (**Figure 7.17**). An attendee can reply by opening the request and clicking the Accept, Tentative, or Decline toolbar button. If an attendee clicks the Accept or Tentative button, the meeting is added to his or her Calendar folder (**Figure 7.18**).

   When an attendee replies, the response is sent back to you by e-mail, and Outlook records the response in the original meeting item in your Calendar folder.

7. If you want to see which attendees have replied and to view their responses, open the meeting item in your Calendar folder, open the Attendee Availability tab, and select the **Show attendee status** option (**Figure 7.19**).

(continued on next page)

✔ Tips

- If an attendee doesn't use Outlook but has an e-mail program that supports the standard *iCalendar* format, you should send the meeting request in this format by choosing Tools > Send As iCalendar in the form (don't choose the command if it's checked, indicating that the option is already on).
- Scheduling meetings won't work if you or an attendee use an e-mail service, such as CompuServe, that doesn't transmit the required information. In this case, the attendee will receive a meeting request e-mail message, but the form won't display the buttons required to reply
- Checking the **All day event** option on the Meeting form converts the meeting to an *invited event*, which is an event to which others are invited.
- Clicking the Cancel Invitation toolbar button 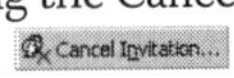 or choosing Actions > Cancel Invitation on the Meeting form converts the meeting into an appointment (or an event if **All day event** is checked).
- If all your attendees have published their free/busy schedules on the Internet or on an Exchange Server network, you can open the Attendee Availability tab on the Meeting form, choose the **Show attendee availability** option, and use the controls to locate times when all attendees are available for your meeting. For more information, type *schedule a meeting* in the Office Assistant.

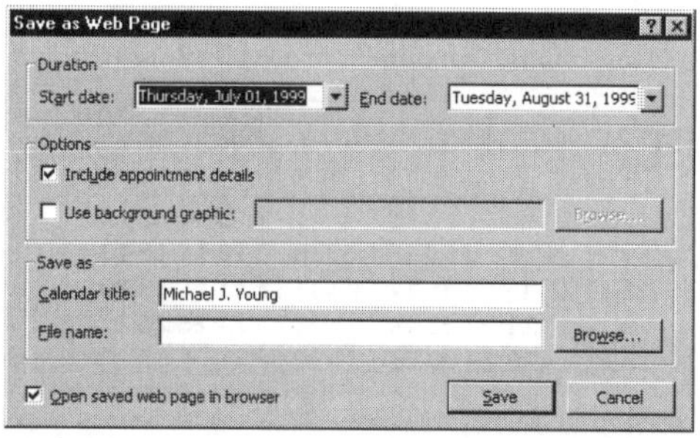

Figure 7.20 The Save As Web Page dialog box.

Working with Items in the Calendar Folder

The most commonly used view of the Calendar folder is Day/Week/Month, which displays your appointments, events, and meetings in a typical calendar or day planner format. In this view, you can display a single day, a work week, a full week, or a month.

✔ Tips

- If you want to publish your Calendar folder on the Internet, you can save it as a Web page by choosing File > Save As Web Page and selecting options in the Save As Web Page dialog box (**Figure 7.20**).
- You can resize or remove any of the panes in the Day/Week/Month view (the time list, the Date Navigator, or the TaskPad) by dragging the appropriate border between panes.

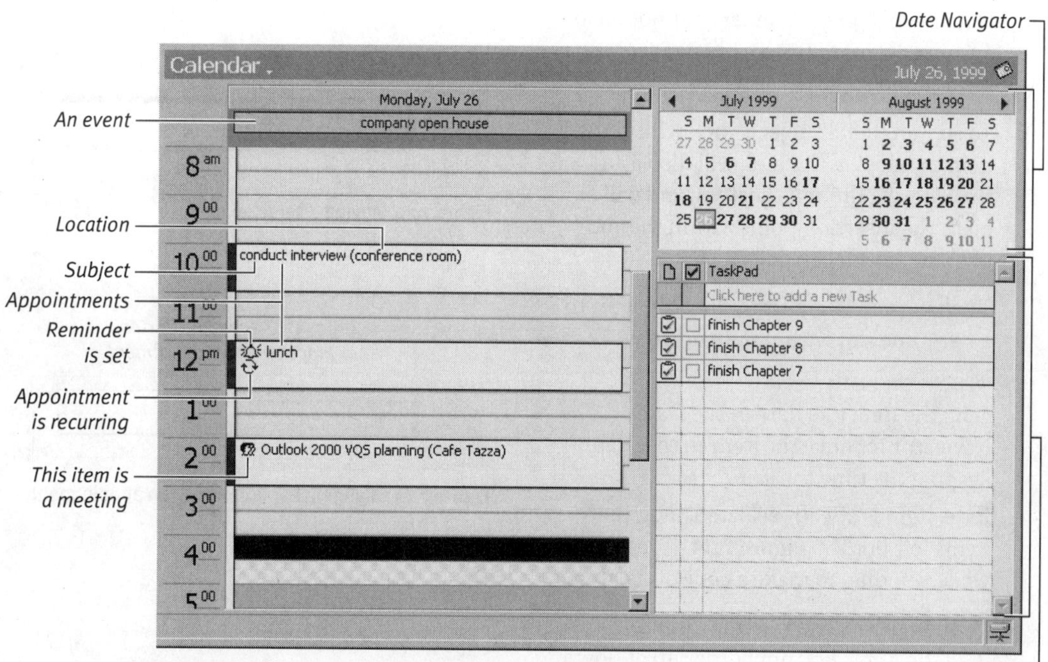

Figure 7.21 Displaying a single day in the Calendar folder.

To work with a single day:

1. Activate the Day/Week/Month view of the Calendar folder.
2. Click the Day button on the Standard toolbar, or choose View > Day.

   Outlook will initially display the current day, in a day planner format (see **Figure 7.21** on the previous page).
3. To view a particular day, click that date in the Date Navigator (**Figure 7.22**).
4. To add a new appointment, click the desired appointment time and type the appointment subject.

   or

   Double-click the time to open a blank Appointment form.
5. To add a new event, click in the banner at the top of the list of times (but not on an existing event) and type the event subject.

   or

   Double-click in the banner (but not on an existing event) to open a blank Event form (**Figure 7.23**).
6. To edit an item's subject, click within the item to select it. Outlook will display a thick border around the item, and will place the insertion point within the subject text so you can edit it.
7. To change an item's time, drag the item to a new time slot within the same day.

   or

   Drag the item to a date in the Date Navigator to move the item to that date, keeping the time the same.

   If the item is already selected, drag the item's left border (**Figure 7.24**). Press Ctrl while you drag to make a *copy* of the item.
8. To change a calendar item's duration, drag the item's bottom border up or down (**Figure 7.25**).

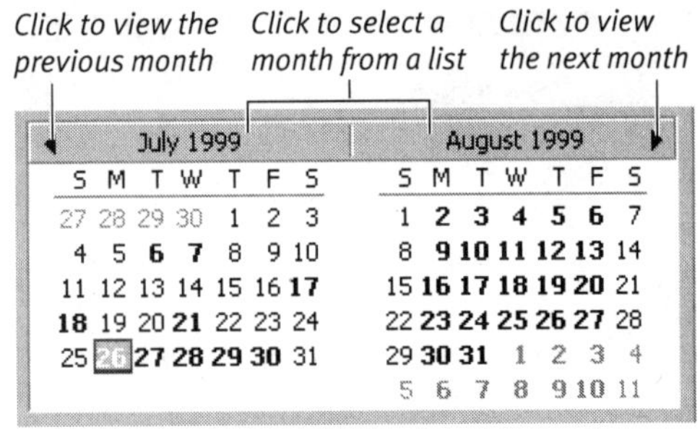

Figure 7.22 The Date Navigator.

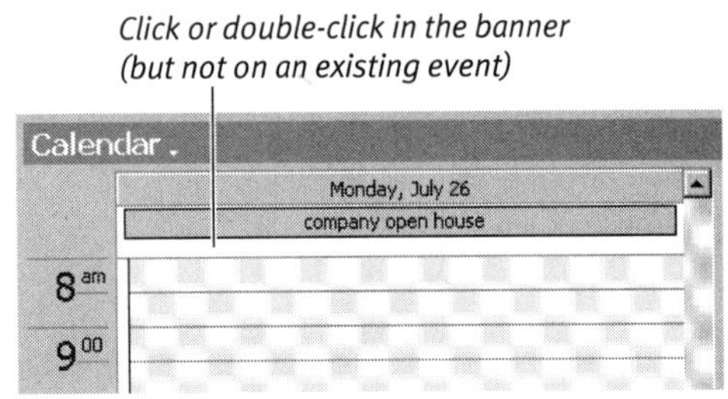

Figure 7.23 Adding a new event.

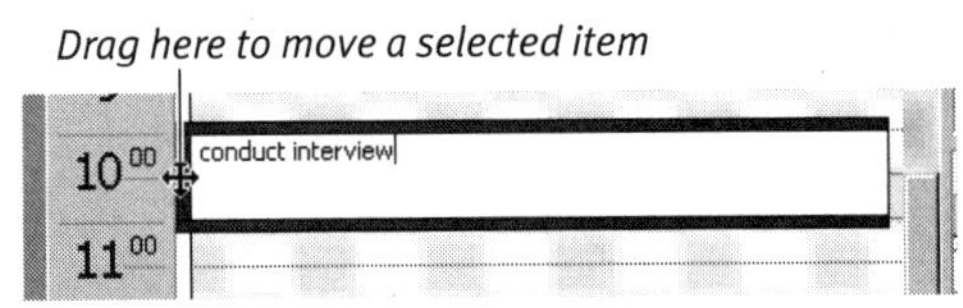

Figure 7.24 Moving a selected item.

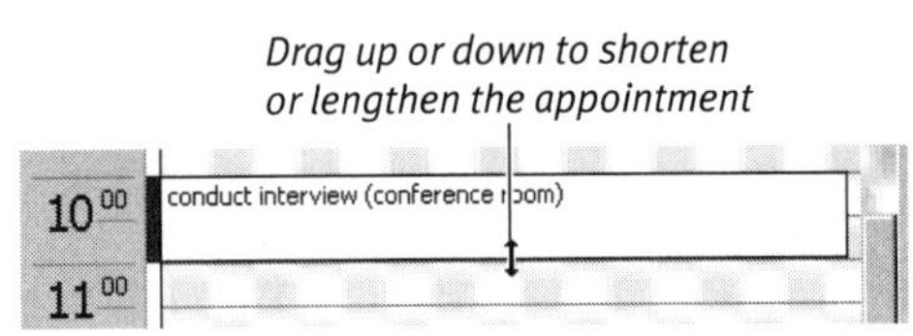

Figure 7.25 Changing the duration of an appointment.

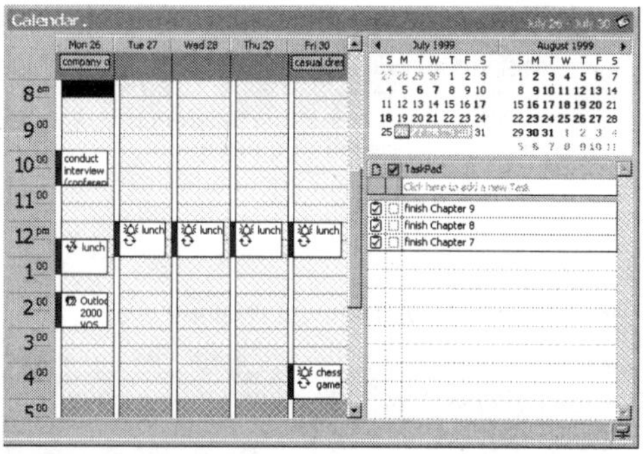

Figure 7.26 Viewing a work week in the Calendar folder.

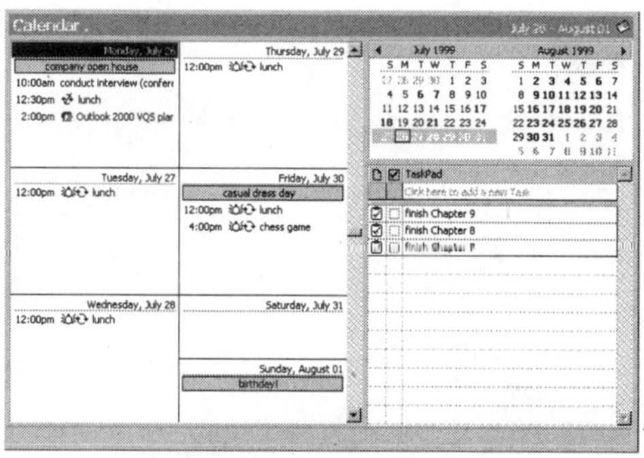

Figure 7.27 Viewing an entire week in the Calendar folder.

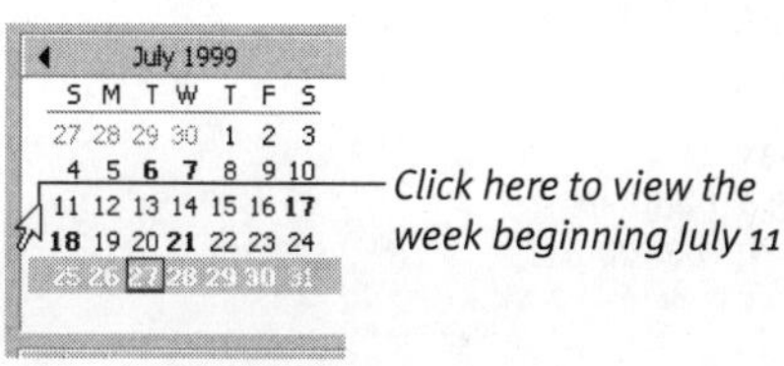

Figure 7.28 Selecting a week to view.

9. To open an item in a form, double-click it or use any of the other methods given in "To open an item" in Chapter 3. (If the item is already selected, double-click its border.)

✔ Tips

- The TaskPad lets you view and work with the tasks in your Tasks folder, which is described in Chapter 9.
- To quickly view the current day, click the Go To Today button  on the Standard toolbar.
- To view a specific date, choose View > Go To > Go To Date, or press Ctrl-G, and enter the date in the Go To Date dialog box.

To work with a week:

1. Activate the Day/Week/Month view of the Calendar folder.
2. To view a work week (Monday through Friday) (**Figure 7.26**), click the Work Week button 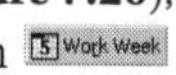 on the Standard toolbar, or choose View > Work Week.

   or

   To view a full week (Monday through Sunday) (**Figure 7.27**), click the Week button  on the Standard toolbar, or choose View > Week.
3. Work with the items using the techniques given in the previous section, "To work with a single day," but keep in mind the following:
   - To view a particular week, click to the left of the week in the Date Navigator (**Figure 7.28**).
   - If you're viewing a full week, clicking on a day and typing a subject adds an *event*, and double-clicking a day opens an Event form.

(continued on next page)

WORKING WITH ITEMS IN THE CALENDAR FOLDER

- If you're viewing a full week, you can drag an item to a different day, but to change an item's time or duration, you have to open the item and edit the times on the form.

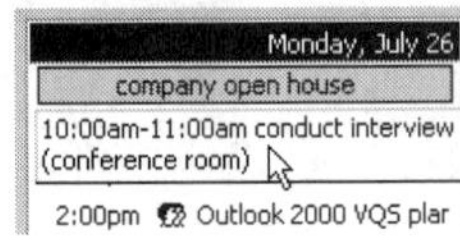

Figure 7.29 Viewing the full item text in a ScreenTip.

✔ Tip

- If the text for an item is cut off, you can point to the item and view the full text in a ScreenTip (**Figure 7.29**).

To work with a month:

1. Activate the Day/Week/Month view of the Calendar folder.
2. Click the Month button on the Standard toolbar, or choose View > Month.

   Outlook will initially display the current month in a standard calendar format (**Figure 7.30**).
3. To view a different month, use the vertical scroll bar to scroll through the months, or pick a month in the Date Navigator (**Figure 7.31**).

   If the Date Navigator is hidden, drag the border at the right of the window toward the left.
4. Work with the items using the techniques given in the earlier section, "To work with a single day," but keep in mind the following:
   - Clicking on a day and typing a subject adds an *event*, and double-clicking a day opens an Event form.
   - You can drag an item to a different day, but to change its time or duration, you have to open the item and edit the times in the form.

Click here to see items that aren't shown

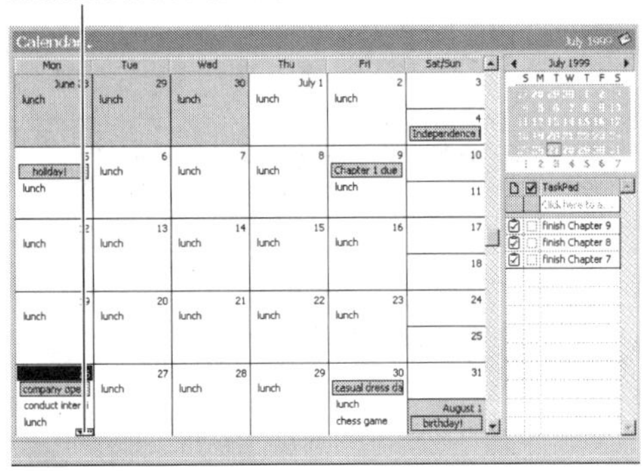

Figure 7.30 Displaying a month in the Calendar folder.

Click to view the previous month

Click to select a month from a list

Click to view the next month

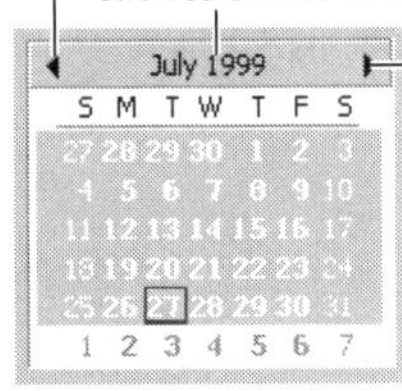

Figure 7.31 Selecting a month in the Date Navigator.

Add a reminder to new items and set the default reminder time

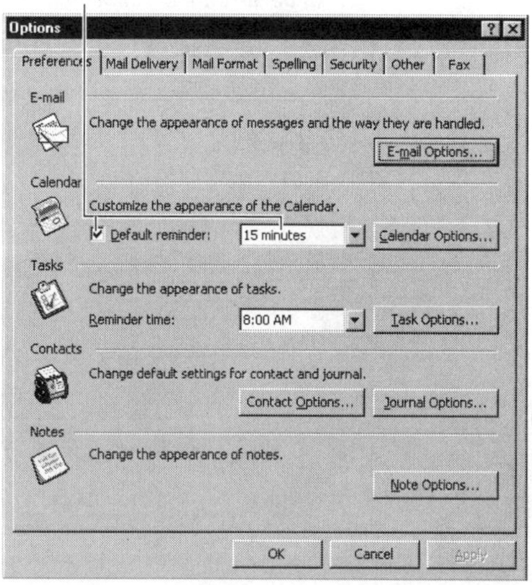

Figure 7.32 The Preferences tab of the Options dialog box.

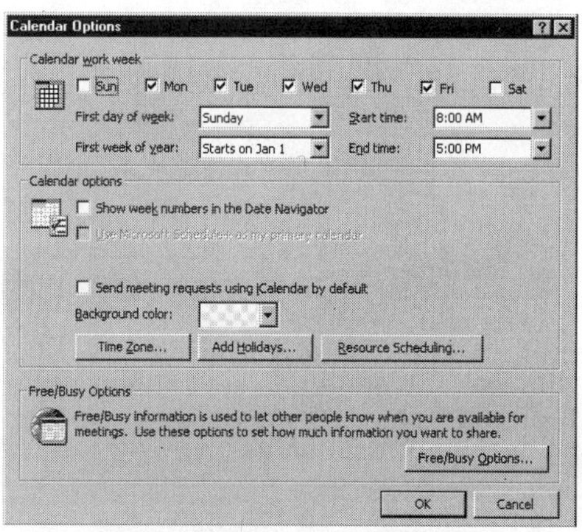

Figure 7.33 The Calendar Options dialog box.

To set Calendar options:

- To have Outlook display a reminder message by default for the new calendar items you create, choose Tools > Options; on the Preferences tab check **Default reminder** and select the default reminder time in the adjoining text box (**Figure 7.32**). (This is only a default setting. If you wish, you can turn off the reminder for a particular calendar item.)

  or

  To change the Calendar work week, to modify the Date Navigator, to change the Calendar background color, or to make other changes, click the **Calendar Options** button in the Preferences tab of the Options dialog box (**Figure 7.32**) and select the desired options in the Calendar Options dialog box (**Figure 7.33**).

(continued on next page)

or

To change the font used in the Date Navigator or to modify the features of reminders, choose Tools > Options, open the Other tab, click the **Advanced Options** button, and select options in the Advanced Options dialog box (**Figure 7.34**).

or

To modify features of the currently active view of the Calendar folder, choose View > Current View > Customize Current View, click the **Other Settings** button, and select the desired options in the Other Settings or Format Day/Week/Month View dialog box (**Figure 7.35**) (the name and contents of the dialog box vary according to the current view).

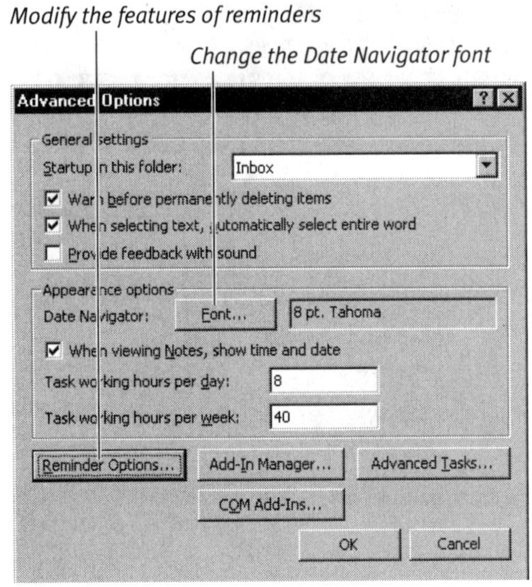

Figure 7.34 Setting Calendar options in the Advanced Options dialog box.

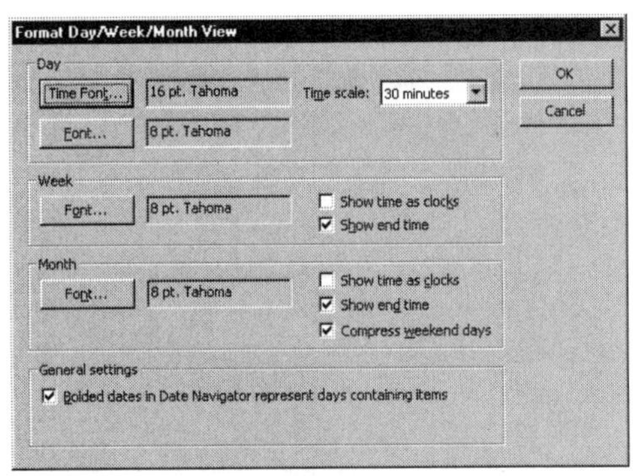

Figure 7.35 The Format Day/Week/Month View dialog box for changing features of the Day/Week/Month view of the Calendar folder.

USING THE CONTACTS FOLDER

8

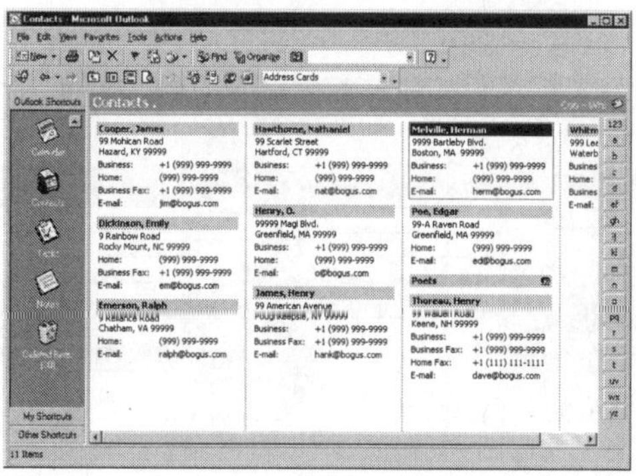

Figure 8.1 The Contact folder in the commonly used Address Cards view.

You can use your Contacts folder to store information about friends, business associates, and companies. This information can include a name; a title; a company name; a Web page address; several street addresses, phone numbers, and e-mail addresses; and many other pieces of information (**Figure 8.1**).

You can use the items in your Contacts folder to look up information on people or companies, to send them e-mail, to dial their phone numbers, to visit their Web sites, or to contact them in other ways.

In this chapter, you'll learn:

- How to create a new contact item: a contact or a distribution list
- How to find a contact
- How to send a messages to a contact, dial a contact's phone number, visit a contact's Web site, and reach a contact in other ways
- How to set options for the Contacts folder

✔ Tip

- You can use most of the instructions given in this chapter either with the default Contacts folder or with another contact-item folder that you've created.

Creating Contact Items

You can create two different types of items in your Contacts folder (**Figure 8.2**):

- A **contact**, which stores information on a single person or company.
- A **distribution list**, which stores a list of names and addresses or fax numbers. You can use a distribution list to send an e-mail or fax message, a meeting request, or a task assignment to an entire group of people (for example, everyone in your workgroup). To address one of these items to the group, you select the name of the distribution list rather than selecting or entering an individual address.

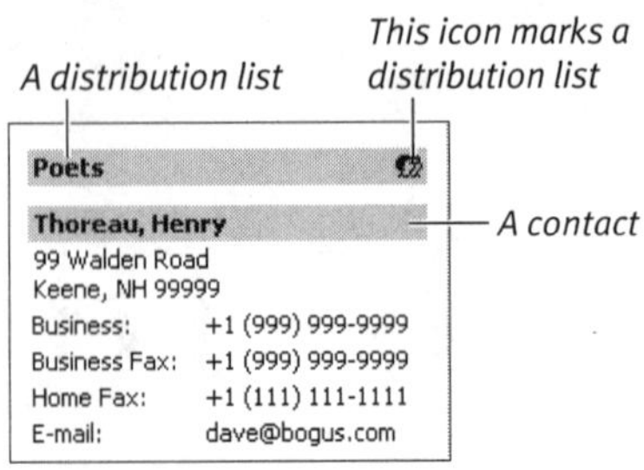

Figure 8.2 A contact and a distribution list in the Contacts folder (Address Cards view).

To create a contact:

1. Open the Contacts folder.
2. Click the New button [New] on the Standard toolbar, or choose Actions > New Contact, or press Ctrl-N.

   Outlook will open a Contact form (**Figure 8.3**).

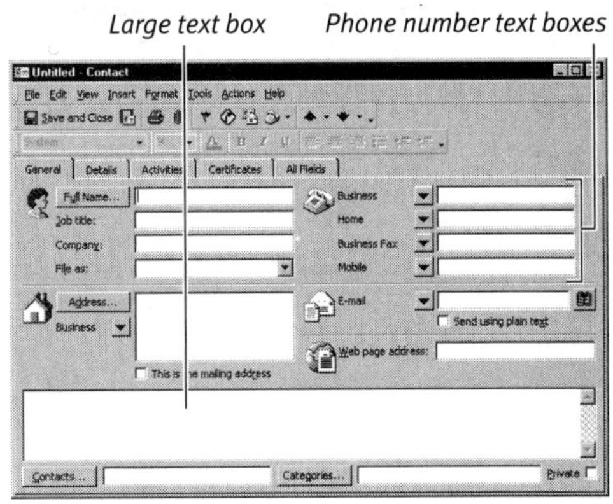

Figure 8.3 A Contact form, ready to define a new contact.

3. Enter the desired information into the controls on the General tab of the Contact form:
   - Type the contact's full name in the **Full Name** text box (see the first tip in the following set).
   - Type the contact's job title and company (if any) in the **Job title** and **Company** text boxes.
   - Use the **Address** text box to enter up to three street or post office box addresses, as shown in **Figure 8.4** (see the first tip in the following set).
   - If the contact receives mail at the address shown in the **Address** text box, check the **This is the mailing address** option.

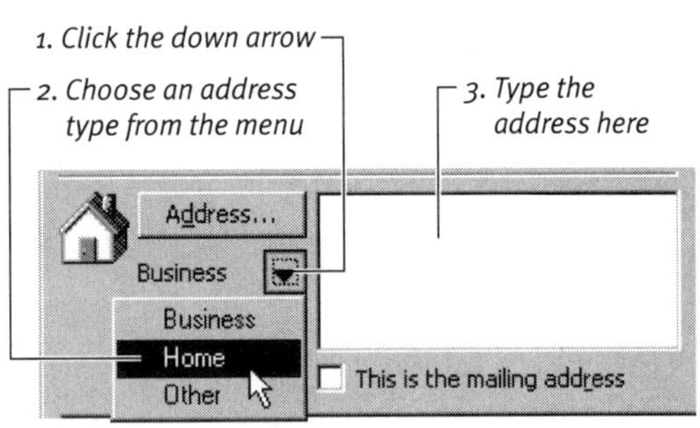

Figure 8.4 Entering a street or post office box address.

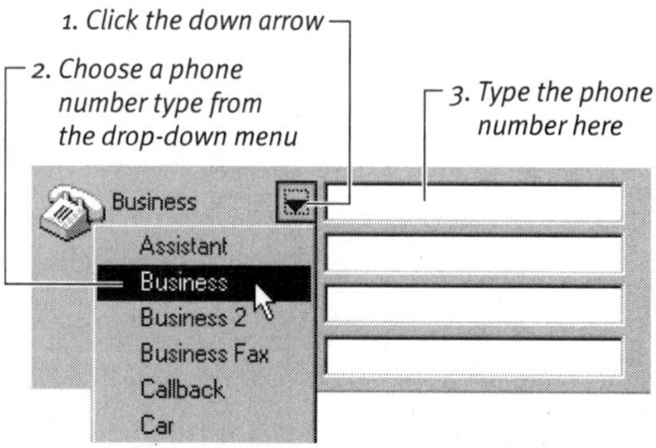

Figure 8.5 Entering a phone number in one of the phone number text boxes.

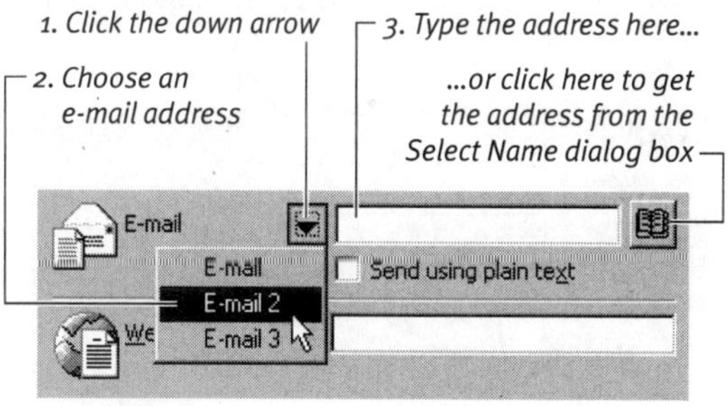

Figure 8.6 Entering an e-mail address.

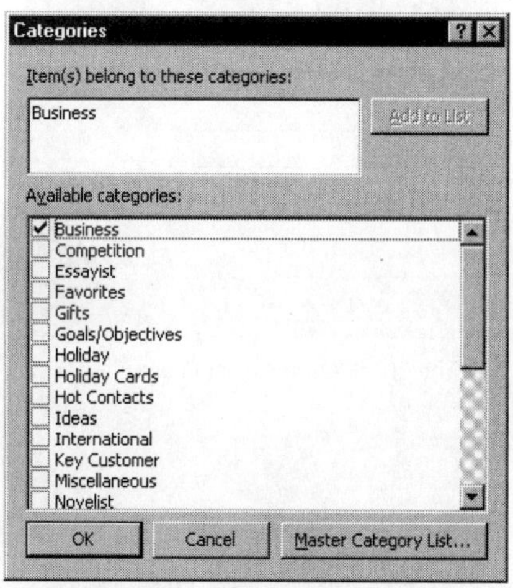

Figure 8.7 Selecting one or more categories for a contact in the Categories dialog box.

- Use the phone number text boxes to enter up to four phone numbers, as shown in **Figure 8.5**.
- Use the **E-mail** text box to enter up to three e-mail addresses for the contact, as shown in **Figure 8.6** (see the second tip in the following set).
- If the contact's e-mail service or software doesn't support the Rich Text or HTML e-mail format, check the **Send using plain text** option so that all e-mail messages will be sent to the contact in plain text.
- If the contact has a Web site, type the full address of the home page in the **Web page address** text box.
- If you want to enter any general information (such as instructions on finding the contact's house), type it in the large text box.
- If you want to link another contact to the current contact, type the other contact's name in the **Contacts** text box or click the **Contacts** button to select that contact from your Contacts folder. You'll then be able to open the other contact by double-clicking the name in the **Contacts** list box. Also, the Activities tab of the Contact form for the other contact will list the current contact, along with any other linked Outlook items.
- If you want to assign a category to the contact, type it in the **Categories** text box or click the **Categories** button to select a category from the Categories dialog box (**Figure 8.7**). You can use a category to sort, filter, group, or find contacts (these operations are discussed in Chapter 3).
- If you're sharing your Contacts folder but you want the contact to be hidden, check the **Private** option. (Sharing folders is discussed in "Sharing Outlook

(continued on next page)

Folders over the Internet" and "E/S Sharing Outlook Folders over a Network" in Chapter 4.)

4. To enter the contact's department, office, profession, nickname, and other less commonly used information, open the Details tab.

   Figure 8.8 shows a completed Contact form.

5. Click the Save And Close button on the form's Standard toolbar to save the new contact in the Contacts folder and to close the form.

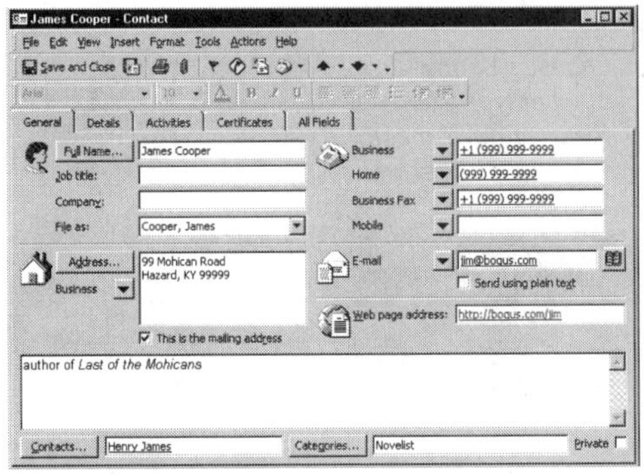

Figure 8.8 A completed Contact form.

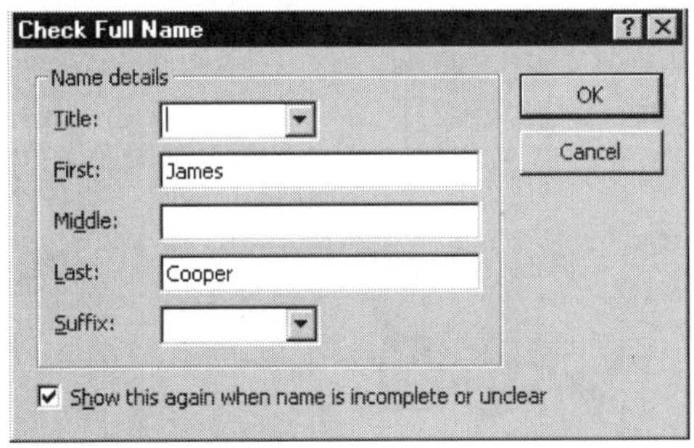

Figure 8.9 The Check Full Name dialog box.

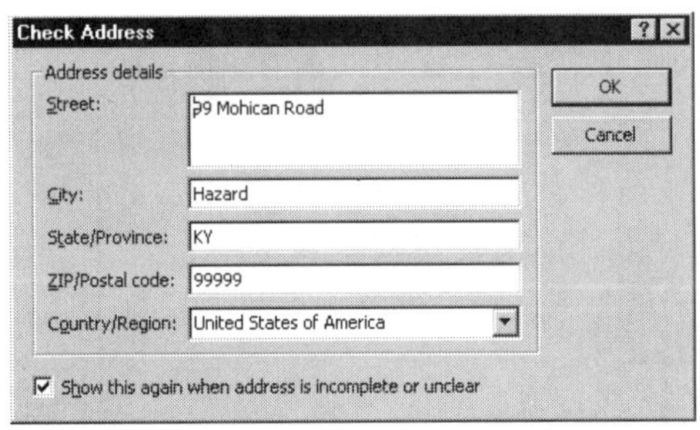

Figure 8.10 The Check Address dialog box.

✔ Tips

- Outlook divides the name and the address you type into separate fields, such as *first name* and *last name* or *street* and *city*. You can sort, filter, group, search, or perform other operations using these individual fields. To see how Outlook has divided the name or address you typed—and to make corrections if necessary—click the **Full Name** or **Address** button to display the Check Full Name (**Figure 8.9**) or Check Address (**Figure 8.10**) dialog box. Outlook will show one of these dialog boxes automatically if the name or address you type appears to be incorrectly formatted.
- Entering an e-mail address in the **E-mail** text box uses the same basic techniques as entering an e-mail address in the **To** text box of a message. For instructions, see "I/O To address a message" or "C/W To address a message" in Chapter 6.
- You can enter several names in the **Contacts** or **Categories** text boxes. If you type the names, separate them using commas or semicolons.

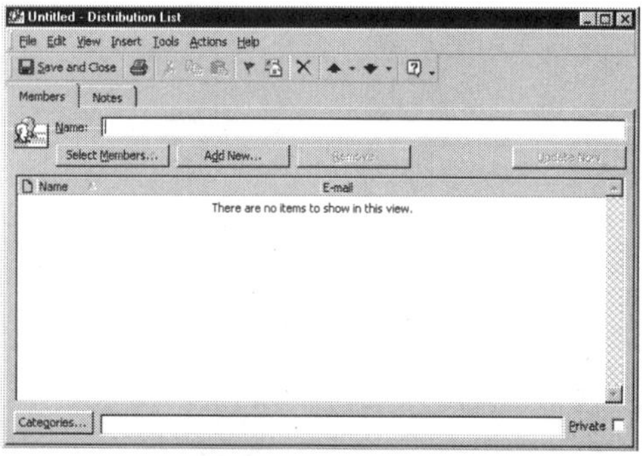

Figure 8.11 A Distribution List form, ready to define a new distribution list.

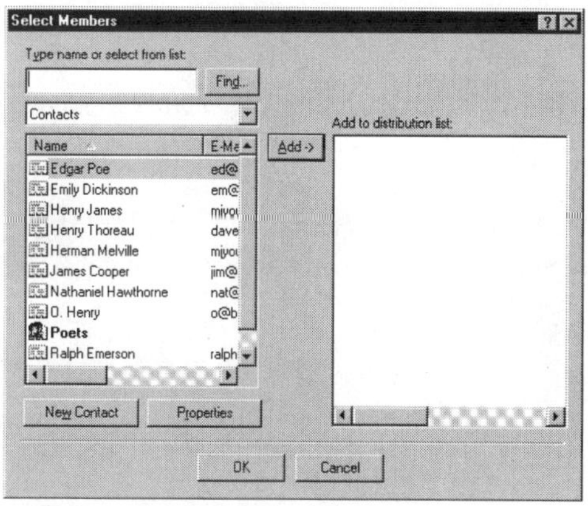

Figure 8.12 The Select Members dialog box as it appears in the Internet Only configuration.

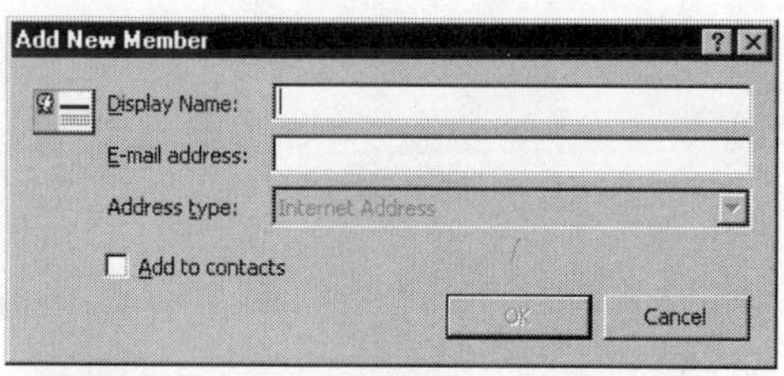

Figure 8.13 The Add New Member dialog box as it appears in the Internet Only configuration.

To create a distribution list:

1. Open the Contacts folder.
2. Choose Actions > New Distribution List, or press Ctrl-Shift-L.

   Outlook will open a Distribution List form (**Figure 8.11**).
3. Define the distribution list by entering information into the controls:
   - Type a name for the distribution list in the **Name** text box—for example, *Marketing Department* or *Camera Club Members*.
   - To add one or more distribution list members by picking them from your Contacts folder, from another address list, or from an Internet directory service, click the **Select Members** button to open the Select Members dialog box (**Figure 8.12**). This dialog box works just like the Select Names dialog box used to address a message, and it varies according to your e-mail configuration. For instructions, see "I/O To address a message" or "C/W To address a message" in Chapter 6.
   - To add a distribution list member by typing a new name and address, click the **Add New** button and fill in the Add New Member dialog box (**Figure 8.13**). Note that if you are using the Corporate Or Workgroup configuration, you'll need to select an address type in the **Address type** list.
   - To remove a member from the distribution list, select the name in the list and click the **Remove** button.

(continued on next page)

- If you want to assign a category to the distribution list, type it in the **Categories** text box, or click the **Categories** button to select a category from the Categories dialog box (see **Figure 8.7**, earlier in the chapter). You can use a category to sort, filter, group, or find distribution lists (these operations are discussed in Chapter 3).
- If you're sharing your Contacts folder but you want the distribution list to be hidden, check the **Private** option. (Sharing folders is discussed in "Sharing Outlook Folders over the Internet" and "E/S Sharing Outlook Folders over a Network" in Chapter 4.)
- If you want to type a description of the distribution list or enter any other information, open the Notes tab.

4. Click the Save And Close button on the form's Standard toolbar to save the new distribution list in the Contacts folder and close the form.

✔ Tips

- If, after you create a distribution list, you delete a member contact or change a member contact's e-mail address, you can update the information displayed on the Distribution List form by clicking the **Update Now** button.
- You can enter several names in the **Contacts** or **Categories** text boxes. If you type the names, separate them using commas or semicolons.

Figure 8.14 Typing a contact name in the Find A Contact list box.

Figure 8.15 Selecting a previous search item from the Find A Contact list box.

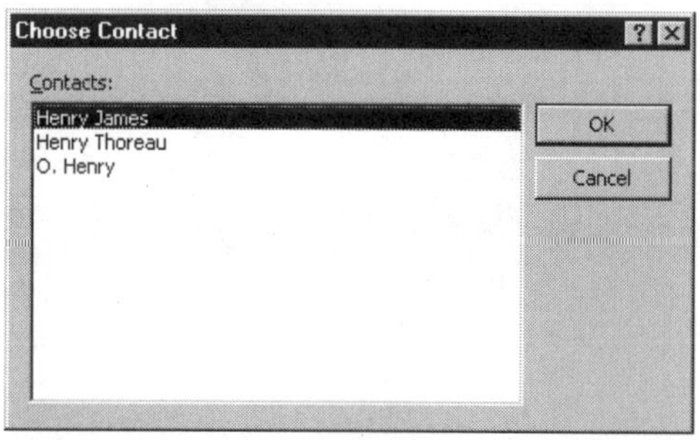

Figure 8.16 Choosing the contact you want to open. (This dialog box was displayed after I typed *henry* in the Find A Contact list box.)

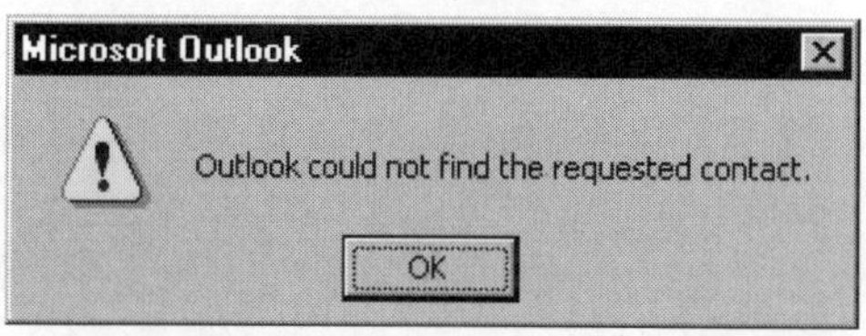

Figure 8.17 The message box that Outlook displays when it doesn't find a matching contact.

Working with Items in the Contacts Folder

In addition to the general ways of working with Outlook items that were discussed in Chapter 3, the Contacts folder provides some unique methods for working with contact items:

- In addition to using the standard Find pane or Advanced Find dialog box, you can quickly find a contact, regardless of which folder is open in Outlook, by using the Find A Contact list box on the Standard toolbar.
- You can use Actions menu commands to quickly "contact a contact" by sending the contact an e-mail message or letter, calling the contact, opening the contact's Web site, or reaching the contact in other ways.

To find a contact using the Find A Contact list box:

- In the Find A Contact list box on the Standard toolbar, type the first or last name or the e-mail address of the contact you want to find (**Figure 8.14**) and press Enter. You don't need to enter the full name.

  or

  Select a previously entered search item from the drop-down list (**Figure 8.15**).

  Outlook will now do one of the following:
  - If it finds a unique matching contact, it will open it in a form.
  - If it finds several matching contacts, it will let you choose one (**Figure 8.16**).
  - If it doesn't find a match, it will tell you so (**Figure 8.17**).

To contact a contact:

1. Open the Contacts folder.
2. Select a contact or a distribution list.
3. Choose the command to carry out the desired action:
   - To send an e-mail or fax message to the contact or distribution list, click the New Message To Contact button on the Standard toolbar or choose Actions > New Message To Contact.
   - To write a letter to the contact, choose Actions > New Letter To Contact. This command requires Microsoft Word and can be used only with a contact, *not* a distribution list.
   - To send a meeting request to the contact or distribution list, click the New Meeting Request To Contact button on the Advanced toolbar or choose Actions > New Meeting Request to Contact. See "Scheduling Meetings" in Chapter 7.
   - To call the contact, click the down arrow on the Dial button on the Standard toolbar and then choose a command from the drop-down menu (**Figure 8.18**), or choose Actions > Call Contact and then choose a command from the submenu. To use Outlook to call a contact, you must have a modem connected to the same line as your telephone.
   - To call the contact using Microsoft NetMeeting, click the Call Using NetMeeting button on the Advanced toolbar or choose Actions > Call Using NetMeeting. You can use this command only for a contact, *not* a distribution list.
   - To display a contact's home page in your Web browser, click the Explore Web Page button on the Advanced toolbar. You can use this command only for a contact, *not* a distribution list.

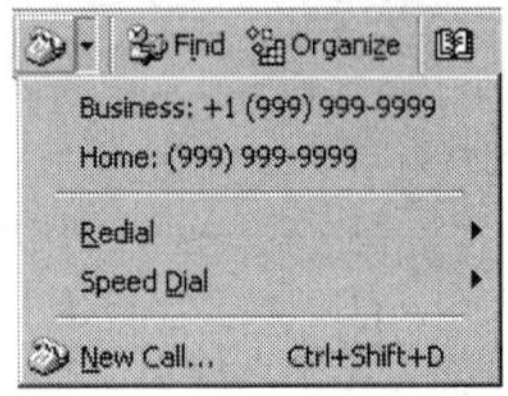

Figure 8.18 The Dial button drop-down menu.

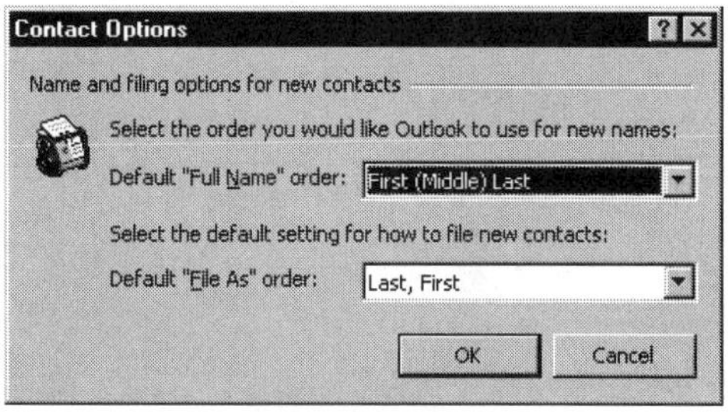

Figure 8.19 The Contact Options dialog box.

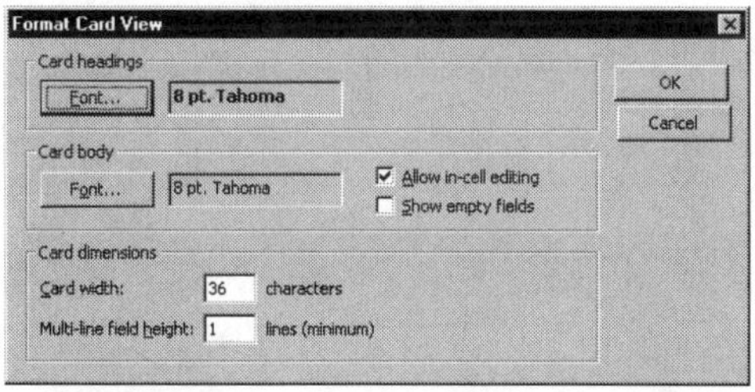

Figure 8.20 The Format Card View dialog box for changing features of the Address Cards view of the Contacts folder.

✔ Tips

- If a contact item is opened in a form, you can perform any of the actions in the preceding list by choosing commands on the form's Actions menu.
- If a contact is opened in a form, you may be able to display a map of the contact's address by clicking the Display Map Of Address toolbar button or by choosing Actions > Display Map Of Address. Outlook will connect to the Microsoft Expedia Web site and attempt to find a map.

To set Contacts options:

◆ To change the order in which you enter names for new contacts or the default way Outlook sorts contacts, choose Tools > Options. Click the **Contact Options** button on the Preferences tab, and select the desired options in the Contact Options dialog box (**Figure 8.19**).

or

To modify features of the currently active view of the Contacts folder, choose View > Current View > Customize Current View. Click the **Other Settings** button, and select the desired options in the Other Settings dialog box (for a table view) or the Format Card View dialog box (for the Address Cards view) (**Figure 8.20**).

✔ Tip

- In the Address Cards view, you can adjust the width of the cards by dragging one of the vertical separators between columns of cards, or you can double-click a separator to have Outlook adjust the card width so an even number of columns will just fit within the Outlook window.

9

USING THE TASKS FOLDER

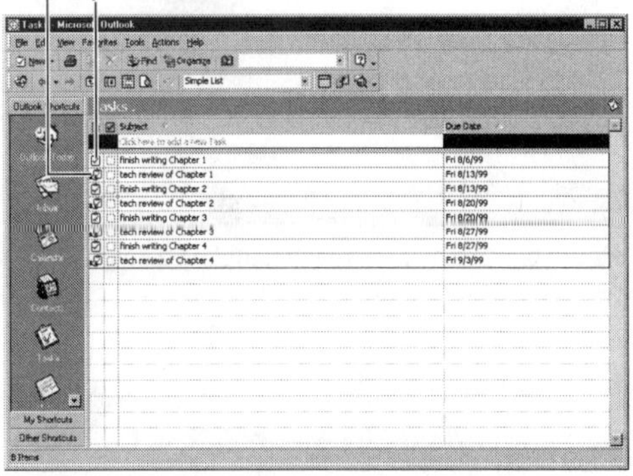

Figure 9.1 The Tasks folder in the Simple List view.

You can use the Tasks folder to keep track of personal tasks that you need to complete or to manage projects that involve other people (**Figure 9.1**).

In this chapter, you'll learn:

- How to create a personal task for tracking a job you have to complete yourself
- How to create a task request for assigning a task to someone else
- How to work with your personal and assigned tasks in the Tasks folder, in a table or in a timeline
- How to set options for the Tasks folder

✔ Tip

- You might want to create a separate task-item folder for each of your main projects. The techniques given in this chapter apply to the default Tasks folder as well as to any new task-item folders that you've created.

Creating Task Items

You can create two types of items in your Tasks folder (**Figure 9.2**):

- A **personal task**, which is stored in your own Tasks folder and is used for tracking a job you need to complete by yourself. You are the *owner* of a personal task.
- An **assigned task**, which you create and assign to someone else by sending that person a task request via e-mail. The person who is assigned the task becomes its *owner* and is responsible for completing it. The task is stored in the owner's Tasks folder, although you can keep a copy in your own Tasks folder. Outlook will automatically update your copy whenever the owner modifies the task. To manage a group project, you can assign tasks to various members of your workgroup in this way.

To create a personal task:

1. Open the Tasks folder.
2. Click the New button on the Standard toolbar, or choose Actions > New Task, or press Ctrl-N.

   Outlook will open a Task form (**Figure 9.3**).
3. Enter the desired information into the controls in the Task tab of the Task form:
   - Type a brief task description into the **Subject** text box.
   - If you want to enter a full task description or any other information, type it into the large text box.
   - If the task is due on a particular date, type or select that date in the **Due date** list box (**Figure 9.4**). (If the task doesn't have a due date, leave **None** selected in the list box.)

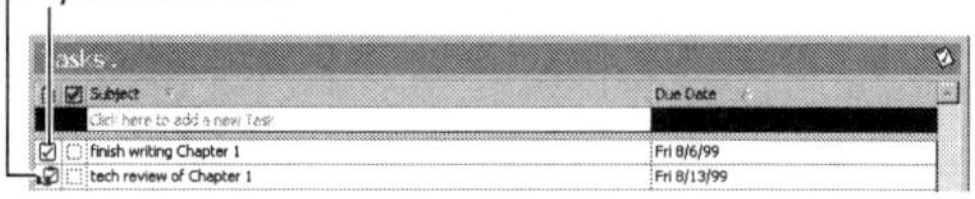

Figure 9.2 A personal task and a copy of an assigned task in the Tasks folder (Simple List view).

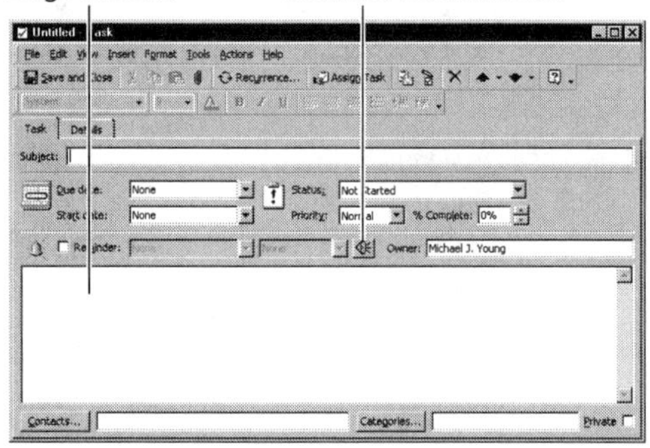

Figure 9.3 A Task form, ready to define a new personal task.

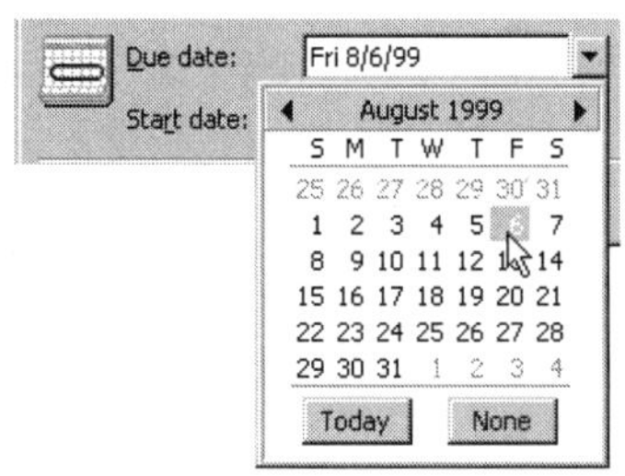

Figure 9.4 Selecting a task due date.

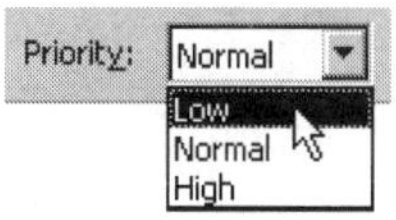

Figure 9.5 Selecting the task's priority.

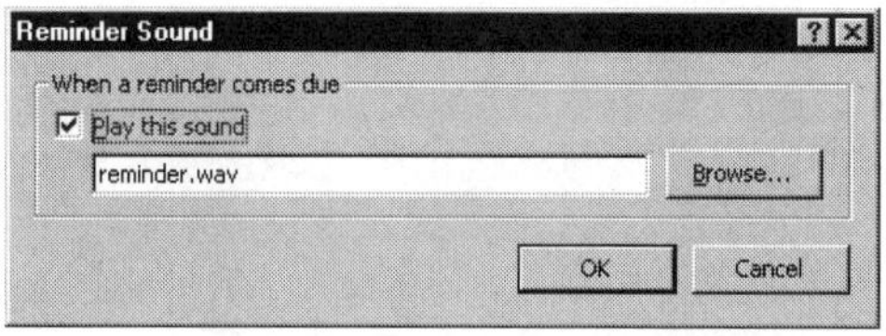

Figure 9.6 The Reminder Sound dialog box.

- If the task is to be started on a particular date, type or select that date in the **Start date** list box. (If the task doesn't have a specific starting date, leave **None** selected in the list box.)
- You generally leave **Not Started** selected in the **Status** list box and **0%** in the **% Complete** text box, and then update these values later as you begin to make progress on the task.
- Specify the task's priority by selecting a value from the **Priority** list box (**Figure 9.5**).
- If you want Outlook to display a reminder message box before the task is due, check the **Reminder** option and type or select the date and the time that the reminder is to be displayed in the following two list boxes. Also, if you want to turn the reminder sound off or on, or select a different sound, click the Reminder Sound button to open the Reminder Sound dialog box (**Figure 9.6**).
- Make sure your name is displayed in the **Owner** text box, because you are the owner of a personal task. (If you assign the task to someone else, as described later, Outlook will change the owner for you.)
- If a contact in your Contacts folder is associated with the task (for example, the client you're performing the task for), type the contact's name into the **Contacts** text box or click the **Contacts** button to select that contact from your Contacts folder. This will link the task to the contact. You'll then be able to open the contact by double-clicking the name. Also, the Activities tab of the Contact form for that contact will list the task along with any other linked Outlook items.

(continued on next page)

- If you want to assign a category to the task, type it into the **Categories** text box or click the **Categories** button to select a category from the Categories dialog box (**Figure 9.7**). You can use a category to sort, filter, group, or find tasks (these operations are discussed in Chapter 3).
- If you're sharing your Tasks folder but you want the task to be hidden, check the **Private** option. (Sharing folders is discussed in "Sharing Outlook Folders over the Internet" and "E/S Sharing Outlook Folders over a Network" in Chapter 4.)

Figure 9.8 shows a completed Task tab.

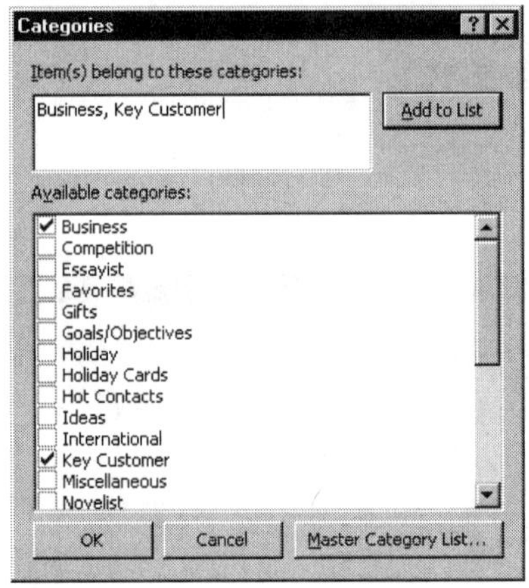

Figure 9.7 The Categories dialog box.

4. To further define the task, open the Details tab (**Figure 9.9**) and enter the desired information into the controls:
   - Enter the estimated number of hours required to complete the task into the **Total work** text box.
   - Enter appropriate information into the **Mileage**, **Billing Information**, and **Companies** text boxes.
   - You normally don't enter information into the **Date completed** and **Actual work** fields until the task is completed.
   - The **Update list** and **Create Unassigned Copy** controls are used only for assigned tasks, described later in the chapter.

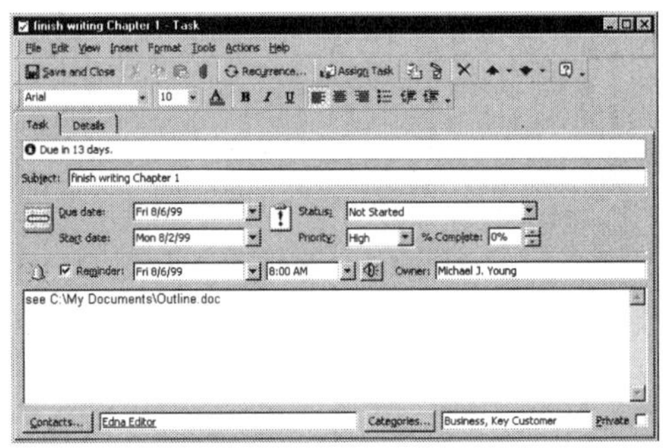

Figure 9.8 A completed Task tab.

5. If you want the task to be recurring, click the Recurrence toolbar button  or choose Actions > Recurrence, and in the Task Recurrence dialog box define the recurrence pattern and range (**Figure 9.10**).

   A recurring task is a series of tasks (all with the same description and options) that are due on the dates that you specify. When you mark one task as completed,

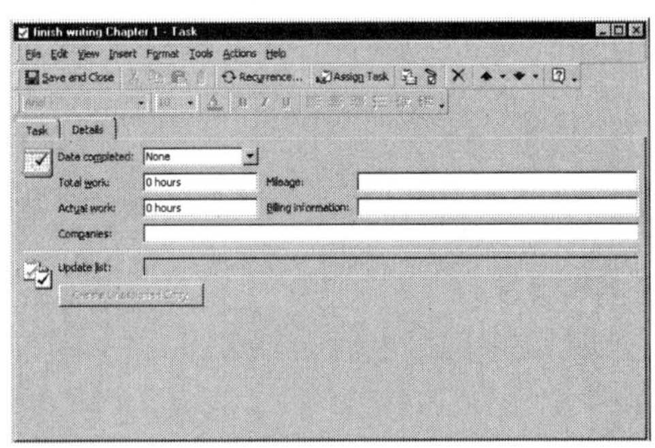

Figure 9.9 The Details tab of the Task form.

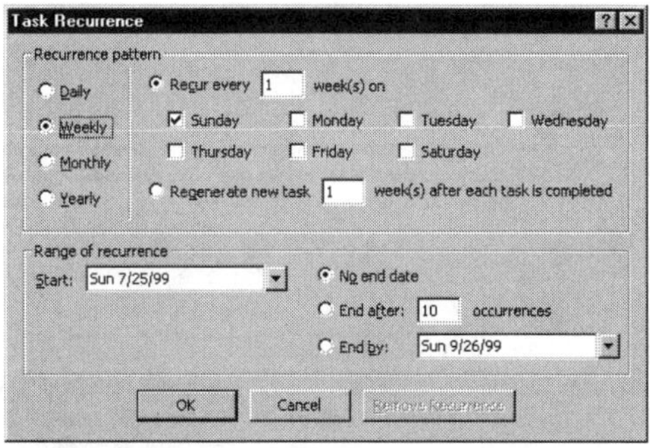

Figure 9.10 The Task Recurrence dialog box.

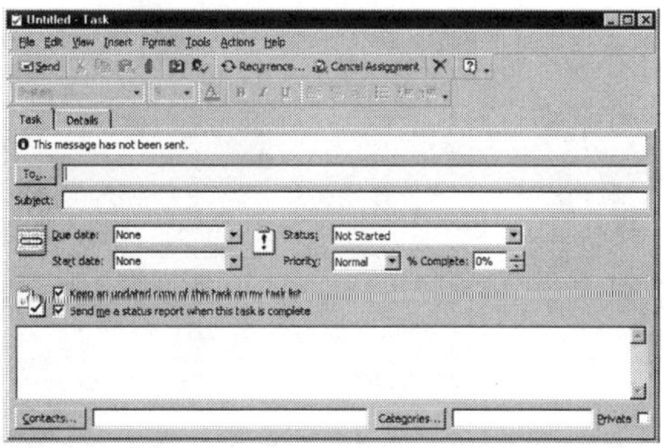

Figure 9.11 A Task form, ready to define a new assigned task.

Outlook automatically generates the next task in the series and adds it to your Tasks folder.

6. Click the Save And Close toolbar button [Save and Close] to save your new task in the Tasks folder and to close the form.

✔ Tips

- You can enter several names into the **Contacts** or **Categories** text boxes. If you type the names, separate them using commas or semicolons.
- With a recurring task, you can generate the next task without having to mark the current task as completed. To do this, open the task and choose Actions > Skip Occurrence in the form. The task's due date will be changed to the due date for the next task in the series.
- Clicking the Assign Task toolbar button [Assign Task] converts the personal task into an assigned task, as discussed next.

To create an assigned task:

1. Open the Tasks folder.
2. Choose Actions > New Task Request, or press Ctrl-Shift-U.

   Outlook will open the Task form shown in **Figure 9.11**.
3. In the **To** text box, enter the address of the person you want to assign the task to. Follow the instructions given in "I/O To address a message" or "C/W To address a message" in Chapter 6.

   The person to whom you assign the task becomes the task owner.
4. If you want to keep a copy of the assigned task in your own Tasks folder, check the **Keep an updated copy of this task on my task list** option.

(continued on next page)

You won't be able to modify your copy of the task, but it will be updated automatically whenever the task owner modifies his or her copy.

5. If you want to receive an e-mail message when the task owner marks the task as completed, check the **Send me a status report when this task is complete** option.

6. Finish defining the task by entering information into the other controls in the Task and Details tabs, following the instructions in "To create a personal task," earlier in the chapter.

   Notice, however, that the Task tab doesn't contain controls for setting a reminder (only the task owner can set a reminder), nor does it contain an **Owner** text box (Outlook automatically assigns this field the name of the owner).

   Figure 9.12 shows a completed Task form.

7. Click the **Send** button.

   Outlook will send the task to its owner, close the form, and (if you checked **Send me a status report when this task is complete**) save a copy of the task in your Tasks folder.

Here's what happens next:

- The owner receives a task request message in his or her Inbox (**Figure 9.13**).
- The owner clicks the Accept or the Decline toolbar button in the task request form to take on or to refuse the task. In either case, you'll receive a message in your Inbox notifying you of the owner's response.
- If the owner clicked the Accept button, the task is added to his or her Tasks folder.

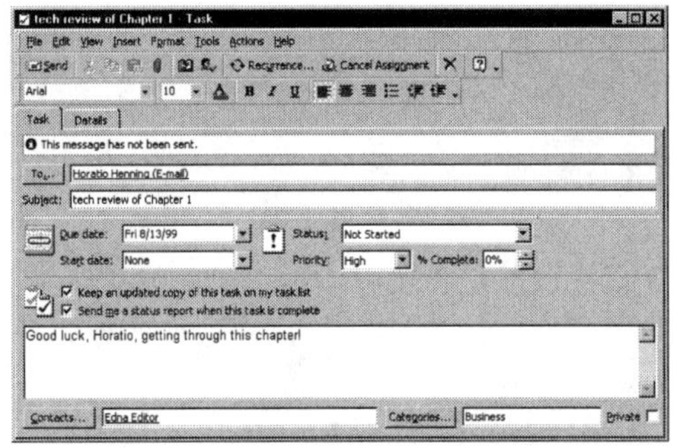

Figure 9.12 A completed Task form for assigning a task to another person.

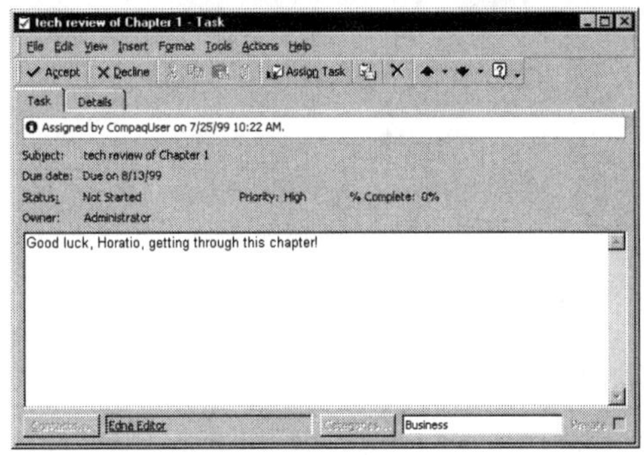

Figure 9.13 A Task request message received by the task owner (this task request resulted from sending the form shown in Figure 9.12).

- If the owner clicked the Accept button and you originally checked the **Send me a status report when this task is complete** option, Outlook will automatically update your copy of the task whenever the owner modifies the task. (Outlook uses special e-mail messages to keep your copy updated.)
- If the owner clicked the Accept button and you originally checked the **Send me a status report when this task is complete** option, you'll get a "Task Completed" message in your Inbox when the owner marks the task as completed.

✔ Tips

- Clicking the Cancel Assignment  button in the Task form for an assigned task converts the task to a personal task.
- Assigning a task won't work if you or the intended owner uses an e-mail service that doesn't transmit the required information, such as CompuServe.

Working with Items in the Tasks Folder

You can work with the tasks in your Tasks folder in a table or in a timeline. A timeline view arranges the tasks according to their due dates, along a horizontal timeline.

To work with your tasks in a table:

1. Open the Tasks folder and switch to any of the standard views *except* Task Timeline (**Figure 9.14**).
2. To sort the tasks, use the sorting techniques in "To sort items" in Chapter 3.
3. To arrange the tasks in any order you wish (that is, not sorted by a particular field), first clear all sorting and then drag each task up or down in the list to the position where you want it.

   To clear all sorting, choose View > Current View > Customize Current View, click the **Sort** button, and then click the **Clear All** button (**Figure 9.15**).
4. To quickly create a new task, click in the **Click here to add a new Task** box at the top of the task list (**Figure 9.16**) and enter information into the fields shown in the view. (To enter additional information, you'll have to open the task.)
5. To quickly modify any of the task information displayed in the table, click the field and then type or select a new value.

   To designate a task as completed in the Simple List view, check the box in the second column (**Figure 9.17**).

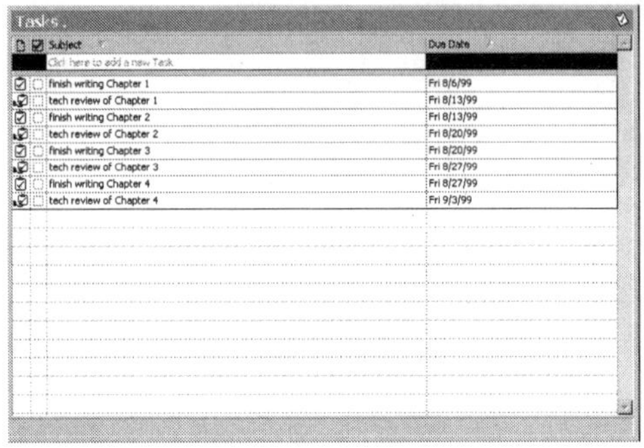

Figure 9.14 The Tasks folder in the commonly used Simple List table view.

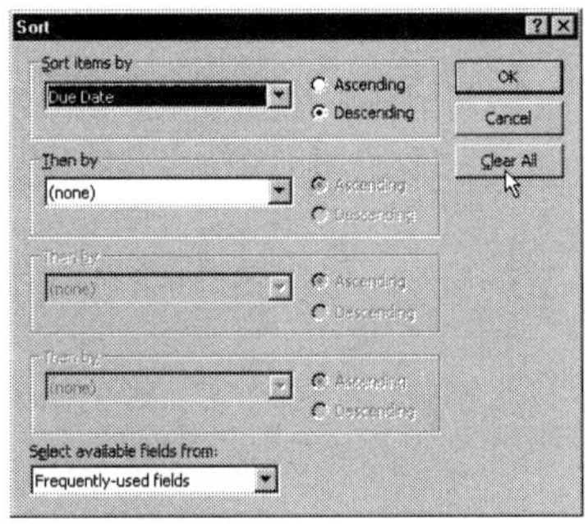

Figure 9.15 Removing all sorting by clicking the Clear All button in the Sort dialog box.

Click anywhere in this box

Figure 9.16 Adding a new task.

This box indicates that the task was completed

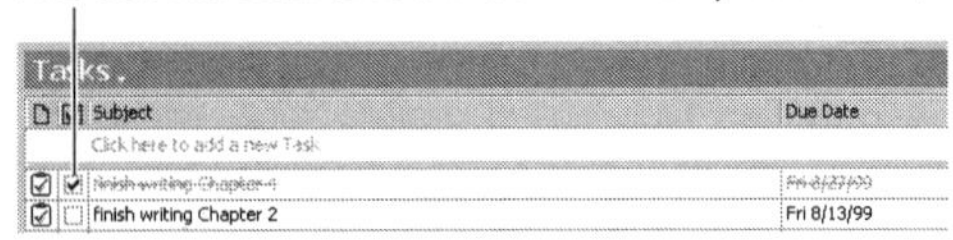

Figure 9.17 A completed task.

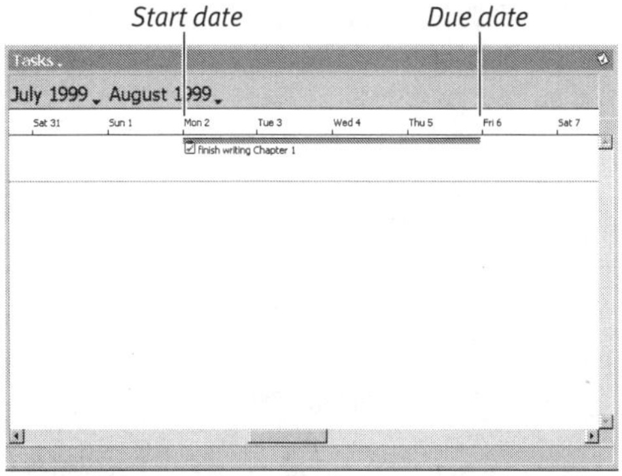

Figure 9.18 The Tasks folder in the Task Timeline view, showing one week.

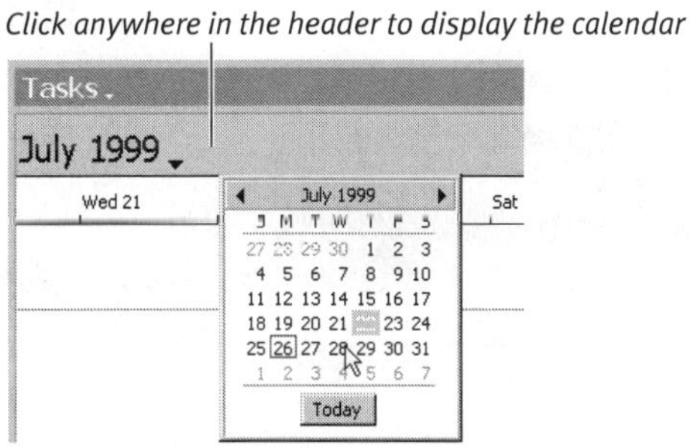

Figure 9.19 Using the pop-up calendar to go to a particular date.

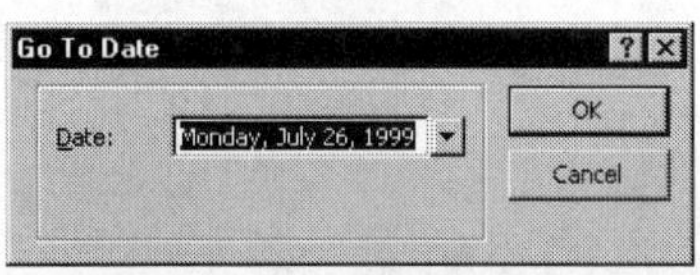

Figure 9.20 The Go To Date dialog box.

✔ Tip

- To add new tasks and to modify existing ones in a particular table view, the **Allow in-cell editing** and **Show "new item" row** options must be checked. To access these options, choose View > Current View > Customize Current View and click the **Other Settings** button.

To work with your tasks in a timeline:

1. Open the Tasks folder and switch to the standard Task Timeline view (**Figure 9.18**).
2. To adjust the amount of detail shown in the timeline, click the Day , Week , or Month  button on the Standard toolbar.
3. To view a particular period of time, scroll using the horizontal scroll bar.

   or

   Click the header (the horizontal gray bar at the top of the Information Viewer, which displays the months), and click a date on the pop-up calendar (**Figure 9.19**).

✔ Tips

- To quickly view today's date, click the Go To Today button  on the Standard toolbar, or choose View > Go To > Go To Today.
- To view any date, choose View > Go To > Go To Date, or press Ctrl-G, and enter the date into the Go To Date dialog box (**Figure 9.20**).

To set Tasks options:

- To change the default task reminder time, choose Tools > Options, and in the Preferences tab, type or select a time in the **Reminder time** list box (**Figure 9.21**).

  or

  To modify the colors used for overdue and completed tasks displayed in the Outlook window, choose Tools > Options, click the **Task Options** button in the Preferences tab, and select new colors in the Task Options dialog box (**Figure 9.22**).

  or

  To modify the number of hours per day or per week that Outlook uses for calculating the values you enter into the **Total work** and **Actual work** text boxes in the Task form, choose Tools > Options, open the Other tab, click the **Advanced Options** button, and type new values into the **Task working hours per day** and **Task working hours per week** text boxes in the Advanced Options dialog box (**Figure 9.23**). (For example, if you specify 10 hours per day, and you subsequently enter 20 hours into the **Total work** task field, Outlook will convert the value to 2 days.)

  or

  To modify the features of reminders, click the **Reminder Options** button in the Advanced Options dialog box.

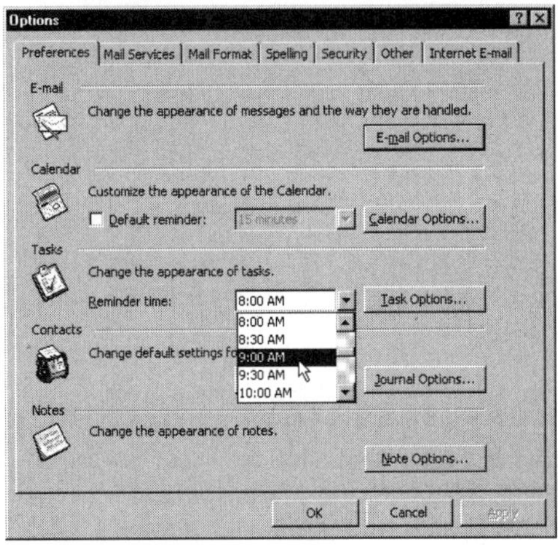

Figure 9.21 Changing the default task reminder time.

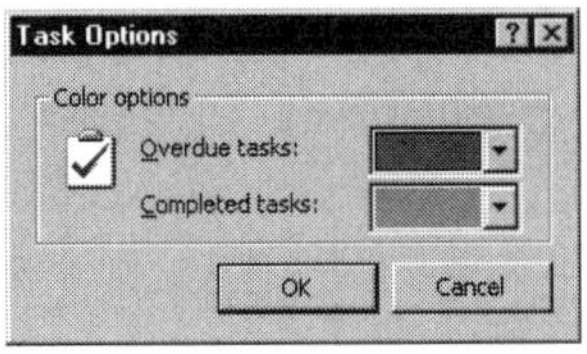

Figure 9.22 The Tasks Options dialog box.

Enter a new value into either text box

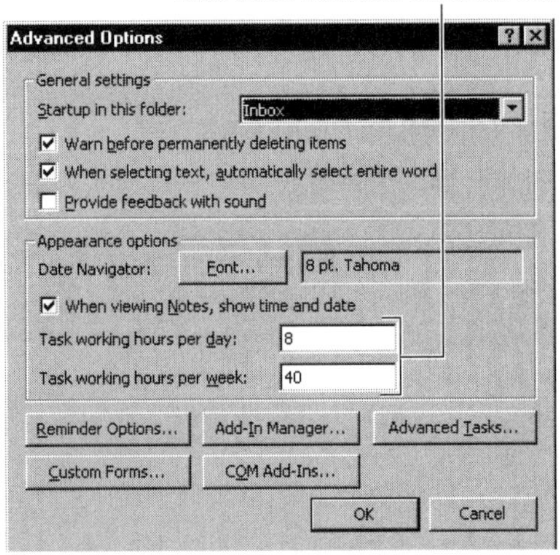

Figure 9.23 Changing the hours per day or week that Outlook uses, in the Advanced Options dialog box.

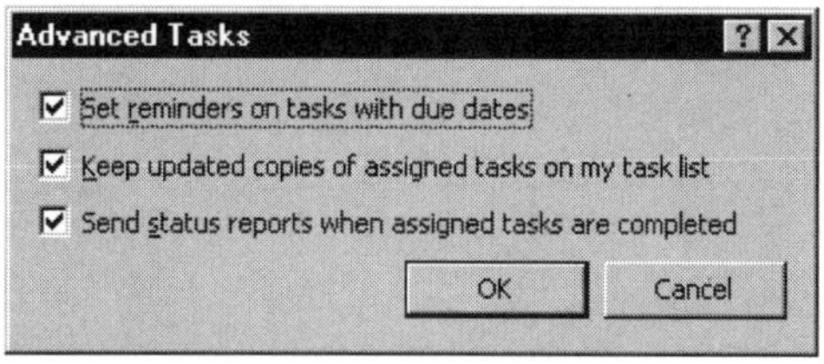

Figure 9.24 The Advanced Tasks dialog box.

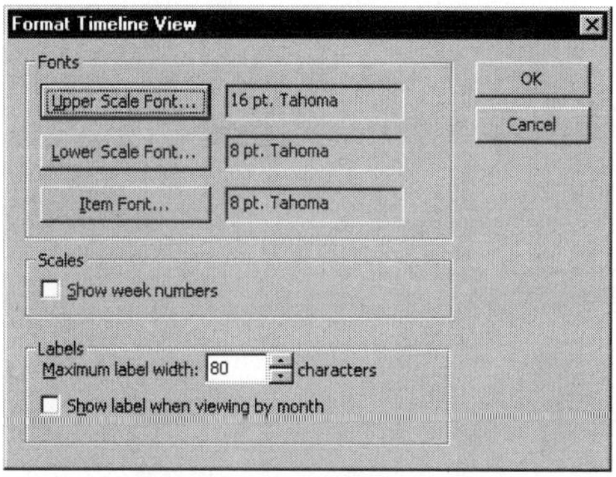

Figure 9.25 The Format Timeline View dialog box for changing features of the Task Timeline view of the Tasks folder.

or

To set additional default options, click the **Advanced Tasks** button in the Advanced Options dialog box, and in the Advanced Tasks dialog box (**Figure 9.24**) check each option you want Outlook to turn on by default in new tasks. (If you wish, you can turn off any of these options for a particular task.)

or

To modify features of the currently active view of the Tasks folder, choose View > Current View > Customize Current View, click the **Other Settings** button, and select the desired options in the Other Settings dialog box (for a table view) or in the Format Timeline View dialog box (for the Task Timeline view) (**Figure 9.25**).

10

USING THE JOURNAL

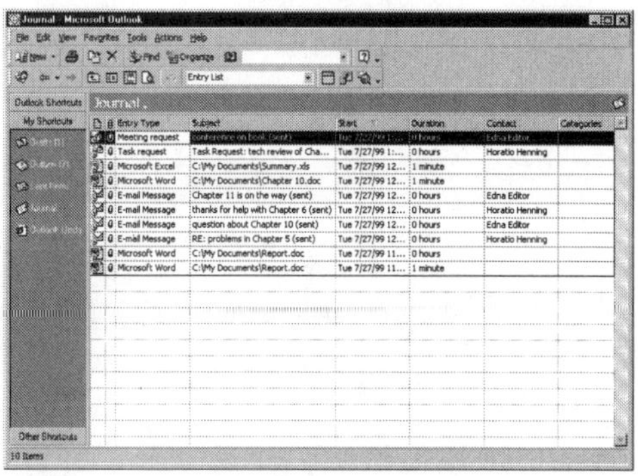

Figure 10.1 The Journal folder in the Entry List view.

You can use the Journal folder to keep a record of various activities in your business or personal life (**Figure 10.1**). The following are examples of activities that you could record in the Journal:

- Receiving an important e-mail message
- Assigning a task to your assistant
- Creating a document in Word
- Working on an Excel worksheet
- Making a phone call
- Paying a utility bill
- Selling shares of a stock

In this chapter, you'll learn:

- How to have Outlook automatically record journal entries
- How to create journal entries manually
- How to work with your journal entries in a table or timeline view
- How to open either a journal entry or the item or file that's associated with an entry
- How to set options for the Journal folder.

Recording Journal Entries

You can create journal entries in two different ways:

- You can have Outlook **automatically** record a journal entry each time a particular activity occurs that is associated with a selected contact, such as sending or receiving an e-mail message from your editor. You can also have Outlook automatically record a journal entry each time you create or modify a document using a selected Office program, such as Microsoft Excel.
- You can **manually** create a journal entry to record *any* type of activity, such as making a phone call, receiving a fax, or writing a letter. When you manually create a journal entry, you can use the Journal Entry form to time the activity so that you can record its exact duration.

✔ Tip

- Automatic journal entries can slow operations on your computer and can consume a large amount of space in your Personal Folders file or your Exchange Server mailbox. To reduce these problems, you can minimize the number of entries Outlook automatically generates and you can frequently archive all but the most recent entries. Archiving is discussed in "Removing and Archiving Items" in Chapter 3.

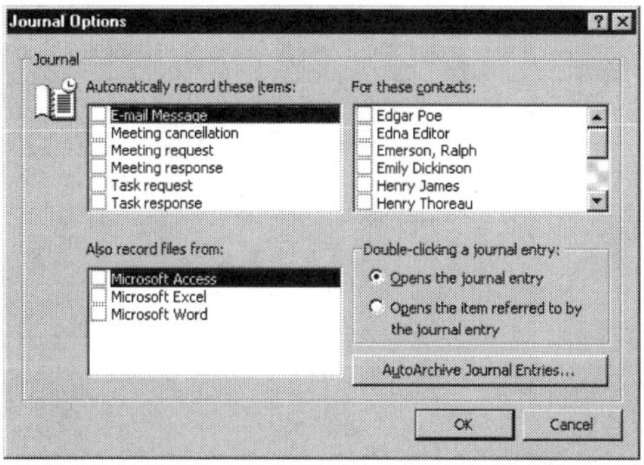

Figure 10.2 The Journal Options dialog box.

To record journal entries automatically:

1. Open the Journal folder.

   Outlook puts the shortcut for the Journal folder in the My Shortcuts group.

   If you haven't previously set up automatic journal entries, Outlook will display the Journal Options dialog box (**Figure 10.2**).

2. If Outlook doesn't automatically display the Journal Options dialog box, display it now by choosing Tools > Options and clicking the **Journal Options** button in the Preferences tab.

3. To have Outlook record specific activities associated with particular contacts, check the activities in the **Automatically record these items** list and check the contacts in the **For these contacts** list.

   For example, if you selected **E-mail Message** and **Task request** in the first list and **Edna Editor** and **Horatio Henning** in the second, Outlook would generate a journal entry whenever you send or receive an e-mail message or a task request to or from either of these two contacts.

4. To have Outlook create a journal entry whenever you create or modify an Office document, check the specific document types in the **Also record files from** list.

   The document types are identified by the name of the Office application that creates them. Only the applications you currently have installed will appear in the list.

5. Click the **OK** button.

✔ Tip

- The **For these contacts** list displays only the contacts in your default Contacts folder, *not* those in a contact-item folder you've created.

To record journal entries manually:

1. Open the Journal folder.
2. Click the New button on the Standard toolbar, or choose Actions > New Journal Entry, or press Ctrl-N.

   Outlook will open a Journal Entry form (**Figure 10.3**).
3. Enter the desired information into the controls in the Journal Entry form:
   - Type a brief description of the journal entry into the **Subject** text box.
   - If you want to enter a full description or any other information, type it into the large text box.
   - Select the type of activity you're recording in the **Entry type** list box (**Figure 10.4**).
   - Type the name of any company associated with the entry into the **Company** text box.
   - Type or select the starting date and time of the activity in the **Start time** list boxes.
   - Type the amount of time required by the activity into the **Duration** list box, or select a time from the drop-down list. Alternatively, you can time an activity that's currently taking place (such as a phone call) by clicking the **Start Timer** button when the activity begins and clicking the **Pause Timer** button when the activity ends or pauses.
   - If a contact in your Contacts folder is associated with the journal entry (for example, the person you're calling on the phone), type the contact's name into the **Contacts** text box or click the **Contacts** button to select that contact from your Contacts folder. This will link the journal entry to the contact. You'll then be able to open the contact

Large text box

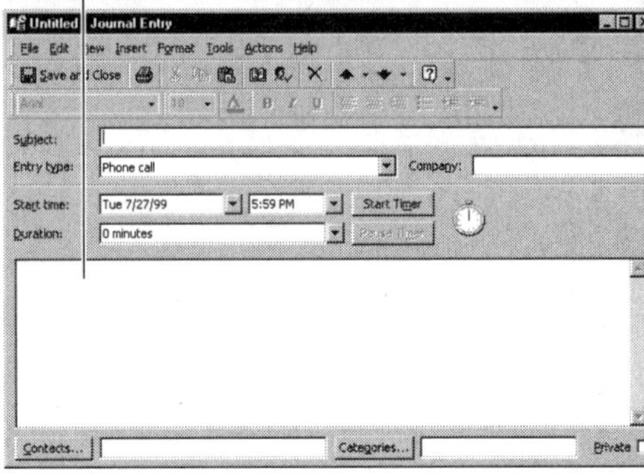

Figure 10.3 A Journal Entry form, ready to define a new manual journal entry.

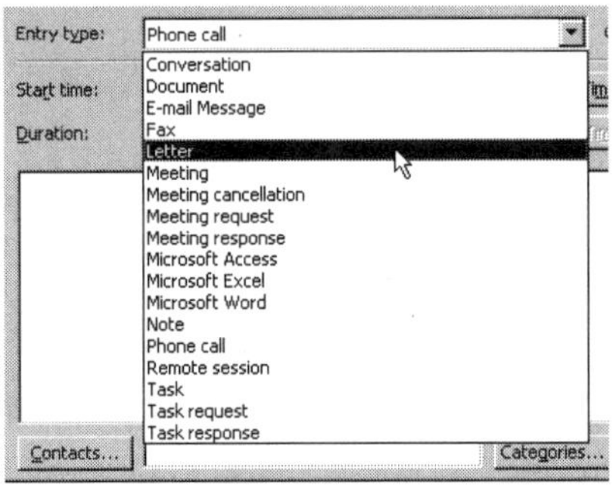

Figure 10.4 Selecting the type of activity.

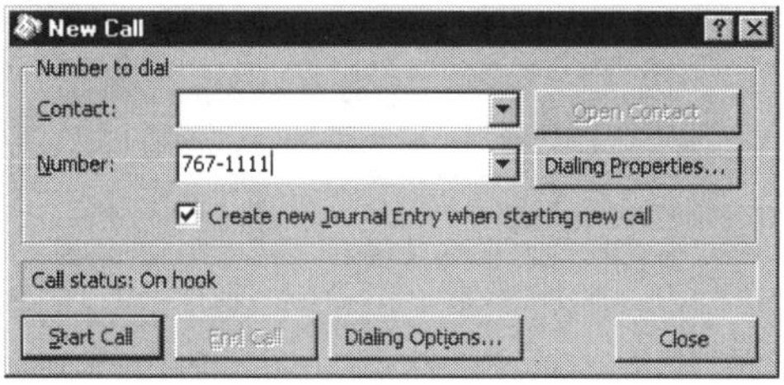

Figure 10.5 Making a call and recording it in a journal entry.

by double-clicking the Activities tab of the Con that contact will list the jo along with any other linked items.

- If you want to assign a category journal entry, type it into the **Categories** text box or click the **Categories** button to select a category from the Categories dialog box (refer to **Figure 9.7**). You can use a category to sort, filter, group, or find journal entries (these operations are discussed in Chapter 3).
- If you're sharing your Journal folder but you want the journal entry to be hidden, check the **Private** option. (Sharing folders is discussed in "Sharing Outlook Folders over the Internet" and "E/S Sharing Outlook Folders over a Network" in Chapter 4.)

4. Click the Save And Close toolbar button to save your new journal entry in the Journal folder and to close the form.

✔ Tips

- You can enter several names into the **Contacts** or **Categories** text boxes. If you type the names, separate them using commas or semicolons.
- You can make a telephone call and record it in a journal entry using a single command. Open the Contacts folder, choose Actions > Call Contact > New Call or press Ctrl-Shift-D, check the **Create new Journal Entry when starting new call** option, and use the New Call dialog box to make your call (**Figure 10.5**).

Working with Items in the Journal Folder

You can work with your journal entries either in a table or in a timeline.

When you open an item in the Journal folder, you can either open the journal entry itself in a form or open any item or document that's associated with the journal entry.

To work with your journal entries in a table:

1. Open the Journal folder and switch to the standard Entry List, Last Seven Days, or Phone Calls view. (The Entry List view is shown in **Figure 10.1**, earlier in the chapter.)

   Entry List shows all entries, while Last Seven Days and Phone Calls apply filters to display subsets of your entries.

2. To quickly create a new journal entry, click in the **Click here to add a new Journal entry** box at the top of the table (**Figure 10.6**) and enter information into the fields shown in the particular view. (To enter additional information, you'll have to open the journal entry in a form.)

3. To quickly modify any of the journal entry information displayed in the table, click the field and then type the change.

✔ Tip

- To add new journal entries and to modify existing entries in a particular table view, the **Allow in-cell editing** and **Show "new item" row** options must be checked. To access these options, choose View > Current View > Customize Current View and click the **Other Settings** button.

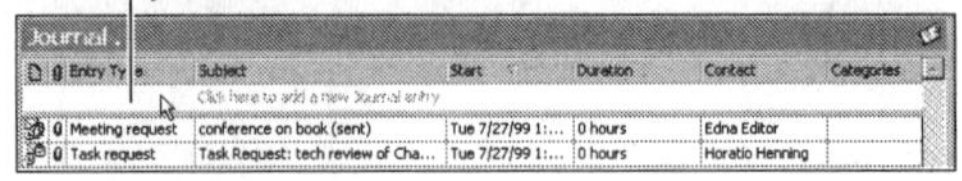

Figure 10.6 Clicking to create a new journal entry.

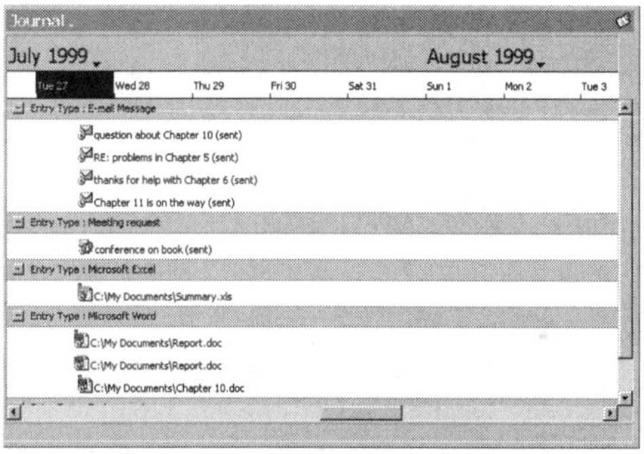

Figure 10.7 The By Type view of the Journal folder, showing one week with all groups expanded.

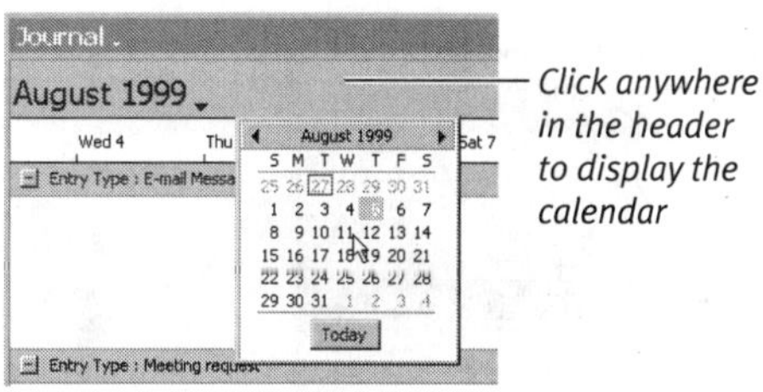

Figure 10.8 Using the pop-up calendar to go to a particular date.

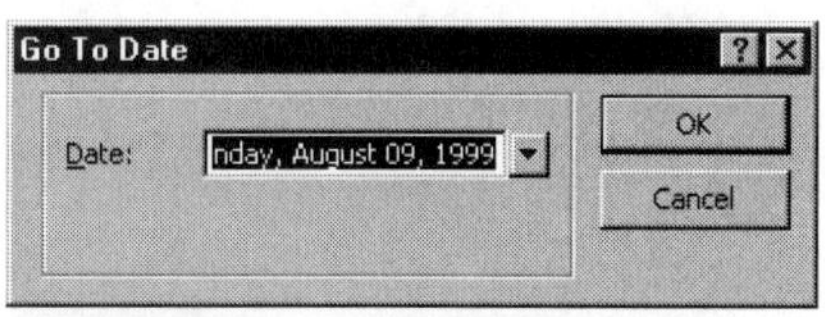

Figure 10.9 The Go To Date dialog box.

To work with your journal entries in a timeline:

1. Open the Journal folder and switch to the standard By Type, By Contact, or By Category view (**Figure 10.7**).

   Each of these views groups your journal entries using a different field. (For information on working with groups, see "To group items" in Chapter 3.)

2. To adjust the amount of detail shown in the timeline, click the Day, Week, or Month toolbar button.

3. To view a particular period of time, scroll using the horizontal scroll bar.

   or

   Click the header (the horizontal gray bar at the top of the Information Viewer, which displays the months), and then click a date on the pop-up calendar (**Figure 10.8**).

✔ Tips

- To quickly view today's date, click the Go To Today button on the Standard toolbar, or choose View > Go To > Go To Today.
- To view any date, choose View > Go To > Go To Date or press Ctrl-G, and then enter the date into the Go To Date dialog box (**Figure 10.9**).

To open a journal entry:

- If the **Opens the journal entry** option is selected (see the following tip), double-click the entry or use any of the other methods discussed in "To open an item" in Chapter 3.

(continued on next page)

or

If the **Opens the item referred to by the journal entry** option is selected (see the tip below), right-click the entry and choose Open Journal Entry from pop-up menu (**Figure 10.10**).

The entry will be opened in the Journal Entry form, where you can view and edit it.

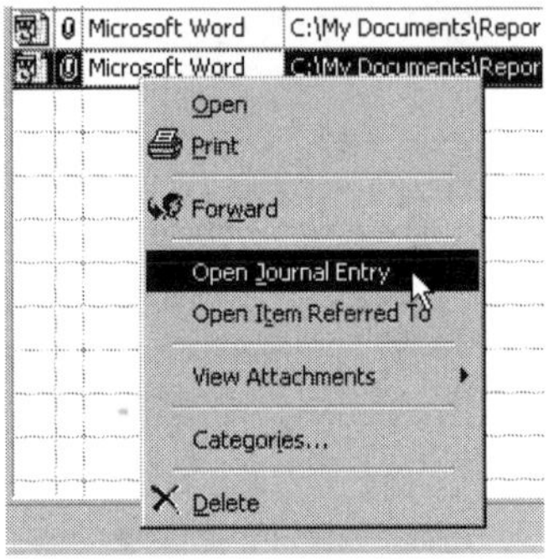

Figure 10.10 Opening the journal entry itself.

✔ Tip

- The two options mentioned in this section are explained in "To set Journal options," on the following page.

To open the item or document associated with a journal entry:

- If the **Opens the item referred to by the journal entry** option is selected (see the tip below), double-click the entry or use any of the other methods discussed in "To open an item" in Chapter 3.

  or

  If the **Opens the journal entry** option is selected (see the tip below), right-click the entry and choose Open Item Referred To from the pop-up menu (**Figure 10.11**).

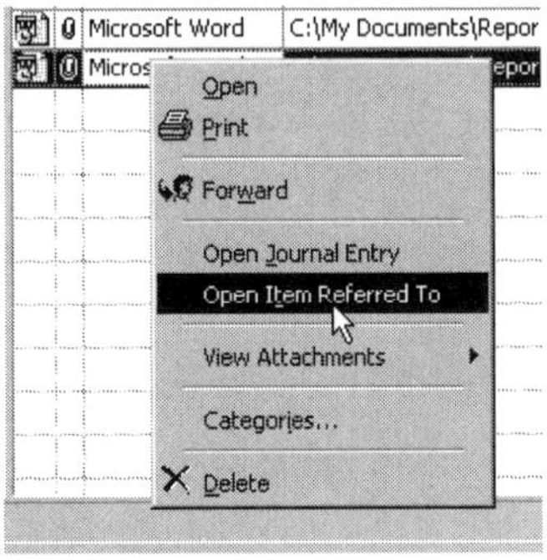

Figure 10.11 Opening the item or document associated with the journal entry.

An item associated with the entry will be opened in a Outlook form, and a document associated with the entry will be opened by the application used to create it (for example, a Word document will be opened in Microsoft Word).

✔ Tips

- The two options mentioned in this section are explained in the next section, "To set Journal options."
- To open an item or document as described here, the large text box of the journal entry must contain a shortcut to

Select one of these options

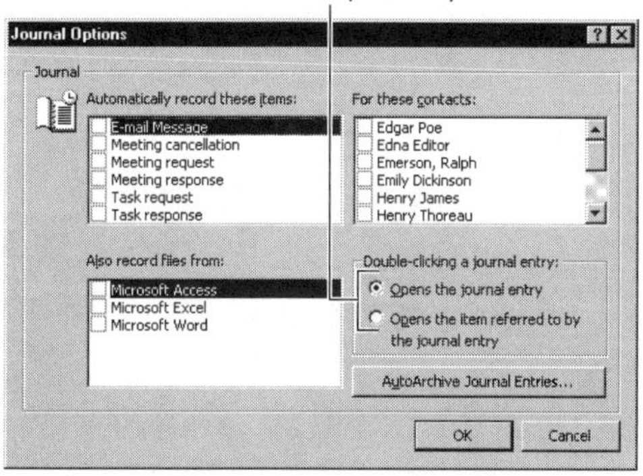

Figure 10.12 Choosing what happens when you double-click a journal entry.

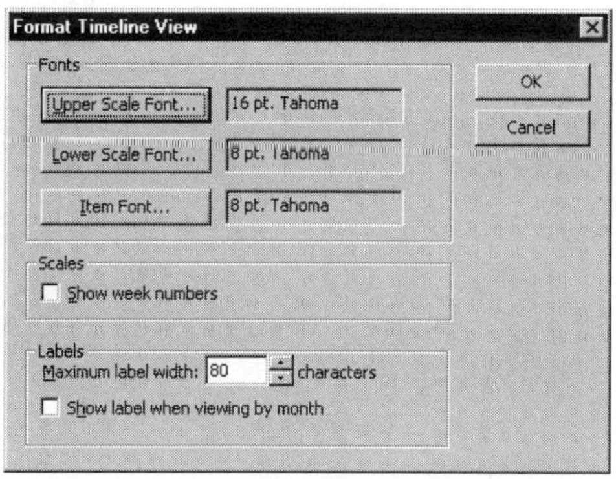

Figure 10.13 The Format Timeline View dialog box for changing features of the By Type view of the Journal folder.

the item or document. When Outlook automatically generates a journal entry, it adds the shortcut. You can also add a shortcut (or attachment, which will work as well) if you create the entry manually. See "Inserting files, items, and objects" in Chapter 3.

To set Journal options:

- To select what happens when you double-click a journal entry (or use another method to open it), choose Tools > Options, click the **Journal Options** button in the Preferences tab, and select the option you want in the Journal Options dialog box (**Figure 10.12**).

  or

  To modify features of the currently active view of the Journal folder, choose View > Current View > Customize Current View, click the **Other Settings** button, and select the desired options in the Other Settings dialog box (for a table view) or the Format Timeline View dialog box (for a timeline view) (**Figure 10.13**).

11

USING THE NOTES FOLDER

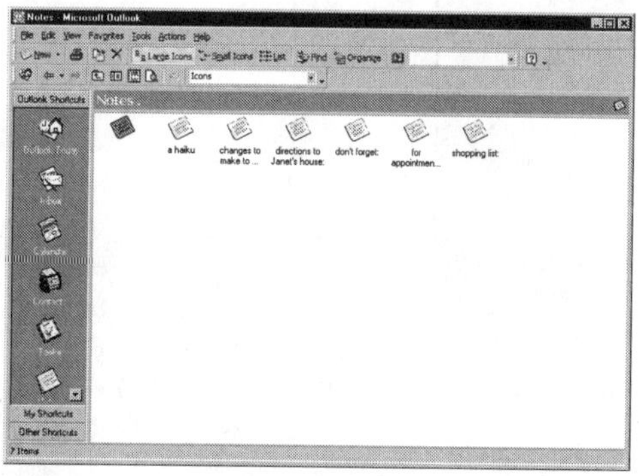

Figure 11.1 The Notes folder in the Icons view, displaying large icons.

You can use the Notes folder to quickly create text notes (**Figure 11.1**). You can use notes to store information that doesn't fit into any of the other Outlook folders (for example, a shopping list). You can also quickly type information into a note that you'll later transfer to another Outlook folder. (For example, while talking on the phone, you could jot down a name and address, and then when you have more time, transfer that information to the Contacts folder.)

In this chapter, you'll learn:

- How to create new notes
- How to work with notes displayed as icons
- How to work with notes in a table view
- How to set options for the Notes folder

✔ Tip

- You can use the instructions given in this chapter either with the default Notes folder or a with another note-item folder that you've created.

Creating New Notes

Notes are the simplest of Outlook items. A note consists of a single text box, in which you can enter plain text only. You can't insert graphics or format the text in a note.

Figure 11.2 A blank note.

To create a new note:

1. Open the Notes folder.
2. Click the New button on the Standard toolbar, or choose Actions > New Note, or press Ctrl-N.
   Outlook will open a blank note (**Figure 11.2**).
3. Type any text you want into the note.
   When the text you type reaches the right-hand border of the note, Outlook automatically wraps it to the next line. To create a new line at any position in the text, press Enter.
4. To open the note's menu, click the note icon in the upper-left corner of the note (**Figure 11.3**). To change features of the note, or to include additional information, choose appropriate commands from this menu:
   - Choose a command on the Color submenu to set the background color of the note (**Figure 11.4**).
   - If you want to assign one or more categories to the note, choose the Categories command to open the Categories dialog box (**Figure 11.5**). You can use a category to sort, filter, group, or find notes (these operations are discussed in Chapter 3).

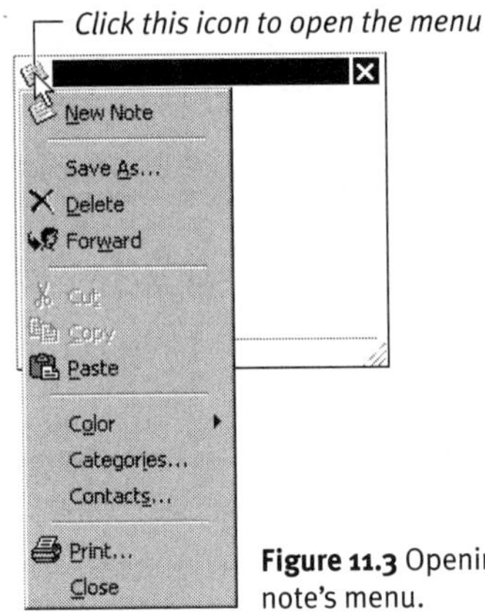

Figure 11.3 Opening a note's menu.

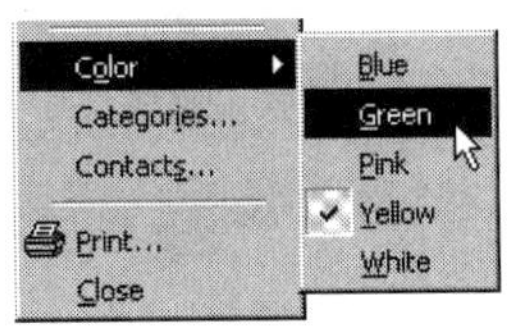

Figure 11.4 Changing the background color of a note.

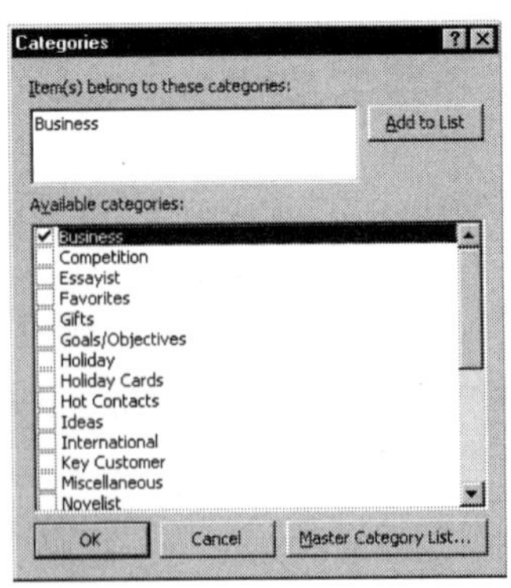

Figure 11.5 The Categories dialog box.

Figure 11.6 The Contacts For Note dialog box.

- If a contact is associated with the note, choose the Contacts command to open the Contacts For Note dialog box (**Figure 11.6**). Then type the contact's name into the text box, or click the **Contacts** button to select the contact from your Contacts folder. This will link the note to the contact. As a result, the Activities tab of the Contact form for that contact will list the note along with any other linked Outlook items. You can enter several contacts (if you type them, separate them using commas or semicolons).

5. If you want to remove the note from the screen and display it only as an item in the Notes folder, click the Close button ☒ in the note's upper-right corner, or press Esc.

✔ Tips

- Unlike other types of Outlook forms, all changes you make in a note are saved automatically, as soon as you make them.
- You can quickly create a note in Outlook, regardless of the currently opened folder, by pressing Ctrl-Shift-N.
- You might want to leave a note open for handy reference while you work in another Outlook folder or in another program.

Working with Items in the Notes Folder

You can display the notes in your Notes folder either as icons or in a table.

To work with note icons:

1. Open the Notes folder and switch to the Icons view.
2. To change the size of the icons, click the Large Icons, Small Icons, or List button on the Standard toolbar; or choose the equivalent commands on the View menu. These options are shown in **Figures 11.7**, **11.8**, and **11.9**.
3. To rearrange the icons (only with the Large Icons or Small Icons option), drag each icon to the position where you want it.
4. To have Outlook align the icons in rows and columns, choose View > Line Up Icons.

✔ Tip

- Steps 3 and 4 assume that the default **Do not arrange** option is applied to the Icons view (this option is shown in **Figure 11.13**, later in the chapter).

To work with notes in a table:

◆ Open the Notes folder and switch to the Notes List, Last Seven Days, By Category, or By Color view.

Notes List shows all your notes (**Figure 11.10**), Last Seven applies a filter, and By Category and By Color group your notes.

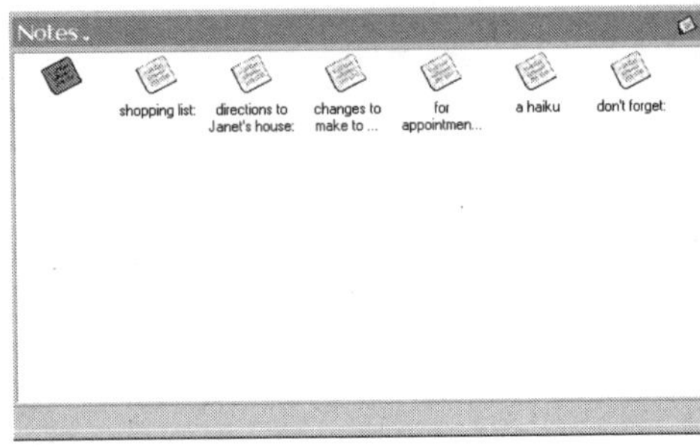

Figure 11.7 The Icons view showing large icons.

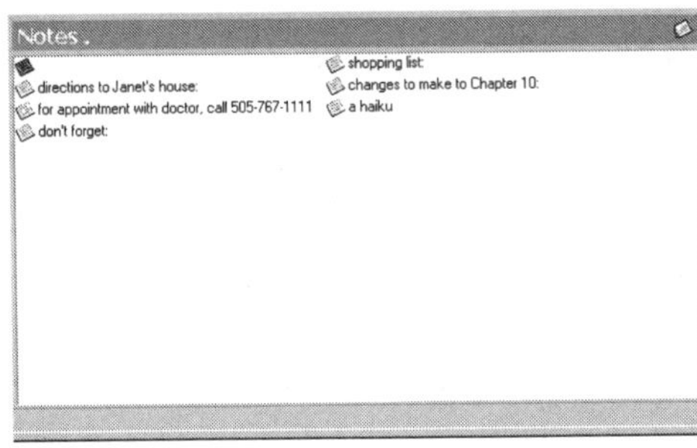

Figure 11.8 The Icons view showing small icons.

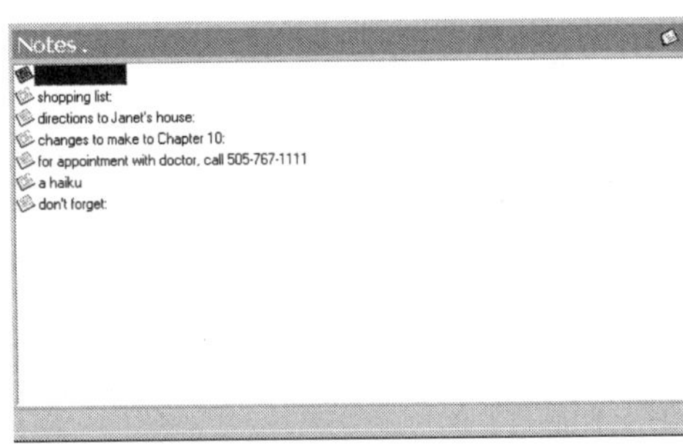

Figure 11.9 The Icons view showing an icon list.

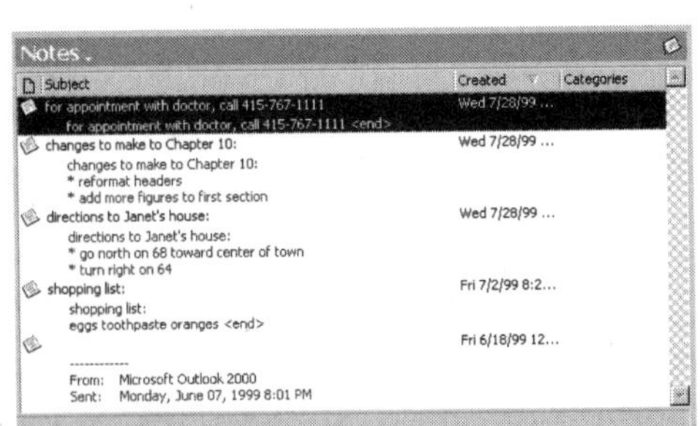

Figure 11.10 The Notes List view of the Notes folder.

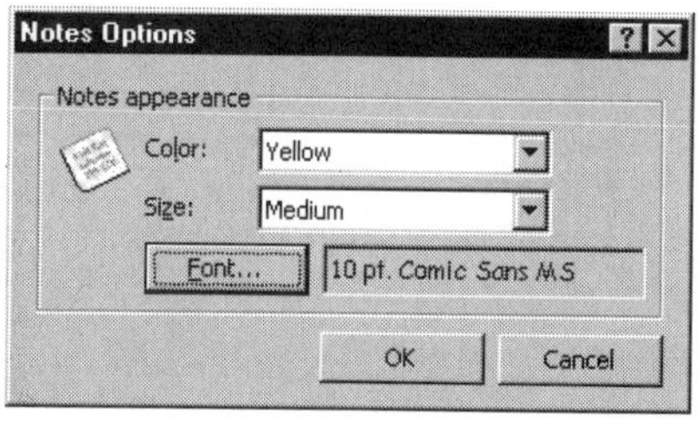

Figure 11.11 The Notes Options dialog box.

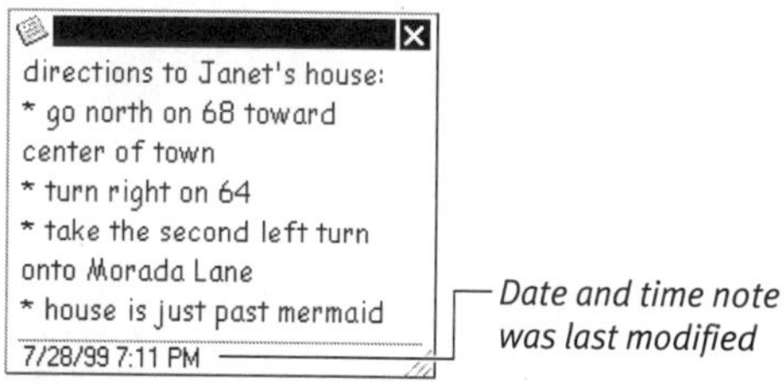

Figure 11.12 A note showing date and time.

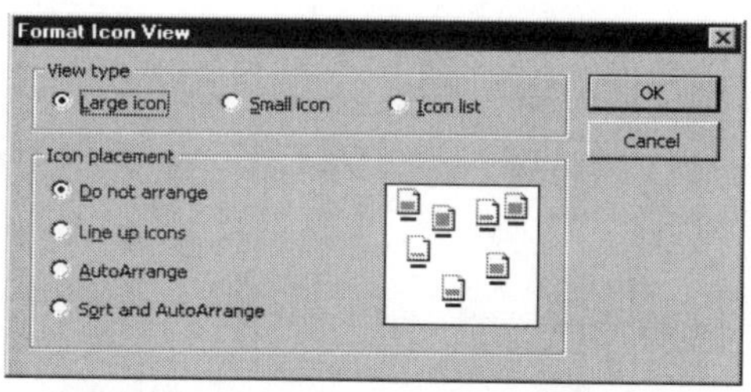

Figure 11.13 The Format Icon View dialog box for changing features of the Icons view of the Notes folder.

To set Notes options:

- To change the note background color, size, or font, choose Tools > Options, click the **Note Options** button in the Preferences tab, and select options in the Notes Options dialog box (**Figure 11.11**).

  The background color and note size that you select will be used as the defaults for the notes you subsequently create (you can override either for a particular note). The font you select will be applied to the text in *all* notes.

  or

  To hide or show the date and time at the bottom of your notes, choose Tools > Options, open the Other tab, click the **Advanced Options** button, and uncheck or check the **When viewing Notes, show time and date** option. The date and time tell you when the note was last modified (**Figure 11.12**).

  or

  To modify features of the currently active view of the Notes folder, choose View > Current View > Customize Current View, click the **Other Settings** button, and select the desired options in the Other Settings dialog box (for a table view) or the Format Icon View dialog box (for the Icons view) (**Figure 11.13**).

MANAGING YOUR DISK FILES AND FOLDERS

12

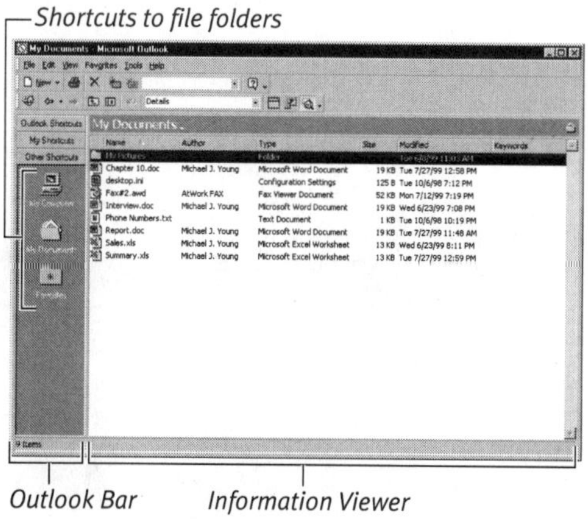

Figure 12.1 Displaying the My Documents file folder in Outlook, using the Details view.

You can work with your disk files and folders using Outlook's integrated file management feature. This feature lets you access your disk files and folders within the Outlook window, using the familiar Outlook interface, rather than having to switch to a separate file management program such as Windows Explorer (**Figure 12.1**).

In this chapter, you'll learn:

- How to open a file folder
- How to open, run, copy, move, rename, view, print, or delete a file; and how to view or change a file's properties
- How to create a new file folder
- How to copy, move, rename, print, or delete a file folder; and how to view or change a file folder's properties
- How to modify the way you view a file folder in Outlook

✔ Tips

- You can perform almost any of the operations discussed in this chapter by right-clicking a file or folder displayed in the Information Viewer or Folder List and choosing a command from the pop-up menu.
- You can often work with several files or folders at once by selecting all of them prior to issuing a command. The techniques for selecting several files or folders are the same as those for selecting multiple Outlook items, which are described in "To open an item" in Chapter 3.

Working with Files

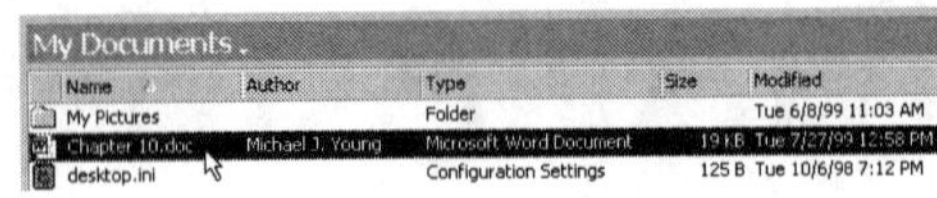

Figure 12.2 Selecting a file name prior to opening the file or performing some other operation on it.

To work with a particular file, you must first open the file folder that contains it and then use the appropriate procedure. To open a file folder, you can click its shortcut in the Outlook Bar or use any of the other methods given in the sections "To open a file folder" and "Other ways to open folders" in Chapter 2. In the initial Outlook setup, the Outlook Bar shortcuts to file folders are generally in the Other Shortcuts group.

✔ Tips

- You can open a subfolder of the currently opened file folder by double-clicking the subfolder name in the Information Viewer.
- If you're not sure which file folder contains a particular file, you can use the Advanced Find dialog box to locate the file. For instructions, see "To use the Advanced Find dialog box" in Chapter 3.

To open or run a file:

1. Click on the file name in the Information Viewer to select it (**Figure 12.2**).
2. Press Enter.

Or

- ◆ Double-click the file name.

If the file is a document or other data file, it will be opened in the program that created it. For example, a Word document (which has a .DOC file name extension) will be opened in Microsoft Word. If the file is a program or a shortcut to a program, the program will begin running.

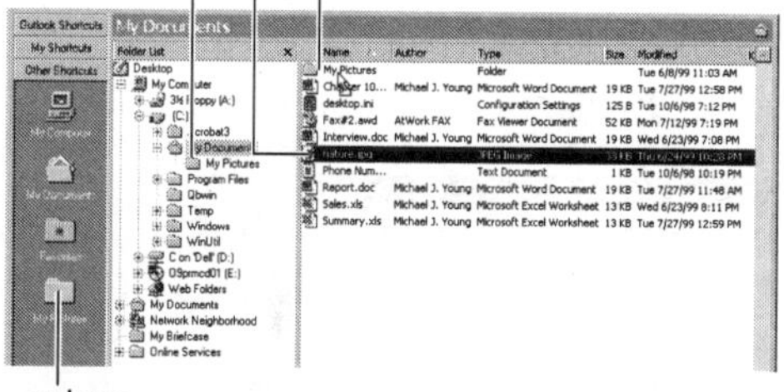

Figure 12.3 Moving file nature.jpg to the My Pictures folder.

✔ Tips

- In "To create an Outlook Bar shortcut to a file" in Chapter 14, you'll learn how to create an Outlook Bar shortcut to a file so that you can open or run the file by simply clicking the shortcut.
- Outlook provides commands for quickly running several related programs. Choose View > Go To, and then from the submenu choose News to run the Outlook Express Internet newsreader program; choose Web Browser to run your default Web browser; or choose Internet Call to run Microsoft NetMeeting.

To copy or move a file:

1. Select the file name.
2. To copy the file, choose Edit > Copy or press Ctrl-C.

   or

   To move the file, choose Edit > Cut or press Ctrl-X.
3. If you're copying the file to a different folder, or if you're moving the file, open the destination folder.
4. Choose Edit > Paste, or press Ctrl-V.

Or

- To move the file, drag it and drop it on the destination folder. You can drop it on the name of the destination folder in the Information Viewer or Folder List, or you can drop it on the shortcut for the folder in the Outlook Bar (**Figure 12.3**). To copy the file, press Ctrl while you drag.

To change a file's name or properties:

1. Select the file name.
2. To rename the file, choose File > Rename and type a new name into the Rename dialog box (**Figure 12.4**).
3. To view or modify the file's properties, choose File > Properties to open the Properties dialog box **Figure 12.5**).

Figure 12.4 The Rename dialog box.

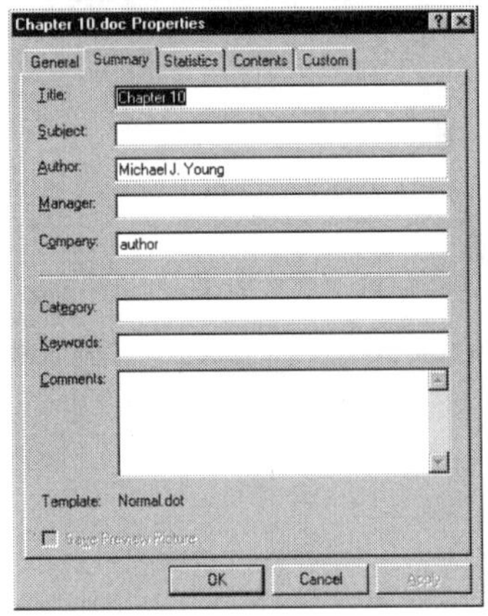

Figure 12.5 The Properties dialog box.

To view or print a file:

1. Select the file name.
2. To view the file, choose File > Quick View (**Figure 12.6**).

   This command is available only if Quick View is capable of viewing the selected file.
3. To print the file, choose File > Print or press Ctrl-P, and In the Print dialog box, select the **Selected File(s)** item in the **Print style** list (**Figure 12.7**) and click the **OK** button.

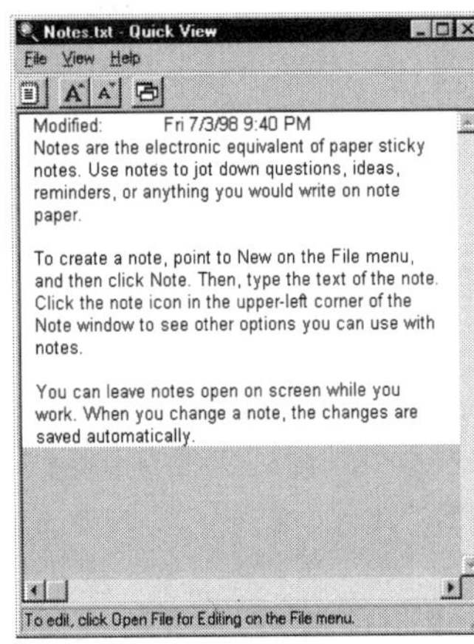

Figure 12.6 Viewing a text file in the Quick View file viewing program.

To delete a file:

1. Select the file name.
2. Press the Delete key, or click the Delete button on the Standard toolbar; or choose Edit > Delete; or press Ctrl-D.

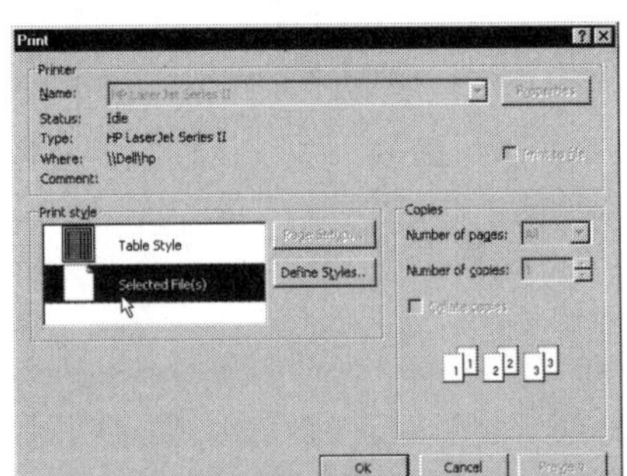

Figure 12.7 Printing the selected file.

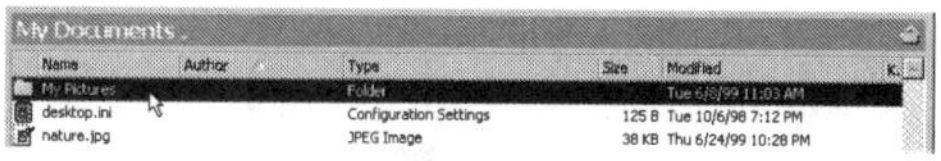

Figure 12.8 Selecting a folder.

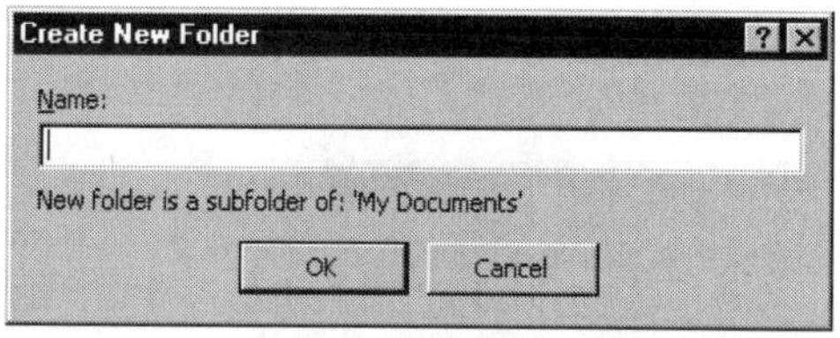

Figure 12.9 The Create New Folder dialog box.

Working with File Folders

In the following procedures, sometimes you need to *open* the file folder while at other times you need to *select* it.

- To **open** a file folder means to display its contents in the Information Viewer, by clicking on the shortcut for the folder in the Outlook Bar or by using any of the other methods given in "To open a file folder" and "Other ways to open folders" in Chapter 2.
- To **select** a file folder means to click on the folder's name in the Information Viewer. The folder that *contains* the folder you want to work with must be opened (**Figure 12.8**).

To create a new file folder:

1. Open the folder in which you want to create the new folder. (The new folder will become a subfolder of the opened folder.)
2. Choose File > New > Folder, or press Ctrl-Shift-E.
3. Type a name for the new folder in the Create New Folder dialog box (**Figure 12.9**) and click the **OK** button.

To copy or move a file folder:

1. Select the folder.
2. To copy the folder, choose Edit > Copy, or press Ctrl-C.

   or

   To move the folder, choose Edit > Cut or press Ctrl-X.
3. If you're copying the folder to a different folder, or if you're moving the folder, open the destination folder.
4. Choose Edit > Paste, or press Ctrl-V.

(continued on next page)

Or

- To move the folder, drag the folder name from the Information Viewer or from the Folder List, and drop it on the destination folder. You can drop it on the destination folder name in the Information Viewer or Folder List, or on the shortcut for the destination folder in the Outlook Bar. Or, if the destination folder is opened in the Information Viewer, you can drop it anywhere in the Information Viewer, except on a folder name. To copy the file, press Ctrl while you drag.

Figure 12.10 The Rename dialog box for renaming a file folder.

To change a file folder's name or properties:

1. Open the folder.
2. Choose File > Folder, and then choose a command on the submenu:
   - Choose **Rename** to change the folder's name in the Rename dialog box (**Figure 12.10**).
   - Choose **Properties** to view or change the folder's properties, including its sharing properties, in the Properties dialog box (**Figure 12.11**).

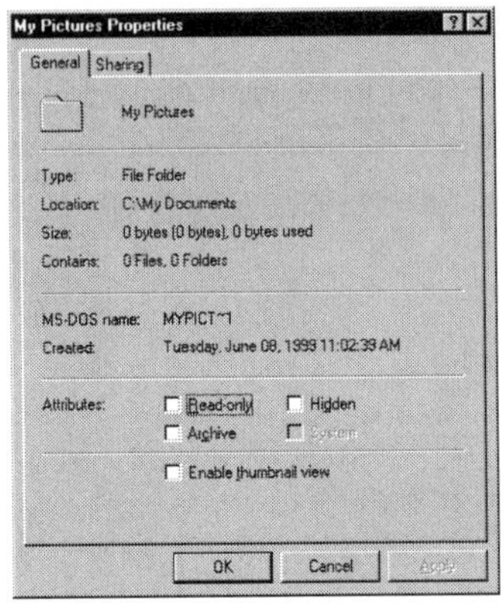

Figure 12.11 The Properties dialog box, showing the properties of the opened folder.

To print a file folder:

1. Open the folder.
2. Activate a table view.

   A table view arranges the files in rows and columns (as shown in **Figure 12.1**, earlier in the chapter). The Details, By Author, By File Type, and Programs standard views are all table views.
3. Choose File > Print.
4. In the Print dialog box, select **Table Style** in the **Print style** list (**Figure 12.12**) and click the **OK** button.

Outlook will print the contents of the opened folder, as it's displayed in the current table view.

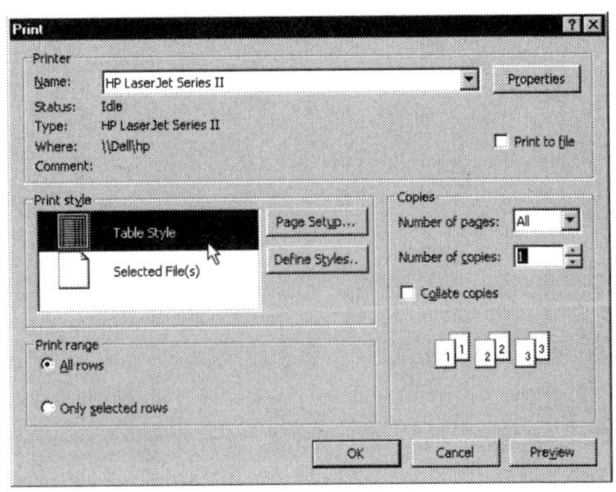

Figure 12.12 Printing the opened folder.

Figure 12.13 Selecting a view for a file folder.

Click one of these buttons to modify the size and arrangement of the icons

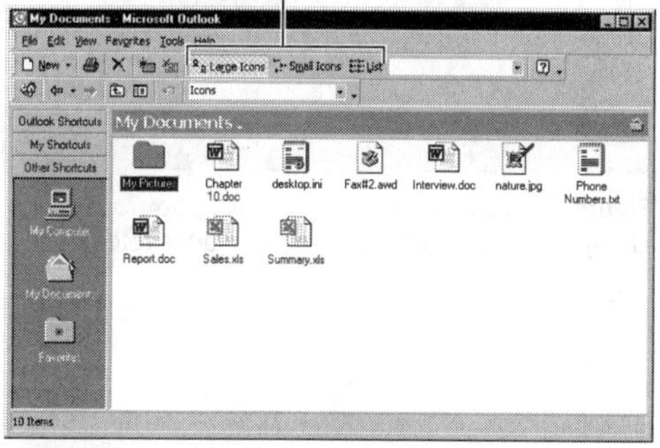

Figure 12.14 The Icons view of a file folder.

✔ Tip

- For more information on printing and print previewing, see "To print an Outlook folder or folder items" in Chapter 4.

To delete a file folder:

- Select the folder in the Information Viewer. Then press the Delete key, or click the Delete button on the Standard toolbar; or choose Edit > Delete; or press Ctrl-D.

  or

  Open the folder and choose File > Folder > Delete.

To modify the view of a file folder:

1. Open the folder.
2. To activate a different view of the folder, select a view in the Current View list box on the Advanced toolbar (**Figure 12.13**), or choose View > Current View and then choose the view from the submenu.
   - The **Icons** view displays all files and folders as icons (**Figure 12.14**).
   - The **Details** view shows all files and folders in a table, listing the properties of each (see **Figure 12.1**, earlier in the chapter).
   - The **By Author**, **By File Type**, and **Programs** views show files and folders in a table, with a grouping or a filter applied.
   - The **Document Timeline** view arranges all files and folders in a timeline according to their creation dates.

(continued on next page)

WORKING WITH FILE FOLDERS

3. To modify features of the current view of the opened file folder, choose View > Current View > Customize Current View, click the **Other Settings** button, and select the desired options in the Format Timeline View dialog box (for the Document Timeline view), the Format Icon View dialog box (for the Icons view), or the Other Settings dialog box (for a table view) (**Figure 12.15**).

✔ Tip

- If you've made a change in a file folder that isn't yet shown in the current view, choose View > Refresh or press F5 to update the view.

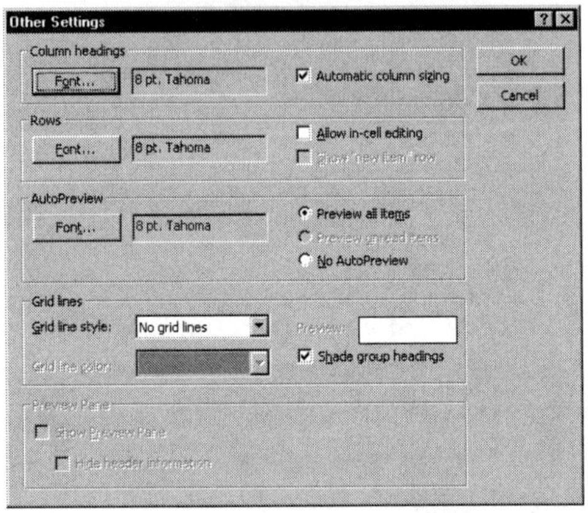

Figure 12.15 The Other Settings dialog box for changing features of a table view of a file folder.

EXPLORING THE WEB IN OUTLOOK

13

You can use Outlook as a tool for exploring the Web. You can view Web pages within the Outlook window, or you can use Outlook to open pages in your default Web browser program (for example, Microsoft Internet Explorer or Netscape Navigator).

In this chapter, you'll learn:

- How to display a Web page in the Outlook window by using the Favorites menu, and how to add a Web page to this menu
- How to display a Web page in your browser by opening an Internet shortcut file
- How to use the Web toolbar to open and navigate through Web pages
- How to create a shortcut to a Web page in your Outlook Bar, so you can display the page in the Outlook window by simply clicking the shortcut

Displaying a Web Page

When you open a Web page using Outlook, either the page will be displayed within the Outlook window (**Figure 13.1**) or it will be displayed in your Web browser (**Figure 13.2**), depending on which of the methods in this chapter that you use.

Once you've opened a Web page, you can view other pages by clicking any hyperlinks that are displayed within the original page.

✔ Tips

- If a Web page is displayed in the Outlook window, you can open the same page in your Web browser by choosing File > Open In Default Browser.
- If you click a Web-page hyperlink inserted in an Outlook item, the page will be opened in your browser. See "To edit a new or existing item" and **Figure 3.17** in Chapter 3.
- You can open a contact's Web page in your browser by selecting the contact in the Outlook window and clicking the Explore Web Page button on the Advanced toolbar, or by pressing Ctrl-Shift-X. See "To contact a contact" in Chapter 8.
- You can run your default Web browser by choosing View > Go To > Web Browser.
- You can attach a Web page to an Outlook folder and display it rather than the folder's normal contents. See "Attaching a Home Page to an Outlook Folder" in Chapter 14.

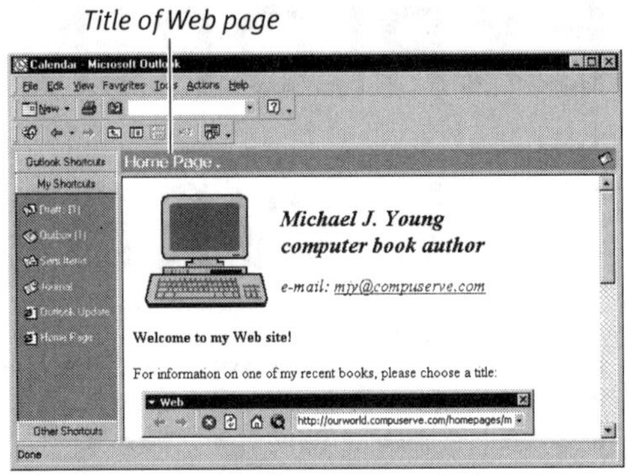

Figure 13.1 A Web page displayed within the Outlook window.

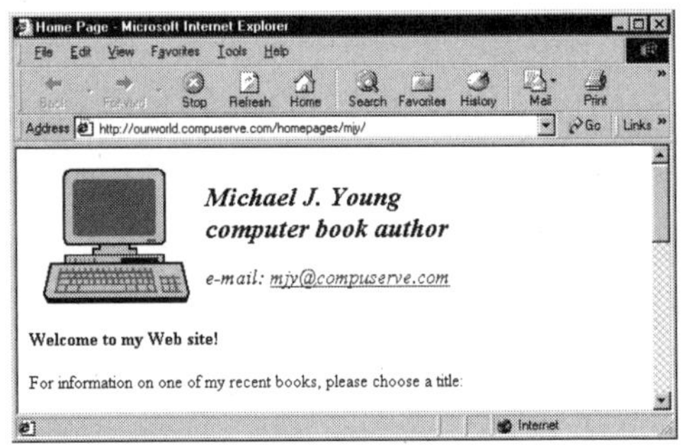

Figure 13.2 The same Web page displayed in the Microsoft Internet Explorer browser.

Figure 13.3 Opening the "Windows" Web page by choosing a command from a submenu of the Favorites menu.

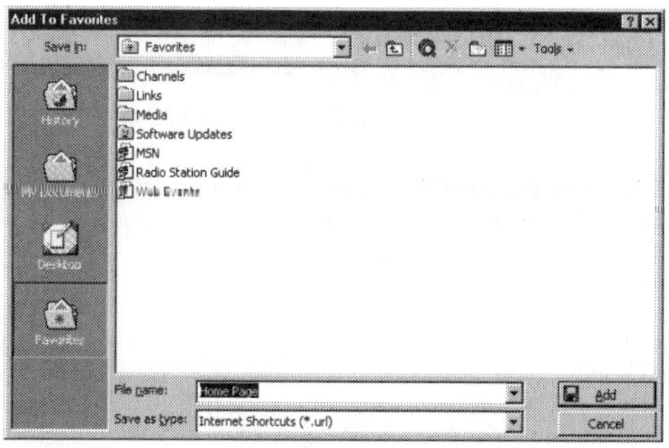

Figure 13.4 The Add To Favorites dialog box.

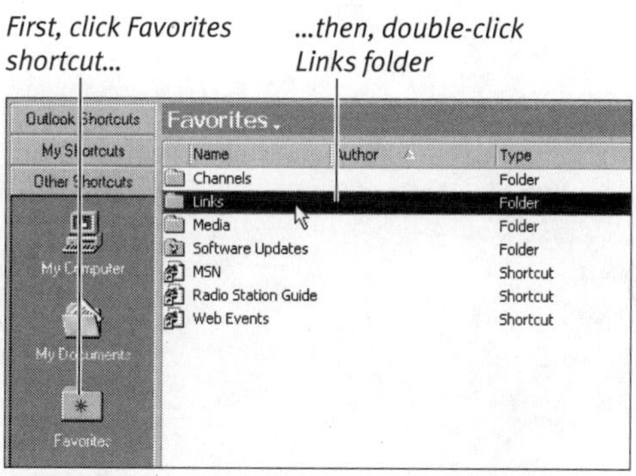

Figure 13.5 Opening the Links subfolder of the Favorites folder.

To open a Web page using the Favorites menu:

- Choose the name of the page you want to open from the Favorites menu or from one of its submenus (**Figure 13.3**).

  Outlook will display the page within the Outlook window.

✔ Tips

- The Web pages displayed on your Favorites menu correspond to the Internet shortcuts that are stored in your \Windows\Favorites file folder.
- You can add an Internet shortcut to your Favorites file folder, thereby adding the Web page to your Favorites menu, by opening the page in Outlook, choosing Favorites > Add To Favorites, and specifying a name and location for the shortcut in the Add To Favorites dialog box (**Figure 13.4**).

To open a Web page using an Internet shortcut:

1. Open the file folder that contains the Internet shortcut to the Web page you want to view.

   To open a file folder, click its shortcut in the Outlook Bar or use any of the other methods given in the sections "To open a file folder" and "Other ways to open folders" in Chapter 2.

   Internet shortcuts are generally stored in your \Windows\Favorites folder or in one of its subfolders (although you can store an Internet shortcut in *any* file folder). You can open Favorites by clicking the Favorites shortcut in the Other Shortcuts group of the Outlook Bar. You can then open a Favorites subfolder by double-clicking it in the Information Viewer (**Figure 13.5**).

(continued on next page)

2. Double-click the Internet shortcut.

   An Internet shortcut has an icon that displays an arrow and a symbol for your default Web browser (for example, if you're using Internet Explorer, the icon displays an *e*) (**Figure 13.6**).

The Web page will be opened in your default Web browser.

Figure 13.6 A shortcut for opening the "Windows" Web site (as displayed with the Large Icons option). Here, Internet Explorer is the default browser.

To use the Web toolbar:

1. If the Web toolbar (**Figure 13.7**) isn't already displayed, choose View > Toolbars > Web.

   Outlook normally displays the Web toolbar when you open a Web page in the Outlook window, and it removes the Web toolbar when you're no longer viewing a Web page.

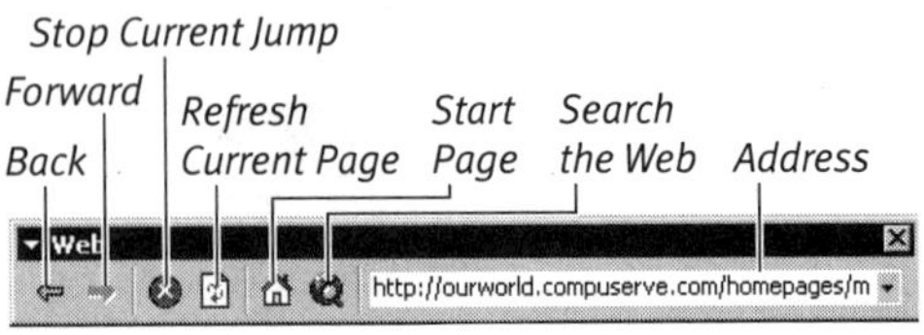

Figure 13.7 The Web toolbar.

2. To open a particular Web page in the Outlook window, type the Internet address into the **Address** list box on the Web toolbar.

   or

   Select a previously typed address from the drop-down list of the **Address** list box (**Figure 13.8**).

Figure 13.8 Selecting a previously typed address from the **Address** list box.

3. To navigate through the Web pages you've viewed in the Outlook window, click the Back or Forward button on the Web toolbar.

4. To stop loading the current page (for example, if your Internet connection has bogged down and loading is taking too long), click the Stop Current Jump button.

5. To reload the current page, click the Refresh Current Page button.

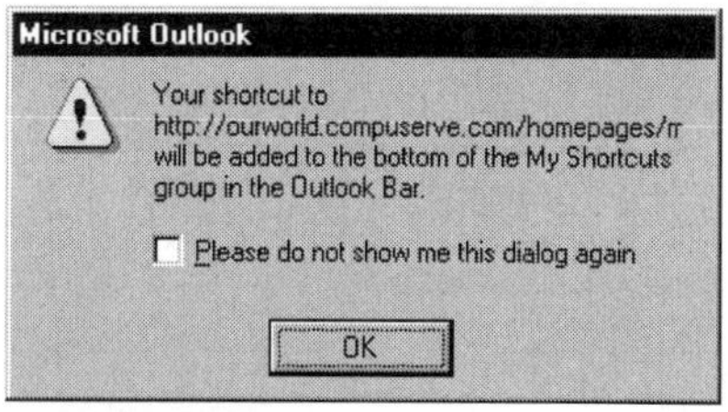

Figure 13.9 Confirming adding an Internet shortcut to the Outlook Bar.

To create a shortcut to a Web page in your Outlook Bar:

1. Open the Web page *in the Outlook window*, using the Favorites menu or the Web toolbar, or by following hyperlinks to the page.
2. In the Outlook Bar, open the shortcut group where you want to add the new shortcut.
3. Choose File > New > Outlook Bar Shortcut To Web Page.
4. If Outlook displays a confirmation dialog box, click the **OK** button (**Figure 13.9**).
5. If you want to rename the shortcut, right-click it and choose Rename Shortcut from the pop-up menu.

You can click the new shortcut to quickly open the Web page and display it in the Outlook window.

✔ Tip

- For information on creating and managing Outlook Bar shortcuts and shortcut groups, see "Modifying the Outlook Bar" in Chapter 14.

CUSTOMIZING OUTLOOK

14

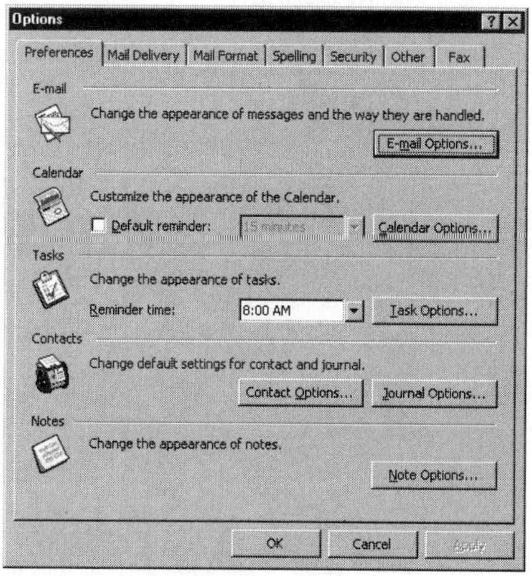

Figure 14.1 The Options dialog box.

In this chapter, you'll learn some of the useful ways that you can customize Outlook. Specifically, you'll learn:

- How to customize the Outlook toolbars and menus to suit your working style
- How to change the Office Assistant to make it look and behave the way you want
- How to modify the Outlook Bar to organize your information and make it easier to access your folders
- How to adjust Outlook views to enhance the way Outlook displays information
- How to attach a home page to an Outlook folder, so that you can display Web-style information in that folder in addition to the folder's contents

✓ Tip

- You can modify many features of Outlook by choosing Tools > Options and changing settings in the tabs of the Options dialog box (**Figure 14.1**). Most of these settings are discussed in this book, each in the appropriate context. You can obtain help on any setting by clicking the Help button [?] near the upper-right corner of the dialog box and then clicking the setting.

Customizing the Toolbars and Menus

Like the other major Office applications, Outlook lets you extensively customize the toolbars and the menu bar. Before delving into the details, you'll need to understand a few definitions:

- A **built-in toolbar** is one of the toolbars supplied with the program. The built-in toolbars available in the main Outlook window are Standard, Advanced, and Web.
- A **custom toolbar** is one that you create yourself.
- The Outlook **menu bar** initially displays the main program menus: File, Edit, View, Favorites, Tools, Actions, and Help (**Figure 14.2**). You can use and customize the menu bar just like a built-in toolbar. The primary difference between the menu bar and a built-in toolbar is that the menu bar can't be hidden.
- This chapter uses the general term **command** to refer to *any* item on a toolbar or on the menu bar. The term includes a button or a menu on a toolbar, a menu on the menu bar, as well as a command or a submenu on a menu.

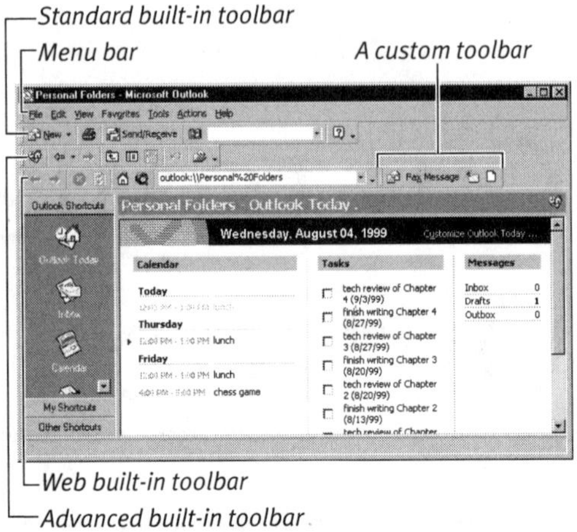

Figure 14.2 The Outlook menu bar, the built-in toolbars, and a custom toolbar.

✔ Tips

- Instructions for using menus and toolbars are given in "Learning Basic Windows and Office Techniques" in Chapter 2.
- You can use the instructions in this chapter to modify either the toolbars and menus in the main Outlook window or those in Outlook forms. To modify the toolbars and menus in the main Outlook window, activate that window before following the instructions. To modify the toolbars and menus in Outlook forms,

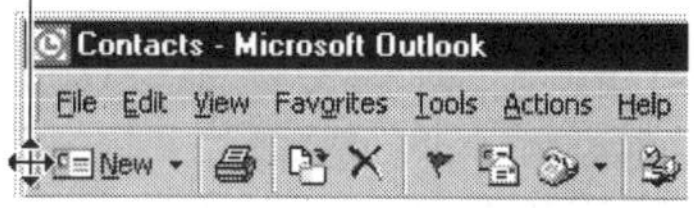

Figure 14.3 Dragging a move handle to move a toolbar.

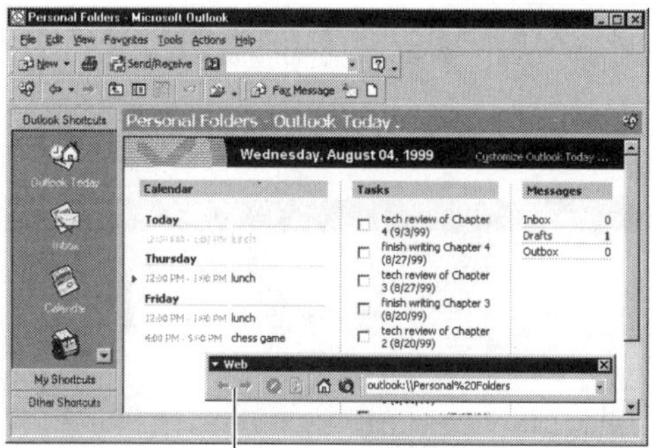

Figure 14.4 The Web toolbar positioned as a floating toolbar.

Figure 14.5 Moving a floating toolbar.

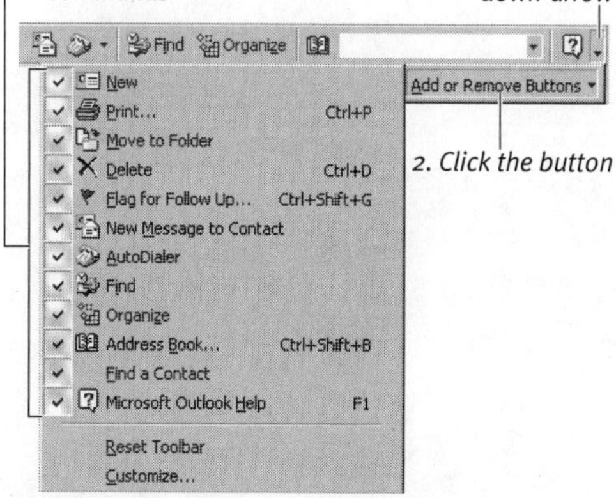

Figure 14.6 Displaying or removing standard commands on a built-in toolbar that is docked.

open any form except a note before following the instructions. Modifications you make in any form (such as a Message form) will affect all other forms except a note.

To move a toolbar or the menu bar:

- Drag the move handle on the toolbar or menu bar (**Figure 14.3**). If you drop the bar near an edge of the Outlook window or form, the bar will be *docked* (that is, positioned) along that edge. The toolbars and the menu bar in **Figures 14.2** and **14.3** are docked. If you drop the bar anywhere else on the screen, it will *float* at that position (**Figure 14.4**).

  or

  If the toolbar or the menu bar is floating, drag its title bar to move it (**Figure 14.5**).

To modify a toolbar or the menu bar:

1. To modify a toolbar that isn't visible, display it by choosing View > Toolbars and then choosing the toolbar name from the submenu.
2. To display or remove standard commands from a built-in toolbar:

   If the toolbar is docked, click the down-arrow on the end of the toolbar, click Add Or Remove Buttons, and then check a command to display it or uncheck a command to remove it (**Figure 14.6**).

(continued on next page)

or

If the built-in toolbar is floating, click the down-arrow in the upper-left corner of the toolbar, click Add Or Remove Buttons, and then check a command to display it or uncheck a command to remove it (**Figure 14.7**).

3. To add *any* available command to the menu bar or to a built-in or custom toolbar, choose Tools > Customize and open the Commands tab (**Figure 14.8**). Choose a command category in the Categories list and then drag the command you want from the Commands list and drop it on the toolbar or menu bar at the desired position.

   You can drop a command on a toolbar, on the menu bar, or on a menu that drops down from a toolbar or the menu bar (the menu will drop down when you drag the command over it).

   To add a custom menu (rather than one of the standard menus in the Commands list), select the New Menu category and then drag the New Menu command to the desired location.

4. To move a command, leave the Customize dialog box open and drag the command to the new position.

   or

   To copy the command, press Ctrl while you drag.

   You can move or copy the command to a different position on the same toolbar or menu bar, or to a different bar.

5. To remove a command, leave the Customize dialog box open, drag the command, and drop it anywhere on the screen *except* on a toolbar or menu bar.

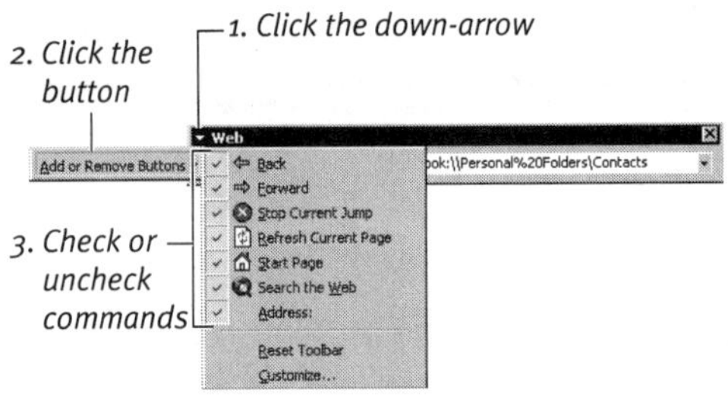

Figure 14.7 Displaying or removing standard commands on a built-in toolbar that is floating.

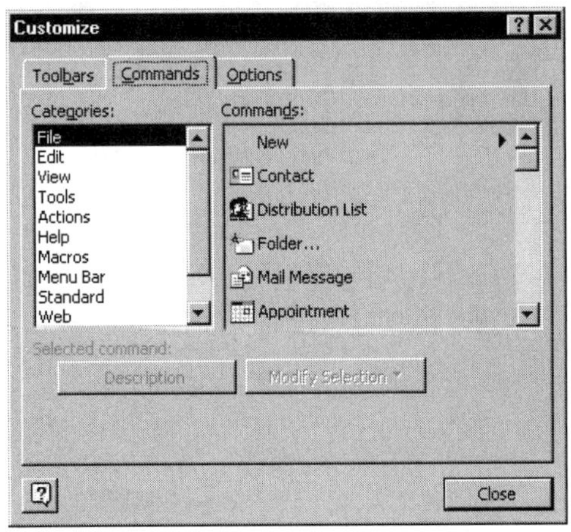

Figure 14.8 The Commands tab of the Customize dialog box.

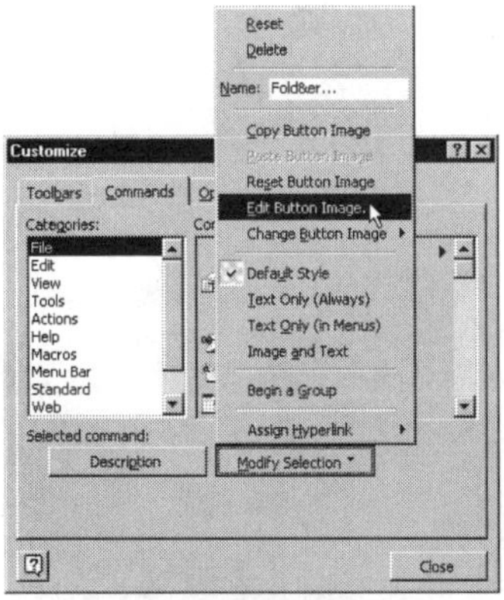

Figure 14.9 Modifying the selected command.

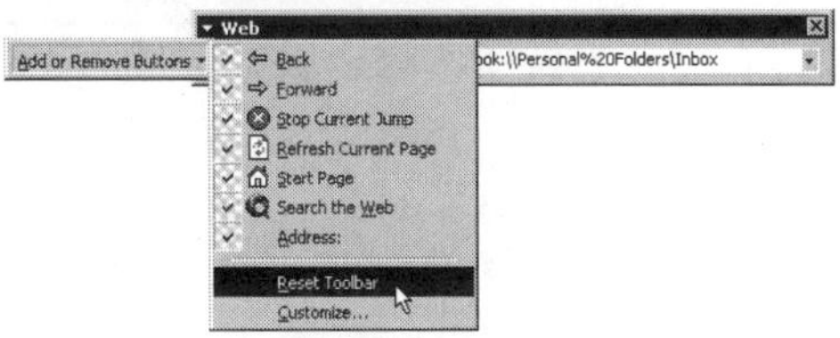

Figure 14.10 Removing modifications from a built-in toolbar.

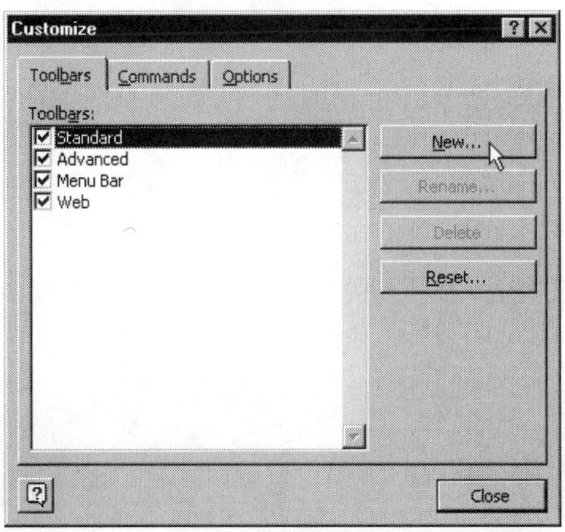

Figure 14.11 Creating a custom toolbar.

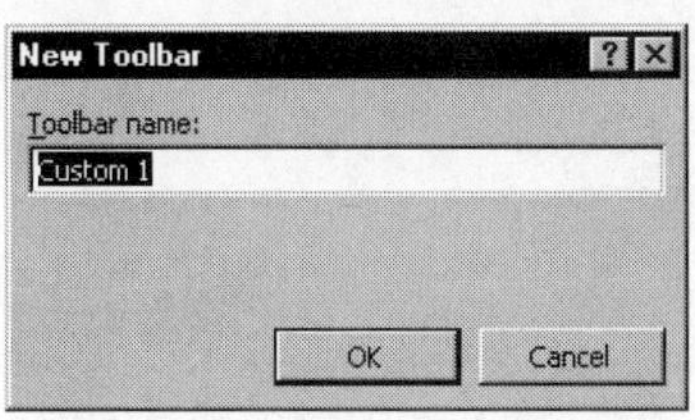

Figure 14.12 The New Toolbar dialog box.

6. To modify a command (for example, to change its image), leave the Customize dialog box open, click the command to select it, click the **Modify Selection** button in the Commands tab, and choose a command from the menu (**Figure 14.9**).

   or

   Leave the Customize dialog box open, right-click the command, and choose a command from the pop-up menu.

6. Click the **Close** button in the Customize dialog box.

✔ Tip

- If you've modified a built-in toolbar, you can restore it to its original "factory" configuration by clicking the down arrow (on the end of a docked toolbar or in the upper-left corner of a floating toolbar), clicking Add Or Remove Buttons, and then choosing Reset Toolbar (**Figure 14.10**).

To create a custom toolbar:

1. If you want to create a toolbar that you can use in Outlook forms, open any form (except a note form).

   or

   If you want to create a toolbar for use in the main Outlook window, activate that window.

2. Choose Tools > Customize, open the Toolbars tab, and click the **New** button (**Figure 14.11**).

3. In the New Toolbar dialog box (**Figure 14.12**) type a name for your new toolbar and click the **OK** button.

   Your new toolbar will initially be devoid of commands. Add the commands you want using the techniques given in the previous section, "To modify a toolbar or the menu bar."

(continued on next page)

4. To rename or delete a custom toolbar, click on the toolbar name (not on the check box) to select the toolbar and then click the **Rename** or **Delete** button.

5. To reset a built-in toolbar that you've modified, click on the toolbar name (not on the check box) to select the toolbar and then click the **Reset** button.

   The toolbar will be restored to its original "factory" configuration.

6. Click the **Close** button in the Customize dialog box.

✔ Tip

- Checking or unchecking a toolbar name in the list in the Toolbars tab provides yet another way to show or hide a toolbar.

To set toolbar and menu options:

1. Choose Tools > Customize and open the Options tab (**Figure 14.13**).

2. Choose options as desired in the Options tab.

   For help with a specific option, click the Help button in the upper-right corner and then click the option. For general help, click the Assistant button in the lower-left corner.

✔ Tip

- The settings you make in the Options tab affect toolbars and menus in both the main Outlook window and in Outlook forms.

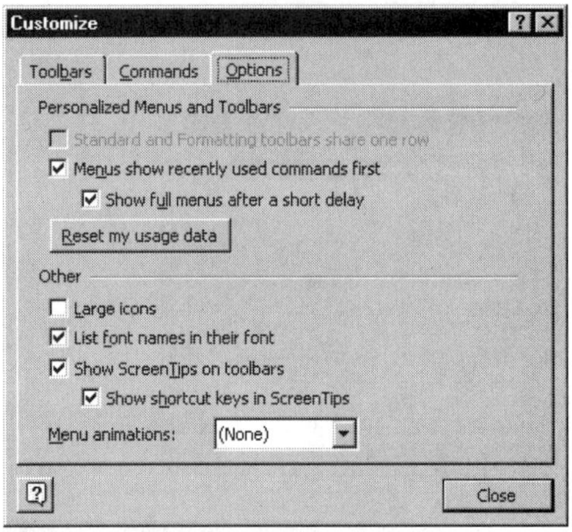

Figure 14.13 The Options tab of the Customize dialog box.

Figure 14.14 Clicking the **Options** button in the Assistant's balloon.

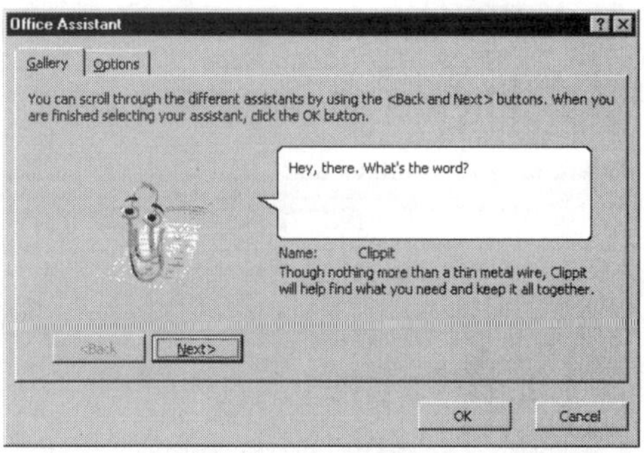

Figure 14.15 The Gallery tab of the Office Assistant dialog box.

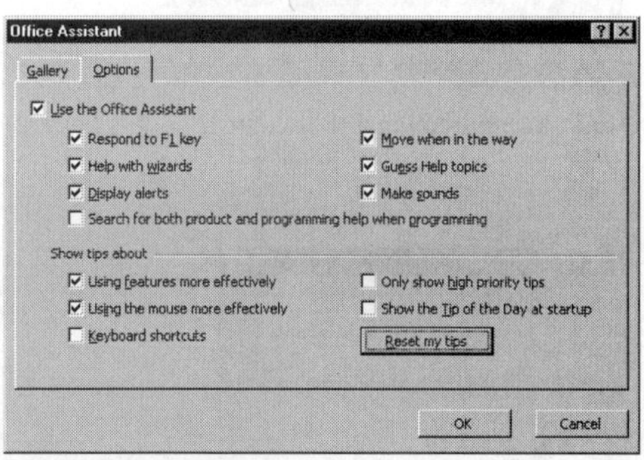

Figure 14.16 The Options tab of the Office Assistant dialog box.

Changing the Office Assistant

You can select a different Outlook Assistant character—for example, Clippit (a paperclip character), F1 (a robot), or Links (a cat). You can also modify the behavior of the Assistant.

✔ Tip

- For instructions on using the Assistant, see "Consulting the Assistant" in Chapter 2.

To change the Office Assistant:

1. If the Assistant isn't currently visible, choose Help > Show The Office Assistant.
2. If the Assistant's balloon isn't visible, click the Assistant.
3. Click the **Options** button in the balloon (**Figure 14.14**).
4. To select a different Assistant character, open the Gallery tab in the Office Assistant dialog box and scroll through the characters by clicking the **Next** and **Back** buttons until you find the character you want (**Figure 14.15**).
5. To change the Assistant's behavior, open the Options tab and check the desired options (**Figure 14.16**).

   Unchecking the **Use the Office Assistant** option disables the Assistant. To reenable it, choose Help > Show The Office Assistant.
6. Click the **OK** button in the Office Assistant dialog box.

Modifying the Outlook Bar

The section "How to Get Around in Outlook" in Chapter 2 explained how to use the shortcuts in the Outlook Bar to open Outlook folders as well as file folders. The following sections explain how to modify the Outlook Bar so that you can streamline your work, organize your information, or accommodate folders you have added or removed (**Figure 14.17**).

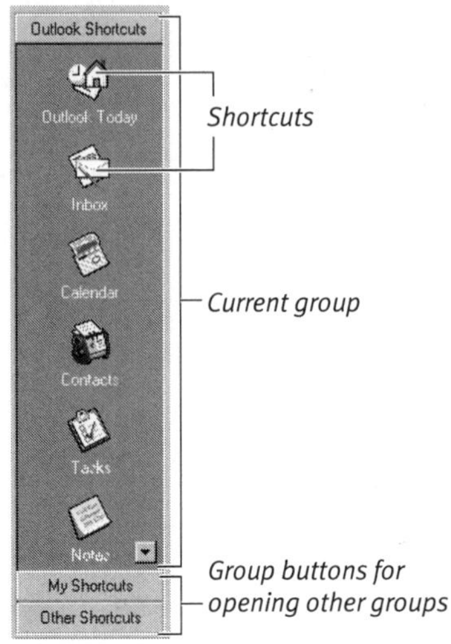

Figure 14.17 The Outlook Bar.

✔ Tip

- For instructions on creating an Outlook Bar shortcut to a Web page (rather than to a folder or to a file), see "To create a shortcut to a Web page in your Outlook Bar" in Chapter 13.

To create an Outlook Bar shortcut to a folder:

1. Display the group in which you want to create the shortcut.
2. Right-click within the current (displayed) group, but *not* on a shortcut, and choose Outlook Bar Shortcut from the pop-up menu (**Figure 14.18**).

   Outlook will open the Add To Outlook Bar dialog box (**Figure 14.19**).
3. In the **Look in** list box, select **Outlook** to create a shortcut to an Outlook folder or select **File System** to create a shortcut to a file folder.
4. Type or select the folder name in the **Folder name** list box.

   or

   Select the folder name in the hierarchical list below the **Folder name** list box.
5. Click the **OK** button.

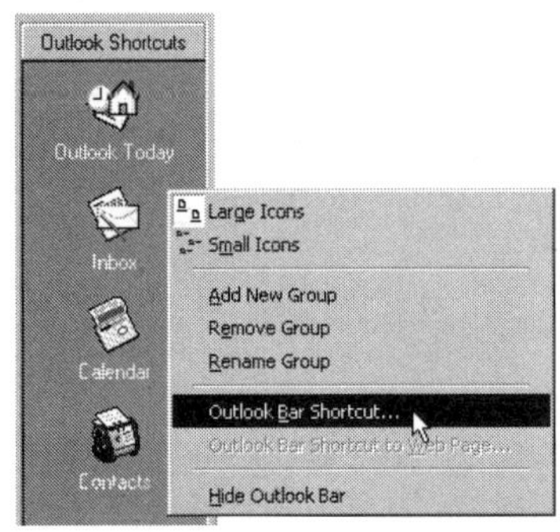

Figure 14.18 Creating a shortcut to a folder.

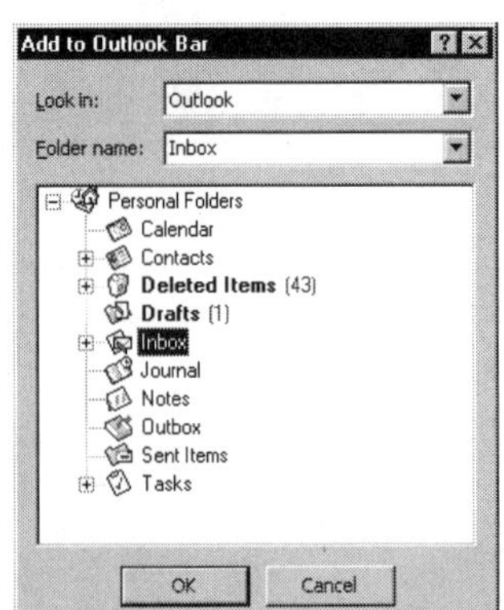

Figure 14.19 The Add To Outlook Bar dialog box.

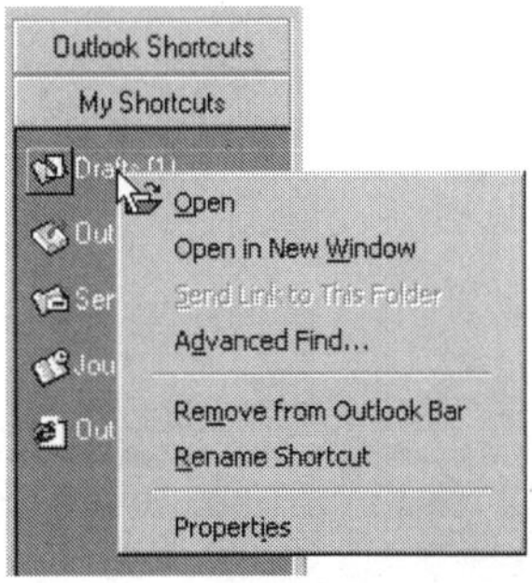

Figure 14.20 Right-clicking a shortcut to display the pop-up menu.

To create an Outlook Bar shortcut to a file:

- Drag the file name and drop at the desired position in the Outlook Bar. You can drag the file name from Windows Explorer, from a file folder that's opened in Windows, or from a file folder that's displayed in Outlook.

✔ Tip

- If the target location for the shortcut isn't visible in the Outlook Bar, while you drag the file you can hold the pointer over the top or bottom of the current group to scroll through that group, or you can hold it over a group button to display a different group. (Keep the mouse button pressed!)

To modify an Outlook Bar shortcut:

1. Right-click the shortcut to display the pop-up menu (**Figure 14.20**).
2. To rename the shortcut, choose Rename Shortcut.
3. To remove the shortcut, choose Remove From Outlook Bar.

✔ Tip

- To move a shortcut, drag it to the desired position. To make a copy of the shortcut, press Ctrl while you drag. If the target location isn't visible in the Outlook Bar, while you drag you can hold the pointer over the top or bottom of the current group to scroll through that group, or you can hold it over a group button to open a different group. (Keep the mouse button pressed!)

To modify Outlook Bar groups:

1. Right-click the group you want to work with.

   To work with the current group, right-click anywhere within it except on a shortcut. To work with one of the other groups, right-click the group button.

   Outlook will display a pop-up menu (**Figure 14-21**).

2. To remove or rename the group you right-clicked, choose Remove Group or Rename Group.

3. To change the size of the shortcut icons in the *current* group (regardless of which group you right-clicked), choose Large Icons or Small Icons.

4. To create a new group, choose Add New Group.

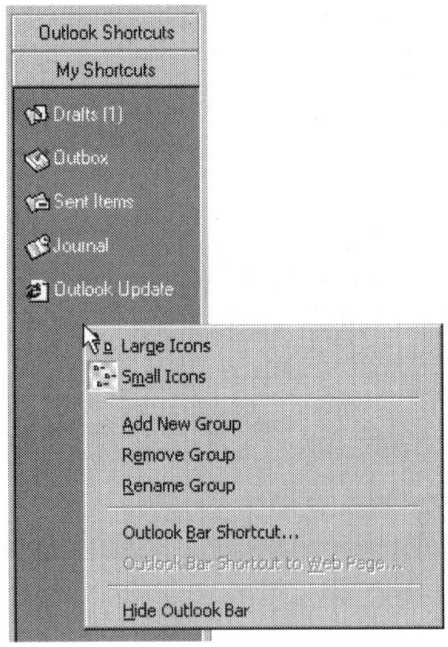

Figure 14.21 Right-clicking in the current group to display the pop-up menu for modifying that group.

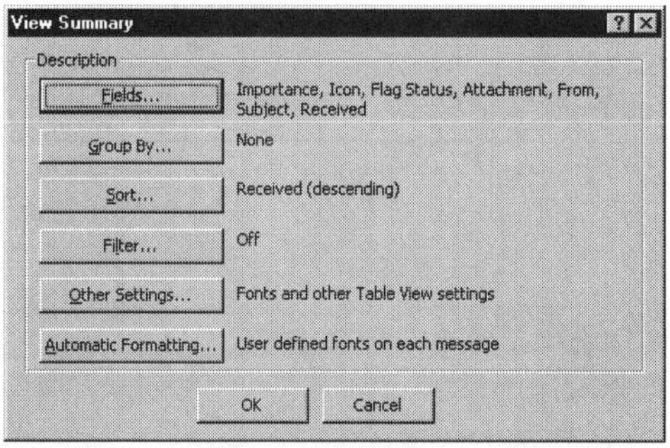

Figure 14.22 The View Summary dialog box, as displayed for the Messages view of the Inbox folder.

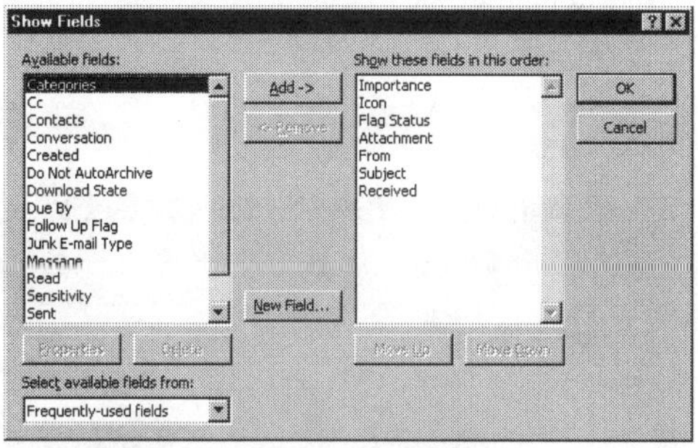

Figure 14.23 The Show Fields dialog box, as displayed for the Messages view of the Inbox folder.

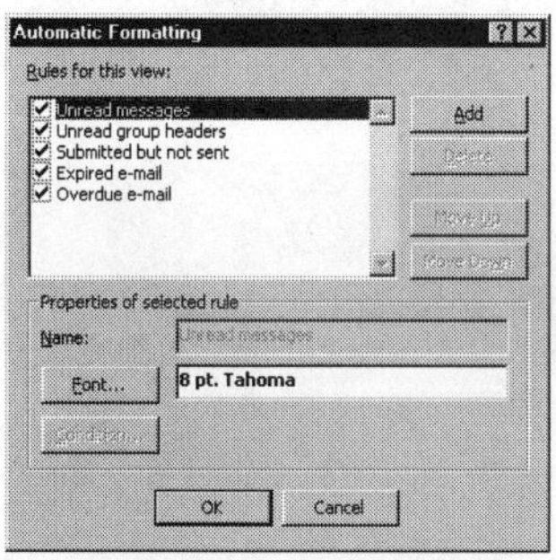

Figure 14.24 The Automatic Formatting dialog box, as displayed for the Messages view of the Inbox folder.

Adjusting Views

Chapter 3 (the section "Using Different Views") explained how to work with the different views of a folder. Chapter 3 (the section "Sorting, Filtering, and Grouping Items") also described how to sort, filter, or group the items in a particular view, which are some of the most common ways to modify a view. In the following sections, you'll learn about some additional ways to modify the current view.

To customize the current view:

1. Choose View > Current View > Customize Current View.

   Outlook will open the View Summary dialog box (**Figure 14.22**). The buttons that are available in this dialog box, and their descriptions, depend upon the current folder and view.

2. To change the particular fields that are displayed, or to change the order of the fields, click the **Fields** button and select options in the Show Fields dialog box (**Figure 14.23**).

3. To modify the way Outlook formats various types of items—for example, the font and color it uses for unread messages—click the **Automatic Formatting** button and select options in the Automatic Formatting dialog box (**Figure 14.24**).

4. To group, sort, or filter the items in the current view, click the **Group By**, **Sort**, or **Filter** button, and follow the instructions given in "Sorting, Filtering, and Grouping Items" in Chapter 3.

5. To change other features of the view, click the **Other Settings** button and select options in the dialog box that Outlook displays.

(continued on next page)

The name of the dialog box and its contents depend upon the current view. Chapters 6 through 11 show examples of this dialog box for different folders and views.

To manage views:

- Choose View > Current View > Define Views to open the Define Views dialog box (**Figure 14.25**) and select the desired options:
  - Create a new custom view, or make a copy of an existing view.
  - Modify any view.
  - Reset any of the built-in views to restore it to its original "factory" settings.
  - Delete or rename a custom view that you've created.

To format columns in a table view:

1. Activate the table view in which you want to format the columns.
2. Choose View > Current View > Format Columns to open the Format Columns dialog box (**Figure 14.26**).
3. Select the desired options in the dialog box.

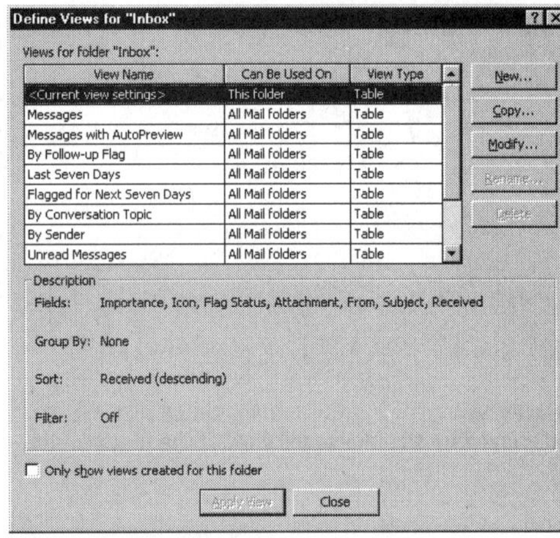

Figure 14.25 The Define Views dialog box, as displayed for the Inbox folder.

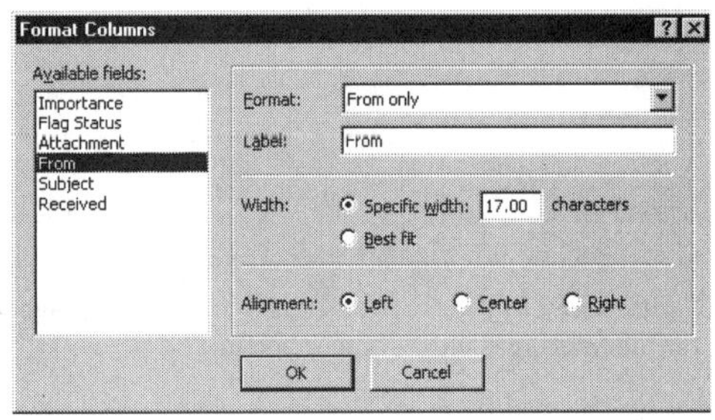

Figure 14.26 The Format Columns dialog box, as displayed for the Messages view of the Inbox folder.

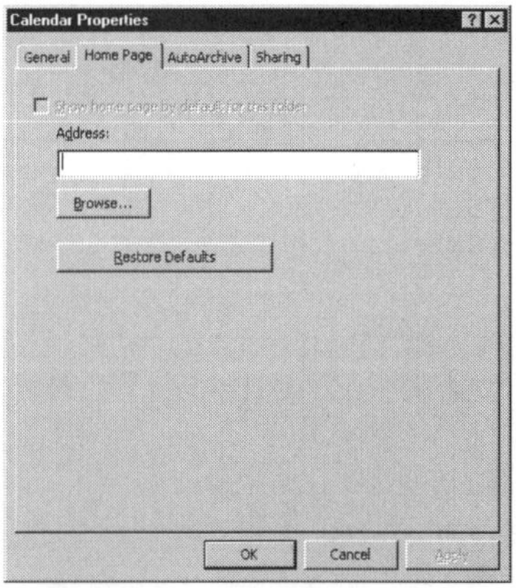

Figure 14.27 The Home Page tab of the Properties dialog box.

Attaching a Home Page to an Outlook Folder

As explained in Chapter 5, the Outlook Today folder has a home page that is displayed by default whenever the folder is opened. You can also assign a home page to any other Outlook folder, such as Inbox or Calendar. You can use a home page to display any information you want—for example, instructions for working with the folder. You can have the page displayed automatically when the folder is opened or have it displayed through a command.

✔ Tip

- The home page you assign to a folder must be contained in a Web-page (HTML) file. You can use an existing HTML file on a local or network disk or on the Web. Or, you can create an HTML file using Microsoft Word, Microsoft FrontPage, or another Web-page designer.

To assign a home page to an Outlook folder:

1. Open the Outlook folder.
2. Choose File > Folder > Properties For "*Folder*" where *Folder* is the name of the opened folder.
3. Open the Home Page tab in the Properties dialog box (**Figure 14.27**).
4. Type the full file path of the Web-page file you want to use into the **Address** text box (for example, *C:\My Documents\CalendarInfo.htm*).

   or

   Click the **Browse** button and select the Web-page file on a local or network disk.

(continued on next page)

or

If the page is located on the Web, type its full Internet address (for example, *http://ourworld.compuserve.com/homepages/mjy/*).

5. If you want the home page displayed automatically whenever you open the folder, check **Show home page by default for this folder**.

   If you don't check this option, the normal folder contents will be displayed when you open the folder.

6. Click the **OK** button in the Properties dialog box.

✔ Tips

- When the folder is opened, you can switch between displaying the home page and displaying the normal folder contents by choosing View > Show Folder Home Page.
- Keep in mind that if the home page is on the Web and if you have a dial-up Internet connection, Outlook will have to dial your service provider each time it displays the page.

Configuring Outlook

A

The instructions in this appendix will help you complete some of the more technical tasks that you might encounter when you first set up Outlook. (Setting up Outlook is described in Chapter 1.) They will also help you modify the Outlook setup after you've already begun using the program. Here, you'll learn how to:

- Switch your basic e-mail configuration between the Internet Only configuration and the Corporate Or Workgroup configuration
- Set up or modify Outlook settings if you're using the Internet Only configuration
- Set up or modify Outlook settings if you're using the Corporate Or Workgroup configuration
- Import e-mail settings, messages, or addresses from another e-mail program that you've been using on your computer
- Add or remove individual Outlook components, such as Help, Stationery, and Integrated File Management

Changing Your Basic E-mail Configuration

As you learned in Chapter 1, you might need to select a basic e-mail configuration when you first set up Outlook. Or, if Outlook uses existing e-mail settings during setup, it might choose the basic configuration for you. In either case, you can later switch between the Internet Only and the Corporate Or Workgroup configurations. You might want to do this, for example, if you change to a new e-mail service that requires the other configuration. See the section "To complete the E-mail Service Options dialog box" in Chapter 1 for an explanation of these two configurations.

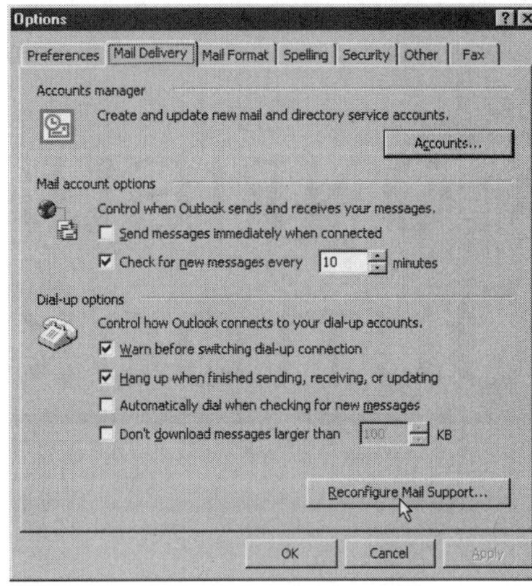

Figure A.1 Clicking the **Reconfigure Mail Support** button to switch e-mail configurations.

To switch e-mail configurations:

1. Choose Tools > Options to display the Options dialog box.
2. In the Options dialog box, open the Mail Delivery tab (Internet Only configuration) or the Mail Services tab (Corporate Or Workgroup configuration).
3. Click the **Reconfigure Mail Support** button near the bottom of the Mail Delivery tab (**Figure A.1**).

   Outlook will display the E-mail Service Options dialog box (**Figure A.2**). In this dialog box, the current e-mail configuration will initially be selected.

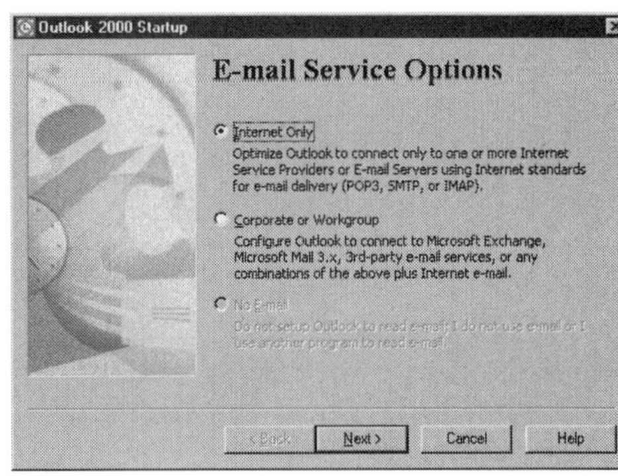

Figure A.2 The E-mail Service Options dialog box.

4. Select the e-mail option you want to switch to and click the **Next** button. (Notice that you don't have the option of choosing **No E-mail** to eliminate e-mail support.)

   Outlook will display a message box informing you that it is about to switch configurations (**Figure A.3**).

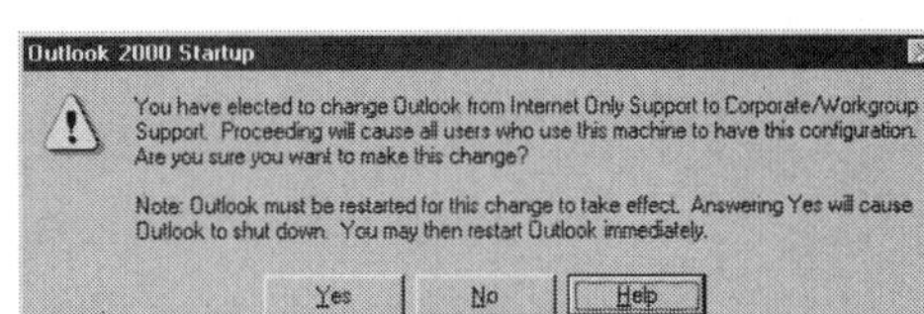

Figure A.3 The message box that Outlook displays before it switches from the Internet Only configuration to the Corporate Or Workgroup configuration.

Figure A.4 The About Microsoft Outlook dialog box.

5. Click the **Yes** button in the message box to proceed with the switch. Outlook will now shut down.

6. Restart Outlook. The program will reconfigure itself and begin running.

✔ Tips

- If you haven't used the new configuration before, and if Outlook lacks setup information, it will prompt you for the required data just as it does during initial program setup. Follow the instructions given in the section "Supplying Setup Information" in Chapter 1.
- To switch e-mail configurations, you need to insert your product CD, because Outlook needs to copy files from it.
- If you switch to the Internet Only configuration, and if you haven't previously set up the fax feature, the Symantec WinFax Starter Edition Setup Wizard will begin running. See "I/O To add a fax account," later in this appendix.
- You can find out your current e-mail configuration by choosing Help > About Microsoft Outlook. The current configuration will be displayed near the top of the About Microsoft Outlook dialog box (**Figure A.4**).

I/O Setting Up and Modifying the Internet Only E-mail Configuration

With the Internet Only Configuration, you send and receive messages and other information by means of *accounts*. There are several different types of accounts:

- A **mail** account for sending and receiving e-mail messages.
- A **directory service** account (also known as LDAP, or lightweight directory access protocol account) for obtaining e-mail addresses and other information on people from an Internet directory service. You can use a directory service account to look up information on people in the Select Names or Address Book dialog box or to verify the recipient addresses you type into your outgoing e-mail messages. For more information, see "I/O To address a message" in Chapter 6.
- A **fax** account, which is a special type of mail account that allows you to send, receive, and manage faxes with a fax modem, using the Symantec WinFax Starter Edition that's provided with Outlook.

✔ Tips

- A mail account for e-mail and a directory service account are both added using the Internet Connection Wizard. However, there are special procedures (described later) for adding or modifying a fax account.
- You can set up several mail or directory service accounts. Outlook will let you select the specific accounts that are used.

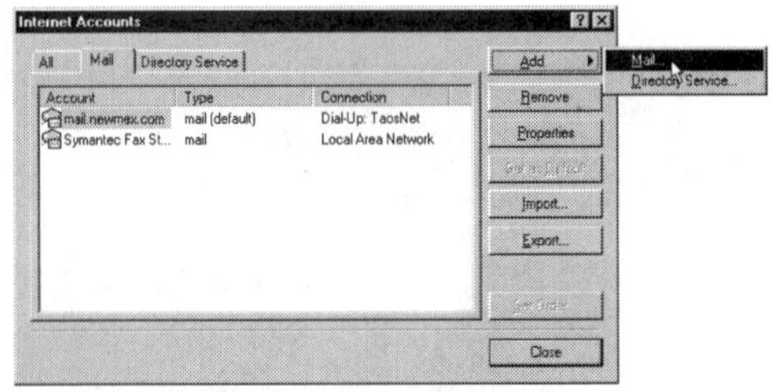

Figure A.5 Choosing Mail to run the Internet Connection Wizard to add a mail account.

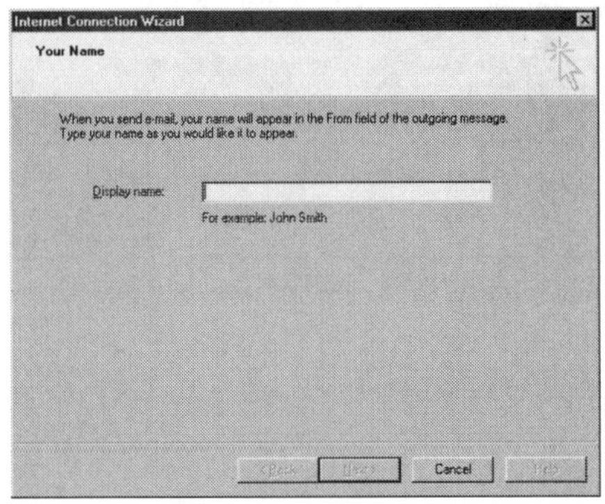

Figure A.6 In the first Internet Connection Wizard dialog box, type your name as you would like it to appear in the From field of your outgoing e-mail messages.

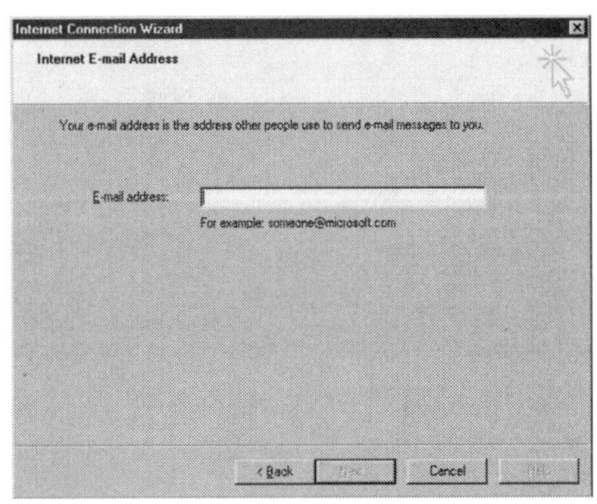

Figure A.7 In the second Internet Connection Wizard dialog box, type the e-mail address assigned to you by your e-mail service. For example, *ace@myisp.com*.

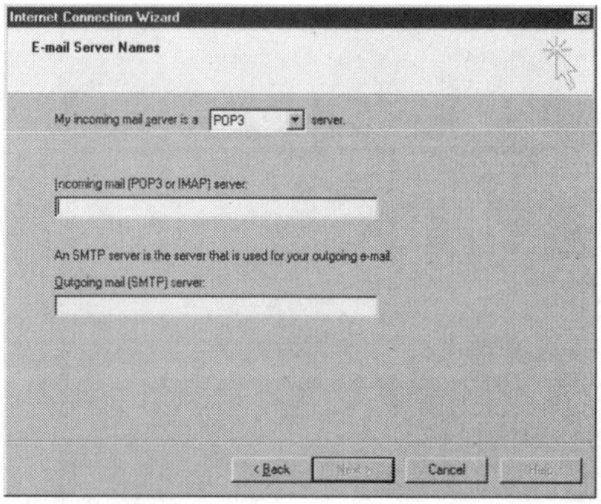

Figure A.8 Select the protocol used by your incoming mail server and enter the addresses for your incoming and outgoing mail servers (often the same address). Get this information from your e-mail service or network administrator.

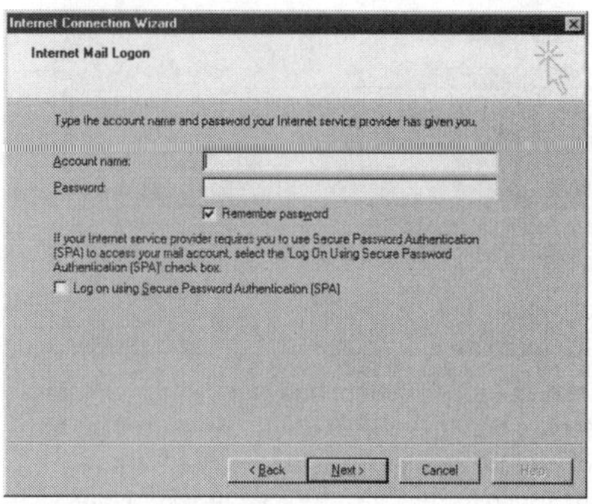

Figure A.9 Type the account name and password that your e-mail service has assigned to you.

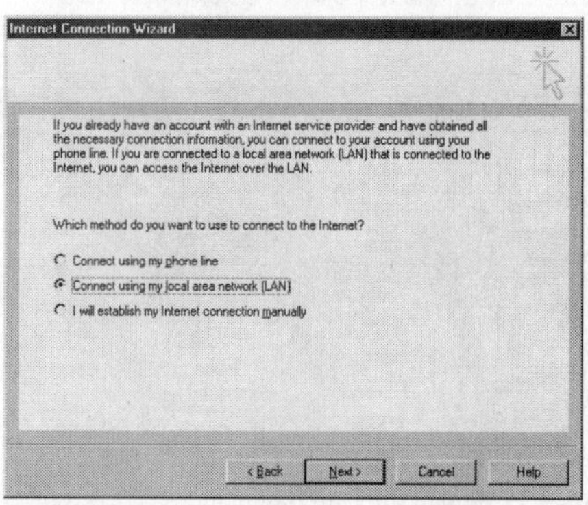

Figure A.10 Select the way that you connect to the Internet to access your e-mail service.

To add a mail account with the Internet Connection Wizard:

1. Run the Internet Connection Wizard in one of the following ways:
   - During initial Outlook setup, the Internet Connection Wizard will run automatically if you're using the Internet Only configuration and if you don't already have an e-mail account set up.
   - If you switch from the Corporate Or Workgroup configuration to the Internet Only configuration, the Internet Connection Wizard will run automatically if you don't already have an e-mail account set up.
   - You can run the Internet Connection Wizard at any time by choosing Tools > Accounts, clicking the **Add** button, and choosing Mail (**Figure A.5**).
2. Complete the Internet Connection Wizard as shown in **Figures A.6** through **A.10**.

   In the fifth dialog box (**Figure A.10**), you need to specify how you're going to get onto the Internet to access your e-mail service. Select one of the following three options:
   - Select **Connect using my phone line** if you want to connect to the Internet using a modem and the Windows Dial-Up Networking facility. This is the most common way to connect with a modem.

   or
   - Select **Connect using my local area network (LAN)** if your computer is attached to a network and you access the Internet through the network (rather than using a modem).

(continued on next page)

or

- Select **I will establish my Internet connection manually** if you use a modem and your own dialing program (Microsoft Internet Explorer's or one provided by another company) to connect to the Internet.

If you selected **Connect using my phone line** in the fifth wizard dialog box (**Figure A.10**), the Internet Connection Wizard will display the Dial-Up Connection dialog box (**Figure A.11**).

3. If the Dial-Up Connection dialog box appears, select **Use an existing dial-up connection** and highlight a connection name if you've previously defined a dial-up connection to an Internet service provider and you want to use it to access your e-mail service.

   or

   Select **Create a new dial-up connection** if you need to define a new dial-up Internet connection to access your e-mail service.

4. If you selected **Create a new dial-up connection**, complete the remaining Internet Connection Wizard dialog boxes as shown in **Figures A.12** through **A.14** to define your new connection.

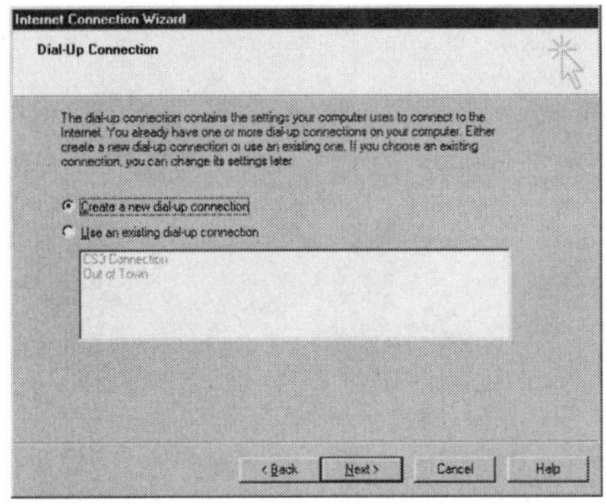

Figure A.11 The Dial-Up Connection dialog box.

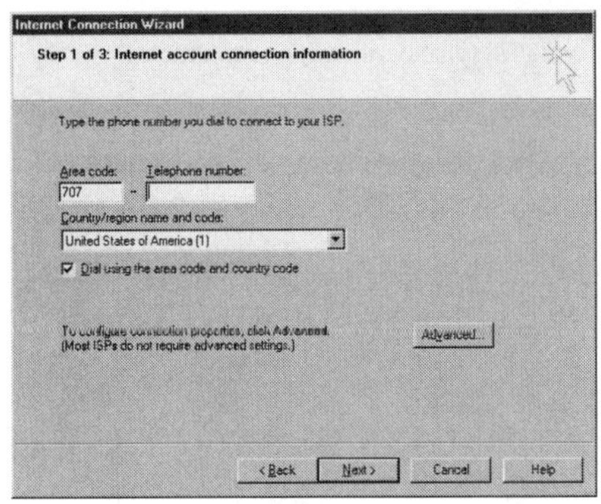

Figure A.12 Type the telephone number of your Internet service provider (ISP). Click the **Advanced** button only if your ISP requires you to specify advanced settings such as the "DNS server address." (Your ISP will tell you exactly what you need to specify.)

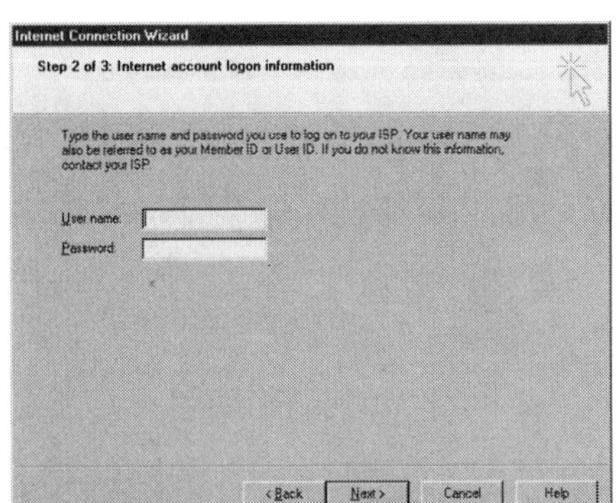

Figure A.13 Type in the user name and password assigned to you by your ISP. (Your user name is also known as your *login ID*.)

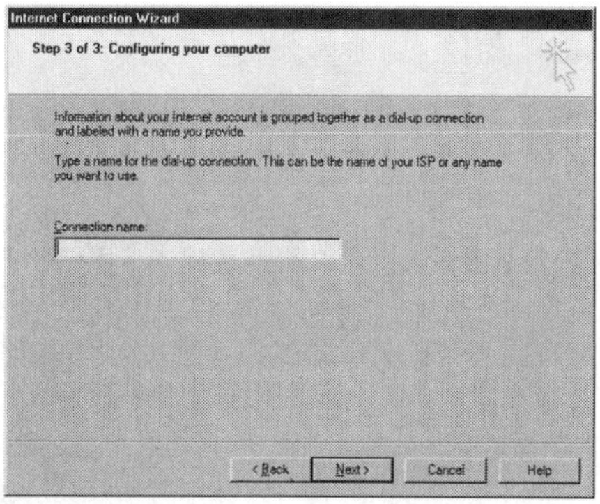

Figure A.14 Type in a name—any name—for your new connection. For example, you might type the name of your ISP.

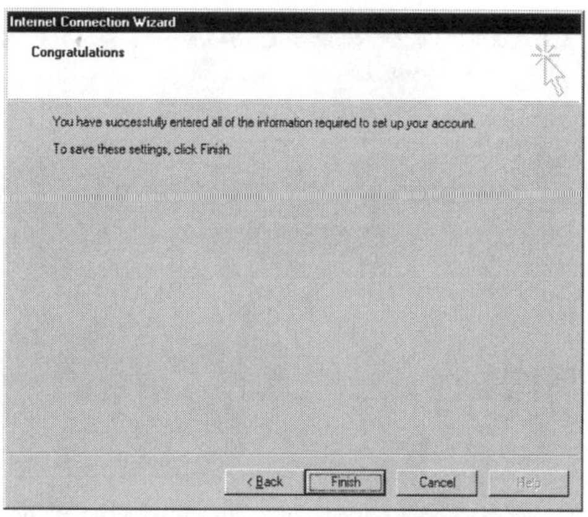

Figure A.15 The final Internet Connection Wizard dialog box.

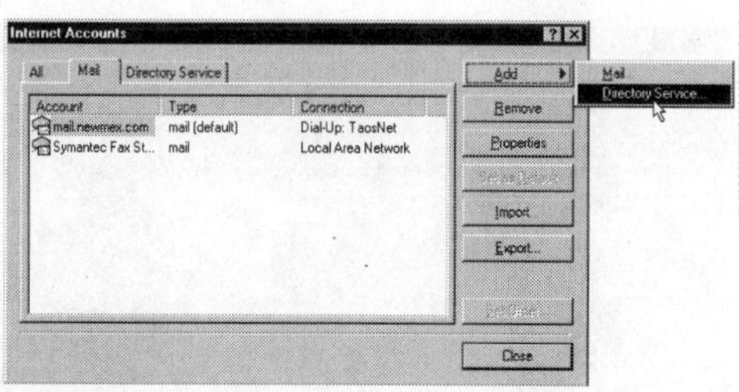

Figure A.16 Running the Internet Connection Wizard to add a directory service account.

When you've entered all the required information, the Internet Connection Wizard displays the Congratulations dialog box (**Figure A.15**).

5. Click the **Finish** button in the Congratulations dialog box and you're done!

I/O To add a directory service account with the Internet Connection Wizard:

1. Choose Tools > Accounts to open the Internet Accounts dialog box.
2. Click the **Add** button and choose Directory Service (**Figure A.16**).

(continued on next page)

3. Complete the Internet Connection Wizard as shown in **Figures A.17** through **A.19**. (These dialog boxes show the actual data you would enter to establish an account for using the public Internet directory service named Bigfoot.)

✔ Tips

- Your Internet service provider (ISP) or your network administrator should be able to supply the addresses for any Internet directory services provided by your ISP or located on your network.
- You should be able to locate the addresses of public directory services by searching for "LDAP servers" or "directory services" on the Internet using a search site such as Yahoo.

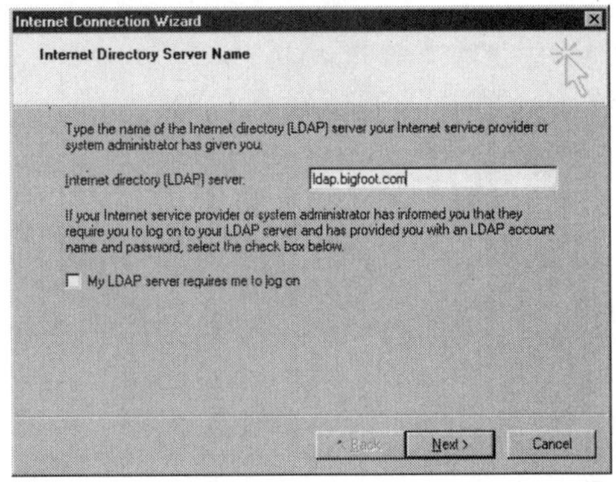

Figure A.17 In the first Internet Connection Wizard dialog box, enter the Internet address of the directory service you want to access.

I/O To modify or remove a mail or directory service account:

1. Choose Tools > Accounts to open the Internet Accounts dialog box.
2. Open the All tab or the tab for the type of account you want to modify or remove—Mail or Directory Service.
3. Click on the account to select it.
4. To modify the account, click the **Properties** button and make the changes you want in the tabs of the Properties dialog box.

   or

   To remove the account, click the **Remove** button.

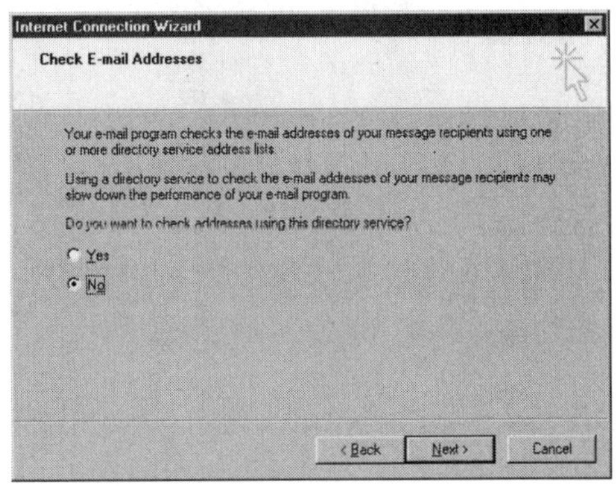

Figure A.18 Select **Yes** if you want Outlook to use this directory service to check the recipient addresses you type into your outgoing e-mail messages.

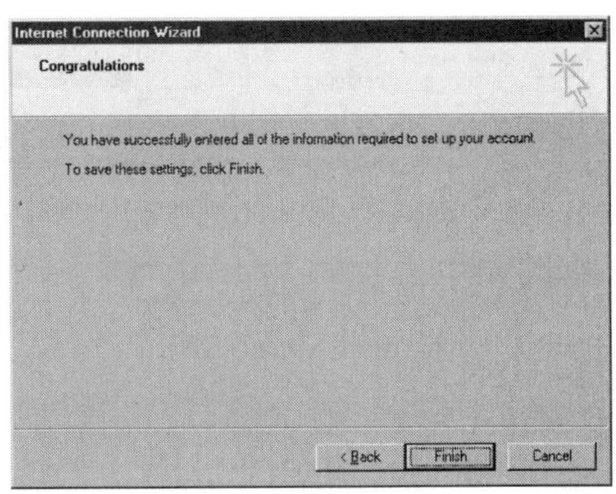

Figure A.19 Click the **Finish** button.

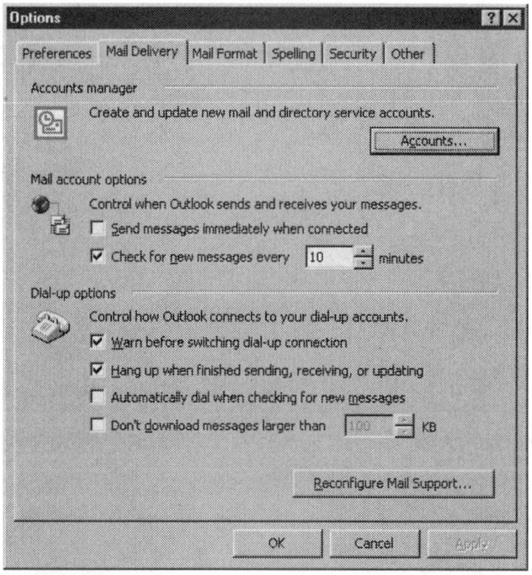

Figure A.20 The Mail Delivery tab of the Options dialog box.

✔ Tips

- The *default* mail account is the one that Outlook uses by default to send your outgoing e-mail messages. To designate a particular mail account as the default, select it in the Internet Accounts dialog box and click the **Default** button.
- If you designated more than one directory service account to be used for validating outgoing e-mail addresses (in the second Internet Connection Wizard dialog box, **Figure A.18**), you can modify the order in which these accounts are used by selecting a directory service account in the Internet Accounts dialog box and clicking the **Set Order** button.
- You can modify the way Outlook uses mail accounts by choosing Tools > Options and opening the Mail Delivery tab (**Figure A.20**).

To add a fax account:

1. Start the Symantec WinFax Starter Edition Setup Wizard in one of the following ways:
   - If you change e-mail configurations from Corporate Or Workgroup to Internet Only, and if you haven't already created a fax account, the wizard will run automatically. (See "Changing Your Basic E-mail Configuration," earlier in this appendix.)
   - You can force the wizard to run by opening the Inbox or another mail-item folder, choosing Actions > New Fax Message, and in the message box that Outlook displays clicking **Yes** to have it install WinFax. You'll need to stop and restart Outlook after you're done.
2. Complete the Symantec WinFax Starter Edition Setup Wizard as shown in **Figures A.21** through **A.26**.
3. The Registration Wizard will start (**Figure A.27**). You can click the **Next** button to register the product or just click **Skip** to return immediately to Outlook.

✔ Tips

- Because it's a type of mail account, a fax account is listed in the All and Mail tabs of the Internet Accounts dialog box (opened by choosing Tools > Accounts), where you can modify or remove it.
- The important fax settings, however, are made by choosing Tools > Options and opening the Fax tab (this tab appears only after you've installed WinFax) (**Figure A.28**).

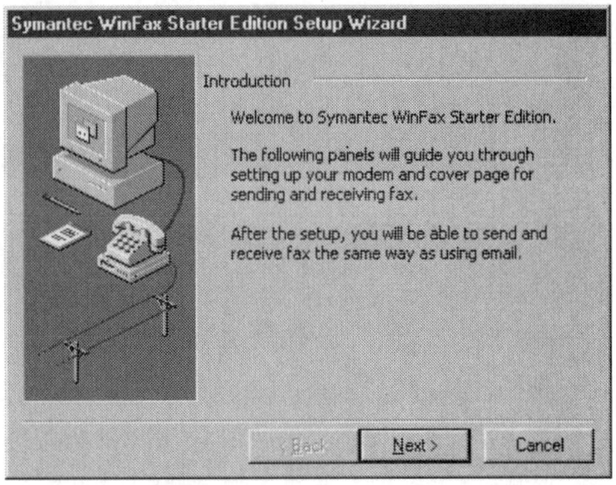

Figure A.21 The first Symantec WinFax Starter Edition Setup Wizard dialog box.

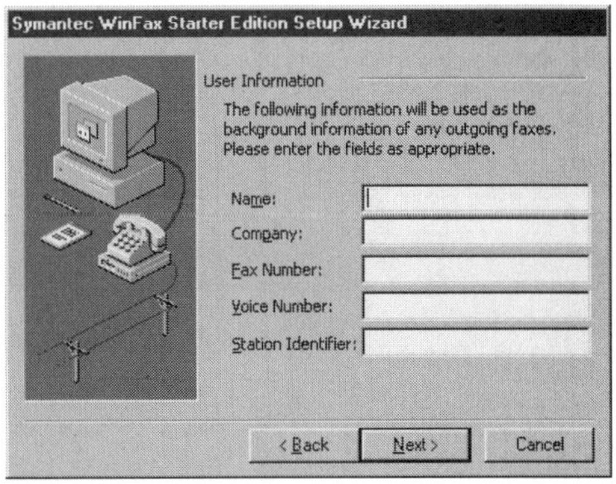

Figure A.22 Enter your personal information, which can be displayed on your outgoing faxes.

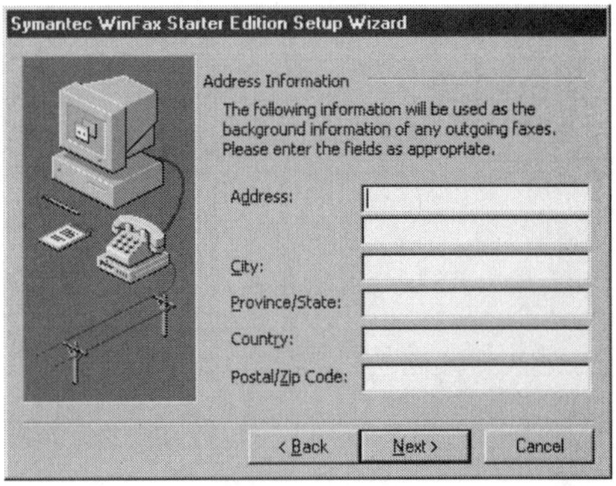

Figure A.23 Enter your address, which can also be displayed on your outgoing faxes.

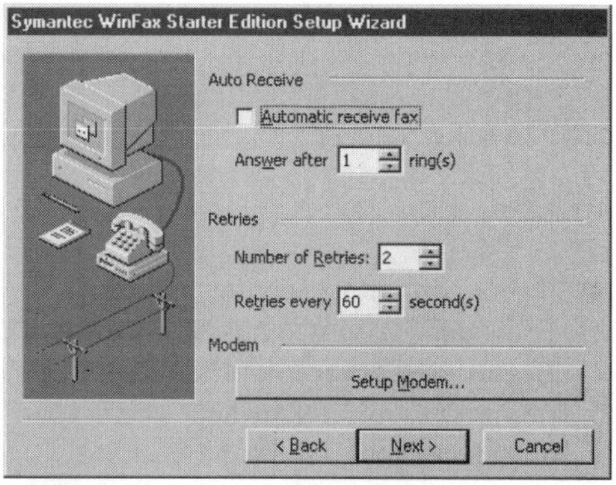

Figure A.24 Select options to control the operation of your fax modem. Check **Automatic receive fax** if you want the fax modem to automatically answer incoming fax calls.

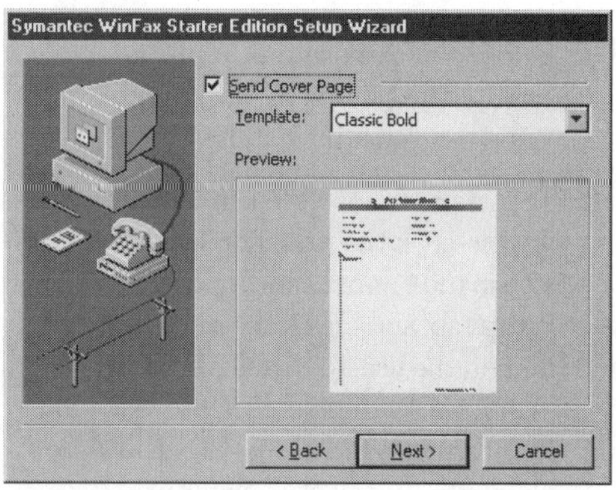

Figure A.25 If you want WinFax to add a cover sheet to your outgoing faxes check **Send Cover Page** and select the cover sheet style in the **Template** list box.

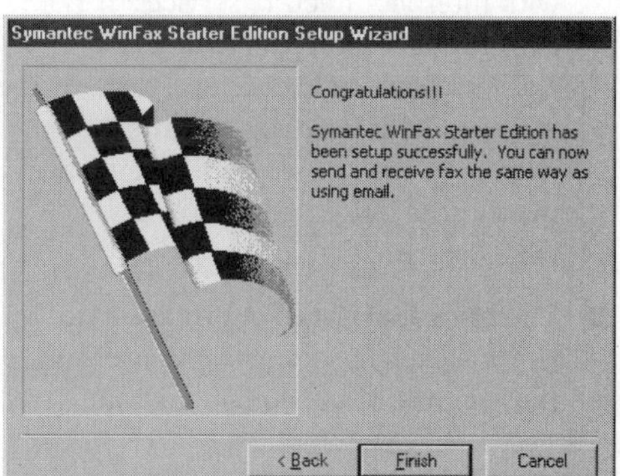

Figure A.26 Click the **Finish** button.

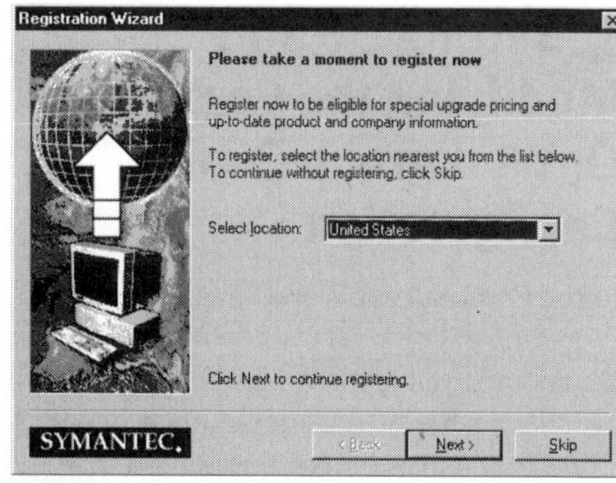

Figure A.27 The Symantec WinFax Starter Edition Registration Wizard.

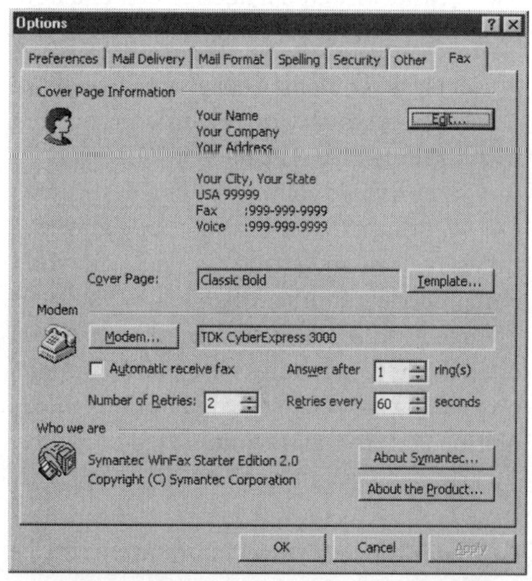

Figure A.28 The Fax tab of the Options dialog box.

Setting Up and Modifying the Corporate Or Workgroup E-mail Configuration

In the Corporate Or Workgroup e-mail configuration of Outlook, your personal settings are kept in a *user profile*, often called simply a *profile*. Each time you start Outlook, it opens a profile and uses the settings it contains (this profile is known as the *current profile*). If your computer already has a user profile when you set up Outlook (perhaps from a previous Outlook installation), Outlook will use it. Otherwise, you'll need to create a new profile by running the Inbox Setup Wizard.

A user profile contains a collection of *information services*, which Outlook uses to connect with the outside world. Each information service provides a source of—or a destination for—information. For example, one information service might let you connect with your e-mail service, another might allow you to you send and receive faxes, another might offer access to an address list, another might provide the file where all your Outlook information is stored, and so on.

✔ Tips

- The **Internet E-mail** information service allows you to send and receive e-mail messages from an e-mail provider that uses the standard SMTP and POP3 Internet protocols. (If your provider employs the IMAP Internet e-mail protocol for incoming messages, you'll have to use the Internet Only e-mail configuration rather than the Corporate Or Workgroup configuration.)
- If your computer is connected to an Exchange Server network, the **Microsoft Exchange Server** information service makes Outlook an Exchange Server client and allows you to share information, collaborate on projects, schedule meetings, and exchange e-mail with other users on the network and on the Internet.
- The **Microsoft Fax** information service lets you send and receive faxes in Outlook. Before you can use this information service, the Microsoft Fax component of Windows must be installed.
- To install Microsoft Fax in Windows 95, double-click the Add/Remove Programs icon in the Control Panel, open the Windows Setup tab, and check the Microsoft Fax item in the list. To install Microsoft Fax in Windows 98, double-click the following file on your Windows 98 CD: \tools\oldwin95\message\us\awfax.exe.
- The **Microsoft LDAP Directory** information service allows you to connect with Internet directory services to look up information on people from the Address Book dialog box and to verify the recipient addresses you type into your outgoing e-mail messages. For more information, see "C/W To address a message" in Chapter 6.
- The **Microsoft Mail** information service lets you exchange e-mail with users of the Microsoft Mail e-mail program.

- The **MS Outlook support for Lotus cc:Mail** information service lets you exchange e-mail with users of the Lotus cc:Mail e-mail program.
- The **Outlook Address Book** information service lets you access the e-mail and fax addresses that are stored in your Outlook Contacts folder, when you send a message or when you open the Address Book dialog box.
- To use the Outlook Address Book information service to access your Contacts folder, right-click the Contacts shortcut in the Outlook Bar, choose Properties from the pop-up menu, open the Outlook Address Book tab, and check the **Show this folder as an e-mail Address Book** option.
- The **Personal Address Book** information service stores (in a .PAB disk file) individual names and addresses as well as distribution lists that let you send a message to an entire group of people (for example, everyone in your marketing department). I recommend, however, that you use the more powerful Outlook Contacts folder and the *Outlook Address Book* information service instead. The Contacts folder now supports distribution lists as well as many other features.
- The **Personal Folders** information service stores all your Outlook information (messages, appointments, contacts, notes, and so on) in a .PST file on your hard drive. This information service is required unless you use the Microsoft Exchange Server information service, which normally stores your Outlook information in a mailbox on the Exchange Server computer. (If you use Exchange Server, you can also add a Personal Folders information service to store additional Outlook folders on a disk on your computer.)
- You might also be able to obtain an information service from an e-mail provider so that you can use Outlook as your e-mail program. For example, CompuServe provides a product you can download called **CompuServe Mail for Microsoft Exchange**. When you install it, it adds an information service to your profile called CompuServe Mail, which lets you use Outlook to send and receive e-mail via CompuServe.
- Before you can use an information service, you must add it to your user profile, as described later in this chapter.

To create a user profile with the Inbox Setup Wizard:

1. Run the Inbox Setup Wizard in one of the following ways:
   - The Inbox Setup Wizard runs automatically during the initial Outlook setup if you're using the Corporate Or Workgroup configuration and a profile hasn't already been created on your computer.
   - The Inbox Setup Wizard also runs automatically if you switch from the Internet Only configuration to the Corporate Or Workgroup configuration and a profile hasn't already been created.
   - You can run the Inbox Setup Wizard at any time by double-clicking the Mail icon in your Windows Control Panel folder (**Figure A.29**), clicking the **Show Profiles** button in the Services tab of the Properties dialog box (**Figure A.30**), and clicking the **Add** button in the Mail dialog box (**Figure A.31**).
2. In the first wizard dialog box (**Figure A.32**), select the **Use the following information services** option, and then in the list check the particular services you want to use. (This list contains the most common information services that allow you to exchange e-mail.) I recommend selecting this option because the wizard will quickly create a user profile for you, add the service or services you selected, and also add any required supplemental information services. (You can later change this profile by following the instructions given in the following sections.)

   or

   Select **Manually configure information services** if you want to select each information service yourself. I advise against using this option unless you are quite familiar with information services.

Figure A.29 Double-clicking the Mail icon in the Windows Control Panel.

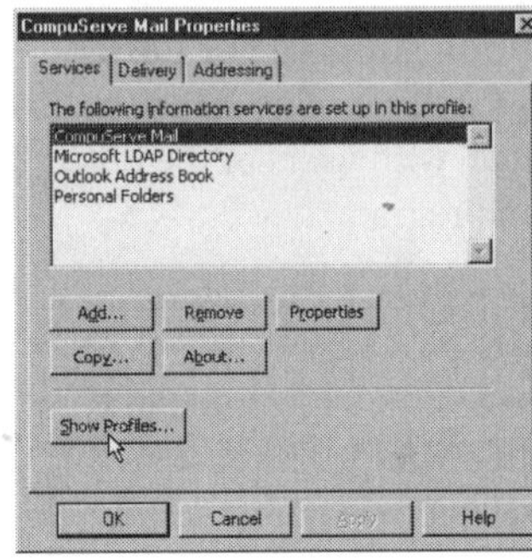

Figure A.30 Clicking the **Show Profiles** button.

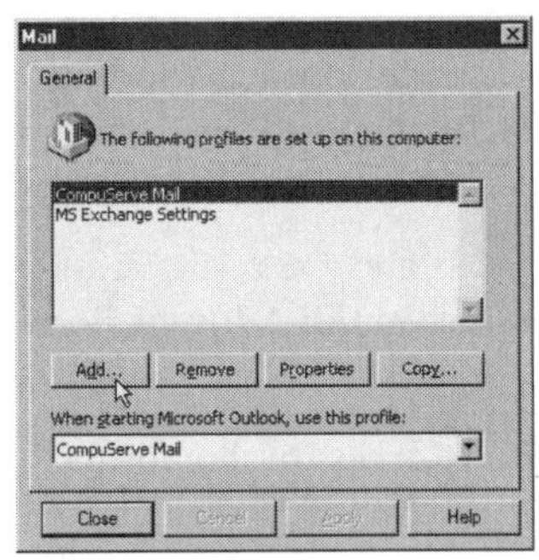

Figure A.31 Clicking the **Add** button.

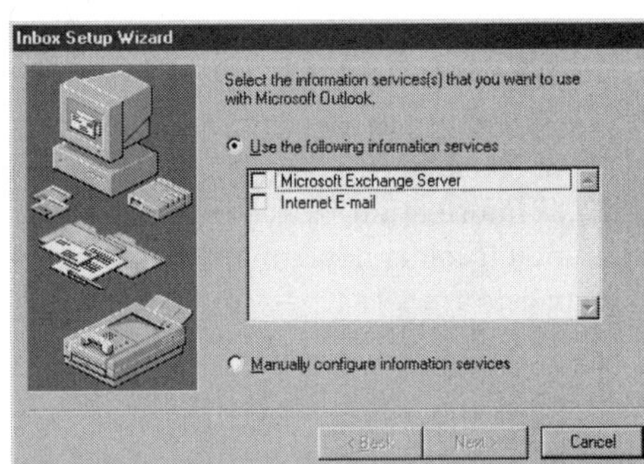

Figure A.32 The first Inbox Setup Wizard dialog box.

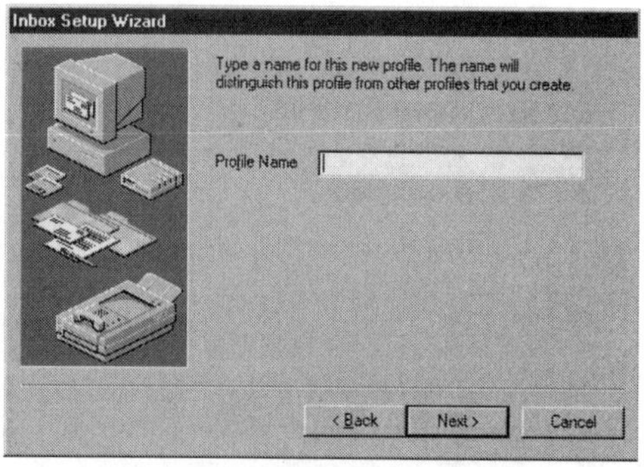

Figure A.33 The second Inbox Setup Wizard dialog box.

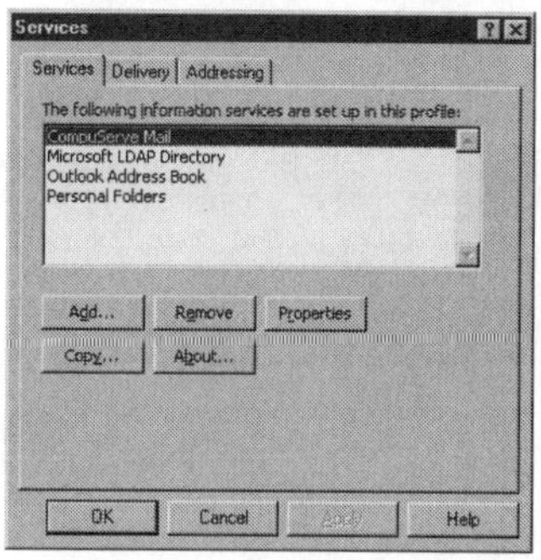

Figure A.34 The Services dialog box.

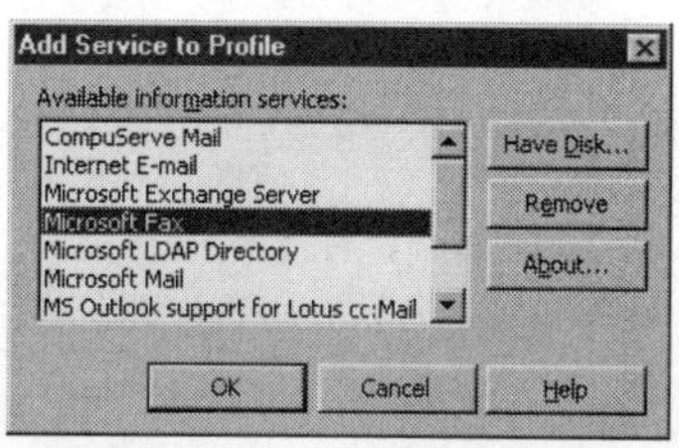

Figure A.35 The Add Service To Profile dialog box.

3. In the second wizard dialog box (**Figure A.33**), type a name for your new profile (for example, *Business Settings*).

4. If you selected the **Use the following information services** option in the first wizard dialog box, complete the dialog boxes that the wizard shows for setting up each information service. The particular dialog boxes you see depend upon the service or services you chose.

   or

   If you selected the **Manually configure information services** option, in the profile Properties dialog box add and configure each service that you want, following the instructions given in the next section.

To add, modify, or remove individual information services in the current Outlook profile:

1. Choose Tools > Services to open the Services dialog box.

2. The Services dialog box displays a list of the information services that have already been added to the current user profile (**Figure A.34**). Use this dialog box as follows:

   - To add a new information service, click the **Add** button, select the service you want in the Add Service To Profile dialog box (**Figure A.35**), click the **OK** button, and then fill in the dialog box or boxes for setting up the service. The new service might not become available until you quit and restart Outlook.
   - To modify an information service, click its name to select it in the list and then click the **Properties** button.
   - To remove an information service from the current user profile, click its name to select it in the list and then click the **Remove** button.

(continued on next page)

✔ Tip

- If you have received an information service on a disk, or if you have downloaded one, or if one is located on your network, click the **Have Disk** button in the Add Service To Profile dialog box (**Figure A.35**) and specify the disk and folder containing the information service files.

C/W To modify settings for the current Outlook profile:

In addition to adding or removing information services from the current Outlook profile, you can also change the way Outlook uses the profile, as follows:

1. Choose Tools > Services.
2. To modify the way Outlook delivers e-mail or fax messages, open the Delivery tab (**Figure A.36**) and set options as desired:
   - **Deliver new mail to the following location** specifies where your e-mail messages are delivered. If you're using the Exchange Server information service, you can have Outlook deliver your messages either to the Inbox in your mailbox on the server or to the Inbox in a Personal Folders file on your computer (provided you've set up a Personal Folders information service).
   - **Recipient addresses are processed by these information services in the following order:** If you have several messaging information services, Outlook will send an outgoing message using the first appropriate service that it finds going down this list. To change the position of a service in the list, click it and then click the up- or down-arrow to the right of the list.

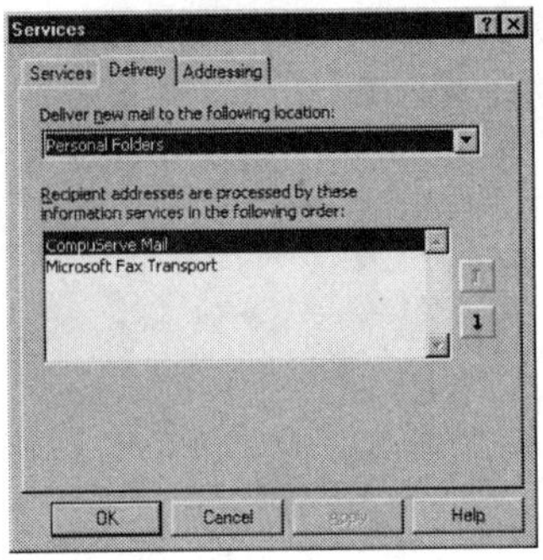

Figure A.36 The Delivery tab of the Services dialog box.

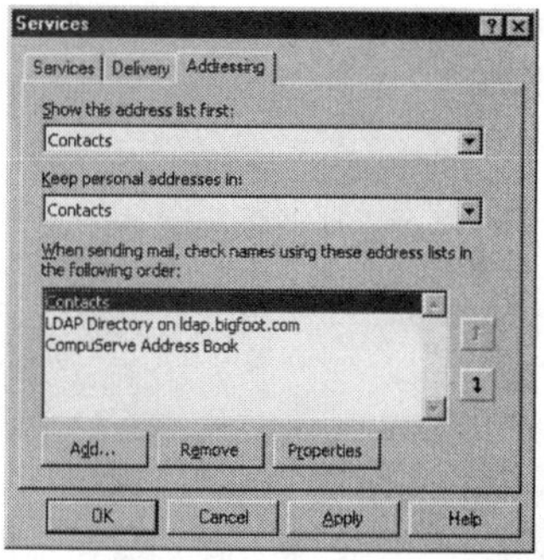

Figure A.37 The Addressing tab of the Services dialog box.

3. To modify the way Outlook displays, stores, and verifies addresses for your outgoing messages, open the Addressing tab (**Figure A.37**) and set options as desired:
   - **Show this address list first** changes the list of addresses you first see when you open the Address Book. (If you wish, you can then view other address lists.)
   - **Keep personal addresses in** changes the default address list to which the Address Book adds new addresses. (If you wish, you can override the default and save an address in a different address list.)
   - **When sending mail, check names using these address lists in the following order** changes the order in which Outlook uses address lists to verify the recipient e-mail and fax addresses you type into your outgoing messages.
   - **Add** adds an address list to those that Outlook uses for verifying recipient addresses.
   - **Remove** removes the selected address list from those that Outlook uses for verifying recipient addresses.
   - **Properties** displays features of the selected address list.

C/W Using Several Profiles

You might want to create more than one user profile. For example, if several people use Outlook on a single computer, each person can have a separate profile with personalized settings. Or, you might want to have one profile for your business settings and another for your personal settings.

To set up several profiles:

1. Create one or more additional profiles following the directions that were given in the section "C/W To Create a user profile with the Inbox Setup Wizard."
2. Choose Tools > Options and open the Mail Services tab (**Figure A.38**).
3. Select either of the following two options in the **Startup settings** area:
   - **Prompt for a profile to be used** causes Outlook to prompt you for the profile it will use, each time you start the program.
   - **Always use this profile** causes Outlook—each time you start the program—to automatically use the profile you select in the adjoining list box.

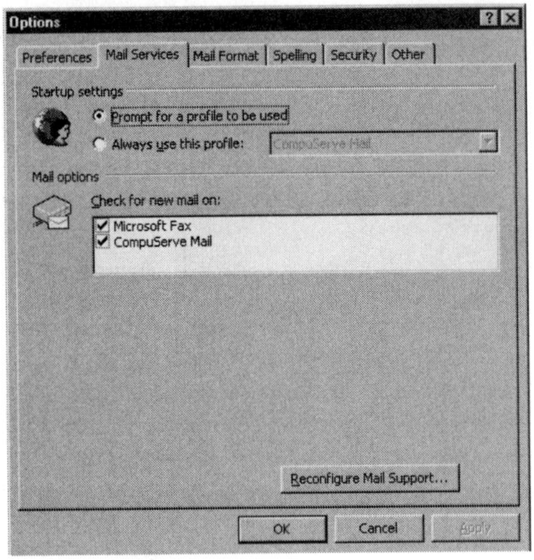

Figure A.38 The Mail Services tab of the Options dialog box.

✔ Tips

- You can work with your profiles by double-clicking the Mail icon in the Windows Control Panel folder, and then clicking the **Show Profiles** button to open the Mail dialog box (**Figure A.30**). Then, by selecting a profile and clicking the appropriate button, you can remove, change properties, or make a copy of the profile. Also, by selecting an item in the **When starting Microsoft Outlook use this profile** list box, you can change Outlook's default profile.
- You can copy an information service from the current profile to another profile by choosing Tools > Services to open the Services dialog box (**Figure A.34**) and then selecting the information service in the list and clicking the **Copy** button.

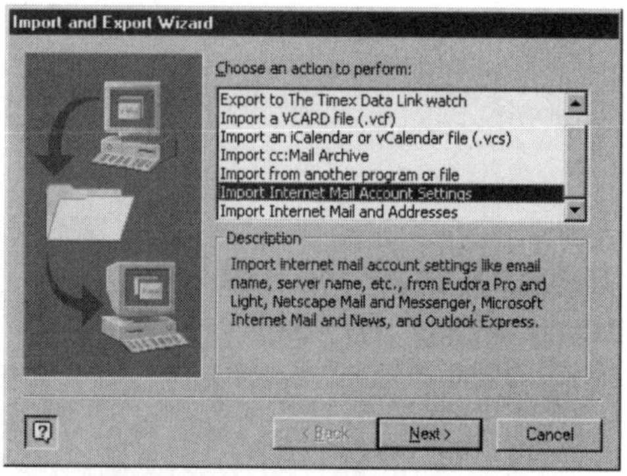

Figure A.39 The first Import And Export Wizard dialog box.

Importing Settings or Data from Another E-Mail Program

As explained in Chapter 1, during initial Outlook setup, you might be given the opportunity to import the e-mail messages, stored addresses, and settings from another e-mail program that is already installed on your computer (that is, to "upgrade" that program). You can also do this at any time after Outlook has been set up. The programs you can upgrade include Qualcomm Eudora, Netscape Mail, Netscape Messenger, Microsoft Outlook Express, and other popular e-mail programs.

To import settings or mail and addresses from another e-mail program:

1. Choose File > Import And Export.
2. In the first Import And Export Wizard dialog box (**Figure A.39**) select the **Import Internet Mail Account Settings** list item to import settings from another e-mail program.

   or

   Select the **Import Internet Mail and Addresses** item to import messages and stored addresses from another e-mail program.
3. Click the **Next** button.

   If Outlook finds one or more e-mail programs it can upgrade installed on your computer, it will prompt you for further information.
4. Select the program you want to import from and supply the other requested information.

Adding or Removing Outlook Components

If you're missing an Outlook feature you require, you might need to install an additional Outlook program component. You might also want to uninstall a program component that you never use.

Figure A.40 Double-clicking the Add/Remove Programs icon, which is found in your Windows Control Panel folder.

To install or uninstall Outlook components:

1. Quit Outlook and any other Office application that's running.
2. Double-click the Add/Remove Programs icon in your Windows Control Panel (**Figure A.40**).
3. In the Install/Uninstall tab, select the name of the Microsoft product that Outlook came with (for example, *Microsoft Outlook 2000* or *Microsoft Office 2000 Premium*) (**Figure A.41**) and click the **Add/Remove** button.
4. Follow the instructions that are displayed for adding or removing Outlook program features.

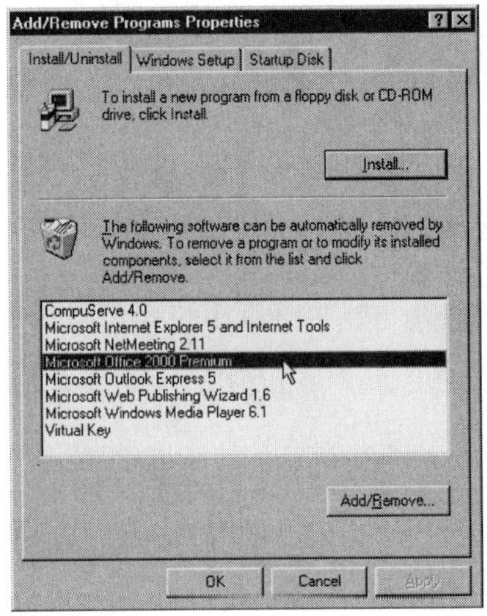

Figure A.41 Selecting the product Outlook was supplied with, in the Install/Uninstall tab of the Add/Remove Programs Properties dialog box.

INDEX

Note: *References to (I/O) and (C/W) denote Internet Only and Corporate or Workgroup configurations, respectively.*

... (ellipsis) after menu commands, 21
% Complete text box on Task form, 183
+ (plus) symbol next to subfolders, 91
? (question mark) next to mouse pointer, 31

A

Accept button, using with Tasks folder, 186–187
Actions menu, creating items with, 44–45
Add Entries to Subscriber Database dialog box, 96
Add New button in Distribution List dialog box, 175
Add/Remove Programs icon, 256
Add Service to Profile dialog box (C/W), 251
Add to Outlook Bar dialog box, 230
Address Book, opening with keyboard command, 26
Address Book button
  (C/W), 141
  (I/O), 137
Address Book dialog box
  (C/W), 143
  (I/O), 139
Address Cards view, 70, 171, 179
Address list box on Web toolbar, 220
Address text box on Contact form, 172
addresses, displaying maps of, 179
addresses (C/W), 253
  copying from address lists, 141
  locating in long lists, 141
  viewing in different address lists, 141
adult-content e-mail messages, color-coding, 153
Advanced E-mail Options dialog box
  (C/W), 142
  (I/O), 138
Advanced Find dialog box, 82–85
Advanced Options dialog box, using with Tasks folder, 190
Advanced Tasks dialog box, 191
Advanced toolbar, 16, 23
Align Left and Align buttons in Formatting toolbar, 53
All Day Event option on Event form, 161, 164
Alt key, 26
Always Use This Profile option on Mail Services tab (C/W), 254
Answer After radio button in Fax Modem Properties dialog box, 128
appointment duration, changing in Calendar folder, 166
Appointment items
  in Calendar folder, 155
  in Create New Folder dialog box, 89
appointment locations, entering in Calendar folder, 156
Appointment Recurrence dialog box, 159
appointment reminders, identifying in Calendar folder, 165

appointments
- adding to Calendar folder, 166
- color-coding, 158
- creating in Calendar folder, 156–160
- marking in Calendar folder, 157

archive files, 66–67, 69
archived items, recovering, 68
arrow mouse pointer, 20
Ascending radio button
- in Group By dialog box, 78
- in Sort dialog box, 76
- on Outlook Today page, 113

Assign Task button, 185
assigned tasks, creating, 181–182, 185–187
Assistant, 29–31, 229
attachments to e-mail messages
- creating, 135
- identifying, 130
- inserting files as, 58
- inserting items as, 59
- opening, 124–125
- saving in disk files, 125–126

attendees for meetings, entering addresses in Calendar folder, 162–163
Author permission level, setting in Microsoft Exchange Server, 101
AutoArchive feature, 65–67, 105–106
automatic archiving
- enabling, 66
- limitations of, 68

Automatic Formatting dialog box, 233
automatic journal entries, 194–195
AutoPreview button, 73

B

Back button on Web toolbar, 220
background color, changing for notes, 204, 207
Bcc message field
- (C/W), 141
- (I/O), 138

Bold button in Formatting toolbar, 53
bold e-mail messages, 123
Browse button in Insert Object dialog box, 60
built-in toolbars, 224
- displaying commands on, 225–226
- removing commands from, 225–226
- resetting, 228
- restoring after modification, 227

Bullets button in Formatting toolbar, 53
business e-mail accounts (I/O), receiving messages from, 119
By Author view for file folders, 215
By Category view, 70
By File Type view for file folders, 215
By Type view for journal entries, 199

C

calendar
- displaying in Task Timeline view, 189
- using with journal entries, 199

Calendar column of Outlook Today page, changing number of days of Calendar items in, 112
Calendar folder, 17, 41, 44, 107
- publishing on Internet, 165
- setting options for, 169–170

calendar items, 155
Calendar items, manipulating in Outlook Today, 110
Calendar Properties dialog box, setting permissions in, 100
Cancel Assignment button, using with Tasks folder, 187
Cancel button in dialog boxes, 28
Cancel Invitation button, 164
categories, 157
- assigning to contacts, 173
- assigning to distribution lists, 176
- assigning to journal entries, 197
- assigning to notes, 204
- assigning to tasks, 184
- entering in Tasks folder, 185

Cc field of Message form, 133–134, 138
Center button in Formatting toolbar, 53
Change and Change All buttons in Spelling dialog box, 55
Check Address dialog box in Contacts folder, 174
check boxes in dialog boxes, 27
Check Full Name dialog box in Contacts folder, 174
check mark next to toolbars, 23

Check Names button
(C/W), 142
(I/O), 139
Choose Contact dialog box, 177
Choose Folders button on Outlook Today page, 112
City field on Contact form, 174
clicking with mouse, 20
Clipboard toolbar, pasting text from, 54
Close button, 16
Close button in dialog boxes, 28
Close Find button, 83
Close Organize button, 151
CNG tone, 128–129
color-coding
changing for overdue and completed tasks, 190
e-mail messages, 152–153
columns, formatting in table view, 234
commands, 224
adding to menu bar, 226
applying to forms, 43–44
choosing from menus, 21
copying, 226
displaying on built-in toolbars, 225–226
displaying on menus, 21–22
dropping on menu bar, 226
dropping on toolbars, 226
executing from toolbars, 24
modifying, 227
moving, 226
removing, 226
removing from built-in toolbars, 225–226
Company text box on Contact form, 172
Compose New Fax Wizard (C/W), 149
CompuServe Mail (C/W)
automatic receipt of messages with, 121–122
limitations when assigning tasks, 187
for Microsoft Exchange, 249
Connection Times dialog box in CompuServe, 121–122
Contact form, 172
contact items
in Create New Folder dialog box, 89
creating, 172–177
Contact Options dialog box, 179
contacts
assigning categories to, 173
calling, 178
contacting, 178–179
entering in Calendar folder, 159
entering in Tasks folder, 185
finding with Find A Contact list box, 177
identifying in Contacts folder, 172
linking, 173
linking to appointments in Calendar folder, 157
linking to journal entries, 196–197
linking to notes, 205
linking with tasks, 183
Contacts folder, 17, 41, 44, 173–174
Contacts options, setting, 179
context menus, 22
Copies area of Print dialog box, 104
Copy Folder dialog box, 92
Copy Items dialog box, 62
copy operations, undoing, 63
Copy Selected Text button in Clipboard toolbar, 54
copying commands, 226
copying text with keyboard command, 26
Corporate or Workgroup configuration, 10
cover sheets (I/O), setting up in WinFax, 247
Create from File option button in Insert Object dialog box, 60
Create New Folder dialog box, 89, 213
Create New option button in Insert Object dialog box, 60
Ctrl key, 26
current date
viewing in Journal Timeline view, 199
viewing in timelines, 189
current day, viewing, 167
current group of Outlook Bar, 230
current profiles (C/W), 248
custom menus, adding, 226
custom toolbars, 224
creating, 227–228
renaming, 228
Customize Outlook Today page, 112

D

Date Navigator in Calendar folder, 165–166
  changing fonts in, 170
  selecting months in, 168
dates
  entering in forms, 50
  hiding and showing in notes, 207
  specifying for appointments in Calendar folder, 158
  viewing, 167
  viewing in Journal Timeline view, 199
  viewing in timelines, 189
Day button, 166, 199
Day button in Task Timeline view, 189
Day/Week/Month view in Calendar folder, 165
Decline button, using with Tasks folder, 186
Decrease Indent button in Formatting toolbar, 53
Default Archive File option in AutoArchive dialog box, 67
default mail account (I/O), 245
default options, setting for Tasks folder, 191
default Outlook folders, copying, 91
Default permission, assigning in Microsoft Exchange Server, 100
Define Styles button in Print dialog box, 105
Define Views dialog box, 234
Delete button, 64
Delete Expired Items... option in AutoArchive dialog box, 67
Deleted Items folder, 17, 41, 94
  recovering items from, 65
  removing all items from, 65–66
Descending radio button
  in Group By dialog box, 78
  in Sort dialog box, 76
  on Outlook Today page, 113
Details tab
  on Task form, 184
  on Contact form, 174
Details view for file folders, 215
Detect and Repair command, 6
Dial button, 178
Dial-Up Connection dialog box (I/O), 242
dial-up Internet connection, 117–118, 120
dialog boxes, 26–28
directory service accounts (I/O), 240
  adding with Internet Connection Wizard, 243–244
  modifying, 244–245
  removing, 244
discussion items, managing in Microsoft Exchange Server, 102
disk files, finding, 82–85
disk symbol next to installable components, 2
Display As Icon check box in Insert Object dialog box, 60
Display Map Of Address button, 179
distribution list items, 172, 175–176
distribution lists
  (C/W), 143
  (I/O), 139
Do not AutoArchive This Item option in Archive dialog box, 69
.DOC file name extension, 210
docking toolbars, 225
Document Timeline view for file folders, 215
documents associated with journal entries, opening, 200–201
double-clicking with mouse, 20
Drafts folder, 17, 41, 44
dragging and dropping items, 20, 46, 62
Due date list box on Task form, 182
Duration list box on Journal Entry form, 196

E

e-mail, setting up, 12
e-mail accounts (I/O)
  connecting with, 118–119
  specifying for sending messages, 136
e-mail addresses
  types of, 143
  looking up (I/O), 138–139
e-mail configuration
  changing, 238–239
  setting up (C/W), 248–253
e-mail editors, 144–147, changing, 145
e-mail formats, 144–147
e-mail information services, managing, 143

e-mail messages, 118
  addressing
    (C/W), 140–143
    (I/O), 136–138
  automatic receipt of
    (C/W), 120–122
    (I/O), 117–119
  color-coding, 152–153
  creating, 133
  creating rules for automatic moving of, 152
  display of, 16
  editing, 124
  flagging for special attention, 124
  formatting text in, 134
  forwarding, 133–134
  importing, 8–9
  inserting items in, 59
  manipulating in Outlook Today, 110
  manual receipt of
    (C/W), 122
    (I/O), 119
  marking, 123
  reading, 17, 123–126
  receiving from task owners, 186
  replying to, 133–134
  resending, 147
  saving copies of, 132
  selecting options for, 135
  sending, 132–147
  sending to contacts, 178
  setting options for, 124
  transmitting from Outbox, 147
e-mail programs, importing settings or data from, 255
E-mail Service Options dialog box, 10–11
e-mail setup, specifying, 7
E-mail text box on Contact form, 173
E-mail Upgrade Options dialog, 8
ellipsis (...) after menu commands, 21
embedded objects, 57–58
  inserting in forms, 59–60
  modifying properties of, 60
enabled e-mail accounts, 119, 122
Entry List view, for journal entries, 193, 198
Entry type list box on Journal Entry form, 196
errors, detecting and repairing, 6
Esc key, 26
Event form, opening, 166
Event items in Calendar folder, 155
events
  adding to Calendar folder, 166
  defining, 161
  identifying in Calendar folder, 165
Exchange Server, 10, 12, 99, 108, 248
Expand/collapse defaults list box in Group By dialog box, 78
Explore Web Page button, 178, 218

F

F1 key, 26
Favorites, opening, 219
Favorites folder, opening in Other Shortcuts group, 34–35
fax accounts (I/O), 240, 246–247
fax cover page (I/O), modifying, 149
FAX form, 148
fax messages
  changing delivery options in current Outlook profile (C/W), 252
  changing properties of (C/W), 150
  receiving, 127–131
  sending to contacts, 148–150, 178
Fax Modem Properties dialog box, 128, 129
fax numbers
  setting up (C/W), 150
  verifying (I/O), 148–149
Fax tab of Options dialog box (I/O), 149, 246–247
Fax Viewer (C/W), displaying faxes in, 131
faxes
  automatic receipt of, 127–128
  manual receipt of, 128–129
  opening, 130–131
  reading, 130–131
  viewing, 130–131
faxing, setting up, 12
fields, 43
  changing in Group By dialog box, 78
  changing in views, 233
  choosing for sorting, 76
  editing in Information Viewer, 49
  filtering on Contact form, 174
  grouping on Contact form, 174
  searching on Contact form, 174
  sorting on Contact form, 174

file attachments. *See* attachments to e-mail messages.
file folder versus Outlook folder, 18
file folder views, modifying, 215–216
file folders. *See also* folders, Outlook folders.
  changing properties of, 214
  copying, 213–214
  creating, 213
  deleting, 215
  identifying shortcuts to, 209
  moving, 213–214
  opening, 34–35, 210, 213, 219
  opening in separate Outlook windows, 35
  opening subfolders of, 39
  versus Outlook folders, 18
  printing, 214
  renaming, 214
  selecting, 213
  selecting views for, 214–215
file names, changing, 212
file properties, changing, 212
files
  copying, 211
  creating Outlook Bar shortcuts to, 231
  deleting, 212
  inserting as attachments to forms, 58
  inserting in forms, 58
  moving, 211
  printing, 212
  storing, 102
  viewing, 212
Filter Applied message, 77
Filter button in View Summary dialog box, 77
filtering items, 74, 77
filters, removing, 77
Find A Contact list box, 177
Find Page, 82–83
Find People dialog box (I/O), 138
Find Public Folders dialog box, 102
first name field on Contact form, 174
Flag For Follow Up dialog box, 124
floating toolbars, 225
folder banner, 16
Folder contains list box in Create New Folder dialog box, 89
folder hierarchy, 88, 91
  expanding and collapsing in Folder List, 37–38
  opening next folder up, 39
folder items, printing, 103–105
Folder List, 99
  converting from temporary to permanent, 38
  displaying, 37
  hiding, 37
  opening folders from, 36, 37–38
folder properties, changing, 105–106
Folder Size button in Tasks Properties dialog box, 105–106
folders. *See also* file folders, Outlook folders.
  adding shortcuts for, 91
  archiving, 106
  copying, 91–92
  creating, 88–90
  creating Outlook Bar shortcuts to, 230
  deleting, 94
  displaying contents when open, 17
  displaying names when open, 16
  moving, 91–92
  moving items between, 63
  navigating, 36, 39
  opening, 36–39
  opening one level up, 36
  recovering from Deleted Items folder, 94
  removing, 94
  renaming, 93
  searching in forms, 84
  sharing over networks, 99–103
  storing items in, 62–63
  switching between home pages and, 236
  types of, 17, 18
Font Color button in Formatting toolbar, 53
Font dialog box, 53
Font list in Formatting toolbar, 53
Font Size list in Formatting toolbar, 53
fonts
  changing for notes, 207
  changing in Date Navigator, 170
  choosing for e-mail messages, 145
For These Contacts list in Journal Options dialog box, 195
Format Card View dialog box in Contacts folder, 179

Format Columns dialog box, 234
Format Icon View dialog box in Notes folder, 207
Format Timeline View dialog box
- in Journal folder, 201
- in Tasks folder, 191

Formatting toolbar, 53
forms, 43
- displaying toolbars in, 43
- opening items in, 167
- saving work in, 50
- undoing edits in, 50

Forward button, 134, 220
Full Name text box on Contact form, 172
full-time Internet connection, 117, 120

G

Gallery tab of Office Assistant, 229
General tab
- on Contact form, 172
- in Tasks Properties dialog box, 105

Go To Date dialog box
- in Journal Timeline view, 199
- in Task Timeline view, 189

Go To Folder dialog box, 36, 38
Go To Today button, 167
graphics, copying and moving, 54
grayed out commands, 21, 25
group buttons, 16, 33, 230
Group By dialog box, 78
Group By This Field option in Information Viewer, 79
grouping, removal of, 79
grouping items, 74–79
groups, nesting, 78

H

hand mouse pointer, 20, 110
help
- Assistant type of, 29–31
- for searching, 84
- viewing with keyboard command, 26

help balloon, displaying in Assistant, 29
Help button, 28, 223, 228
help topics, printing in Assistant, 30
Home page tab
- in Properties dialog box, 235
- in Tasks Properties dialog box, 105–106

home pages
- attaching to Outlook folder, 235–236
- automatic display of, 236
- displaying for contacts, 178
- switching between folders and, 236

hours per day or week, changing in Tasks folder, 190
HTML (hypertext markup language) format, 144–145
hyperlink, 20

I

I-beam mouse pointer, 20
icons
- displaying linked and embedded objects as, 60
- listing in Notes folder, 206

Icons view
- for file folders, 215
- for Notes folder, 203

Ignore All button in Spelling dialog box, 55
Ignore button in Spelling dialog box, 55
IMAP Internet protocol (C/W), 248
Import and Export Wizard, 255
importing e-mail, 8–9
Inbox folder, 17, 41, 44, 123
Inbox Setup Wizard, 12, 250–251
Increase Indent button in Formatting toolbar, 53
information services (C/W), 248
- copying between profiles, 254
- managing in current Outlook profile, 251

Information Viewer, 16
Insert as area in Insert Item dialog box, 59
Insert File dialog box, 58, 135
Insert Item dialog box, 59
Insert Object dialog box, 60
insertion point, 51
installing program, 2
Internet Accounts dialog box (I/O), 240
Internet addresses (I/O), adding for directory services, 244

Internet Connection Wizard (I/O), 12
- adding directory service accounts with, 243–244
- adding mail accounts with, 241–243

Internet E-mail (C/W), 121, 248
Internet Only e-mail configuration (I/O), setting up and modifying, 10, 240–247
Internet shortcuts
- adding to Favorites file folder, 219
- opening Web pages with, 219–220

Invite Attendees button, 159
invited events, 164
ISP (Internet service provider) (I/O), entering telephone number for, 242
Italic button in Formatting toolbar, 53
italic e-mail messages, 136
item duration, changing in Calendar folder, 166
item types, defaults for Outlook folders, 44
items, 16–17, 41
- archiving, 64–69
- copying, 46, 61–63
- creating, 43–46
- creating in table view, 45
- creating with New button, 46
- editing, 49–51
- expanding and collapsing groups of, 79
- filtering, 74, 77
- filtering in current view, 233
- finding, 82–85
- grouping, 74, 78
- grouping in current view, 233
- inserting as attachments to e-mail messages, 59
- inserting in e-mail messages, 59
- inserting in forms, 59–60
- modifying formats of, 233
- moving, 61–63
- opening, 47–48
- opening in forms, 167
- preventing archiving of, 68
- printing in forms, 105
- removing, 64–69
- removing from archives, 67
- renaming in Calendar folder, 166
- saving changes made to, 49–50
- saving in archives, 66
- selecting, 48
- sorting, 74–76
- sorting in current view, 233
- viewing, 48
- viewing full text for, 168

items associated with journal entries, opening, 200–201
Items list in Insert Item dialog box, 59

J

Job title text box on Contact form, 172
journal entries
- automatic recording of, 194–195
- creating, 198
- hiding, 197
- linking to contacts, 196–197
- managing with tables, 198
- managing with timelines, 198–199
- manual recording of, 194, 196–197
- modifying in tables, 198
- opening, 199–200

Journal Entry form, 196
Journal folder, 17, 41, 44
Journal Items in Create New Folder dialog box, 89
Journal Options dialog box, 195, 201
journal timelines, adjusting detail shown in, 199
junk e-mail messages, color-coding, 153

K

keyboard commands, 26, 46
keyboard shortcuts, displaying, 26

L

Large Icons button, using with Notes folder, 206
last name field on Contact form, 174
Last Seven Days view for journal entries, 198
LDAP (lightweight directory access protocol), 142, 240
letters, writing to contacts, 178
light bulb icon in Assistant, 30

Link check box in Insert Object dialog box, 60
linked data, editing, 60
linked objects, 57–58
  inserting in forms, 59–60
  modifying properties of, 60
links to Web pages, entering in forms, 51
list boxes in dialog boxes, 27–28
List button, using with Notes folder, 206
lists in dialog boxes, 27–28
locations for events, identifying in Calendar folder, 165
login ID (I/O), entering in Internet Connection Wizard, 242
Look for list box
  in Advanced Find dialog box, 83
  in Go To Folder dialog box, 38
Look in list in Insert Item dialog box, 59
Lotus cc:Mail, 10, 249

M

mail accounts (I/O)
  adding with Internet Connection Wizard, 240–243
  modifying, 244–245
  removing, 244
Mail Delivery tab of Options dialog box, 245
Mail Format tab in Options dialog box, 145
mail items, 18, 89
Mail Usage dialog box, completing, 7
mailbox, hierarchy of folders in, 108
manual journal entries, 196–197
Maximize button, 16
meeting attendees, entering addresses in Calendar folder, 162–163
Meeting form, 162
Meeting items in Calendar folder, 155
meeting requests, sending to contacts, 178
meetings
  identifying in Calendar folder, 165
  scheduling, 162–164
members
  adding to distribution lists, 175
  removing from shared folders, 97
  sharing folders with, 95
Memo Style option in Print dialog box, 103
menu bar, 16, 224
  adding commands to, 226
  modifying, 225
  moving, 225
menu commands
  applying to forms, 43–44
  choosing, 21–22
  executing with keyboard, 26
menu options, setting, 228
menus, customizing, 226
Message forms, 133
  caution about creating e-mail messages in, 58
  completing, 134–135
  reading messages in, 123
message header, 123, 141
  hiding and displaying, 136
  hiding and showing, 124
Message Options dialog box, 124
messages. *See* e-mail messages.
Messages column of Outlook Today page, changing folders displayed in, 112
Messages folder, 107
Microsoft Exchange Server, 10, 12, 99, 108, 248
Microsoft Fax information service (C/W), 127, 150, 248
Microsoft LDAP Directory information service (C/W), 248
Microsoft Mail 3.*x*, using Outlook 2000 on, 10
Microsoft Mail information service (C/W), 248
Microsoft NetMeeting
  calling contacts with, 178
  running, 211
Microsoft Outlook dialog box (I/O), 118
Microsoft Word editor, 144–147
Minimize button, 16
Minimum permission level, 97
Month button, 168, 199
Month button in Task Timeline view, 189
months, managing with Calendar folder, 168
mouse operations, 20–23
Move Folder dialog box, 92
move handle, 225
move operations, undoing, 63

Move To Folder button, 63
moving commands, 226
My Computer shortcut in Other Shortcuts group, 35
My Documents shortcut in Other Shortcuts group, 35
My Shortcuts group, 32

N

name checking (C/W), automating, 142
Name option in Create New Folder dialog box, 89
Name text box in Distribution List form, 175
names
  entering in distribution lists, 176
  locating in address lists (I/O), 141
  locating in contacts list (I/O), 138
  searching in e-mail messages
    (C/W), 142
    (I/O), 139
  separating, 174, 176, 185, 197
nesting groups, 78
Net Folder Wizard, 96–98
NetMeeting
  calling contacts with, 178
  running, 211
networks
  sharing folders on, 99–103
  using Outlook 2000 on, 10
New button, 44, 133
New Call dialog box in Journal folder, 197
New Toolbar dialog box, 227
Next Folder button, 39
Next Item button, 48
No E-mail configuration, 11
None list box on Task form, 182–183
None permission level, setting in Microsoft Exchange Server, 100
nonstandard e-mail protocols, using Corporate or Workgroup configuration with, 10
note, opening menu for, 204
note icons, 206
Note Items in Create New Folder dialog box, 89
notes
  changing background color for, 204, 207
  creating, 204–205
  displaying as items in Notes folder, 205
  linking contacts to, 205
  managing with tables, 206
  removing from screen, 205
  saving, 205
Notes folder, 17, 41, 44
Notes items, limitations of, 53, 56
Notes List view, 206
Notes options, setting, 207
notes views, modifying features of, 207

O

Object Type list in Insert Object dialog box, 60
objects, dragging between windows, 58
Office Assistant, 29–31, 229
offline versus online management of e-mail (I/O), 118
OK button in dialog boxes, 28
one-time appointments, creating, 156–158
online meetings, setting in Calendar folder, 158
online versus offline management of e-mail (I/O), 118
open folders
  displaying contents of, 17
  displaying names of, 16
Open Other User's Folder dialog box, 101
Open Recurring Item message box, 160
Opening Mail Attachment dialog box, 125, 131
option buttons in dialog boxes, 27
Options button, using when creating e-mail messages, 135
Options dialog box
  fax settings in, 127
  setting mail delivery options in (I/O), 118
Organize button, 81, 151–152
Organize Page feature, 80–81, 151
Other Settings dialog box
  modifying file folder views in, 216
  modifying Messages view in, 154
Other Shortcuts group, displaying, 34

Outbox, transmitting e-mail messages from, 147
Outbox folder, 17, 41, 44
Outlook 2000 program file, locating, 4–5
Outlook Address Book information service (C/W), 249
Outlook Bar, 16
  creating shortcut to Web pages in, 221
  hiding and displaying, 33
  modifying, 230–232
  opening shortcut group in, 33
Outlook Bar shortcuts
  copying, 231
  creating to files, 231
  creating to folders, 230
  modifying, 231
  moving, 231
Outlook components
  adding, 256
  installing, 2
  removing, 256
Outlook editor, 144–147
Outlook Express Internet newsreader program, 8, 211
Outlook folders. *See also* file folders, folders.
  attaching home pages to, 235–236
  attaching Web pages to, 218
  copying, 91
  versus file folders, 18
  opening, 32–34
  opening in separate Outlook windows, 33
  printing, 103–105
  sharing over the Internet, 95–98
Outlook items. *See* items.
Outlook menu bar, 224
Outlook profiles (C/W)
  adding information services to, 251
  modifying information services in, 251
  modifying settings for, 252–253
  removing information services from, 251
Outlook Shortcuts group, 32
Outlook Today folder, 17, 42
  customizing, 111–113
  displaying home page for, 109
  opening, 36, 109
  saving settings made to, 113
  selecting styles for, 113
  undoing settings made to, 113
Outlook window, identifying parts of, 31
Owner text box on Task form, 183
owners of tasks, 182

P

.PAB disk files (C/W), 249
Page Setup button in Print dialog box, 105
paperclip button, 124, 130
paragraph alignment, changing, 53
Paragraph dialog box, 53
password (I/O), entering in Internet Connection Wizard, 242
Paste All button in Clipboard toolbar, 54
Pause Timer button on Journal Entry form, 196
performance, maximizing, 10
Permissions area of Calendar Properties dialog box, 100
Personal Address Book information service (C/W), 249
personal e-mail account, sending and receiving e-mail messages with, 147
personal folders, 99
Personal Folders information service (C/W), 249
personal task items, creating, 181–185
phone calls, recording in journal entries, 197–198
Phone List view, 70
phone number text boxes on Contact form, 173
plain text format, 144
pointing with mouse, 20
pop-up menus, 22–23
POP3 Internet protocol (C/W), 248
Post Reply button, 102
Preview pane, 16–17
  adjusting height of, 72
  displaying, 72–73
  modifying features of, 73
  reading messages in, 123–126
Preview Pane button, 72, 123
Previous Folder button, 39
Previous Item button, 48
Print button, 104, 105
Print dialog box, 103, 212, 214
Print options, selecting, 104

Print style area of Print dialog box, 103–105
printers, selecting, 104
printing
  file folders, 214
  files, 212
  help topics in Assistant, 30
Priority list box on Task form, 183
private appointments, setting up, 158
private folders, 99
  accessing in Microsoft Exchange Server, 101
  sharing in Microsoft Exchange Server, 100
Private option
  using with Contacts folder, 173–174
  using with distribution lists, 176
  using with journal entries, 197
  using with Tasks folder, 184
profiles (C/W), 248, 254
program files, fixing errors in, 6
program organization, 17
program window, 16
Programs view for file folders, 215
Prompt before AutoArchive option in AutoArchive dialog box, 67
Prompt for a Profile to Be Used option on Mail Services tab (C/W), 254
Properties dialog box, 106, 212
  opening for folders, 100, 106
  using with folders, 214
.PST files, 66–67, 69, 96, 99
  (C/W), 249
  hierarchy of folders in, 108
public folders, 99.
  accessing in Microsoft Exchange Server, 102
  creating in Microsoft Exchange Server, 101
  locating in Microsoft Exchange Server, 102
push buttons in dialog boxes, 27
push pin button, 38

Q

question mark (?) next to mouse pointer, 31
Quick Fax Viewer window (I/O), 130
Quick View dialog box, 212

R

radio buttons in dialog boxes, 27
RE: appearing in message Subject line, 133
Recurrence button, 159, 161, 184
recurring appointments
  creating and removing, 159–160
  identifying in Calendar folder, 165
recurring events, creating, 161
recurring meetings, creating, 163
recurring tasks, creating, 184
red wavy lines under names (C/W), 140
Refresh Current Page button on Web toolbar, 220
Registration Wizard for Symantec WinFax Starter Edition (I/O), 246–247
reminder messages, setting in Calendar folder, 157, 169
Reminder Sound button
  in Calendar folder, 157
  in Tasks folder, 183
reminders, modifying in Tasks folder, 190
removed items, restoring, 65
Rename dialog box, 93
  changing file folder names in, 214
  changing file names in, 212
Reply and Reply to All buttons, 133–134
Reviewer permission level, 97
rich text format, 144–145
right-clicking with mouse, 20
Roles list box, selecting permission level from, 100
root folder, 36, 88
running Outlook 2000, 3–6

S

Save All Attachments dialog box, 126
Save And Close button, 158, 161, 174
Save as Web Page dialog box, 165
Save Attachment dialog box, 125
Save Changes button in Outlook Today, 113
ScreenTips, displaying, 24
scroll bars, 16
search criteria, saving, 85
Search for the word(s) text box in View Summary dialog box, 77
Search the Web button on Web toolbar, 220

search tools, 82–85
searches, speeding up, 83
Select available fields from list box in Sort dialog box, 76
Select Folder dialog box in Outlook Today, 113
Select Members button in Distribution List dialog box, 175
Select Members dialog box in Contacts folder, 175
Select Names dialog box
  (C/W), 141
  (I/O), 137
Select where to place the folder area of Create New Folder dialog box, 90
Send button, 50, 135, 136
Send/Receive button, 119, 122, 147
Send Using Plain Text option on Contact form, 173
Sent Items folder, 17, 41, 44
Services dialog box in CompuServe, 121
Setup program, running, 2
shared folders, removing members from, 97
Sharing tab of Task Properties dialog box, 106
shortcut menus, 22
shortcuts, 16
  adding for folders, 91
  displaying, 17
  on Outlook Bar, 230
Show Attendee Availability option on Meeting form, 164
Show Fields dialog box, 233
Show Outlook Today in this style list box, 113
Show this number of days in my calendar list box on Outlook Today page, 112
Simple List view of Tasks folder, 181, 188
single days, managing in Calendar folder, 166
Small Icons button, using with Notes folder, 206
SMTP Internet protocol (C/W), 248
Sort my task list by list box on Outlook Today page, 113
sorting items, 74–76, 188
spelling checker, 55–56
spin buttons in dialog boxes, 27
Standard style for Outlook Today, 108, 113
Standard toolbar, 16, 23
Start date list box on Task form, 183
Start menu, running Outlook 2000 from, 3
Start Page button on Web toolbar, 220
Start Timer button on Journal Entry form, 196
starting Outlook 2000, 3–6
status bar, 16
Status list box on Task form, 183
Stop Current Jump button on Web toolbar, 220
street field on Contact form, 174
subfolders, 88, 210
subject, identifying in Calendar folder, 165
Subject text box, 135, 182
subjects, editing in items for Calendar folder, 165–166
submenu, 21
Suggestions list in Spelling dialog box, 55
Summer style for Outlook Today, 113
Symantec WinFax Starter Edition Setup Wizard (I/O), starting, 246

T

Table Style option in Print dialog box, 103
table view
  adding new tasks in, 189
  adjusting column width in, 71
  creating new items in, 45
  displaying file folders in, 214
  displaying text in, 73
  formatting columns in, 234
  modifying tasks in, 189
  sorting items in, 76
tables
  managing journal entries with, 198
  managing notes with, 206
  managing tasks with, 188–189
  managing with timelines, 189
tabs in dialog boxes, 28
task descriptions, entering in Task forms, 182
task due date, selecting, 182
Task form, 182
task information, modifying, 188
task items, 89, 182–187
task priority, selecting on Task form, 183

Task Recurrence dialog box, 184–185
task reminder time, changing default for, 190
Task Timeline view, 189
tasks
- arranging in tables, 188
- assigning categories to, 184
- changing sort order in Outlook Today, 113
- clearing sorting in tables, 188
- creating, 45, 188
- designating completion of, 188
- hiding, 184
- linking with contacts, 183
- managing with tables, 188–189
- manipulating in Outlook Today, 110
- recurring type of, 184–185
- sending to owners, 186

Tasks folder, 17, 41, 44, 107, 191
tasks for current day, showing on Outlook Today page, 113
Tasks options, setting, 190–191
Tasks Properties dialog box, 105
text
- copying, 54
- deleting, 54
- formatting in forms, 53
- moving, 54
- searching in forms, 51
- selecting in forms, 52

text boxes, 27
- editing text in, 51
- entering text in, 51

Then by area
- of Group By dialog box, 78
- of Sort dialog box, 76

then by list box on Outlook Today page, 113
This is the mailing address check box on Contact form, 172
time periods
- viewing in Journal Timeline view, 199
- viewing in timelines, 189

timelines
- managing journal entries with, 198–199
- managing tasks with, 18

times
- changing in Calendar folder, 166
- entering for appointments in Calendar folder, 156
- entering in forms, 50
- hiding and showing in notes, 207

title bar, 16
To box in Message form (I/O), 136–137
To message field (I/O), 138
toolbar buttons, displaying and identifying, 24
toolbar options, setting, 228
toolbars
- appearance of, 24
- displaying, 23
- displaying in forms, 43
- hiding, 23
- hiding and showing, 228
- modifying, 225
- moving, 225
- showing and hiding, 228
- types of, 23–25

Toolbars submenu, 23
Total work text box on Details tab of Tasks folder, 184
triangle
next to toolbar button, 24
on submenu, 21

U

underlined names (C/W), 140
Undo button, 63, 65
Undo Last button in Spelling dialog box, 55
undoing edits in forms, 50
unread messages
- displaying in Folder List, 38
- identifying, 123

Up One Level button, 36, 39
upgrading e-mail options, 8
user name (I/O), entering in Internet Connection Wizard, 242
user profiles (C/W), 248, 250–251

V

View menu, opening folders from, 36
View Summary dialog box, 75, 77, 78, 233
views
- adjusting, 233–234
- changing, 70–73
- customizing in Calendar folder, 170
- managing, 234

modifying, 154
modifying for file folders, 215–216
selecting for file folders, 214–215

W

Web browsers
opening Web pages in, 218
running, 211, 218
Web page address text box on Contact form, 173
Web page shortcuts, renaming in Outlook Bar, 221
Web pages
canceling loading of, 220
creating shortcuts to, 221
displaying, 218–221
navigating with Web toolbar, 220
opening with Internet shortcuts, 219–220
reloading, 220
Web toolbar, 23, 220
Week button
in Task Timeline view, 189
using with Journal Timeline view, 199
weeks
managing with Calendar folder, 167–168
viewing, 167
work weeks, changing in Calendar folder, 167–169